Critical Thinking Handbook:

High School

A Guide for Redesigning Instruction

by
**Richard Paul, A.J.A. Binker, Douglas Martin,
& Ken Adamson**

Center for Critical Thinking and Moral Critique
Sonoma State University
Rohnert Park, CA 94928
707-664-2940
© 1989

Acknowledgements

We wish to acknowledge the many helpful suggestions and criticisms of Jennifer Adrian, Heidi Kreklau, Chris Vetrano, Thomas McCurry, and Jane Kelsberg. They are, of course, not responsible for any errors, mistakes, or misconceptions.

ISBN # 0-944583-03-2
Library of Congress Catalog Card Number: 89-062293

Contents

Part II: Achieving the Deeper Understandings

Appendices

Introduction

The Design of the Book

This Handbook has one basic objective: to demonstrate that it is possible and practical to integrate instruction for critical thinking into the teaching of all subjects. We focus on language arts, social studies, and science, but we believe that the range of sample *before* and *after* lessons we provide will prove to any open-minded person that teaching so as to cultivate the critical thinking of students is eminently *practical*. We also believe that it should be given the highest priority, for it is *necessary* if we genuinely want our students to be prepared for the real world which awaits them personally, politically, and vocationally.

Of course, to say that it is practical is not to say that it is simple and easy. To teach for critical thinking requires that teachers themselves think critically, and very often teachers have not been encouraged to do so. Furthermore, sometimes they do not feel competent to do so. Every teacher interested in fostering critical thinking must be prepared to undergo an evolutionary process over an extended period of time. Mistakes will be made along the way. Many didactic teaching habits have to be broken down, to be replaced by ones more in line with coaching than lecturing. In any case, there are many dimensions of critical thinking, and one needs to be patient to come to terms with them. Of course, since critical thinking is essential in the life of adults as well as children, teachers will find many uses for their emerging critical thinking abilities in their everyday life outside the classroom: as a consumer, citizen, lover, and person.

We have divided this handbook into two parts: "Putting Critical Thinking into Instruction," and "Achieving the Deeper Understandings." We have put a good deal of the theory of critical thinking instruction in Part Two because most teachers like to get a good look at application before they spend much time on theory. In a way this makes good sense. Why learn a theory if you're not happy with what the theory makes possible? On the other hand, it is sometimes hard to understand and appreciate the application if one is not clear about the theory that underlies it. How and why are often deeply intertwined. We hope therefore that the reader will feel free to move back and forth between parts one and two, as needed. It would probably be a good idea to thumb through the book as a whole, familiarizing yourself with what's there, so that when you run into a problem you will be apt to remember sections of the book that are likely to shed light upon it. For example, notice that the glossary of critical thinking terms may be of use if you run across a term in critical thinking whose use and importance is not perfectly clear to you. In fact, reading randomly in the glossary is a good way to stimulate your sense of what critical thinking is.

Each of the chapters makes the transition from a didactic paradigm of education to a critical one a little easier. For example, it is important that we get a clear idea of what education is and is not (chapter 8, "Thinking Critically About Teaching: From Didactic to Critical Teaching"). Too often it has been unwittingly assumed that any kind of learning is educational. We forget that in school we learn bad habits as well as good ones, absorb misconceptions and prejudices as well as truths and insights. Or again, if we want instruction to accentuate and stimulate independent student thought, we need to design the curriculum with this in mind (chapter 9, "Redesigning Curriculum"). We need a clear articulation of critical thinking principles along with their applications (chapter 3, "Strategies"). We need to get a rich sense of the teacher as a questioner, including a variety of questioning strategies (chapter 2, "Global Strategies: Socratic Questioning & Role-Playing"). We need to stimulate students to analyze their personal experiences and relate that analysis to subject matter learning (chapter 2, "Global Strategies: Socratic Questioning & Role-Playing"). We need to provide for the affective life of the student, for feelings, values, and emotions are as essential to education as they are to all human life and activities (the Affective strategies, chapter 3, "Strategies"). We need to get a sense of how different teachers can articulate their own unique understandings of critical thinking while at the same time all capture the essence of the idea (chapter 12, "What Critical Thinking Means to Me: Teachers' Own Formulations"). We need a host of staff development strategies so that school districts can take advantage of some of the many practical ideas being developed for facilitating staff development in critical thinking (chapters 10 and 11, "Remodelling: A Foundation For Staff Development," and "The Greensboro Plan: A Sample Staff Development Plan"). Finally, the vocabulary of critical thinking needs to be organized and made available for easy reference (chapter 14, "Glossary: Educators' Guide to Critical Thinking Terms and Concepts").

Why Critical Thinking Is Essential to Education

If we consider some of the many complaints of classroom teachers concerning their pupils and then contrast them with what we look for in the ideal student, we will recognize that the fundamental missing element in schooling today is *thinking students*, or, more precisely, *critically thinking* students.

Here are some of the many complaints we hear from teachers:

✓ "Most students aren't motivated; they don't want to study or work. They look for chances to goof off, clown around, disrupt class. They'd rather talk about music, clothes, cars, ..."

✓ "Students forget what they've learned. We have to keep going over the same points, reminding them of what they've learned, rather than building on past learning. Each class begins at square one."

✓ "Most students are obsessed with grades and don't care about learning."

✓ "They're impatient. They want clear simple answers and they want them fast."

✓ "They make the same mistakes over and over again. They don't learn to correct their own mistakes."

✓ "They don't use what they've learned."

✓ "They need to be told every little thing. They don't even try to figure things out. They want us to do all of their thinking for them."

✓ "When I ask if there are questions they don't have any; but they haven't understood."

✓ "When assigned position papers, many students just write facts. The rest simply state and repeat their feelings."

✓ "They hate to read. (It's boring.)"

✓ "They hate to write. (It's too hard.)"

✓ "Instead of explaining or developing their ideas, they just repeat themselves."

✓ "They can't seem to stay on topic for long without going off on tangents."

The kind of students teachers would like to have are equally easy to describe:

✓ Students who are motivated to learn, get excited by ideas, don't need to be reprimanded, pay attention by choice.

✓ Students who remember what they learned yesterday, last month, last year; who don't have to be reminded over and over again what was covered before.

✓ Students who see grades as a by-product of learning; who put learning on a par with grades.

✓ Students who recognize that they can't completely understand everything at once, who are willing to delve; who are unsatisfied with pat answers.

✓ Students who learn from their mistakes, correct themselves.

✓ Students who *use* what they've learned.

✓ Students who can and will try to figure things out for themselves and don't expect me to do all of the thinking.

✓ Students who recognize when they don't understand something and can ask questions for clarification.

✓ Students who can get beyond the facts and the surface to explore their meaning; students who respond thoughtfully, go beyond knee-jerk reactions and first impressions.

✓ Students who like to read and talk about what they've read.

✓ Students who recognize the need to write in order to develop their ideas.

✓ Students who know the difference between explaining themselves and repeating themselves.

✓ Students who can and do stick to the point.

If we look closely at how teaching is typically structured, we will see that at the root of it are conceptions of knowledge, learning, and teaching that unwittingly take the motivation to *think* away from students. In most of the classes most of the time, teachers are talking and actively engaged, while students are listening passively. Most teacher utterances are statements, not questions. When teachers ask questions, they typically wait only a couple of seconds before they answer their own questions. Knowledge is taken to be equivalent to recall, so that when students can repeat what the teacher or text said, they are thought to have knowledge. Attempt is continually made to reduce the complex to the simple, giving students formulas, procedures, and algorithms to memorize and practice in hopes that understanding will emerge at the same time.

Schoenfeld reports on an experiment in which elementary students were asked questions like this, "There are 26 sheep and 10 goats on a ship. How old is the captain?" 76 of the 97 students "solved" the problem by adding, subtracting, multiplying or dividing. (Schoenfeld, 1989.) They felt they were expected to do so as quickly and "correctly" as possible. They did *not* feel they were expected to *make sense of* the problem. Instruction and practice had not emphasized *understanding* the problem.

Schoenfeld cites many similar cases, including a study that demonstrated that "word problems" in math tend to be approached by students by using the key word algorithm, that is, by reading problems like "John had eight apples. He gave three to Mary. How many does John have left?" and looking for the words like 'left' to tell them what operation to perform. As Schoenfeld puts it, "... the situation was so extreme that many students chose to subtract in a problem that began 'Mr. Left ...'." (Schoenfeld, 1982.) Giving students such short cuts as indicator words, though it appears to help by making learning easier, actually interferes with learning in a deeper sense. Students are, in effect, taught that problems can be solved by circling data, and going through steps practiced before ("I'm supposed to do this, then this, then this."); that they shouldn't slow down and think things through. They have had much more practice going through the steps than they have at thinking things through.

This tendency toward robotic, mindless responses becomes obsessive in many students. Hence, in their minds, history class becomes a place where they hear names, dates, events, and judgments about them, and try to repeat what they have heard on tests. Literature becomes uninteresting stories to remember along with what the teacher said is important about them, such as, foreshadowing.

Consider how students are generally taught factual detail. Students are continually presented with easily retainable facts (for example, foreign countries' main exports), and merely expected to reiterate them. They do not clearly understand *why* they should remember these facts. The collections of facts become merely sets of words in their heads, with no meaning, significance, or use. However, they *can* have meaning to students, can become *intelligible* to students, when they tell students something important, something students make sense of or want to know. If, when trying to understand a country's economic problems, students realize they need to know its chief exports, then that fact isn't just sitting there in the student's head as a bunch of words, it has meaning. It has a place in a broader picture; it has consequences; it helps that student understand that country's problem. It is *context*, not the mere fact itself, that gives it meaning, that makes it intelligible.

Values and principles tend to be treated as though they were facts. They are stated, and students are expected to reiterate them. This sort of process does not produce *understanding*. Principles (such as, "Write clearly!" and, "Stick to the point!") have their meaning, their justification, their very life in application, in *use*. I may know that I'm supposed to stick to the point, but this principle is little more than words to me if I don't know *how* to stick to the point, if I don't learn how to recognize *for myself* when I'm focused and when I stray. I can only learn how by practice, by *thinking* — by trying, sometimes succeeding, sometimes failing, by seeing for myself when I succeeded, when I failed, and by *understanding* the differences between the successes and failures. Present instructional practices rarely allow this kind of process.

A Critical model of education, then, acts to reverse these patterns at every point. Students are continually asked to think about what they learn, to try to apply their new ideas, to compare their own ideas with what they are presented in school, to practice explaining what they learn and what they think by listening to their peers as they try to understand new ideas.

The underlying assumption in present education is that knowledge consists of bits of information, concepts, and skills which, by being verbally presented to students, enable students to learn and know them. Educators assume that students automatically replace ignorance with knowledge, misconception with truth. We reject this assumption. We suggest it be replaced by the notion that beliefs are interdependent; that individual beliefs make up larger systems of which they are parts; that, in order to learn, students must actively reshape these systems.

One main consequence of this idea is that being told something, however clear the explanation, does not guarantee understanding. If you tell me something that contradicts or is incompatible with my present system of beliefs, I'm unlikely to replace my whole belief system with that new idea. I will often distort what you've said so that it fits my belief system; I may simply "tack it on" to my beliefs, ignoring the incompatibility between old and new, bouncing back and forth between them, sometimes using one, sometimes the other, willy-nilly; or I may simply fail to take it in at all. To really learn the new idea, I have to struggle through the problems the idea creates for me, *build* a new mental structure or system of beliefs. This process requires me to make my present beliefs explicit (figure out what I really think), and slowly reshape the old system into a new and better body of thought. Hence, to understand the new idea, concept, or principle, I have to think my way through to it, internalize it. I can do so through extended discussion, talking and listening to others as they internalize new knowledge. Consider how this conception of learning works.

When I put things into words, and hear myself, I think again about what I'm saying, realize that this isn't saying what I mean; I think of a new example; I put the point in a slightly better way, or different way, and thus come to see new sense to it. When I have to convince others, (such as classmates), I have to communicate convincing grounds for thinking as I do. The people I'm talking to react: understanding some parts of what I've said better than others, forcing me to rephrase my point and so think it through again in a slightly different way, with the result that I understand it more clearly. My audience says things in response that had never occurred to me; they ask questions, raise objections, and so on. As I answer, I find myself saying things I hadn't realized I believed. Sometimes I say things I know are wrong, and so I have to change my original idea somewhat. My audience may suggest new examples, or expand on my ideas in a new way. In short, while I'm discussing things with my classmates *I am learning*. By listening to me, reacting, and hearing my replies, my classmates are learning. We're all thinking things though together. As a group, we know more, can figure out more, and have more and better ideas than any one of us individually. Having done our own thinking and produced our own knowledge, we understand deeply; the knowledge becomes part of us rather than bunches of words we have collected and which we may easily lose.

This is at the heart of education for critical thought. Students learn to think by thinking, learn to learn by learning, learn to judge by judging and by assessing their thinking, learning, and judging. (Does this make sense? Is this clear? Is it true? Is it well reasoned?) Students come to use the power of their minds to clarify, judge, and reason.

When teachers begin to integrate critical thinking into their instructional practice, they have experiences like the following (taken from *The Greensboro Plan: Infusing Reasoning and Writing into the K-12 Curriculum*):

Beth:

> I teach North Carolina History and 8th grade English, and I am always trying to bridge the gap and use an interdisciplinary approach. What critical thinking helps me do is go

beyond the textbook and find things we can really discuss using the Socratic method — to go beyond just the facts and try to analyze the situation — to put ourselves in the other person's shoes — to look at a lot of different components.

Here is an article on slavery which I have copied and brought with me to show how you do not have to rewrite all your lesson plans to infuse critical thinking into your curriculum. Instead, you go further and bring in other things to enhance what you're teaching and give opportunities for discussion. This article is about slavery and slave trading. I have the students become one of the slaves on the ship and write a diary about how it would feel to be a slave. Later on in English, students write an essay on whether or not the ship captains should have been tried as criminals. This asks students to look at ideas from different viewpoints. For a final activity, I asked students to assume that they were a member of the English Parliament of 1807 and to write a persuasive essay on whether or not slavery should be banned and why.

Mandy:

Since I have taken part in this project, I have become a much more critical thinker. That's helped me tremendously in my classroom.

I always explain to my students how all our subjects are overlapping; this helps them in real life. One revised science lesson we used this year was building a rain forest in our room in a terrarium. We turned it into a vivarium by adding an anole, a small lizard.

The students decided they wanted to write a book about the anole, and the first thing they wanted to do was go to the library to *copy* information. Instead of this, we brainstormed to find out what we already knew and what we could learn just by observation. All my students became motivators for others while we worked with words.

After the pre-writing exercises, I took them to the media center for research. Again, they wanted to fall into the trap of copying from the encyclopedia. But I allowed them only to write down words — single words or maybe a phrase, rather than copying down sentences. It was difficult for them — it was difficult for me, too.

They came back from the media center with ideas rather than with things they had copied. We talked about the ideas and categorized — and then I told them to write down ideas in their own words. It was amazing what happened! If I had given this assignment a year ago, a description of the anole would be only a few sentences long. My students this year wrote pages — they really did — and they were excited. This was their work; this was their description; it was not *World Book's* description. And it made it much more real to them — and of course real to me too.

In the first example, notice how students had to grapple again and again with the concept of slavery from different angles: What was it like? In what ways were different people partly responsible? What do I think of it? How can I convince others to agree with me? Each time students explored the issue, they were learning and using facts, probing and clarifying values, using principles, and were putting these pieces together.

The second example above illustrates the difference between merely taking statements in and giving them back, and restructuring belief systems. Students first publicly shared their original beliefs, ideas, and suggestions. Then, when they consulted resources, they wrote only the barest bones of the information, and were thus forced to *reconstruct* the new knowledge. Notice that, though this process was more difficult, the students themselves produced more writing and were more pleased with the results.

Finally, consider two more experiences of teaching students to learn deeply.

Sylvia

My involvement in the Reasoning and Writing project came about because I believe the following: *1)* students are faced with an explosion of information; *2)* given a limited time in which learn, students must choose *what* information they need and learn *how* to acquire it; *3)* to make intelligent choices, students must exercise good judgment; *4)* successful living in today's world requires high order thinking and reasoning skills; *5)* writing can be used as a tool to improve thinking and reasoning skills in all curriculum areas. ...

I have incorporated two new ideas this year: Socratic questioning and writing to aid concept development. I have worked primarily with one class, using questioning techniques to encourage students to think critically. The results have been encouraging: class discussions became more animated, students offered ideas freely, criticism was constructive, helpful, and resulted in better ideas. I believe that the entire class benefitted.

One high school teacher tried to focus on critical thinking in a sophomore English class. This teacher designed small group and paired discussions only to have the students complain, "You're supposed to use the grammar book. You're supposed to start on the first page and give us the sentences to do and then check them and then we do the next sentence ...."

The students insisted that "doing the sentences" was the top priority. One of the students said, in defense of this method, "We learned about prepositions." However, when the instructor asked the class *what* they had learned about prepositions, the class went silent. When asked, "Do you remember what prepositions are? Can you name some?" nobody could. Though this teacher continued her emphasis on critical thinking, she also gave students "sentences to do" for part of the class time. After the fourth day, no students objected when she neglected to assign more sentences. On their final exam, these students were asked, "Why is it better for a school to teach you how to find answers than to teach you the answers?" Among their responses were the following:

- ✓ So you can get in the habit of doing it yourself and not depend on someone else.
- ✓ When you teach people the answer, they will never try to find the answer thereself. They will look for somebody to give them the answer instead of looking for it because they don't know how to find it.
- ✓ When you get a job, they will expect you to find the answers yourself.
- ✓ Because it makes you feel good about yourself when you can look up something by yourself and get the answer correct. You feel more independent in school.
- ✓ School is not going to be with you all your life.
- ✓ So you can learn how to find the answers to *your* problems because one day you're going to have to find the answers yourself. Nobody is going to be able to give you the answers.
- ✓ Because it won't help you to know the answers and not know what they mean.
- ✓ Because in the future there won't be a teacher to hold your hand or to tell you everything you should know. You should learn on your own.

As you consider the rest of the material in this book, we ask you to apply these basic ideas to each facet of the task of incorporating critical thought into instructional practice. Just as students must struggle through a process of restructuring their thought to incorporate new facts, skills, and principles, so must teachers grapple with the problems of restructuring their conceptions of education, and learn to apply principles underlying it. We encourage you to work your way through our ideas — reading, explaining, listening, questioning, writing, applying, assessing — figuring out what you think about what we say.

The Spirit of Critical Thinking

Before we introduce you to the remodelling process, you may want to read through this section on the spirit of critical thinking. It provides an introduction to our concept of critical thinking. However it freely uses the vocabulary of critical thinking — assumption, reason, argument, contradiction, relevant, point of view, conclusion, ... — and is somewhat abstract. So if it doesn't seem perfectly clear to you at the outset, don't be discouraged. Simply come back to it later on after you have had more exposure to concrete examples. Indeed, you should keep in mind throughout that we have designed this handbook with the thought that teachers will want to return to various sections of it over time for deeper understandings. It is definitely not the kind of book that a person can simply absorb at one reading.

The term 'critical,' as we use it, does not mean thinking which is negative or finds fault, but rather thinking which evaluates reasons and brings thought and action in line with our evaluations, our best sense of what is true. The ideal of the critical thinker could be roughly expressed in the phrase 'reasonable person'. Our use of the term 'critical' is intended to highlight the intellectual autonomy of the critical thinker. That is, as a critical thinker, I do not simply accept conclusions (uncritically). I evaluate or critique reasons. My critique enables me to distinguish poor from strong reasoning. To do so to the greatest extent possible, I make use of a number of identifiable and learnable skills. I analyze and evaluate reasons and evidence; make assumptions explicit and evaluate them; reject unwarranted inferences or "leaps of logic;" use the best and most complete evidence available to me; make relevant distinctions; clarify; avoid inconsistency and contradiction; reconcile apparent contradictions; and distinguish what I know from what I merely suspect to be true.

The uncritical thinker, on the other hand, doesn't reflect on or evaluate reasons for a particular set of beliefs. By simply agreeing or disagreeing, the uncritical thinker accepts or rejects conclusions, often without understanding them, and often on the basis of egocentric attachment or unassessed desire. Lacking skills to analyze and evaluate, this person allows irrelevant reasons to influence conclusions, doesn't notice assumptions and therefore fails to evaluate them, accepts any inference that "sounds good;" is unconcerned with the strength and completeness of evidence, can't sort out ideas, confuses different concepts, is an unclear thinker, is oblivious to contradictions, and feels certain, even when not in a position to know. The classic uncritical thinker says, "I've made up my mind! Don't confuse me with facts." Yet, critical thinking is more than evaluation of simple lines of thought.

As I evaluate beliefs by evaluating the evidence or reasoning that supports them (that is, the "arguments" for them), I notice certain things. I learn that sometimes I must go beyond evaluating small lines of reasoning. To understand an issue, I may have to think about it for a long time, weigh many reasons, and clarify basic ideas. I see that evaluating a particular line of thought often forces me to re-evaluate another. A conclusion about one case forces me to come to a certain conclusion about another. I find that often my evaluation of someone's thinking pivots around the meaning of a concept, which I must clarify. Such clarification affects my understanding of other issues. I notice previously hidden relationships between beliefs about different issues. I see that some beliefs and ideas are more fundamental than others. As I think my way through my beliefs, I find I must orchestrate the skills I have learned into a longer series of moves. As I strive for consistency and understanding, I discover opposing sets of basic assumptions which underlie those conclusions. I find that, to make my beliefs reasonable, I must evaluate not individual beliefs but, rather, large sets of beliefs. Analysis of an issue requires more work, a more extended process, than that required for a short line of reasoning. I must learn to use my skills, not in separate little moves but together, coordinated into a long sequence of thought.

Sometimes, two apparently equally strong arguments or lines of reasoning about the same issue come to contradictory conclusions. That is, when I listen to one side, the case seems strong. Yet when I listen to the other side, that case seems equally strong. Since they contradict each other, they cannot both be right. Sometimes it seems that the two sides are talking about different situations or speaking different languages, even living in different "worlds." I find that the skills which enable me to evaluate a short bit of reasoning do not offer much help here.

8

Suppose I decide to question two people who hold contradictory conclusions on an issue. They may use concepts or terms differently, disagree about what terms apply to what situations and what inferences can then be made, or state the issue differently. I may find that the differences in their conclusions rest, not so much on a particular piece of evidence or on one inference, as much as on vastly different perspectives, different ways of seeing the world, or different conceptions of such basic ideas as, say, human nature. As their conclusions arise from different perspectives, each, to the other, seems deluded, prejudiced, or naive. How am I to decide who is right? My evaluations of their inferences, uses of terms, evidence, etc. also depend on perspective. In a sense, I discover that *I have a perspective.*

I could simply agree with the one whose overall perspective is most like my own. But how do I know I'm right? If I'm sincerely interested in evaluating beliefs, should I not also consider things from other perspectives?

As I reflect on this discovery, I may also realize that my perspective has changed. Perhaps I recall learning a new idea or even a system of thought that changed the way I see myself and the world around me in fundamental ways, which even changed my life. I may remember how pervasive this change was — now I began to interpret a whole range of situations differently, continually used a new idea, concept or phrase, paid attention to previously ignored facts. I realize that I now have a new choice regarding the issue under scrutiny.

I could simply accept the view that most closely resembles my own. But I realize that I cannot reasonably reject the other perspective unless I understand it. To do so would be to say, "I don't know what you think, but whatever it is, it's false." The other perspective, however strange it seems to me now, may have something both important and true, which I have overlooked and without which my understanding is incomplete. Thinking along these lines, I open my mind to the possibility of change of perspective. I make sure that I don't subtly ignore or dismiss these new ideas; I realize I can make my point of view richer, so it encompasses more. As I think within another perspective, I begin to see ways in which it is right. It points out complicating factors I had previously ignored, makes useful distinctions I had missed, offers plausible interpretations of events I had never considered, and so on. I become able to move between various perspectives, freed from the limitations of my earlier thought.

One of the most important stages in my development as a thinker, then, is a clear recognition that I have a perspective, one that I must work on and change as I learn and grow. To do this, I can't be inflexibly attached to any particular beliefs. I strive for a consistent "big picture." I approach other perspectives differently. I ask how I can reconcile the points of view. I see variations between similar but different perspectives. I use principles and insights flexibly and do not approach analysis as a mechanical, "step one, step two" process. I pursue new ideas in depth, trying to understand the perspectives from which they come. I am willing to say, "This view sounds new and different; I don't yet understand it. There's more to this idea than I realized; I can't just dismiss it."

Looked at another way, suppose I'm rethinking my stand on an issue. I re-examine my evidence. Yet, I cannot evaluate my evidence for its completeness unless I consider evidence cited by those who disagree with me. Similarly, I find I can discover my basic assumptions by considering alternative assumptions, alternative perspectives. I use fairmindedness to clarify, enhance, and improve my perspective.

A narrowminded critical thinker, lacking this insight, says, not, "This is how *I* see it," but, "This is how *it is.*" While working on pieces of reasoning, separate arguments, and individual beliefs, this person tends to overlook the development of perspective as such. Such thinking consists of separate or fragmented ideas and the examination of beliefs one at a time without appreciation for connections between them. While conscious and reflective about particular conclusions, this type of thinker is unreflective about his or her own point of view, how it affects his or her evaluations of reasoning, and how it is limited. When confronted with alternative perspectives or points of view, this person assesses them by their degree of agreement with his or her own view and lumps together similar, though different, perspectives. Such an individual is given to sweeping acceptance or sweeping rejection of points of view and is tyrannized by the words he or she uses. Rather than trying to understand why others think as they do, he or she dismisses new ideas, assuming the objectivity and correctness of his or her own beliefs and responses.

As I strive to think fairmindedly, I discover resistance to questioning my beliefs and considering those of others. I find a conflict between my desire to be fairminded and my desire to feel sure of what I think. It sometimes seems a lot easier to avoid the confusion, frustration, and embarrassment that I feel when reassessing my beliefs. Simply trying to ignore these feelings doesn't make them go away. I realize that without directly addressing these obstacles to critical thought, I tend to seek its appearance rather than its reality, that I tend to accept rhetoric rather than fact, that without noticing it, I hide my own hypocrisy, even from myself.

By contrast, the critical thinker who lacks this insight, though a good arguer, is not a truly reasonable person. Giving good-sounding reasons, this person can find and explain flaws in opposing views and has well-thought-out ideas, but this thinker never subjects his or her own ideas to scrutiny. Though giving lip service to fairmindedness and describing views opposed to his or her own, this thinker doesn't truly understand or seriously consider them. One who often uses reasoning to get his or her way, cover up hidden motives, or make others look stupid or deluded is merely using skills to reinforce his or her own views and desires, without subjecting them to scrutiny. Such people are not truly reasonable. By cutting themselves off from honestly assessing their own perspectives or seriously considering other perspectives, these people are not using their mental capacities to their fullest extent.

To sum up, the fully reasonable person, the kind of critical thinker we want to foster, contrasts with at least two other kinds of thinkers. The first kind has few intellectual skills of any kind and tends to be naive, easily confused, manipulated, and controlled, and so easily defeated or taken in. The second has skills, but only of a restricted type, which enable pursuit of narrow, selfish interests and effective manipulation of the naive and unsuspecting. The first we call 'uncritical thinkers' and the second 'weak sense,' or selfish, critical thinkers. What we aim at, therefore, are "strong sense" critical thinkers, those who use the fullest powers of their minds in the service of sincere, fairminded understanding and evaluation of their beliefs.

Introduction to Remodelling: Components of Remodels and Their Functions

The basic idea behind lesson plan remodelling as a strategy for staff development in critical thinking is simple. Every practicing teacher works daily with lesson plans of one kind or another. To remodel lesson plans is to critique one or more lesson plans and formulate one or more new lesson plans based on that critical process. To help teachers generalize from specific remodelling moves, and so facilitate their grasp of strong sense critical thinking and how it can be taught, we have devised a list of teaching strategies. Each strategy highlights an aspect of critical thought.

Each use illustrates how that aspect can be encouraged in students. In the chapter, "Strategies," we explain the thirty-five strategies illustrated in the remodels. Each is linked to the idea of strong sense critical thinking, in the "Principle" section. For each we explain some ways the aspect of critical thought can be encouraged, in the "Application" section.

Complete remodelled lessons have three major components: an *Original Lesson,* or statement of the *Standard Approach* (which describes the topic and how it is covered, including questions and activities); the *Critique* (which describes the significance of the topic and its value for the educated thinker, evaluates the original, and provides a general idea of how the lesson can be remodelled); and the *Remodelled Lesson* (which describes the new lesson, questions to be posed to students and student activities, and cites the critical thinking strategies by number). The strategy number generally follows the questions or activities it represents. When an entire remodel or section develops one dimension of critical thought in depth, the number appears at the top of the remodel or section. Complete remodel sets also include a list of *Objectives* which integrate the objectives of the original with the critical thinking goals; and the list of critical thinking *Strategies* applied in the remodel (listed in order of first appearance). Note the functions of these parts in the example below. Each component can serve some purpose for both the writer and the reader.

Advertising

Objectives of the remodelled plan

The students will:

- practice listening critically by analyzing and evaluating T.V. commercials
- exercise fairmindedness by considering advertisements from a variety of perspectives
- analyze and evaluate the arguments given in ads
- practice using critical vocabulary to analyze and evaluate ads
- clarify key words
- distinguish relevant from irrelevant facts in ads
- examine assumptions in ads
- develop insight into egocentricity by exploring the ways in which ads appeal to unconscious desires

Standard Approach

Very few texts actually address the issue of advertising. Those that do touch upon indicators to watch for which signal the use of some sort of reasoning — such indicators as "if ... then," "because," "since," "either ... or," and "therefore." Students are to decide if the reasoning presented is logical or illogical. Some lessons on ads focus on finding and decoding the factual information regarding sales. Students are often asked to write their own ads.

Critique

We chose this lesson for its subject: advertising. Ads are a natural tie-in to critical thinking, since many are designed to persuade the audience that it needs or wants a product. Ads provide innumerable clear-cut examples of irrelevance, distortion, suppressed evidence, and vague uses of language. Analysis of ads can teach students critical thinking micro-skills and show their use in context. Practice analyzing and evaluating ads can help students develop ability to listen critically. The standard approach, however, is not done in a way which best achieves these results.

Such lessons often focus more on writing ads than critiquing them. They tend to treat neutral and advertising language as basically equivalent in meaning, though different in effect, rather than pointing out how differences in effect arise from differences in meaning. They downplay the emptiness, irrelevance, repetition, questionable claims, and distortion of language in most ads. Their examples bear little resemblance to real ads. By rarely addressing ads aimed at students, texts minimize useful transfer.

Since most students are exposed to more television commercials than other ads, we recommend that students discuss real commercials aimed at them. We also provide suggestions for using ads to practice use of critical vocabulary and to discuss the visual and audio aspects of commercials.

Strategies used to remodel

S-22 listening critically: the art of silent dialogue
S-9 developing confidence in reason
S-18 analyzing or evaluating arguments, interpretations, beliefs, or theories
S-14 clarifying and analyzing the meanings of words or phrases
S-16 evaluating the credibility of sources of information
S-3 exercising fairmindedness
S-31 distinguishing relevant from irrelevant facts
S-2 developing insight into egocentricity or sociocentricity
S-29 noting significant similarities and differences
S-28 thinking precisely about thinking: using critical vocabulary
S-35 exploring implications and consequences
S-30 examining or evaluating assumptions

Remodelled Lesson Plan S-22

Due to the number of ads to which students are exposed, and their degree of influence, we recommend that the class spend as much time as possible on the subject. As students learn to approach ads thoughtfully and analytically, and practice applying critical insight to their lives, they develop confidence in their reasoning powers and their ability to see through attempts to irrationally manipulate them. **S-9**

To focus on ads and language, begin by having students give complete descriptions of what is said in a variety of television commercials. Put the quotes on the board. For each commercial, the class can evaluate the arguments presented in ads by discussing the following questions: What ideas does it give you about the product (or service) and owning or using it? Does it give reasons for buying the product? If so, what reasons? Are they good reasons?

What are the key words? Do they have a clear meaning? What? **S-14** What other words could have been chosen? Who made this ad? Why? Do they have reason to distort evidence about the worth of the product? **S-16** How might someone who wasn't trying to sell the product describe it? How might a competitor describe it? **S-3** What would you need to know in order to make a wise decision about whether to buy it? Does the commercial address these points? **S-31** Why or why not? Has anyone here had experience with the product? What? **S-18**

When the commercials have been discussed, have students group them by the nature of the ads (repetition, positive but empty language, etc.) or of the appeals made (to the desires to have fun, be popular, seem older, etc.) Have students fill out the groups by naming similar commercials not previously discussed. Students could discuss why these appeals are made. "How do ads work? Why do they work? Do they work on you? On whom? Why? What are slogans for? Jingles? Why are running stories and continuing characters used? Why are the various techniques effective?" **S-2**

The teacher interested in developing students' critical vocabulary can have students practice while critiquing ads. Use questions like the following: What does the ad imply? **S-35** Does the ad make, or lead the audience to make, any assumptions? Are the assumptions true, questionable, or false? **S-30** Does the ad contain an argument? If so, what is the conclusion? Is the conclusion stated or implied? Does the ad misuse any concepts or ideas? To judge the product, what facts are relevant? Are the relevant facts presented? **S-31** Does it make any irrelevant claims? **S-28**

The class could also compare different ads for the same product, aimed at different audiences (e.g., fast food ads aimed at children, and at adults). **S-29** The class could compare ads for different brands of the same or similar products; compare ads to what can be read on ingredients labels; or design and conduct blind taste tests. **S-18**

To gain further insight into listening critically, the class could also discuss aspects of the ads other than use of language. What does the ad show? What effect is it designed to achieve? How? Why? What is the music like? Why is it used? Do the actors and announcers use tone of voice to persuade? Facial expression? How? Are these things relevant to judging or understanding the product? **S-22**

The teacher may also have the class critique ads for any stereotyping (e.g., sexual stereotyping). **S-2**

For further practice, if a VCR is available, watch and discuss taped commercials. Students could jot notes on critical points and share their insights.

The *Standard Approach* (or *Original Lesson*) describes how the subject is treated. As a summary, it provides focus for the critique and remodel. Teachers who share their work can better follow the remodel when the original is clearly described. The critical thinking infused is better highlighted — for both the writer and the reader — when the original is available for contrast with the remodel.

The *Critique* generally begins by explaining the use of having students study the subject, the role such study has in the life of the critical thinker, and how critical thinking applies to the topic. It then provides a critique of the original from the point of view of education for critical thinking. Given the reasons for studying the topic, and the role such study should have for the critical thinker, the ways the original fosters and fails to foster such understanding is explicated. Thus, the analysis of the significance of the topic provides a focus for and basis of the evaluation. The evaluation, then, mentions parts of the original that can be kept, and parts that should be changed or dropped, and *why*. The critique often includes a general statement suggesting what must be added to raise deeper issues and develop insight into the material.

The *Remodelled Lesson* then follows, based on the analysis and evaluation of the topic and its treatment in the original. It reflects the reasoning given in the critique. It includes teacher questions and student activities designed to overcome the problems in the original. Citing the strategy numbers helps make the critical thinking infused explicit, and offers cross-referencing for others to better see what is being done in the new lesson and why. Readers of the remodel can refer to the strategy descriptions given in the Strategy chapter, if the function of the strategy is unclear to them. Furthermore, citing the strategy provides a check for the writer, who, during the writing and revision process, can evaluate the questions and activities to make sure that they do in fact engage the students in that particular dimension of critical thought.

The list of *Strategies used to remodel* helps readers who want to better understand a particular strategy, or want ideas for applying it, to easily find examples. As the readers read the Remodelled Plan, they can easily refer to this list for the names of the strategies cited.

The *Objectives* provide an opportunity for writers of remodels to summarize their work, and show the readers how the strategies apply to the content, that is, to show the relationship between the content and critical thought. Writing objectives, and looking at what you've written, making the goals explicit as a list of what students will do, helps the writer ensure that the remodel does achieve the goals as stated. If not, the goals should be added to the remodel or dropped from the objectives. (Does the activity as described *really* have students carefully and fairmindedly evaluate these assumptions?) Objectives can also show relationships between the strategies as they apply to that lesson, they make explicit that, in this case, this one strategy is (or these three strategies are) used in the service of this main strategy. Reading through objectives of other people's remodels can make it easier to find ideas in them to use in one's own work. When confronted with a particular remodelling problem, reading objectives of other remodels is an easy way of finding out which remodels can provide help or inspiration.

The finished form of the complete remodel sets, and separation and order of their elements, is not intended to suggest the precise order in which the elements are developed or written. Generally, the three major components are begun in rough form: an initial statement of key parts of the original and their functions, its most obvious strengths and weaknesses, and provisional revisions are usually jotted down first.

The writer can then step back and evaluate these rough ideas and begin to analyze the situation more deeply. Does my critique really get at the heart of the matter? Is the evaluation fair, accurately stated, and properly justified? Does my remodel really address the flaws I've identified? Could I add something to take the lesson more deeply into the subject? Am I missing a good opportunity to encourage careful honest thought? Are the main points of the remodel explained or justified by what I've said in the critique?

The remodellers may also want to review pertinent strategies, skim other remodels for ideas, and share their work with colleagues for comments and ideas before beginning a final rewrite. When the three main components are in relatively finished form, the writer can list the strategies used. The final version of the Objectives is usually written last, and checked to ensure that it reflects the remodel.

Although going through an extended process like this may seem like a lot of unnecessary work, and you needn't write up every instance of infusing critical thinking in polished form, we encourage you to put at least some of your work in this form for the following reasons:

- First impressions and initial ideas about what to do may be misleading and are rarely as valuable for either students or colleagues as a finished product which has been carefully evaluated and revised.

- The evaluation, revision, double-checking, and analysis provide crucial opportunities for teachers to develop the ability to engage in careful critical thought.

- Having to organize one's ideas and express them clearly helps the writer to more thoroughly probe those ideas, and discover other ideas.

- An extended process creates a finished product which is clearer and more helpful to colleagues with whom it is shared, than rough notes and scattered ideas would be.

- The objectives most worthwhile to pursue in the remodel will rarely be apparent until after the analysis and critique of the original material and plan, and development of a remodelled lesson.

- Revision after further analysis can correct such mistakes as failing to include crucial points, or covering the material in a superficial or tangential way. It's remarkably easy to blast a critique for missing an important opportunity for developing critical thought, but then neglect to take advantage of the opportunity oneself. It's easy to miss the main point, purpose, or context of a topic, principle, or skill, when first considering it. It's easy to write wonderful sounding objectives and then fail to fulfill them.

We therefore recommend a more extended process of producing remodels, with the elements given above, whether done in that order or not. (For example, the first step might be to confer with colleagues. With some lessons, one might have to review some strategies, remodels, or the subject introduction, before being able to come with remodel ideas.) Whatever process you use, we strongly encourage you to gain some experience in the careful and complete analysis and evaluation required to produce well written, complete remodel sets.

How To Use This Book

You may choose to read this book as you would any other book, but if you do, you will probably miss a good deal of the benefit that can be derived from it. There are no algorithms or recipes for understanding or teaching critical thinking. Although we separate aspects of critical thinking, the global concept of the truly reasonable person is behind each aspect, and each aspect relates to it and the other dimensions. Thus, to develop critical thought, one must continually move back and forth between the global ideal of the rational and fairminded thinker and the details describing such a thinker. Similarly, although we separate the aspects of staff development for integrating critical thinking into the curriculum (understanding the concept, critiquing present practice, formulating remodels), teachers must continually move back and forth between these activities.

If you are a high school teacher and you want to improve your ability to teach for critical thinking, this book can help you develop the ability to remodel your own lesson plans. Your own teaching strategies will progressively increase as your repertoire of critical thinking strategies grows. As you begin, try to develop a baseline sense of your present understanding of critical thinking and of your ability to critique and redesign lesson plans. The critiques and remodels that follow, and the principles and strategies that precede them, may provide an immediate catalyst for you to take your lesson plans and redesign them. But the longer critiques and remodels here might seem intimidating. Some of the strategies may seem unclear or confusing, and you may bog down as soon as you attempt to redesign your own lessons. Keep in mind that in some of our remodels, we put as many ideas as we could, in order to provide as many examples and varieties of applications as possible. Thus, some of the remodelled plans are longer and more elaborate than you might initially be willing to produce or teach. The purpose of this book is not to simply give you lesson ideas, but to encourage you to develop your own.

We therefore suggest alternative approaches and ways of conceiving the process:

- Read through the strategies and a couple of remodels, then write critiques and remodels of your own. After you have attempted a critique and remodel, read our critique and remodel of a similar lesson. By using this procedure, you will soon get a sense of the difficulties in the critique-remodel process. You will also have initiated the process of developing your own skills in this important activity.

- Another way of testing your understanding of the critical insights is to read the principle section of a strategy, and write your own application section.

- You could review a remodel of ours and find places where strategies were used but not cited and places where particular moves could be characterized by more than one strategy.

- You may want to take several strategies and write a passage about their interrelationships.

- Or you might take a subject or topic and list significant questions about it. Share and discuss your lists with colleagues.

- If, when reviewing a remodel, you find a particular strategy confusing, review the principle and application in the strategy chapter. If, when reading the strategy chapter, you feel confused, review the critiques and remodels of the lessons listed below it. If you are still confused, do not use the strategy. Review it periodically until it becomes clear.

- When remodelling your own lessons, you will probably find that sometimes you can make more drastic changes, or even completely rewrite a lesson, while at other times you may make only minor adjustments. Some of your remodels may make use of many strategies, say, two or more affective strategies, and a macro-ability requiring coordinated use of several micro-skills. For other remodels, you may use only one strategy. It is better to use one clearly understood strategy than to attempt to use more than you clearly understand.

- You may want to begin remodelling by using only one or two strategies clearest to you. After remodelling some lessons, you will likely find ourself spontaneously using those strategies. You could then reread the strategy chapter and begin infusing additional strategies with which you feel comfortable. Thus, as the number of strategies you regularly use grows, your teaching can evolve at the pace most comfortable to you.

- If students don't grasp a critical idea or skill when you introduce it, don't give up. Critical insight must be developed over time. For instance, suppose the first attempt to get students to fairmindedly consider each others' views fails. It is likely that students are not in the habit of seriously considering each other's positions, and hence may not listen carefully to each other. If you make restating opposing views a routine part of discussion, students will eventually learn to prepare themselves by listening more carefully.

- Although the main function of this book is to help you remodel your lesson plans, we have not restricted our suggestions to the remodelling process. We strongly urge you to apply the insights embedded in the strategies to all aspects of classroom experience (including discussions, conflicts, and untraditional lessons — for instance, movies.) You may also use our remodels, or sections of them. Though many of our lessons are too long for one class period, we did not suggest where to break them up. Nor did we provide follow-up questions. If you decide to experiment with any of our remodels, you will probably have to remodel them somewhat to take your own students and text into account.

- We urge you to apply your growing critical insight to the task of analyzing and clarifying your concept of education and the educated person. Of each subject you teach, ask yourself what is most basic and crucial for an educated person to know or to be able to do. Highlight those aspects and teach them in a way that most fosters in-depth and useful understanding.

- Texts often have the same features — whether problems or opportunities for critical thought — occurring over and over again. Hence, remodelling a couple of lessons from a text can give you a basic structure to use many times over the course of the year.

- When comparing your work to ours, keep in mind that this is a flexible process; our remodel is not the only right one. Any changes which promote fairminded critical thought are improvements.

However you use what follows in this book, your understanding of the insights behind the strategies will determine the effectiveness of the remodels. Despite the detail with which we have delineated the strategies, they should not be translated into mechanistic, step-by-step procedures. Keep the goal of the well-educated, fairminded critical thinker continually in mind. Thinking critically involves insightful critical judgments at each step along the way. It is never done by recipe.

Diagram 1

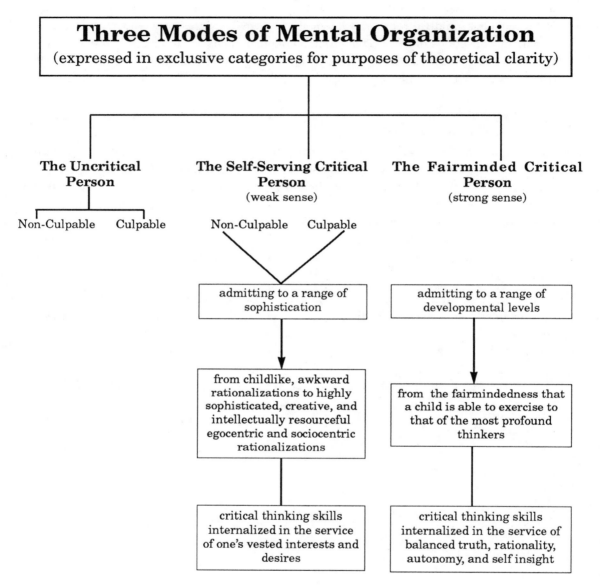

Three Modes of Mental Organization
(expressed in exclusive categories for purposes of theoretical clarity)

The Uncritical Person

Non-Culpable   Culpable

The Self-Serving Critical Person
(weak sense)

Non-Culpable   Culpable

The Fairminded Critical Person
(strong sense)

admitting to a range of sophistication

admitting to a range of developmental levels

from childlike, awkward rationalizations to highly sophisticated, creative, and intellectually resourceful egocentric and sociocentric rationalizations

from the fairmindedness that a child is able to exercise to that of the most profound thinkers

critical thinking skills internalized in the service of one's vested interests and desires

critical thinking skills internalized in the service of balanced truth, rationality, autonomy, and self insight

---

Note

Children enter school as fundamentally non-culpable, uncritical and self-serving thinkers. The educational task is to help them to become, as soon as possible and as fully as possible, responsible, fairminded, critical thinkers, empowered by intellectual skills and rational passions. Most people are some combination of the above three types; the proportions are the significant determinant of which of the three characterizations is most appropriate. For example, it is a common pattern for people to be capable of fairminded critical thought only when their vested interests or ego-attachments are not involved, hence the legal practice of excluding judges or jury members who can be shown to have such interests.

Diagram 2

Critical Thinking Lesson Plan Remodelling

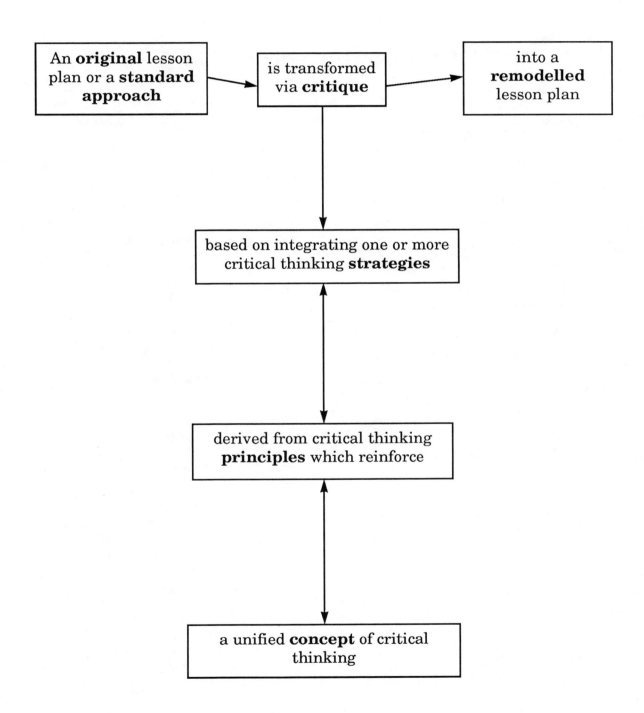

Diagram 3

The Perfections and Imperfections of Thought

clear _____ vs _____unclear

precise _____ vs _____imprecise

specific _____ vs _____vague

accurate _____ vs _____inaccurate

relevant _____ vs _____irrelevant

consistent _____ vs _____inconsistent

logical _____ vs _____illogical

deep _____ vs _____superficial

complete _____ vs _____incomplete

significant _____ vs _____trivial

adequate (for purpose) _____ vs _____inadequate

fair _____ vs _____biased or one-sided

Global Strategies: Socratic Questioning & Role-Playing

I. The Role of the Teacher

A teacher committed to teaching for critical thinking must think beyond compartmentalized subject matter, teaching to ends and objectives that transcend subject matter classification. To teach for critical thinking is, first of all, to create an environment in the class and in the school that is conducive to critical thinking. It is to help make the classroom and school environment a mini-critical society, a place where the values of critical thinking (truth, open-mindedness, empathy, autonomy, rationality, and self-criticism) are encouraged and rewarded. In such an environment, students learn to believe in the power of their own minds to identify and solve problems. They learn to believe in the efficacy of their own thinking. Thinking for themselves is not something they fear. Authorities are not those who tell them the "right" answers, but those who encourage and help them to figure out answers for themselves, who encourage them to discover the powerful resources of their own minds.

The teacher is much more a questioner than a preacher in this model. The teacher learns how to ask questions that probe meanings, that request reasons and evidence, that facilitate elaboration, that keep discussions from becoming confusing, that provide incentive for listening to what others have to say, that lead to fruitful comparisons and contrasts, that highlight contradictions and inconsistencies, and that elicit implications and consequences. Teachers committed to critical thinking realize that the primary purpose of all education is to teach students how to learn. Since there are more details than can be taught and no way to predict which the student will use, teachers emphasize thinking about basic issues and problems. Thus, details are learned as a necessary part of the process of settling such questions, and so are functional and relevant.

The teacher who teaches students how to learn and think about many basic issues gives them knowledge they can use the rest of their lives. This teacher realizes that subject matter divisions are arbitrary and are a matter of convenience, that the most important problems of everyday life

21

rarely fall neatly into subject matter divisions, that understanding a situation fully usually requires a synthesis of knowledge and insight from several subjects. An in-depth understanding of one subject requires an understanding of others. (One cannot answer questions in history, for example, without asking and answering related questions in psychology, sociology, etc.) Students must discover the value of "knowledge" "evidence," and "reasoning" by finding significant payoffs in dealing with their everyday life problems outside of school. Recognizing the universal problems we all face, the teacher should encourage each student to find personal solutions through self-reflective experiences and thought processes:

> Who am I? What is the world really like? What are my parents, my friends, and other people like? How have I become the way I am? What should I believe in? Why should I believe in it? What real options do I have? Who are my real friends? Whom should I trust? Who are my enemies? Need they be my enemies? How did the world become the way it is? How do people become the way they are? Are there any really bad people in the world? Are there any really good people in the world? What is good and bad? What is right and wrong? How should I decide? How can I decide what is fair and what is unfair? How can I be fair to others? Do I have to be fair to my enemies? How should I live my life? What rights do I have? What responsibilities?

The teacher who believes in personal freedom and thinking for oneself does not spoon-feed students with predigested answers to those questions. Nor should students be encouraged to believe that the answers to them are arbitrary and a matter of sheer opinion. Raising probing questions whenever they are natural to a subject under discussion, the teacher realizes that, in finding the way to answers, the student forges an overall perspective into which subject matter discoveries will be fit. Neither the discussion nor the student should be forced to conclusions that do not seem reasonable to the student.

Thus, such teachers reflect upon the subjects they teach, asking themselves, "What ideas and skills are the most basic and crucial in this subject? What do practitioners in this field do? How do they think? Why should students be familiar with this subject? What use does a well-educated person and citizen of a republic make of this subject? How can these uses be made apparent to and real for my students? Where do the various subject areas overlap? How should the tools and insights of each subject inform one's understanding of the others? Of one's place in the world?"

The teacher committed to teaching for critical thinking realizes that the child has two sources of "belief:" beliefs that the child forms as a result of personal experience, inward thinking, and interaction with peers and environment, and beliefs that the child learns through instruction by adults. The first could be called "real" or "operational" beliefs. They are what define the child's real world, the foundation for action, the source of acted-upon values. They are a result of the child making sense of or figuring out the world. They are heavily influenced by what has been called "pleasure-principle thinking." They are in large measure egocentric, unreflective, and unarticulated.

People believe in many things for egocentric, irrational reasons: because others hold the belief, because certain desires may be justified by the belief, because they feel more comfortable with the belief, because they are rewarded for the belief, because they ego-identify with the belief, because others reject them for not acting on the belief, because the belief helps to justify feelings of like or dislike toward others.

Students, of course, also have spontaneously formed reasonable beliefs. Some of those are inconsistent with the expressed beliefs of parents and teachers. As a result of this contradiction with authority, students rarely raise these beliefs to what Piaget calls "conscious realization."

Students have also developed their own theories about psychology, sociology, science, language, and so on, covering most subjects. The totality of these real beliefs is unsynthesized and contains many contradictions which students will discover only if encouraged to freely express them in an atmosphere that is mutually supportive and student-centered.

The other source of belief, didactic instruction from adult authority figures, is an authority's interpretation of reality, not the students'. The students learn to verbalize it but does not synthesize it with operational belief. Therefore, they rarely recognize contradictions between these two belief systems. A student's own theories and beliefs are not necessarily replaced with the knowledge offered in school.

The teacher concerned with this problem, then, provides an environment wherein students can discover and explore their beliefs. Such teachers refrain from rushing students who are struggling to express their beliefs, allow time for thoughtful discussion, refuse to allow anyone to attack students for their beliefs, reward students for questioning their own beliefs, and support students when they consider many points of view.

Unless the teacher provides conditions in which students can discover operational beliefs through reflective thinking, these two systems of beliefs will exist in separate dimensions of their lives. The first will control their deeds, especially private deeds; the second will control their words, especially public words. The first will be used when acting for themselves; the second when performing for others. Neither, in a sense, will be taken seriously. Neither will be subjected to rational scrutiny: the first because it isn't openly expressed and challenged verbally; the second because it is not tested in the crucible of action and practical decision-making. This dichotomy, when embedded in an individual's life, creates a barrier to living an "examined life." Students lack the wherewithal to explore contradictions, double standards, and hypocrisies. They will use critical thinking skills, if at all, as weapons in a struggle to protect themselves from exposure, and to lay bare the contradictions of the "other," the "enemy." When they integrate critical thinking skills into this dichotomous thinking, they become self-serving, not fairminded, critical thinkers.

The role of the teacher could be summarized as follows:

- help break big questions or tasks into smaller, more manageable parts
- create meaningful contexts in which learning is valued by the students
- help students clarify their thoughts by rephrasing or asking questions
- pose thought-provoking questions
- help keep the discussion focussed
- encourage students to explain things to each other
- help students find what they need to know by suggesting and showing students how to use resources
- ensure that students do justice to each view, that no views are cut off, ignored, or unfairly dismissed

II. Socratic Questioning: Wondering Aloud About Meaning and Truth

Introduction

Socratic discussion, wherein students' thought is elicited and probed, allows students to develop and evaluate their thinking by making it explicit. By encouraging students to slow their thinking down and elaborate on it, Socratic discussion gives students the opportunity to develop and test their ideas — the beliefs they have spontaneously formed and those they learn in school. Thus, students can synthesize their beliefs into a more coherent and better-developed perspective.

Socratic questioning requires teachers to take seriously and wonder about what students say and think: what they mean, its significance to them, its relationship to other beliefs, how it can be tested, to what extent and in what way it is true or makes sense. Teachers who wonder about the meaning and truth of students' statements can translate that curiosity into probing questions. By wondering aloud, teachers simultaneously convey interest in and respect for student thought, and model analytical moves for students. Fruitful Socratic discussion infects students with the same curiosity about the meaning of and truth of what they think, hear, and read and gives students the clear message that they are expected to think and to take everyone else's beliefs seriously.

Socratic questioning is based on the idea that all thinking has a logic or structure, that any one statement only partially reveals the thinking underlying it, expressing no more than a tiny piece of the system of interconnected beliefs of which it is a part. Its purpose is to expose the logic of someone's thought. Use of Socratic questioning presupposes the following points: All thinking has assumptions; makes claims or creates meaning; has implications and consequences; focuses on some things and throws others into the background; uses some concepts or ideas and not others; is defined by purposes, issues, or problems; uses or explains some facts and not others; is relatively clear or unclear; is relatively deep or superficial; is relatively critical or uncritical; is relatively elaborated or undeveloped; is relatively monological or multi-logical. Critical thinking is thinking done with an effective, self-monitoring awareness of these points.

Socratic instruction can take many forms. Socratic questions can come from the teacher or from students. They can be used in a large group discussion, in small groups, one-to-one, or even with oneself. They can have different purposes. What each form has in common is that someone's thought is developed as a result of the probing, stimulating questions asked. It requires questioners to try on others' beliefs, to imagine what it would be to accept them and wonder what it would be to believe otherwise. If a student says that people are selfish, the teacher may wonder aloud as to what it means to say that, how the student explains acts others call altruistic, what sort of example that student would accept as an unselfish act, or what the student thinks it means to say that an act or person was unselfish. The discussion which follows should help clarify the concepts of selfish and unselfish behavior, as well as the kind of evidence required to determine whether or not someone is or is not acting selfishly, and the consequences of accepting or rejecting the original generalization. Such a discussion enables students to examine their own views on such concepts as generosity, motivation, obligation, human nature, right, and wrong.

24

Some people erroneously believe that holding a Socratic discussion is like conducting a chaotic free-for-all. In fact, Socratic discussion has distinctive goals and distinctive ways to achieve them. Indeed, any discussion — any thinking — guided by Socratic questioning is structured. The discussion, the thinking, is structured to take student thought from the unclear to the clear, from the unreasoned to the reasoned, from the implicit to the explicit, from the unexamined to the examined, from the inconsistent to the consistent, from the unarticulated to the articulated. To learn how to participate in it, one has to learn how to listen carefully to what others say, to look for reasons and evidence, to recognize and reflect upon assumptions, to discover implications and consequences, to seek examples, analogies, and objections, to seek to discover, in short, what is really known and to distinguish it from what is merely believed.

Socratic Questioning

- raises basic issues
- probes beneath the surface of things
- pursues problematic areas of thought
- helps students to discover the *structure* of their own thought
- helps students develop sensitivity to clarity, accuracy, and relevance
- helps students arrive at judgment through their own reasoning
- helps students note claims, evidence, conclusions, questions-at-issue, assumptions, implications, consequences, concepts, interpretations, points of view: the elements of thought

---

Three Kinds of Socratic Discussion

We can loosely categorize three general forms of Socratic questioning and distinguish three basic kinds of preparation for each: the spontaneous, the exploratory, and the issue-specific.

Spontaneous or unplanned

Every teacher's teaching should be imbued with the Socratic spirit. We should always keep our curiosity and wondering alive. If we do, there will be many occasions in which we will spontaneously ask students questions about what they mean and explore with them how we might find out if something is true. If one student says that a given angle will be the same as another angle in a geometrical figure, we may spontaneously wonder how we might go about proving or disproving that. If one student says Americans love freedom, we may spontaneously wonder about exactly what that means (Does that mean, for example, that we love freedom more than other people do? How could we find out?). If in a science class a student says that most space is empty, we may be spontaneously moved to raise some question on the spot as to what that might mean and how we might find out.

Such spontaneous discussions provide models of listening critically as well as exploring the beliefs expressed. If something said seems questionable, misleading, or false, Socratic questioning provides a way of helping students to become self-correcting, rather than relying on correction by the teacher. Spontaneous Socratic discussion can prove especially useful when students become interested in a topic, when they raise an important issue, when they are on the brink of grasping or integrating something, when discussion becomes bogged down or confused or hostile.

Socratic questioning provides specific moves which can fruitfully take advantage of the interest, effectively approach the issue, aid integration and expansion of the insight, move a troubled discussion forward, clarify or sort through what appears confusing, and diffuse frustration or anger.

Although by definition there can be no pre-planning for a particular spontaneous discussion, teachers can prepare themselves by becoming familiar and comfortable with generic Socratic questions, and developing the art of raising probing follow-up questions and giving encouraging and helpful responses. Ask for examples, evidence, or reasons, propose counter-examples, ask the rest of class if they agree with a point made, suggest parallel or analogous cases, ask for a paraphrase of opposing views, rephrase student responses clearly and succinctly. These are among the most common moves.

- If you see little or no relevance in a student comment, you may think, "I wonder why this student mentioned that now?" and ask, "What connection do you see between our discussion and your point that ...?" or "I'm not sure why you mentioned that now. Could you explain how it's related to this discussion?" or "What made you think of that?" Either the point is germane so you can clarify the connection, or only marginally related, so you can rephrase it and say "A new issue has been raised." That new issue can be pursued then, or tactfully postponed, or can generate an assignment.

- If a student says something vague or general, you may think, "I wonder about the role of that belief in this student's life, the consequences of that belief, or how the student perceives the consequences, or if there are any practical consequences at all" and so may ask, "How does that belief affect how you act? What, for example, do you do or refrain from doing because you believe that?" You might have several students respond and compare their understandings, or suggest an alternative view and have students compare its consequences.

To summarize: Because we begin to wonder more and more about meaning and truth, and so think aloud in front of our students by means of questions, Socratic exchanges will occur at many unplanned moments in our instruction. However, in addition to these unplanned wonderings we can also design or plan out at least two distinct kinds of Socratic discussion: one that explores a wide range of issues and one that focuses on one particular issue.

Exploratory

What we here call *exploratory* Socratic questioning enables teachers to find out what students know or think and to use it to probe into student thinking on a variety of issues. Hence you may use it to learn students' impressions of a subject in order to assess their thought and ability to articulate it, you may use it to see what students value, or to uncover problematic areas or potential biases, or find out where students are clearest and fuzziest in their thinking. You may use it to discover areas or issues of interest or controversy, or to find out where and how students have integrated school material into their belief systems. Such discussions can serve as preparation in a general way for later study or analysis of a topic, as an introduction, as review, to see what students understood from their study of a unit or topic preparatory to taking a test, to suggest where they should focus study for test, as a basis for or guide to future assignments, or to prepare for an assignment. Or, again, you might have students take (or pick) an issue raised in discussion and give their own views, or have students form groups to discuss the issue or topic.

This type of Socratic questioning raises and explores a broad range of interrelated issues and concepts. It requires minimal pre-planning or pre-thinking. It has a relatively loose order or structure. You can prepare by having some general questions ready to raise when appropriate by considering the topic or issue, related issues and key concepts. You can also prepare by predict-ing students' likeliest responses and preparing some follow-up questions. Remember, however, that once students' thought is stimulated there is no predicting exactly where discussion will go.

What follows are some suggestions and possible topics for Socratic discussions:

• "What is social studies?" If students have difficulty, ask, "When you've studied social studies, what have you studied/talked about?" If students list topics, put them on the board. Then have students discuss the items and try to group them. "Do these topics have something in common? Are there differences between these topics?" Encourage students to discuss details they know about the topics. If, instead of listing topics, they give a general answer or definition, or if they are able to give a statement about what the topics listed have in common, suggest examples that fit the definition but are not social studies. For example, if a student says, "It's about people," mention medicine. Have them modify or improve their definition. "How is social studies like and unlike other subjects? What basic questions does the subject address? How does it address them? Why study social studies? Is it important? Why or why not? How can we use what we learn in social studies? What are the most important ideas you've learned from this subject?"

• When, if ever, is violence justified? Why are people as violent as they are? What effects does violence have? Can violence be lessened or stopped?
• What is a friend?
• What is education? Why learn?
• What is most important?
• What is right and wrong? Why be good? What is a good person?
• What is the difference between living and non-living things?
• Of what sorts of things is the universe made?
• What is language?
• What are the similarities and differences between humans and animals?

There may be occasions when you are unsure whether to call a discussion exploratory or issue-specific. Which you call it is not important. What is important is what happens in the dis-cussion. For example, consider this group of questions:

• What does 'vote' mean?
    How do people decide whom to elect? How should they decide? How could people pre-dict how a potential leader is likely to act? If you don't know about an issue or the candidates for an office, should you vote?
    Is voting important? Why or why not? What are elections supposed to produce? How? What does that require? What does that tell us about voting?
    Why are elections considered a good idea? Why is democracy considered good? What does belief in democracy assume about human nature?
    How do people become candidates?
    Why does the press emphasize how much money candidates have? How does having lots of money help candidates win?
    Why do people give money to candidates? Why do companies?

These questions could be the list generated as possible questions for an exploratory discus-sion. Which of them are actually used would depend on how students respond. For an issue-spe-cific discussion, these questions and more could be used in an order which takes students from ideas with which they are most familiar to those with which they are least familiar.

Issue-Specific

Much of the time you will approach your instruction with specific areas and issues to cover. This is the time for issue-specific Socratic questioning. To really probe an issue or concept in depth, to have students clarify, sort, analyze and evaluate thoughts and perspectives, distinguish the known from the unknown, synthesize relevant factors and knowledge, students can engage in an extended and focused discussion. This type of discussion offers students the chance to pursue perspectives to their most basic assumptions and through their furthest implications and consequences. These discussions give students experience in engaging in an extended, ordered, and integrated discussion in which they discover, develop, and share ideas and insights. It requires pre-planning or thinking through possible perspectives on the issue, grounds for conclusions, problematic concepts, implications, and consequences. You can further prepare by reflecting on those subjects relevant to the issue: their methods, standards, basic distinctions and concepts, and interrelationships — points of overlap or possible conflict. It is also helpful to be prepared by considering likeliest student answers. This is the type of Socratic questioning most often used in the lesson remodels themselves. Though we can't provide the crucial follow-up questions, we illustrate pre-planning for issue-specific Socratic questioning in numerous remodels.

All three types of Socratic discussion require development of the art of questioning. They require the teacher to develop familiarity with a wide variety of intellectual moves and sensitivity to when to ask which kinds of questions, though there is rarely one best question at any particular time.

Some Suggestions for Using Socratic Discussion

• Have an initial exploratory discussion about a complex issue in which students break it down into simpler parts. Students can then choose the aspects they want to explore or research. Then have an issue-specific discussion where students share, analyze, evaluate, and synthesize their work.

• The class could have a "fishbowl" discussion. One third of the class, sitting in a circle, discusses a topic. The rest of the class, in a circle around the others, listens, takes notes, then discusses the discussion.

• Assign an essay asking students to respond to a point of interest made in a discussion.

• Have students write summaries of their discussions immediately afterwards. They could also add new thoughts or examples, provide further clarification, etc. They could later share these notes.

A Taxonomy of Socratic Questions

It is helpful to recognize, in light of the universal features in the logic of human thought, that there are identifiable categories of questions for the adept Socratic questioner to dip into: questions of clarification, questions that probe assumptions, questions that probe reasons and evidence, questions about viewpoints or perspectives, questions that probe implications and consequences, and questions about the question. Here are some examples of generic questions in each of these categories:

Questions of Clarification

- What do you mean by _____?
- What is your main point?
- How does ____ relate to ___?
- Could you put that another way?
- What do you think is the main issue here?
- Is your basic point _____ or _____?
- Let me see if I understand you; do you mean _____ or _____?
- How does this relate to our discussion/ problem/ issue?
- What do you think John meant by his remark? What did you take John to mean?
- Jane, would you summarize in your own words what Richard has said? ... Richard, is that what you meant?

- Could you give me an example?
- Would this be an example: _____?
- Could you explain that further?
- Would you say more about that?
- Why do you say that?

Questions that Probe Assumptions

- What are you assuming?
- What is Karen assuming?
- What could we assume instead?
- You seem to be assuming _____. Do I understand you correctly?
- All of your reasoning is dependent on the idea that ____. Why have you based your reasoning on _____ rather than _____?
- You seem to be assuming ____. How would you justify taking this for granted?
- Is it always the case? Why do you think the assumption holds here?

Questions that Probe Reasons and Evidence

- What would be an example?
- What are your reasons for saying that?
- What other information do we need to know?
- Could you explain your reasons to us?
- But is that good evidence to believe that?
- Are those reasons adequate?
- Is there reason to doubt that evidence?
- Who is in a position to know if that is the case?
- What would you say to someone who said ___?
- Can someone else give evidence to support that response?
- By what reasoning did you come to that conclusion?
- How could we go about finding out whether that is true?

- How do you know?
- Why did you say that?
- Why do you think that is true?
- What led you to that belief?
- Do you have any evidence for that?
- How does that apply to this case?
- What difference does that make?
- What would convince you otherwise?

Questions About Viewpoints or Perspectives

- You seem to be approaching this issue from ____ perspective. Why have you chosen this rather than that perspective?
- How would other groups/types of people respond? Why? What would influence them?
- How could you answer the objection that _____ would make?
- Can/did anyone see this another way?
- What would someone who disagrees say?
- What is an alternative?
- How are Ken's and Roxanne's ideas alike? Different?

Questions that Probe Implications and Consequences

- What are you implying by that?
- When you say _____, are you implying _____?
- But if that happened, what else would also happen as a result? Why?
- What effect would that have?

- Would that necessarily happen or only probably happen?
- What is an alternative?
- If this and this are the case, then what else must also be true?

Questions About the Question

- How can we find out?
- How could someone settle this question?
- Is the question clear? Do we understand it?
- Is this question easy or hard to answer? Why?
- Would _____ put the question differently?
- Does this question ask us to evaluate something?
- Do we all agree that this is the question?
- To answer this question, what questions would we have to answer first?
- I'm not sure I understand how you are interpreting the main question at issue.
- Is this the same issue as _____?
- Can we break this question down at all?
- How would _____ put the issue?
- What does this question assume?
- Why is this question important?

Wondering (And Wondering About Your Wonderings)

As a blossoming critical thinker, you will find yourself wondering in many directions. You will often, however, be unsure about how many of these wonderings to share with your students. You certainly don't want to overwhelm them. Neither do you want to confuse them or lead them in too many directions at once. So when do you make the wonderings explicit in the form of a question and when do you keep them in the privacy of your mind?

There is no pat formula or procedure for answering these questions, though there are some principles:

- "Test and find out." There is nothing wrong with some of your questions misfiring. You won't always be able to predict what questions will stimulate students thought. So you must engage in some trial-and-error questioning.
- "Tie into student experience and perceived needs." You may think of numerous examples of ways students can apply what they learn, and formulate questions relating academic material to students' lives.
- "Don't give up too soon." If students don't respond to a question, wait. If they still don't respond, you could rephrase the question or break it down into simpler questions.

The teacher must use care and caution in introducing students to Socratic questioning. The level of the questions should match the level of the students' thought. It should not be assumed that students will be fully successful with it, except over a considerable length of time. Nevertheless, properly used, it can be introduced in some form or other at virtually any grade level.

Socratic Interludes in Class

#1 Helping Students Organize Their Thoughts for Writing

Introduction

The following Socratic interlude represents an initial attempt to get students to think about what a persuasive essay is and how to go about preparing to write one. Of course, like all Socratic questioning it goes beyond one objective, for it also stimulates students to think critically in general about what they are doing and why. It helps them to see that their own ideas, if developed, are important and can lead to insights.

Transcript

(A Reconstruction)

T: you are all going to be writing a persuasive essay, so let's talk about what you have to do to get your ideas organized. There are two ways to persuade people of something, by appealing to their reason, a rational appeal, and by appealing to their emotions, an emotional appeal. What is the difference between these? Let's take the rational appeal first, what do you do when you appeal to someone's reason?

John: You give them good reasons for accepting something. You tell them why they should do something or what they can get out of it or why it's good for them.

T: But don't they already have reasons why they believe as they do? So why should they accept your reasons rather than theirs?

Bob: Well, maybe mine are better than theirs.

T: But haven't you ever given someone, say your mother or father, good reasons for what you wanted to do, but they just did not accept your reasons even though they seemed compelling to you.

Susan: Yeah, that happens a lot to me. They just say that I have to do what they say whether I like it or not because they are my parents.

T: So is it hopeless to give people good reasons for changing their minds because people will never change their minds?

Grace: No, people sometimes do change their minds. Sometimes they haven't thought about things a lot or they haven't noticed something about what they're doing. So you tell them something they hadn't considered and then they change their minds....sometimes.

T: That's right, sometimes people do change their minds after you give them a new way of looking at things or reasons they hadn't considered. What does that tell you about one thing you want to be sure to do in deciding how to defend your ideas and get people to consider them? What do you think, Tom?

Tom: I guess you want to consider different ways to look at things, to find new reasons and things.

T: Well, but where can you find different ways to look at things? What do you think, Janet?

Janet: I would look in the library.

T: But what would you look for, could you be more specific?

Janet: Sure. I'm going to write about why women should have the same rights as men, so I'll look for books on feminism and women.

T: How will that help you to find different ways to look at things, could you spell that out further?

Janet: I think that certainly there will probably be different ideas in different books. Not all women think alike. Black women and white women and religious women and Hispanic women all have their own point of view. I will look for the best reasons that each give and try to put them into my paper.

T: OK, but so far we have just talked about giving reasons to support your ideas, what I called in the beginning a rational appeal. What about the emotional side of things, of appealing to people's emotions? John, what are some emotions and why appeal to them?

John: Emotions are things like fear and anger and jealousy, what happens when we feel strongly or are excited.

T: *Right, so do you know anyone who appeals to our emotions? Are your emotions ever appealed to?*

Judy: Sure, we all try to get people involved in feeling as we do. When we talk to friends about kids we don't like we describe them so that our friends will get mad at them and feel like we do.

T: *How do we do this, could you give me an example, Judy?*

Judy: OK, like I know this girl who's always trying to get her hands on boys, even if they already have girl friends. So I tell my friends how she acts. I give them all the details, how she touches them when she talks to them and acts like a dip. We really get mad at her.

T: *So what do you think, should you try to get your reader to share your feeling? Should you try to get their emotions involved?*

Judy: Sure, if you can.

T: *But isn't this the way propaganda works? How we get people emotional so that they go along with things they shouldn't? Didn't Hitler get people all emotional and stir up their hate?*

Judy: Yeah, but we do that too when we play the national anthem or when we get excited about Americans winning medals at the Olympics.

T: *So what do you think of this Frank, should we or shouldn't we try to get people's emotions stirred up?*

Frank: If what we are try to get people to do is good we should do it, but if what we are trying to get them to do is bad we shouldn't.

T: *Well, what do you think about Judy's getting her friends mad at a girl by telling them how she flirts with boys?*

Frank: Are you asking me?....I think she ought to clean up her own act first. (laughter)

Judy: What do you mean by that?!

Frank: Well, you're one of the biggest flirts around!

Judy: I never flirt with boys who have girl friends and anyway I'm just a friendly person.

Frank: Yes you are, *very* friendly!

T: *OK, calm down you guys, I think you better settle this one in private. But look, there's an important point here. Sometimes we do act inconsistently, sometimes there are contradictions in our behavior, and we criticize people for doing what we do. And that's one thing we should think about when writing our papers, are we willing to live by what we are preaching to others? Or another way to put this is by asking whether our point of view is realistic. If our point of view seems too idealistic then our reader may not be persuaded.*

We don't have much time left today, so let me try to summarize what I see as implied in what we have talked about. So far, we have agreed about a number of things important to persuasive writing: 1) you need to give good reasons to support your point of view, 2) you should be clear about what your reasons are, 3) you should consider the issue from more than one point of view, including considering how your reader might look at it, 4) you should check out books or articles on the subject to get different points of view, 5) you should consider how you might reach your reader's feelings, how what you say ties into what they care about, 6) following Judy's example you should present specific examples and include the details that make your example realistic and moving, 7) in line with Frank's point, you should watch out for contradictions and inconsistencies, and 8) you should make sure that what you are arguing for is realistic. For next time I would like you all to write out the introductory paragraph to your paper in which you basically tell the reader what you are going to try to persuade him or her of and how you are going to do it, that is, how the paper will be structured. Don't worry that your first draft is rough; you will be working in groups of threes to sharpen up what you have written.

#2: Helping Students to Think More Deeply about Basic Ideas

Introduction

We tend to pass by basic ideas quickly in order to get into more derivative ideas. This is part of the didactic mind set of school-is-giving-students-content-to-remember. What we need to do, in contrast, is to stimulate student's thinking right from the beginning, especially about the most basic ideas in a subject so that they are motivated from the beginning to use their thinking in trying to understand things, and so that they base their thinking on foundational ideas that make sense to them.

Transcript

(A Reconstruction)

Teacher: This is a course in Biology. What kind of a subject is that? What do you know about Biology already? Kathleen, what do you know about it?

Kathleen: It's a science.

T: And what's a science?

Kathleen: Me? A science is very exact. They do experiments and measure things and test things.

T: Right, and what other sciences are there besides Biology? Marisa, could you name some?

Marisa: Sure, there's Chemistry and Physics.

T: What else?

Blake: There's Botany and Math?

T: Math...math is a little different from the others, isn't it? How is math different from Biology, Chemistry, Physics, and Botany? Blake, what would you say?

Blake: You don't do experiments in math.

T: And why not?

Blake: I guess cause numbers are different.

T: Yes, studying numbers and other mathematical things is different from studying chemicals or laws in the physical world or living things and so forth. You might ask your math teacher about why numbers are different or do some reading about that, but let's focus our attention here on what are called the life sciences. Why are Biology and Botany called life sciences?

Peter: Because they both study living things.

T: How are they different? How is Biology different from Botany? Jennifer, what do you think?

Jennifer: I don't know.

T: *Well, let's all of us look up the words in our dictionaries and see what is said about them.*

(Students look up the words)

T: *Jennifer, what did you find for Biology?*

Jennifer: It says: "The science that deals with the origin, history, physical characteristics, life processes, habits, etc...of plants and animals: It includes Botany and Zoology".

T: *So what do we know about the relationship of Botany to Biology? Rick?*

Rick: Botany is just a part of Biology.

T: *Right, and what can we tell about Biology from just looking at its etymology. What does it literally mean? If you break the word into two parts "bio" and "logy". Blake, what does it tell us?*

Blake: The science of life or the study of life.

T: *So, do you see how etymology can help us get an insight into the meaning of a word? Do you see how the longer definition spells out the etymological meaning in greater detail? Well, why do you think experiments are so important to biologists and other scientists? Have humans always done experiments do you think? Marisa.*

Marisa: I guess not, not before there was any science.

T: *Right, that's an excellent point, science didn't always exist. What did people do before science existed? How did they get their information? How did they form their beliefs? Peter.*

Peter: From religion.

T: *Yes, religion often shaped a lot of what people thought. Why don't we use religion today to decide, for example, what is true of the origin, history, and physical characteristics of life?*

Peter: Some people still do. Some people believe that the Bible explains the origin of life and that the theory of evolution is wrong.

T: *What is the theory of evolution, Jose?*

Jose: I don't know.

T: *Well, why don't we all look up the name Darwin in our dictionaries and see if there is anything there about Darwinian theory.*

(Students look up the words)

T: *Jose, read aloud what you have found.*

Jose: It says "Darwin's theory of evolution holds that all species of plants and animals developed from earlier forms by hereditary transmission of slight variations in successive generations and that the forms which survive are those that are best adapted to the environment."

T: *What does that mean to you....in ordinary language? How would you explain that? Jose.*

Jose: It means the stronger survive and the weaker die?

T: *Well, if that's true why do you think the dinosaurs died out? I thought dinosaurs were very strong?*

Shannon: They died because of the ice age, I think.

34

T: So I guess it's not enough to be strong, you must also fit in with the changes in the environment. Perhaps fitness or adaptability is more important than strength. Well, in any case why do you think that most people today look to science to provide answers to questions about the origin and nature of life rather than to the Bible or other religious teachings?

Shannon: Nowadays most people believe that science and religion deal with different things and that scientific questions cannot be answered by religion.

T: And by the same token, I suppose, we recognize that religious questions cannot be answered by science. In any case, how were scientists able to convince people to consider their way of finding answers to questions about the nature of life and life processes. Kathleen, you've been quiet for a while, what do you think?

Kathleen: To me science can be proved. When scientists say something we can ask for proof and they can show us, and if we want we can try it out for ourselves.

T: Could you explain that further?

Kathleen: Sure, in my chemistry class we did experiments in which we tested out some of the things that were said in our chemistry books. We could see for ourselves.

T: That's right, science is based on the notion that when we claim things to be true about the world we should be able to test them to see if, objectively, they are true. Marisa, you have a question?

Marisa: Yes, but don't we all test things. We test our parents and our friends. We try out ideas to see if they work.

T: That's true. But is there any difference between the way you and I test our friends and the way a chemist might test a solution to see if it is acidic?

Marisa: Sure, ... but I'm not sure how to explain it.

T: Blake, what do you think?

Blake: Scientists have laboratories; we don't.

T: They also do precise measurements and use precise instruments, don't they? Why don't we do that with our friends, parents, and children? Adrian, do you have an idea why not?

Adrian: We don't need to measure our friends. We need to find out whether they really care about us.

T: Yes, finding our about caring is a different matter than finding out about acids and bases, or even than finding out about animal behavior. You might say that there are two different kinds of realities in the world, the qualitative and the quantitative, and that science is mostly concerned with the quantitative, while we are often concerned with the qualitative. Could you name some qualitative ideas that all of us are concerned with? Rick, what do you think?

Rick: I don't know what you mean.

T: Well, the word qualitative is connected to the word quality. If I were to ask you to describe your own qualities in comparison to your brother or sister, would you know the sort of thing I was asking you?

Rick: I guess so.

T: Could you, for example, take your father and describe to us some of his best and some of his worst qualities as you see them?

Rick: I guess so.

T: OK, why don't you do it. What do you think some of your father's best qualities are?

Rick: To me he is generous. He likes to help people out when they are in trouble.

T: And what science studies generosity?

Rick: I don't know. None, I guess.

T: That's right, generosity is a human quality, it can't be measured scientifically. There is no such thing as generosity units. So science is not the only way we can find things out. We can also experience qualities in the world. We can experience kindness, generosity, fear, love, hate, jealousy, self-satisfaction, friendship, and many, many other things as well. In this class we are concerned mainly with what we can find out about life quantitatively or scientifically. For next time, I want you to read the first chapter in your text book and I want you to be prepared to explain what the first chapter says. I will be dividing you up into groups of four and each group of four will develop a short summary of the first chapter (without looking at it, of course) and then we will have a spokesperson from each group explain your summary to the class. After that, we will have a discussion of the ideas mentioned. Don't forget today's discussion, because I'll be asking you some questions that will see if you can relate what we talked about today with what was said in your first chapter. Any questions? ... OK, ... See you next time.

#3: Helping Students to Think Seriously about Complex Social Issues

Introduction

In the following extended discussion, Rodger Halstead, Homested High School Social Studies teacher, Socratically questions students about their views about the Middle East. He links up the issue with the holocaust during WWII and, ultimately, with the problem of how to correct one injustice without committing another.

Part One

I thought what we'd do now is to talk a little about the Middle East. And remember we saw a film, and title of the film was, "Let My People Go." And in the process of seeing that film, we took a look at some of the things that happened in the concentration camps; in the death-camps of Nazi Germany during World War II. Remember that? It's pretty hard to forget, so I'm sure that you do remember that. Who do you hold responsible for what happened to the Jewish people during the holocaust, the Nazi holocaust of the 1940's and the late 1930's? Who do you hold responsible for that? Laura?

Laura: Everyone. Um ...

What do you mean, everyone?

Students: It started in Germany. I would ... My first thought goes to Hitler; then it goes to the German people that allowed him to take control without ... without seeing what he was doing before it was too late.

Let's see if we understand. Are you talking now about what I call moral responsibility, that they hold some moral responsibility for what happened, or are you talking about legal responsibility? What I'd like to really have us talk about is legal responsibility. Who would you punish for the responsibility for what happened to the Jewish people? Would you punish all Germans? No. OK, then who would you punish?

Student: Hitler.

Hitler. OK, if he had been alive and we'd been able to capture him, you would have punished him.

Student: Absolutely.

OK. I think probably we'd all agree to that, alright? Anybody else?

Student: Probably his five top men. I ... I'm not sure ...

Well, whatever. Whether it's five or six or ten or whatever. The top guys, the SS ...

Student: (several talking) Well, that's a good question ... and, there are a lot of Nazis out there.

Well, are you sure everyone was a member of the Nazi party? Not all Germans were.

Student: Well, not all Germans were ... um ...

Want to think about it?

Student: Yeah.

How about somebody else? First of all, we all agree that somebody should have been punished, right? Alright, these are not acts that should have gone unpunished. OK, Steve?

Steve: Well, it'd be kind of hard, but, like, I think that every soldier or whatever, whoever took a life, theirs should be taken. (Several speaking)

Every person who ... every ... every Nazi soldier who was in the camps ...

Steve: Who had something to do with ...

Who had something to do with the killing of the people in the camps. The Jews, the gypsies, the opponents of Hitler, all those people. All the 12 million killed. Anybody that had a direct ... played a direct role. You would punish them. What if we had a corporal here, Steve, and the corporal said, "The reason I did this is because I was ordered to do it. And if I didn't do it, my family was going to be injured, or something was going to happen to my family." Are you going to punish that corporal?

Steve: Well, I guess ... well, I mean ... ah, they ... They still took a life, you know, but they're ... what they're ... You know, they were just following the rules. What ... (Laughter) Yes, but I mean ... I, I, I believe that, you know, if you take a life ...

What if they didn't take a life? What if they just tortured somebody?

Steve: Then they ... then ... then they should be tortured in the same way.

So you say anybody who was directly responsible for any injury, torture, murder, whatever in the camps; they themselves should get a similar kind of punishment. What about the people who were in the beaurocracy of the German government who, ah, set up the trains and the time schedule of the trains? What about the engineer on the train? You're looking at me, Amy. I'm not sure if ...

Amy: Well, yeah, I guess ...

All those people?

Amy: Yeah, because if you think about it, if they hadn't of done that, they couldn't have gotten the people there.

OK, and what about the people standing on the streets while the Jews to get in the trucks ...

Amy: No, I think that's going a little too ...

OK, so anybody who participates in any way in the arrest, the carrying out of all these activities, including even people who, ah ... what about people who typed up the memos?

Amy: Yeah, I guess)

(Several Speaking)

No, says Manual. Why not no? Why no?

Manual: Like, for example, if they're put under a lot of duress. Like, ah, we're going to kill your family, we're going to hurt your family, put them in a concentration camp, too ...

Yes. Yes?

Manual: It, it's just total ... you just can't hold them responsible because their family ... it's just like, ah ... the next, the closest thing to them, and you can't just say you have to punish them because I don't think they did it on purpose. They didn't do it because we hate the Jews, we don't like you ... we're not doing it because we want to see you suffer. They're doing it because they don't want to see their family suffer.

Anybody who enjoyed what they were doing, Manny, clearly needs to be punished, in your? right? What if I do it, but I don't enjoy it? Oh, God! I don't want to do this! Ohhh! But you made me do it.

Manual: I don't think they should be punished.

OK, the war's over, Manny. Let's get the man in here for a second. The war's over, Manny, and we now have the rest of these people. Leslie, did you do that because you wanted to do that? (jumps to Rodger)

(Laughter)

Student: No.

No. Gail, did you do it because you wanted to do it?

Gail: No.

Did you do it because you wanted to do it, Ariel? Did you do it, Laurel? Cuz you wanted, Brad?

Student: No.

Manny, what we got? None of them did it because they wanted to. They all did it because it was orders.

Manual: Well, ah ...

How do we know?

Manual: That's a good question.

You want to get off the hot seat for a second, Manny?

Manual: Yeah.

OK, I don't know ... eeny, meeny, Stacy?

Stacy: Well, ah ... that's why I think that it should maybe just be the leadership because they're the ones ...

Just Hitler, and the ...

Stacy: Yeah, cuz they're the ones who made up the concentration camps, and they're the ones who tell the people to do it. And some people will want to do these things, and some people won't, and you can't determine who wants to do it and who doesn't.

Student: Yeah, but how far do you go down?

Stacy: See ... Well, that's why you just do ... it'd just be those top ...

Student: What's the top ...

Stacy: Hitler and his five or six men.

Stacy, would I gather that you agree with Manny that if somebody really enjoyed doing it and wanted to do it, 'doing it' meaning hurting, killing, torture; if they really wanted to do it and enjoyed it, those people should be punished.

Stacy: Yeah, they should, but you can't decide, you can't tell who really wanted to be ...

OK, someone who did it reluctantly, you shouldn't punish them, is that right?

Stacy: Right.

Suppose you and I are in the mafia. And suppose you and I are in the mafia, and I order you to kill ... ah, Katherine. OK?

Stacy: OK.

You happen to be ... ah, acquaintances with Kathy, and you don't want to do it, but I order you to do it. And, in fact you do, you carry it out because I tell ya, if you don't do it, I'm going to pull your fingernails out, and your toenails, and I'm going to shoot off you kneecap. And so you kill Katherine. Now, along comes Brad. He's a policeman. And he arrests you for killing Katherine, OK? And you say, "I didn't want to do it. My toenails were going to go out, my fingernails were going to go out, my kneecaps were going to go." Should we say, "You're home free, Stacy."

Stacy: No, I'd lead them to you, is what I'd do.

So, they're going to arrest me.

Stacy: Yeah.

Alright. Now should you be arrested? Should we just say, "I'm sorry, Stacy. should you be arrested? Should you be punished?

Stacy: Yeah, I should be arrested but maybe not. ... You should be *really* punished, yeah.

   Really punished

Stacy: Yeah

Should you be punished too?

Stacy: I'm in the Mafia. I shouldn't be in the Mafia

So any body who is in the camp who does these deeds because even though they did it because they did not want to do them they should also be held responsible and punished.

Stacy: You can't. There are too many of them. It's stooping to the Nazi's level by killing, by punishing all these people

So will you let some of them go free because you can't punish all

Stacy: Right, you can't, you can't punish a whole entire group of people that's like millions of people

Why can't you do that?

Stacy: Because it's doing what they were doing to the Jewish people.

We'll we get some disagreement here, Jeannette

Jeannette: If you can't call a person responsible for making a decision, where does that leave society.

What kind of decision?

Jeannette: They made a decision to follow the order

And you are saying we can't be responsible for a major

(voices)

Oh I'm sorry. Oh you have to ... the front row is answering ... why must you hold them responsible?

(Laughter.)

Jeannette: Because they made the decision, they did it.

But what if they did it under duress?

Jeannette: They could've ... faced the responsibilities, you have to face responsibilities either way, you can't just do something.

Suppose, suppose I say to you, "Jeanette you, I want you to ah pull Bill's eyeballs out of his head. (Laughter) And if you don't do that, I am going to kill you, Jeanette."

Jeannette: I am responsible

Are you responsible?

Jeannette: I'm responsible.

You're going to die!

Jeannette: I'm responsible!

So we should punish you because you do this deed even though you would have died if you hadn't done it?

Jeannette: No! it's still my decision.

Student: Yeah.

Stacy: But they, what if they were drafted into being in the Nazi camps and they were forced to do that — and they did not want to do that?

Student: How did they force ...

Stacy: Just like we had American troops in Viet Nam, they were killing people.

Student: And they were drafted. A lot of people ran though ...

Student: A lot of people didn't.

Time out! time out, we have a real important discussion and that is the issue of the people who, what about the people who did not willingly do it who did it because of orders, are they or are they not responsible?

Student: No.

Jody

Jody: I agree with Janet. They are responsible, they made the decision to do it, — they have a choice but some people I'm sure made the choice to die rather than to do this. I'm sure there were people that did that. And that was their decision because they could not go through with the order. You can't live with that. They went through it and made that decision. They have to live with what they did and they have to be punished for it because they took the lives of other people.

Wait a minute, no, no, no, no, no. Do you know the story of Patty Hearst at all? I know its ancient history to you. When she was kidnapped by a group call the SLA. She was brainwashed and she was beaten. She was abused and eventually she joins the group and they rob a bank and she had a part of the bank robbery up in Carmichael, CA, it's up near Sacramento and in the process of doing that after she is freed she argued that during the bank robbery they had a gun on her and she didn't have any choice now she's arrested for the bank robbery and she's going to be put on trial. Is she responsible for her acts in that bank robbery Jody, because if she didn't participate in that, there was gun on her and she could have been killed. Does she go free or do you punish her for the bank robbery?

Jody: That's a hard question. (yeah, no fair) was it proven that there was a gun on her?

Yes they had tape. It was not clear whether there were bullets in the gun or so forth. There is tape of a gun.

Jody: Well, if there's really proof, that's different.

What do you mean that's different?

Jody: Well, than someone who was a Nazi

No, no, no, let's not get to Nazi yet. You're on a jury, Jody, are you going to vote guilty or innocent?

Jody: Innocent

Why?

Jody: Because there was proof that she was forced; it wasn't a threat that something was going to happen. She was forced.

Did she do it under threat of her own life?

Student: Yes

All right. Leslie here is a Nazi. OK, Gayle is just a neutral. Leslie tells Gayle if you don't kill Ariel the Jew, you will be punished. Gayle kills Ariel the Jew. The reason she does is because Leslie told her to do it.

Jody: No, I guess.

Leslie held the gun on her. Are we not going to punish Gayle — Gayle "Patty Hearst"

Jody: No. I would probably have to say that she would have to be responsible.

Patty Hearst Patty Hearst

Jody: Yeah.

Because you see the inconsistency with the previous position and you want to hold the position that in fact everyone who does things even under orders and compulsion are responsible for what they do. Is that right? Would I be clear that in any future argument with your parents, you will not argue a line that might say, "The reason I did that is because somebody else told me I had to do that." You'll never argue that?

Jody: Your parents always say, "But it was your decision."

And you agree to that.

Jody: And you don't have to listen to what everyone else says.

And you believe that.

Jody: Yeah.

And you will follow it.

Jennifer.

Jennifer: Um, I agree with Janet, but I think its conditional because

What is conditional?

Jennifer: Well, that, that the people are ultimately responsible for their actions because in the Patty Hearst case, she umm, it was a bank robbery, and that wasn't directly, I mean that was, — are not supposed to steal people's money and that would affect people but it's not physically, its not physical pain and it's not, you know, killing them, and so I think they should of um punish all the people who are in the Nazi camp because they were responsible for — physical pain and ah their deaths.

Now let's see. Let's change it just slightly to make sure we understand. So far, we have pretty wide — all the leaders get punished, right? We had some disagreement on who in the camps will be punished and some of you think all the people involved in the camps and others think not quite all the people. Anybody beyond that? What about Germans who knew what was going on and did nothing to stop it?

Student: (many voices)

It's too broad.

It's too broad?

Student: Yeah.

Is there anybody in the room right now who thinks that we should punish all the Germans who knew what was going on and did nothing to stop it. OK, so obviously you would not agree to punish Americans who knew about it, right? Or the British, right? So you're keeping your level of punishment to the leaders and those who are directly involved, and you have some disagreement on who is directly involved and should be punished. Have I got it right?

Part Two

You're in the U.N. It's 1947. You have now been given the legal right, whether you believe it is the moral right or not, you have been given the legal right to decide what to do with Palestine. OK, we are not talking about moral. No, we are talking about legal. You are a country, you are going to have to vote on what to do with the state of Palestine. What are you going to do?

Student: Vote for the Arabs

For the Arabs., you are going to vote that the Arabs have — why?

Student: Additionally, I would give the Jews a piece of Germany.

OK, OK, Would you today be somewhat sympathetic to a Palestinian who comes to you and says, "My land has been taken wrongly from me and I have been driven off my land by a people and by an organization for an act that I had no responsibility for." Would you be sympathetic to a Palestinian who said that?

Jeanette: Yes

What would you say to the Palestinian, other than to say that I am sympathetic?

Jeanette: I would say what my Daddy always says to me, that life is not fair.

So the world is not fair and life is not fair. We do the best we can. Do the Palestinians have, in your mind, some right to oppose what was done to them?

Jeanette: Yes

Do they have the right to use force to try to, uh, change what was done to them?

Jeanette: They have a right.

In your mind?

Jeanette: yes, they do.

How do we get out of this dilemma?

Jeanette: I don't know.

It is a real dilemma isn't it?

Jeanette: Yea.

Anybody else? John.

John: No wait, I want to clarify a couple of things first.

OK

John: OK, the land that is, uh, that is in question, Palestine, was once the Jews'. If we go back far enough ... it was their holy land, right?

Yes. Correct.

John: And the Arabs drove them off a long time ago.

Well, actually the Romans drove them off.

John: The Romans drove them off, OK, but they've had a history of persecution, so isn't that ...

Student: The Jews?

John: Isn't that, yea the Jews, isn't that the significance of giving them that piece of land instead of a piece of Germany is because that's originally theirs and they have pride and heritage there and they were driven off ...

John, would you then argue the proposition that anybody who, any group of people, who have been persecuted and driven off their land, at some time in the future should be given that land back?

John: No.

That's not your proposition?

John: That's a Halstead generalization.

Well, I thought that's what you said; did I not get what you said correct?

John: I'm talking about the Jews specifically.

All right, explain it to me again, let's see if I hear it right.

John: OK, the Jews have been burned all through history.

All right.

John: You agree with that?

Yes, I do.

John: OK, and you agree that that was once their holy land,

I agree to that.

John: So, if in fact, the UN decides to give them a piece of land which they did, the significance of giving them that land in contrast to giving them a piece of Germany is because it was once theirs and it was, it had some significant to them, in fact we're trying to compensate for 'em, not just push them into the corner, OK.

I agree to all that, now are you saying to me that you personally, if you had been a delegate in the UN would have voted to give a portion of Palestine to the Jewish people because of that argument?

John: Correct.

Is that an argument that is valid for any other group of people or is that argument only valid to the Jewish people?

John: It's, yea, it depends.

Well, I ... suppose ... suppose I can find, John, suppose I can find another group of people who have been persecuted for a good portion of their life and had their land taken away by another group and now these people are trying to find someplace to live where they in fact can live a fruitful life, would you in fact agree to those people getting their land back?

John: Yea.

All right, let's talk about the American Indian. Were the American Indians persecuted?

Class: Yes.

Were they driven off their land?

Class: Yes.

Were they put in reservations?

Class: Yes.

Have we taken their land away from them?

Class: Yes.

John: And I'm not saying that's right.

Are the, are the American Indians today that are alive basically on land areas where they are not able to survive fruitfully as a people? Should they be given their land back?

Student: Some

John: Seems logical, I mean

Am I correct then that, John, that you're arguing, that you would agree that we in the United States should give this land back to the American Indian because of all those circumstances?

John: They should get something., in proportion to the size of their people.

They should get something, something of the United States ... and they should get something that is worthwhile and fruitful and that they can live and survive not some junk land down in the desert ... is that correct?

Class: Yes.

Would you agree perhaps maybe Santa Clara Valley? Would you personally, John, be willing to move out of your house and turn it over to the Indians?

Class laughs. ... give Ohio.

Well, that's too easy for John to give away Ohio. Would you give away your home?

John: I wouldn't be happy about it.

No you wouldn't, you would feel wronged if it happened, right?

John: Right.

Would you, would you, if the government came down and said "John Rimenshutter and family, your house has just been given away to an Indian couple." would you feel right in taking some force against that Indian couple at a later time to get your house back?

John: Yeah.

Laurel: I wouldn't, I would ...

Laurel, you wouldn't what?

Laurel: I wouldn't

You wouldn't what?

Laurel: I wouldn't feel comfortable using force to get my house back from the Indian couple. I would go to the government.

John: Well, yeah

Laurel: and, and, Well, but the question was would you feel force ...

Laurel, you're in the UN. Would you vote to give a piece of that land to the Jewish people, or would you vote to give it to the Arabs in its entirety?

Laurel: I really ... I want to be able to feel good about giving that homeland to the Jews.

All right.

Laurel: I think they deserve it ... and I think I would vote no because the Arabs are there and it is Arab land.

So then what do we do with the Jews? It's 1946, 1947.

Laurel: And you know a lot of the time ... Jody was telling me a lot of Jews didn't want to go back to their homes that they've been ... they didn't want to go back to their German homes.

Is that rightfully so? Would you, would you agree that there is logical reason why they would not want to go back?

Laurel: Absolutely, oh absolutely ...

So what do we do with them maybe we've got thousands maybe hundreds of thousands of Jews who were in the camps they don't want to go back to Germany, they don't want to go back to Poland.

Laurel: Maybe ...

John has raised what is actually true, they want to go back to where is their historical place.

Laurel: Right, right

You do not believe that's right, because the majority of the people who live there are Arabs now. So what are we going to do with the Jews?

Laurel: Somehow, uh ...

It's a heck of a dilemma, isn't it?

Laurel: Somehow, split up Israel so that, um, the Arabs, but yea, but, but they didn't do that totally, I mean a lot of, there's like what, in Lebannon there's a lot of there's many camps up there for, for ...

Palestinians.

Laurel: Palestinians and I don't think that that's fair.

OK.

Laurel: And, um, I think somehow both sides ...

In trying to correct one injustice have we created another injustice?

Laurel: Yes!

And do we, do we have in the Middle East, two groups of people who believe rightfully so, that they have been injured, and that there is a solution to their problem and that is that the solution to their problem, for both of them, is to have the land of Palestine? Now the Palestinians feel injured because their land was given away and their solution is to give them back Palestine, and the Jews feel that they have been injured historically and specifically the Holocaust and the solution to them is to give them Palestine. Haven't we got a heck of a dilemma on our hands? Yeah, Katherine.

Katherine: Well, not all of the Jews that live in Israel are survivors of the Holocaust.

I agree.

Laurel: I mean they're from, it's their homeland for people from all around the world so now they can practice freely and have a place, a place to be without being persecuted, and, when I was there, the feeling is that they are more than willing to live with the Arabs only as long as they can just be the, but, the Arabs, it seems that the Arabs only they want to be in there and they don't want they don't, they aren't willing to live with the Jews.

To participate effectively in Socratic questioning, one must:

• listen carefully to what others say
• take what they say seriously
• look for reasons and evidence
• recognize and reflect upon assumptions
• discover implications and consequences
• seek examples, analogies, and objections
• seek to distinguish what one *knows* from what one merely *believes*
• seek to enter empathetically into the perspectives or points of view of others
• be on the alert for inconsistencies, vagueness, and other possible problems in thought
• look beneath the surface of things
• maintain a healthy sense of skepticism
• be willing to helpfully play the role of devil's advocate

III. Role Playing and Reconstructing Opposing Views

A fundamental danger for human thought is narrowness. We do not naturally and spontaneously open our minds to the insights of those who think differently from us. We have a natural tendency to use our native intelligence and our cognitive skills to protect and maintain our system of beliefs rather than to modify and expand it, especially when ideas are suggested that have their origin in a very different way of thinking. We can never become fairminded unless we learn how to enter sympathetically into the thinking of others, to reason from their perspectives and eventually to try seeing things as they see them.

Learning how to accurately reconstruct the thinking of others and how to role play their thinking (once reconstructed) are fundamental goals of critical thinking instruction. Very little work has yet been done in giving students opportunities to role play the reasoning of others. So it is not now clear to what extent or in what forms role playing to enhance critical reciprocity is possible.

But imagine some possible experiments. Students could brainstorm two lists, one list of their reasons for being allowed to stay out late and one for the reasons their parents might give forbidding it. A role play might be devised in which two students would pretend that they were parents and were asked, in that role, to give their reasons why their children should not be allowed to stay out late. It would be interesting to see how accurately the students could reconstruct the reasoning of their parents. They will probably find this challenging and should be encouraged to be as clear as possible in their reasons. Socratically questioning them would reveal more about their thinking. If a student gives the reason that "kids can't be trusted," the teacher might ask, "What does trust mean to you?" Or, "What kinds of things can kids not be trusted to do? Do you think that all kids are untrustworthy? What circumstances have caused you not to trust one of your kids?" Then one might experiment with a discussion between a student playing "parent" and another student playing "daughter" or "son." The class might subsequently discuss what the best reasons were on each side of the dispute and who seemed to have the stronger argument.

History lessons might also provide opportunities for initial role playing experiences. For instance, students could role play discussions between Northerners and Southerners on disputed questions of the Civil War period or between a member of the British royalty and a colonist concerning the events that led up to the Boston Tea Party.

An interesting follow-up exercise might be to have the students, either in pairs or singly, compose a dialogue on a given issue or on a chosen one. Remind them to brainstorm lists of reasons for both sides of the issue, being sure to focus on the side they don't hold. Then have them write a dialogue expressing the opposing viewpoints. Some of the pairs of students could present their dialogues to the class.

IV. Analyzing Experiences

The necessary role of insights and intellectual virtues — such traits as intellectual empathy, intellectual courage, intellectual integrity, and confidence in reason — in significant learning has been largely ignored in schooling. This deficiency is intimately connected with another one, the failure of schools to help students recognize the need, not only to test what they "learn" in school against their own experience, but also to test what they experience by what they "learn" in school.

We subject little of our experience to critical analysis. We seldom take our experiences apart, to get some sense of their true worth. We seldom separate experiences into their parts of *raw data* and interpretations of the data. Students need to recognize that the same event or situation is often interpreted differently and therefore experienced differently. Failing to recognize the difference between aspects of our experiences, we ignore how the interests, goals, and desires we bring to those data shape and structure our interpretations. Similarly, we rarely seriously entertain the possibility that our interpretation (and hence the total experience) might be selective, biased, or misleading.

The process of developing intellectual virtues and insights is part of developing an interest in taking our experiences apart, in order to recognize when biased subjectivity is distorting our experience. What is more, we need to continually keep in mind the fact that the world is complex and that there are often a variety of legitimate ways to experience the same event or situation. Meta-experiences become important benchmarks and guides for future thought. They make possible modes of thinking and maneuvers in thinking of which the irrational mind is incapable.

To teach for the intellectual virtues, therefore, one must recognize the significant differences between the higher order critical thinking of a fairminded person and the lower order critical thinking of a self-serving person. Though both kinds of thinkers share a certain command of the micro-skills of critical thinking and hence would, for example, score well on tests such as the Watson-Glaser Critical Thinking Appraisal or the Cornell Critical Thinking Tests, they would be unequal at tasks which presuppose the intellectual virtues. The self-serving (weak sense) critical thinker would lack the insights that underlie and support these virtues.

To reason well in domains in which I am prejudiced — hence, eventually to reason my way out of prejudices — I must develop a set of analyzed examples of such reasoning. Of course, to do so, I must see that when I am prejudiced, it seems to me that I am not, and conversely, that those who are not prejudiced as I am will nevertheless seem to me to be prejudiced — to a prejudiced person an unprejudiced person seems prejudiced. I will realize this only to the degree that I have analyzed experiences in which I have first been intensely convinced that I was correct on an issue, judgment, or point of view, only to find after a series of challenges, reconsiderations, and new reasonings that my previous conviction was, in fact, prejudiced. I must take this experience apart in my mind, clearly understand its elements and how these elements fit together (how I became prejudiced; how I inwardly experienced that prejudice; how intensely that prejudice appeared as insight to me; how I progressively began to break it down by seriously considering opposing lines of reasoning; how I slowly came to new assumptions, new information, and ultimately new conceptualizations).

Only by this special kind of inner experience of reasoning one's way out of prejudices does one gain the sort of higher order abilities a fairminded critical thinker requires. The somewhat abstract articulation of the intellectual virtues will take on concrete meaning in the light of these *analyzed experiences.* We grasp their true meaning only when we take apart our own experience in this way. For example, suppose you had developed a habit of getting angry when other people were late but typically felt justified when you were late. In fact, suppose you felt hostility toward others when they expressed exasperation at your being late. You would probably have a great deal of difficulty in separating your anger and the thinking that fostered that anger from the objective events: you or someone else is late. But if you came to do so, to see inconsistency in your responses to lateness, you could begin to reshape your own responses and be fairer to others. Once we begin to analyze experiences in this way, we begin to develop the insights upon which the intellectual virtues depend.

To generalize, in order to develop intellectual virtues, we must develop a variety of analyzed experiences that represent to us personal models, not only of the pitfalls of our own previous thoughts and experiences, but also of processes we used to reason our way out of or around them. These model experiences must be charged with meaning for us. We cannot be *indifferent* to them. We must sustain them in our minds by our sense of their importance, that they may sustain and guide us in our thought.

What does this imply for teaching? For one thing, it implies a somewhat different content or material focus. Our own minds and experiences must become the subject of our study and learning. Indeed, only to the extent that the content of our own experiences becomes an essential part of what is studied will the "usual" subject matter be truly learned. By the same token, the experiences of others must also become part of our studies. But experiences of any kind should always be critically analyzed, and all students must do their own analysis of the experience to be assessed and recognize what indeed they are doing.

This entails that students grasp the logic of experience and come to see that, for example, every experience has three elements, each of which may require some special scrutiny in the analytic process: *1)* something to be experienced (some actual situation or other); *2)* an experiencing subject (with a point of view, framework of beliefs, attitudes, desires, and values); and *3)* some interpretation or conceptualization of the situation. To take apart any experience, I must ponder three distinctive questions (as well as their interrelation):

1) What are the raw facts, the most neutral description, of the situation?
2) What interests, attitudes, desires, or concerns am I bringing to the situation?
3) How am I conceptualizing or interpreting the situation in light of my point of view?

If students are given a wide range of assignments requiring them to analyze their experiences and the experiences of others along these lines, and are given ample opportunity to argue among themselves about which interpretations make the most sense and why, then they will begin to amass a collection of critically analyzed experiences. As these experiences illuminate the pitfalls of thought, their identification with the analyses will lay the foundation for their intellectual traits and moral character. They will have intellectual virtues because they thought their own way to them and internalized them as concrete understandings and insights. Their basic values and their thinking processes now feed each other. Their intellectual and affective life becomes more integrated. Critical standards for thinking become part of their own thinking rather than external to them in texts, teachers, or the authority of a peer group.

There will be many opportunities in the day-to-day life of school activities to help students develop their intellectual courage, empathy, integrity, perseverance, confidence in reason, and fairmindedness. We need not pressure students to develop these traits, but merely provide conditions which support their growth. The same can be said for fostering essential insights, such as insight into the difference between objective situations and our own special interpretations of them. If we provide situations that call upon students to express their own interpretations while distinguishing basic facts from those interpretations, they will develop crucial insights over time. We must take care, however, not to encourage students to believe either that every interpretation of an event is equally "correct" or that only one interpretation contains *the* truth. Students should learn over time that some interpretations of events are more justified than others (more accurate, relevant, or insightful), while no one interpretation of an event contains *all the truth*.

V. Teaching the Distinction Between Fact, Opinion, and Reasoned Judgment

Many texts claim to foster critical thinking by teaching students to divide all statements into facts and opinions. When they do so, students fail to grasp the significance of dialogical thinking and reasoned judgment. When an issue is fundamentally a matter of fact (e.g., "What is the weight of this block of wood?" or "What are the dimensions of this figure?"), there is no reason to argue about the answer; one should carry out the process that gets us the correct answer. Sometimes this might require following complex procedures. In any case, weighing and measuring, the processes needed for the questions above, are not typically matters of debate.

On the other hand, questions that raise matters of mere opinion, such as, "What sweater do you like better?" "What is your favorite color?" or "Where would you like to spend your vacation?" do not have any one correct answer since they ask us merely to express our personal *preferences*.

But most of the important issues we face in our lives are not exclusively matters of fact or matters of preference. Many require a new element: that we reason our way to conclusions while we take the reasoned perspectives of others into account. As teachers, we should be clear in encouraging students to distinguish these three different situations: the ones that call for facts alone, the ones that call for preference alone, and the ones that call for reasoned judgment. When, as members of a jury, we are called upon to come to a judgment of innocence or guilt, we do not settle questions of pure fact, and we are certainly not expected to express our subjective preferences.

Students definitely need to learn procedures for gathering facts, and they doubtless need to have opportunities to express their preferences, but their most important need is to develop their capacities for reasoned judgment. They need to know how to come to conclusions of their own based on evidence (facts) and reasoning of their own within the framework of their own perspectives. Their values and preferences will, of course, play a role in their perspectives and reasoning, but their perspectives should not be a matter of pure opinion or sheer preference. I should not believe in things or people just because *I want to.* I should have good reasons for my beliefs, except, of course, where it makes sense to have pure preferences. It does make sense to prefer butterscotch to chocolate pudding, but it does not make sense to prefer taking advantage of someone rather than respecting his rights. Over time, students need to distinguish fact, opinion, and reasoned judgment, since they will never be good thinkers if they commonly confuse them as most students now do. (See the section on Text Treatment of Critical Thinking in "Thinking Critically about Teaching: From Didactic to Critical Teaching.")

In passing, be sure not to confuse this distinction with that of convergent and divergent questions. Questions of opinion and questions of reasoned judgment are both divergent, but the first does not involve the question of truth or accuracy (because it calls for expression of preference), while the second does (since reasoned judgment can be more or less reasonable, more or less prejudiced, more or less justified).

We have put this distinction into the Global Strategies section of this handbook to underscore its importance as a pervasive emphasis in all instruction. In any event, we should always keep in mind global, as well as more specific, strategies in fostering critical thinking. When we habitually play the role of Socratic questioner, habitually seek opportunities to have students reconstruct and role play the thinking of others, habitually encourage students to develop intellectual virtues, and habitually encourage students to distinguish preference from reasoned judgment, we will discover new possibilities for critical thinking instruction and will develop global insights that help guide us in understanding and applying the strategies illustrated more specifically in the lesson remodels that follow.

Strategies

Introduction

Each strategy section has three parts. The "principle" provides the theory of critical thinking on which the strategy is based and links the strategy to the ideal of the fairminded critical thinker. The "application" provides examples of when and how the strategy can be used. Our lists of possible questions are often larger and more detailed here than in the remodels. Each strategy description concludes with a list of lesson plans in which we use the strategy.

The reader should keep in mind the connection between the principles and applications on the one hand, and the character traits of a fairminded critical thinker on the other. Our aim, once again, is not a set of disjointed skills, but an integrated, committed, thinking person. The strategies and remodels should be used to illuminate each other. If puzzled by a remodel (ours or your own), see the strategies. If puzzled by a strategy, see the originals and our critiques and remodels for clarification.

The strategies listed below are divided into three categories — one for the affective and two for the cognitive. This of course is not to imply that the cognitive dimension of critical thinking should be given twice as much emphasis. Indeed, the affective dimension is every bit as important to critical thinking. No one learns to think critically who is not motivated to do so. In any case, whatever dimension is emphasized, the other dimension should be integrated. We want students to continually use their emerging critical thinking skills and abilities in keeping with the critical spirit, and the critical spirit can be nurtured only when actually practicing critical thinking in some (cognitive) way. One cannot develop one's fairmindedness, for example, without actually thinking fairmindedly. One cannot develop one's intellectual independence without actually thinking independently. This is true of all the essential critical thinking traits, values, or dispositions. They are developmentally embedded in thinking itself. In teaching for critical thinking in a strong sense, the affective dimension of thinking is fully as important as the cognitive.

Furthermore, just as the cognitive and affective dimensions are interdependent and intertwined, so also are the various individual strategies. For purposes of learning, we articulate separate principles and applications. In the beginning, the connections between them may be obscure. Nevertheless, eventually we begin to discover how progress with any one principle leads inevitably to other principles. To see this let us look first at the individual strategies in the affective dimension.

The Interdependence of Traits of Mind

Affective strategies are interdependent because the intellectual traits they imply develop best in concert with each other. Consider intellectual humility. To become aware of the limits of our knowledge, we need the courage to face our own prejudices and ignorance. To discover our own prejudices in turn, we often must empathize with and reason within points of view toward which we are hostile. To achieve this end, we must typically persevere over a period of time, for learning to empathically enter a point of view against which we are biased takes time and significant effort. That effort will not seem justified unless we have the confidence in reason to believe we will not be "tainted" or "taken in" by whatever is false or misleading in the opposing viewpoint. Furthermore, merely believing we can survive serious consideration of an "alien" point of view is not enough to motivate most of us to consider them seriously. We must also be motivated by an intellectual sense of justice. We must recognize an intellectual responsibility to be fair to views we oppose. We must feel obliged to hear them in their strongest form to ensure that we are not condemning them out of ignorance or bias on our part. At this point, we come full circle back to where we began: the need for intellectual humility.

Or, to begin at another point, consider intellectual good faith or integrity. Intellectual integrity is clearly a difficult trait to develop. We are often motivated, generally, of course without admitting to or being aware of this motivation, to set up inconsistent intellectual standards. Our egocentric or sociocentric tendencies make us ready to believe positive information about those we like, and negative information about those we dislike. We are likewise strongly inclined to believe what serves to justify our vested interest or validate our strongest desires. Hence, all humans have some innate mental tendencies to operate with double standards, which of course is paradigmatic of intellectual bad faith. Such modes of thinking often correlate quite well with getting ahead in the world, maximizing our power or advantage, and getting more of what we want.

Nevertheless, it is difficult to operate explicitly or overtly with a double standard. We therefore need to avoid looking at the evidence too closely. We need to avoid scrutinizing our own inferences and interpretations too carefully. At this point, a certain amount of intellectual arrogance is quite useful. I may assume, for example, that I know just what you're going to say (before you say it), precisely what you are really after (before the evidence demonstrates it), and what actually is going on (before I have studied the situation quite carefully). My intellectual arrogance may make it easier for me to avoid noticing the unjustifiable discrepancy between the standards I apply to you and the standards I apply to myself. Of course, if I don't have to empathize with you, that too makes it easier to avoid seeing my duplicity. I am also better positioned if I lack a keen need to be fair to your point of view. A little background fear of what I might discover if I seriously considered the consistency of my own judgments can be quite useful as well. In this case, my lack of intellectual integrity is supported by my lack of intellectual humility, empathy, and fairmindedness.

Going in the other direction, it will be difficult to use a double standard if I feel a responsibility to be fair to your point of view, see that this responsibility requires me to view things from your perspective empathically, and do so with some humility, recognizing I could be wrong, and you right. The more I dislike you personally, or feel wronged in the past by you or by others who share your way of thinking, the more pronounced in my character the trait of intellectual integrity and good faith must be to compel me to be fair.

Distinguishing Macro-Abilities From Micro-Skills

Our reason for dividing cognitive strategies into macro-abilities and micro-skills is not to create a hard and fast line between the most elementary skills of critical thinking (the micro-skills) and the process of orchestrating those elementary skills, but rather to provide teachers with a way of thinking about two levels of learning. We use these two levels in most complex abilities. For intuitive examples, consider what is involved in learning to play the piano, learning to play good tennis, mastering ballet, or becoming a surgeon. In each of these areas, there is a level of skill learning which focuses on the most elementary of moves. For example, learning to practice the most elementary ballet positions at the bar, learning to play scales on the piano, or learning to hit various tennis strokes on the backboard. One must often return to this micro-level to ensure that one keeps the fundamentals well in hand. Nevertheless, dancing ballet is not practicing at the bar. Playing the piano is not simply playing scales. And hitting tennis balls against a backboard is not playing tennis. One must move to the macro level for the real thing. So, too, in critical thinking. Students have to learn the fundamentals: What an assumption is, what an implication is, what an inference and conclusion are, what it is to isolate an issue, what it is to offer reasons or evidence in support of what one says, how to identify a contradiction or a vague sentence.

But thinking critically in any actual situation is typically doing something more complex and holistic than this. Rarely in thinking critically do we do just one elementary thing. Usually we have to integrate or make use of a variety of elementary critical thinking skills. For example, when we are reading (a macro-ability) we have to make use of a variety of critical thinking micro-skills, and we have to use them in concert with each other. We might begin by reflecting on the implications of a story or book title. We might then begin to read the preface or introduction and start to identify some of the basic issues or objectives the book or story is focused on. As we proceed along, we might begin to identify particular sentences that seem vague to us. We might consider various interpretations of them. As we move along, we would doubtless dip into our own experience for possible examples of what the author is saying. Or we might begin to notice assumptions the author is making. We would be making all of these individual moves as part of one integrated activity: the attempt to make sense of, to follow, what we are reading. As always, the whole is greater than and more important than the parts. We read not to practice our critical thinking micro-skills. We use our critical thinking micro-skills in order to read, or better, in order to read clearly, precisely, and accurately. Keep this principle of interdependence in mind as you read through the various strategies.

Strategy List: 35 Dimensions of Critical Thought

A. Affective Strategies

S-1 thinking independently
S-2 developing insight into egocentricity or sociocentricity
S-3 exercising fairmindedness
S-4 exploring thoughts underlying feelings and feelings underlying thoughts
S-5 developing intellectual humility and suspending judgment
S-6 developing intellectual courage
S-7 developing intellectual good faith or integrity
S-8 developing intellectual perseverance
S-9 developing confidence in reason

B. Cognitive Strategies — Macro-Abilities

S-10 refining generalizations and avoiding oversimplifications
S-11 comparing analogous situations: transferring insights to new contexts
S-12 developing one's perspective: creating or exploring beliefs, arguments, or theories
S-13 clarifying issues, conclusions, or beliefs
S-14 clarifying and analyzing the meanings of words or phrases
S-15 developing criteria for evaluation: clarifying values and standards
S-16 evaluating the credibility of sources of information
S-17 questioning deeply: raising and pursuing root or significant questions
S-18 analyzing or evaluating arguments, interpretations, beliefs, or theories
S-19 generating or assessing solutions
S-20 analyzing or evaluating actions or policies
S-21 reading critically: clarifying or critiquing texts
S-22 listening critically: the art of silent dialogue
S-23 making interdisciplinary connections
S-24 practicing Socratic discussion: clarifying and questioning beliefs, theories, or perspectives
S-25 reasoning dialogically: comparing perspectives, interpretations, or theories
S-26 reasoning dialectically: evaluating perspectives, interpretations, or theories

C. Cognitive Strategies — Micro-Skills

S-27 comparing and contrasting ideals with actual practice
S-28 thinking precisely about thinking: using critical vocabulary
S-29 noting significant similarities and differences
S-30 examining or evaluating assumptions
S-31 distinguishing relevant from irrelevant facts
S-32 making plausible inferences, predictions, or interpretations
S-33 evaluating evidence and alleged facts
S-34 recognizing contradictions
S-35 exploring implications and consequences

S-1 Thinking Independently

Principle:	Critical thinking is autonomous thinking, thinking for oneself. Many of our beliefs are acquired at an early age, when we have a strong tendency to form beliefs for irrational reasons (because we want to believe, because we are rewarded for believing). Critical thinkers use critical skills and insights to reveal and eradicate beliefs to which they cannot rationally assent. In formulating new beliefs, critical thinkers do not passively accept the beliefs of others; rather, they analyze issues themselves, reject unjustified authorities, and recognize the contributions of justified authorities. They thoughtfully form principles of thought and action; they do not mindlessly accept those presented to them. They do not accept as true, or reject as false, beliefs they do not understand. They are not easily manipulated.

Independent thinkers strive to incorporate all known relevant knowledge and insight into their thought and behavior. They strive to determine for themselves when information is relevant, when to apply a concept, or when to make use of a skill.

Application:	A critical education respects the autonomy of the student. It appeals to rationality. Students should be encouraged to discover information and use their knowledge, skills and insights to think for themselves. Merely giving students "facts" or telling them the "right way" to solve a problem interferes with students' critiquing and modifying pre-existing beliefs with new knowledge.

Rather than simply having students discuss ideas in their texts, the teacher can have them brainstorm ideas and argue among themselves, for instance, about problems and solutions to problems. Before reading a section of text that refers to a map, chart, time-line, or graph, students could read and discuss what the map, or the rest, shows. Students could develop their own categories instead of being provided with them. "Types of Literature" lessons could be remodelled so that students group and discuss writings they have read, entertaining different ways to classify them.

When a text tries to do too much of the students' thinking for them, it can be examined in depth. *"Why does the text tell you about this? Why do the authors think this (concept, skill, procedure, step) is worth knowing? Why does the text tell you to do this? What would happen if you didn't"*

When giving written assignments, those assignments should provide many opportunities for the student to exercise independent judgment: in gathering and assembling information, in analyzing and synthesizing it, and in formulating and evaluating conclusions. Have students discuss how to organize their points in essays.

In science, students could put their own headings on charts or graphs they make, or decide what kind of graph would be most illuminating.

Students could review material themselves, rather than relying on their texts for summaries and review questions. The teacher could routinely ask students, *"What are the most important points covered in the passage (chapter, story, etc.)?"* as a discussion beginner. The class could brainstorm about what they learned when studying a lesson or unit. Only after they have exhausted their memories should the teacher try to elicit any crucial points neglected.

When discussing specific countries and periods of history, have students look at and discuss political, population distribution, physical, historical, linguistic, and land use maps before reading their texts. They could also discuss trade routes and difficulty or ease of travel, note what other groups or countries are nearby, predict potential areas of conflict, etc. Whenever they are about to use a map, first ask them what kind of map they need, and how and where to find it.

Lesson plans in which the strategy is used

S-2 Developing Insight Into Egocentricity or Sociocentricity

Principle: Egocentricity is the confusion of immediate perception with reality. It manifests itself as an inability or unwillingness to consider others' points of view, to accept ideas or facts which would conflict with gratification of desire. In the extreme, it is characterized by a need to be right about everything, a lack of interest in consistency and clarity, an all or nothing attitude ("I am 100% right; you are 100% wrong."), and a lack of self-consciousness of one's own thought processes. The egocentric individual is more concerned with the *appearance* of truth, fairness, and fairmindedness, than with actually *being* correct, fair, or fairminded. Egocentricity is the opposite of critical thought.

As people are socialized, egocentricity partly evolves into sociocentricity. Egocentric identification extends to groups. The individual goes from *"I* am right!" to *"We* are right!" To put this another way, people find that they can often best satisfy their egocentric desires through a group. 'Group think' results when people egocentrically attach themselves to a group. One can see this in both children and adults: My daddy is better than your daddy! My school (religion, country, race, etc.) is better than yours.

If egocentricity and sociocentricity are the disease, self-awareness is the cure. In cases in which their own egocentric commitments are not supported, few people accept another's egocentric reasoning. Most can identify the sociocentricity of members of opposing groups. Yet when we are thinking egocentrically or sociocentrically, it seems right to us (at least at the time). Our belief in our own rightness is easier to maintain because we suppress the faults in our thinking. We automatically hide our egocentricity from ourselves. We fail to notice when our behavior contradicts our self-image. We base our reasoning on false assumptions we are unaware of making. We fail to make relevant distinctions, though we are otherwise aware of, and able to make them (when making such distinctions does not prevent us from getting what we want). We deny or conveniently 'forget' facts inconsistent with our conclusions. We often misunderstand or distort what others say.

The solution, then, is to reflect on our reasoning and behavior; to make our assumptions explicit, critique them, and, when they are false, stop making them; to apply the same concepts in the same ways to ourselves and others; to consider every relevant fact, and to make our conclusions consistent with the evidence; and to listen carefully and open-mindedly to those with whom we disagree. We can change egocentric tendencies when we see them for what they are: irrational and unjust. Therefore, the development of students' awareness of their egocentric and sociocentric patterns of thought is a crucial part of education in critical thinking.

Application: Although everyone has egocentric, sociocentric, and critical (or fairminded) tendencies to some extent, the purpose of education in critical thinking is to help students move away from egocentricity and sociocentricity, toward increasingly critical thought. Texts usually neglect obstacles to rationality, content to point out or have students point out irrationality and injustice. We recommend that students repeatedly discuss *why* people think irrationally and act unfairly.

The teacher can facilitate discussions of egocentric or sociocentric thought and behavior whenever such discussions seem relevant. Such discussions can be used as a basis for having students think about their own egocentric or sociocentric tendencies. The class can discuss conditions under which people are most likely to be egocentric and how egocentricity interferes with our ability to think and listen. Students should be encouraged to recognize common patterns of egocentric thought. The class can discuss some of the common false assumptions we all make at times (e.g., "Anyone who disapproves of anything I do is wrong or unfair. I have a right to have everything I want. Truth is what I want it to be.") Teachers can also have students point out the contradictions of egocentric attitudes. ("When I use something of yours without permission, it is 'borrowing'; when you use something of mine, it is 'stealing.' Taking something without asking is O.K. Taking something without asking is wrong.") Sometimes story characters illustrate egocentricity.

The most real and immediate form of sociocentricity students experience is in the mini-society of their peers. Student attitudes present a microcosm of the patterns which exist on a larger scale in societies. All of your students share some attitudes which are sociocentric. Furthermore, students divide themselves into "subcultures" or cliques, each of which is narrower than the school-wide "culture." Honest and realistic exploration of these phenomena allows students to clarify and evaluate the ways in which "group think" limits them.

Often texts attempt to discourage sociocentricity by encouraging tolerance — asking students to agree that people whose ways are different are not necessarily wrong. Yet, by keeping discussion general and not introducing specific advantages of different ways, students are left with a vague sense that they should be tolerant, rather than a clear sense that others have ways worth knowing about and learning from.

Some texts inadvertently foster sociocentricity by presenting only the American side of issues or presenting some groups in a distinctly negative light. The teacher could encourage students to recognize sociocentric bias, reconstruct and consider other views of current and historical issues, and discuss how to avoid thinking sociocentrically.

Texts include many subtle forms of sociocentricity, displaying a narrowly European or American perspective in word choice. For example, societies are described as "isolated" rather than "isolated from contact with Europeans."

Before beginning study of another culture, the teacher could elicit students' ideas of that group, including stereotypes and misconceptions. Ask, *"What are these people like? What do you think of when you think of them? How have you seen them portrayed in movies and on T.V.?"* After study, students could evaluate these ideas in light of what they have learned.

Lesson plans in which the strategy is used

S-3 Exercising Fairmindedness

Principle: To think critically about issues, we must be able to consider the strengths and weaknesses of opposing points of view; to imaginatively put ourselves in the place of others in order to genuinely understand them; to overcome our egocentric tendency to identify truth with our immediate perceptions or long-standing thought or belief. This trait correlates with the ability to reconstruct accurately the viewpoints and reasoning of others and to reason from premises, assumptions, and ideas other than our own. This trait also correlates with the willingness to remember occasions when we were wrong in the past despite an intense conviction that we were right, as well as the ability to imagine our being similarly deceived in a case at hand. Critical thinkers realize the unfairness of judging unfamiliar ideas until they fully understand them.

The world consists of many societies and peoples with many different points of view and ways of thinking. In order to develop as reasonable persons we need to enter into and think within the frameworks and ideas of different peoples and societies. We cannot truly understand the world if we think about it only from one viewpoint, as Americans, as Italians, or as Russians.

Furthermore, critical thinkers recognize that their behavior affects others, and so consider their behavior from the perspective of those others.

Application: The teacher can encourage students to show reciprocity when disputes arise or when the class is discussing issues, evaluating the reasoning of story characters, or discussing people from other cultures.

When disputes naturally arise in the course of the day, the teacher can ask students to state one another's positions. Students should be given an opportunity to correct any misunderstanding of their positions. The teacher can then ask students to explain why their fellow student might see the issue differently than they do. *"What is Sue angry about? Why does that make her mad? Sue, is that right?"*

Students can be encouraged to consider evidence and reasons for positions they disagree with, as well as those with which they agree. For example, have students consider positions from their parents' or siblings' points of view. *"Why doesn't your mother want you to ...? Why does she think it's bad for you (wrong, etc.)? What does she think will happen?"*

Rather then generally having students argue their points of view, call on a student who doesn't have a position on the issue under discussion — that is still thinking things through. Help that student clarify the uncertainty. *"What makes sense about what each side said? What seems wrong? What aren't you sure about?"*

Although texts often have students consider a subject or issue from a second point of view, discussion is brief, rather than extended, and no attempt is made to have students integrate insights gained by considering multiple perspectives. If students write a dialogue about an issue from opposing points of view, or contrast a story character's reasoning with an opposing point of view, or role play discussions, the teacher can have them directly compare and evaluate different perspectives.

When the class is discussing different cultures the teacher can encourage students to consider *why* people choose to do things differently or why other people think their ways are best. For example, ask, *"What would be some advantages to arranged marriages? Why might some people prefer that system to ours? What prob-lems would it solve or lessen?"*

Students can be reminded of, and analyze, times that every member of a group or the class contributed something toward finding or figuring out an answer, solving a problem, or understanding a complex situation.

Lesson plans in which the strategy is used

S-4 Exploring Thoughts Underlying Feelings and Feelings Underlying Thoughts

Principle: Although it is common to separate thought and feeling as if they were independent opposing forces in the human mind, the truth is that virtually all human feelings are based on some level of thought and virtually all thought generative of some level of feeling. To think with self-understanding and insight, we must come to terms with the intimate connections between thought and feeling, reason and emotion. Critical thinkers realize that their feelings are their response (but not the only possible, or even necessarily the most reasonable response) to a situation. They know that their feelings would be different if they had a different understanding or interpretation of that situation. They recognize that thoughts and feelings, far from being different kinds of "things," are two aspects of their responses. Uncritical thinkers see little or no relationship between their feelings and their thoughts.

When we feel sad or depressed, it is often because we are interpreting our situation in an overly negative or pessimistic light. We may be forgetting to consider positive aspects of our life. We can better understand our feelings by asking our-selves "How have I come to feel this way? How am I looking at the situation? To what conclusion have I come? What is my evidence? What assumptions am I mak-ing? What inferences am I making? Are they sound inferences? Are there other pos-sible ways to interpret this situation?" We can learn to seek patterns in our assumptions, and so begin to see the unity behind our separate emotions. Under-standing oneself is the first step toward self-control and self-improvement. This self-understanding requires that we understand our feelings and emotions in rela-tion to our thoughts, ideas, and interpretations of the world.

Application: Whenever a class discusses someone's feelings (e.g., that of a character in a story), the teacher can ask students to consider what the person might be thinking to have that feeling in that situation. *"Why does he feel this way? How is he inter-preting his situation? What led him to that conclusion? Would you have felt the same if you had been in his circumstances? Why or why not? What accounts for the differ-ence? What could he have thought instead? Then how might he have felt?"*

This strategy can be used in the service of developing an intellectual sense of justice and courage. Students can discuss the thoughts underlying passionate commitment to personal or social change. Students can discuss reasons for resis-tance to change: greed, fear, self-interest, and other negative or hampering feelings. *"Why are people greedy? What thoughts underlie greed? Why do people feel they need more money? What does less money mean to them? Why? What assumptions underlie these attitudes? To what further thoughts do these attitudes give rise?"*

When discussing a case of mixed feelings, the teacher could ask, *"What was she feeling? What else? (Encourage multiple responses.) What led to this feeling? That one? Are these beliefs consistent or contradictory? How could someone have contradictory responses to one situation? Is there a way she could reconcile these contradictions?"*

Students can also generalize about thoughts behind various emotions: behind fear, thoughts like — "This is dangerous. I may be harmed;" behind anger, thoughts like — "This is not right, not fair;" behind indifference, thoughts like — "This does not matter;" behind relief, thoughts like — "Things are better now. This won't both-er me anymore."

Lesson plans in which the strategy is used

S-5 Developing Intellectual Humility and Suspending Judgment

Principle: Critical thinkers recognize the limits of their knowledge. They are sensitive to circumstances in which their native egocentrism is likely to function self-deceptive-ly; they are sensitive to bias, prejudice, and limitations of their views. Intellectual humility is based on the recognition that one ought not claim more than one actually knows. It does not imply spinelessness or submissiveness. It implies the lack of intellectual pretentiousness, arrogance, or conceit. It implies insight into the foundations of one's beliefs: knowing what evidence one has, how one has come to believe, what further evidence one might examine or seek out.

Thus, critical thinkers distinguish what they know from what they don't know. They are not afraid of saying "I don't know" when they are not in a position to be sure. They can make this distinction because they habitually ask themselves, "How could one know whether or not this is true?" To say "In this case I must suspend judgment until I find out x and y," does not make them anxious or uncomfortable. They are willing to rethink conclusions in the light of new knowledge. They qualify their claims appropriately.

Application: Texts and testing methods inadvertently foster intellectual arrogance. Most text writing says, "Here's the way it is. Here's what we know. Remember this, and you'll know it, too." Behind student learning, there is often little more thought than "It's true because my textbook said it's true." This often generalizes to, "It's true because I read it somewhere."

Teachers can take advantage of any situation in which students are not in a position to know, to encourage the habit of exploring the basis for their beliefs. When materials call on students to make claims for which they have insufficient evidence, we suggest the teacher encourage students to remember what is said in the materials but also to suspend judgment as to its truth. The teacher might first ask for the evidence or reasons for the claim and have students probe its strength. Students can be encouraged to explain what they would need to learn in order to be more certain. You might have students consider how reasonable people respond to gossip or the news on T.V. They hear what is said, remember what they have heard, but do not automatically believe it.

In exposing students to concepts within a field, we can help students to see how all concepts depend on other, more basic concepts and how each field of knowledge is based on fundamental assumptions which need to be examined, understood, and justified. We can help students to discover experiences in their own lives which help support or justify what a text says. We should always be willing to entertain student doubts about what a text says.

We can model intellectual humility by demonstrating a willingness to admit limits in our own knowledge and in human knowledge generally. Routinely qualify statements: "I believe," "I'm pretty sure that," "I doubt," "I suspect," "Perhaps," "I'm told," "It seems," etc. This trait can be encouraged by frequent discussion in which ideas new to the students are explored for evidence and support.

Students should discuss such experiences as getting a bad first impression, then learning they were wrong; feeling certain of something, then later changing their minds; thinking they knew something, then realizing they didn't understand.

The teacher can have students brainstorm questions they have *after* study. Students could keep question logs during the course of research projects, periodically recording their unanswered questions. Thus, they can come to see for themselves that even when they have learned what is expected of them, there is more to learn.

S-6 Developing Intellectual Courage

Principle: To think independently and fairly, one must feel the need to face and fairly deal with unpopular ideas, beliefs, or viewpoints. The courage to do so arises from the recognition that ideas considered dangerous or absurd are sometimes rationally justified (in whole or in part) and that conclusions or beliefs inculcated in us are sometimes false or misleading. If we are to determine for ourselves which is which, we must not passively and uncritically accept what we have "learned." We need courage to admit the truth in some ideas considered dangerous and absurd, and the distortion or falsity in some ideas strongly held in our social group. It will take courage to be true to our own thinking, for honestly questioning our deeply held beliefs can be difficult and sometimes frightening, and the penalties for non-conformity are often severe.

Application: Intellectual courage is fostered through a consistently openminded atmosphere. Students should be encouraged to honestly consider or doubt any belief. Students who disagree with or doubt their peers or text should be given support. The teacher should raise probing questions regarding unpopular ideas which students have hitherto been discouraged from considering. The teacher should model intellectual courage by playing devil's advocate.

Texts often seem to suggest that standing up for one's beliefs is fairly easy; they ignore the difficulty of "doing the right thing." Students could discuss such questions as these: *"Why is it hard to go against the crowd? If everyone around you is sure of something, why is it hard to question it or disagree? When is it good to do so? When might you hesitate? When should you hesitate? Is it hard to question your own beliefs? Why? Why does this idea bother you?*

Students who have been habitually praised for uncritically accepting others' claims may feel the rug pulled out from under them for a while when expected to think for themselves. Students should be emotionally supported in these circumstances and encouraged to express the natural hesitancy, discomfort, or anxiety they may experience so they may work their way through their fears. A willingness to consider unpopular beliefs develops by degrees. Teachers should exercise discretion beginning first with mildly unpopular rather than with extremely unpopular beliefs.

If, during the course of the year, an idea or suggestion which at first sounded "crazy" was proven valuable, students can be reminded of it, and discuss it at length, and compare it to other events. *"How did this idea seem at first? Why? What made you change your mind about it? Have you had other similar experiences? Why did those ideas seem crazy or stupid at first?"*

S-7 Developing Intellectual Good Faith or Integrity

Principle: Critical thinkers recognize the need to be true to their own thought, to be consistent in the intellectual standards they apply, to hold themselves to the same rigorous standards of evidence and proof to which they hold others, to practice what they advocate for others, and to honestly admit discrepancies and inconsistencies in their own thought and action. They believe most strongly what has been justified by their own thought and analyzed experience. They have a commitment to bringing the self they are and the self they want to be together. People in general are often inconsistent in their application of standards once their ego is involved positively or negatively. When people like us, we tend to over-estimate their positive characteristics; when they dislike us, we tend to underrate them.

Application: Texts often inadvertently encourage the natural split between "school belief" and "real life" belief and between verbal or public belief and belief that guides action. There is an old saying to the effect that "They are good prophets who follow their own teachings." And sometimes parents say, "Do as I say, not as I do." There is often a lack of integrity in human life. Hypocrisy and inconsistency are common. As educators, we need to highlight the difficulties of being consistent in an often inconsistent world.

As teachers, we need to be sensitive to our own inconsistencies in the application of rules and standards, and we need to help students to explore their own. Peer groups often pressure students to judge in-group members less critically than out-group members. Students need opportunities to honestly assess their own participation in such phenomena.

When evaluating or developing criteria for evaluation, have students assess both themselves and others, noting their tendency to favor themselves.

Texts often preach. They unrealistically present goodness and change as easy when it is often not. They ask general and loaded questions ("Do you listen to other views? Is it important to treat others fairly?") to which students are likely to simply respond with a "Yes!" Such questions should be remodelled. For example, ask, *"When have you found it difficult to listen to others?"* or *"Why are people often unfair?"*

Language Arts texts sometimes have students roundly criticize characters without taking into account the difficulties of living up to worthy ideals. Students should be encouraged to give more realistic assessments. *"Would you have done otherwise? Would it have been easy? Why or why not? Why do so few people do this?"*

Social studies texts are harsher judges of other societies than of ours. Students should evaluate their texts' consistency in evaluation. The teacher may have to help students to recognize this problem.

S-8 Developing Intellectual Perseverance

Principle: Becoming a more critical thinker is not easy. It takes time and effort. Critical thinkers are willing to pursue intellectual insights and truths in spite of difficulties, obstacles, and frustrations. They recognize the need to struggle with confusion and unsettled questions over an extended period of time in order to achieve deeper understanding and insight. They recognize that significant change requires patience and hard work. Important issues often require extended thought, research, struggle. Considering a new view takes time. Yet people are often impatient to "get on with it" when they most need to slow down and think carefully. People rarely define issues or problems clearly; concepts are often left vague; related issues are not sorted out, etc. Students need to gain insight into the need for intellectual perseverance.

Application: Critical thinking is reflective and recursive; that is, we often go back in our thoughts to previous problems to re-consider or re-analyze them. Intellectual perseverance can be developed by reviewing and discussing the kinds of difficulties that were inherent in previous problems worked on, exploring why it is necessary to struggle with them over an extended period. Studying the work of great inventors or thinkers through biography can also be of use, with students discussing why long-range commitment was necessary. In time, students will see the value in pursuing important ideas at length.

Raise difficult problems again and again over the course of the year. Design long-term projects for which students must persevere. Of course, it is important to work with students on skills of breaking down complex problems into simpler components, so that they will see how to attack problems systematically.

Students can discuss experiences they have had wherein they came to understand something that at first baffled them, or seemed hopelessly confusing and frustrating. *"What was it like to not understand or be able to do it? How did you come to understand it? What was that like?"*

Texts will sometimes say of a problem that it is hard to solve, and leave it at that. To help students develop the sense that things are not hopeless, you could divide the class into groups and have them discuss various ways in which the problem could be approached, seeing if they can break the problem down into simpler components. It is important to devote considerable time to problem analysis, in order to develop student confidence in their ability to distinguish hard from easy problems and to recognize when a longer term commitment will be necessary. Students will not develop intellectual perseverance unless they develop confidence in their ability to analyze and approach problems with success. You should not overwhelm students with the task of *solving* problems so difficult that they have little hope of making progress.

Take a basic idea within a subject ("well-written," "justice," "culture," "life," "matter," etc.). Have students write their ideas on it and discuss them. Every month or so, have them add to, revise, or write another paper. At the end of the year, they can assess the changes in their understanding from repeated consideration over the course of the year, graphically illustrating progress and development achieved through perseverance.

For students to recognize the need for further study of an idea, they need to have some sense of how their present knowledge is limited. Presenting some problems that are beyond their knowledge can be useful, if the class can come to see what they would have to learn to solve them. In this context, students can successfully uncover what they don't know, thereby fostering intellectual humility as well as laying the foundation for intellectual perseverance.

Illustrate how getting answers is not the only form of progress, show them how having better, clearer questions is also progress. Point out progress made. Sympathize with students' natural frustration and discouragement.

Have students discuss the importance of sufficient thought regarding significant decisions and beliefs, and the difficulty of becoming rational and well-educated, fairminded people.

When study and research fail to settle key questions, due to the inadequacy of available resources, the class could write letters to appropriate faculty of one or two colleges. Have students describe their research and results and pose their unanswered questions.

Lesson plans in which the strategy is used

S-9 Developing Confidence in Reason

Principle: The rational person recognizes the power of reason, the value of disciplining thinking in accordance with rational standards. Virtually all the progress that has been made in science and human knowledge testifies to this power, and so to the reasonability of having *confidence* in reason. To develop this faith is to come to see that ultimately one's own higher interests and those of humankind at large will be served best by giving the freest play to reason, by encouraging people to come to their own conclusions through a process of developing their own rational faculties. It is to believe that, with proper encouragement and cultivation, people can develop the ability to think for themselves, to form reasonable points of view, draw reasonable conclusions, think coherently and logically, persuade each other by reason and, ultimately, become reasonable persons, despite the deep-seated obstacles in the native character of the human mind and in society as we know it. It is to reject force and trickery as standard ways of changing another's mind. This confidence is essential to building a democracy in which people come to genuine rule, rather than being manipulated by the mass media, special interests, or by the inner prejudices, fears, and irrationalities that so easily and commonly tend to dominate human minds.

You should note that the act of faith we are recommending is not to be blind but should be tested in everyday experiences and academic work. In other words, we should have confidence in reason, because reason works. Confidence in reason does not deny the reality of intuition; rather, it provides a way of distinguishing intuition from prejudice.

Application: As a teacher, you can model confidence in reason in many ways. Every time you show your students that you can make rules, assignments, and classroom activities intelligible to them so that they can see that you are doing things for well-thought-out reasons, you help them to understand why confidence in reason is justified. Every time you help them solve a problem with the use of their own thinking or "think aloud" through a difficult problem in front of them, you encourage them to develop confidence in reason. Every time you encourage them to *question* the reasons behind rules, activities, and procedures, you help them to recognize that we should expect *reasonability* to be at the foundation of our lives. Every time you display a patient willingness to hear their reasons for their beliefs and actions you encourage confidence in reason. Every time you clarify a standard of good reasoning, helping them to grasp *why* this standard makes sense, you help them to develop confidence in reason.

One reason students have little faith in reason is that they don't see reason being used in their everyday lives. Power, authority, prestige, strength, intimidation, and pressure are often used instead of reason. Students develop a natural cynicism about reason which educators should help them to overcome.

Give students multiple opportunities to try to persuade each other and you. Insist that students who disagree *reason* with each other, rather than using ridicule, intimidation, peer pressure, etc.

Texts often make knowledge acquisition seem mysterious, as though scholars have some sort of mystical mental powers. Make the reasoning behind what they study clear, and students will feel that knowledge and reason are within their grasp.

Have students compare and contrast the following concepts: intimidate, convince, persuade, trick, brainwash.

Lesson plans in which the strategy is used

S-10 Refining Generalizations and Avoiding Oversimplifications

Principle: It is natural to seek to simplify problems and experiences to make them easier to deal with. Everyone does this. However, the uncritical thinker often oversimplifies, and as a result misrepresents problems and experiences. What should be recognized as complex, intricate, ambiguous, or subtle is viewed as simple, elementary, clear, and obvious. For example, it is typically an oversimplification to view people or groups as *all good* or *all bad*, actions as *always right* or *always wrong*, one contributing factor as *the cause*, etc., and yet such beliefs are common. Critical thinkers try to find simplifying patterns and solutions but not by misrepresentation or distortion. Making a distinction between useful simplifications and misleading oversimplifications is important to critical thinking.

One of the strongest tendencies of the egocentric, uncritical mind is to see things in terms of black and white, "all right" and "all wrong." Hence, beliefs which should be held with varying degrees of certainty are held as certain. Critical thinkers are sensitive to this problem. They understand the relationship of evidence to belief and so qualify their statements accordingly. The tentativeness of many of their beliefs is characterized by the appropriate use of such qualifiers as 'highly likely,' 'probably,' 'not very likely,' 'highly unlikely,' 'often,' 'usually,' 'seldom,' 'I doubt,' 'I suspect,' 'most,' 'many,' and 'some.'

Critical thinkers scrutinize generalizations, probe for possible exceptions, and then use appropriate qualifications. Critical thinkers are not only clear, but also *exact* or *precise*.

Application: Whenever students or texts oversimplify, the teacher can ask questions which raise the problem of complexity. For instance, if a student or text over-generalizes, the teacher can ask for counter-examples. If a text overlooks factors by stating one cause for a problem, situation, or event, the teacher can raise questions about other possible contributing factors. If different things are lumped together, the teacher can call attention to differences. If interconnected or overlapping phenomena are too casually separated, the teacher can probe overlaps or connections. If only one point of view is expressed, though others are relevant, the teacher can play devil's advocate, bringing in other points of view.

Texts often state such vague generalities as "People must work together to solve this problem." Such a statement glosses over complications which could be clarified in a discussion. *"Why don't people work together on this? How should they? Why? Why wouldn't this seemingly obvious solution work? So, what else must be done? How could these needs and interests be reconciled?"*

Among the most common forms of oversimplification found in social studies texts is that of vaguely expressed explanations. Students can better understand explanations and descriptions of historical events, and peoples' reactions to them, by considering offered explanations in depth. For example, texts often say that citizens of a former colony resented the rule they lived under. Students could discuss questions like the following: *Why do many people resent being ruled by others? What, exactly made them unhappy with their situation? How would present day Americans feel about being conquered and ruled? What consequences might arise from our being taken over? Why? How might Americans respond? Why? Why would a country want to rule another group? What would it get out of it? Why wouldn't they want to give it up? What do they say are their reasons for not giving it up? Why don't the people they rule accept those reasons? Was this group's treatment of that group consistent with those reasons?*

Another common form of oversimplification in history texts occurs when texts describe the reason or cause of present or historical situations. This treatment serves texts' sociocentric bias when discussing the causes of wars in which the U.S. has been involved; the enemy bears total responsibility. Students have had a sufficient number of experiences with conflict to be able to see how sometimes both sides are partly to blame. By discussing these experiences, and drawing analogies, students can learn to avoid simple, pat, self-serving interpretations of events.

When discussing generalizations, the teacher could ask students for counter-examples. The class can then suggest and evaluate more accurate formulations of the claim. *"Is this always the case? Can you think of a time when an x wasn't a y? Given that example, how could we make the claim more accurate?"* ("Sometimes ...." "When this is the case, that happens ...." "It seems that...." "When this *and* that are *both* true, then ....)

The teacher can encourage students to qualify their statements when they have insufficient evidence to be certain. By asking for the evidence on which student claims are based and encouraging students to recognize the possibility that alternative claims may be true, the teacher can help students develop the habits of saying "I'm not sure," and of using appropriate probability qualifiers.

Analogies, and models (for example, in science) simplify the phenomena they represent. The class can examine ways such analogies and models break down. *"In what ways is this a poor analogy? How does this model break down? Why? What accounts for the differences? What does that tell us about our subject? Could the analogy or model be improved? How? Why is that better?"*

Lesson plans in which the strategy is used

S-11 Comparing Analogous Situations: Transferring Insights to New Contexts

Principle: An idea's power is limited by our capacity to see its application. Critical thinkers' ability to use ideas mindfully enhances their ability to transfer ideas critically. They practice using ideas and insights by appropriately applying them to new situations. This allows them to organize materials and experiences in different ways, to compare and contrast alternative labels, to integrate their understanding of different situations, and to find fruitful ways to conceptualize novel situations. Each new application of an idea enriches understanding of both the idea applied and the situation to which it is applied.

70

Application: Critical teaching, focussing more on basic concepts than on artificial organization of material, encourages students to apply what they have just learned to different but analogous contexts. It provides for more than one way to organize material. Using similar information from different situations makes explanations clearer, less vague.

When students master a new skill, or discover an insight, they can be encouraged to use it to analyze other situations. Combine the strategy with independent thought by asking students to name or find analogous situations.

Students can find analogies between historical events or beliefs and present day actions and claims. Such parallel situations can be compared, and insights into each applied to the other.

When students have learned a scientific law, concept, or principle, they can enrich their grasp of it by applying it to situations not mentioned in the text. By exploring student understanding of such situations, teachers can discover misunderstandings.

Lesson plans in which the strategy is used

S-12 Developing One's Perspective: Creating or Exploring Beliefs, Arguments, or Theories

Principle: The world is not given to us sliced up into categories with pre-assigned labels on them. There is always a large number of ways that we can "divide up" and so experience the world. How we do so is essential to our thinking and behavior. Uncritical thinkers assume that their perspective on things is the only correct one. Selfish critical thinkers manipulate the perspectives of others to gain advantage for themselves. Fairminded critical thinkers learn to recognize that their own way of thinking and that of all other perspectives are subject to error. They learn to develop their point of view through a critical analysis of their experience. They learn to question commonly accepted ways of understanding things and avoid uncritically accepting the viewpoints of their peer groups or society. They know what their perspectives are and can talk insightfully about them. To do this, they must create and explore their own beliefs, their own reasoning, and their own theories.

Application: Perspective is developed through extended thought, discussion, and writing. Students who are unsure what to think can be given time to reflect and come to tentative conclusions. Students who have definite conclusions about the subject at hand can consider ideas from other perspectives, answer questions about what they think, or reflect on new situations or problems. Students can compare what they say they believe with how they act.

One-to-one Socratic questioning may facilitate development of perspective, especially for students who think they've exhausted their ideas. This strategy will often coincide with evaluating actions and policies, arguments, or assumptions.

Students could explain how what they have learned has changed their thinking in some way. A written assignment could be used as an opportunity for a student to explore an idea in depth, and either come to conclusions, or clarify issues and concepts.

In general, we should look for opportunities to ask students what *they* believe, how *they* see things, what reasons seem most persuasive to *them*, what theory *they* think best explains what we are trying to explain, and so forth. We should look for occasions in which they can name and describe their own perspectives, philosophies, and ways of thinking.

Lesson plans in which the strategy is used

S-13 Clarifying Issues, Conclusions, or Beliefs

Principle: The more completely, clearly, and accurately an issue or statement is formulated, the easier and more helpful the discussion of its settlement or verification. Given a clear statement of an issue, and prior to evaluating conclusions or solutions, it is important to recognize what is required to settle it. And before we can agree or disagree with a claim, we must understand it clearly. It makes no sense to say "I don't know what you are claiming, but I deny it, whatever it is." Critical thinkers recognize problematic claims, concepts, and standards of evaluation, making sure that understanding precedes judgment. They routinely distinguish facts from interpretations, opinions, judgments, or theories. They can then raise those questions most appropriate to understanding and evaluating each.

Application: Teachers should encourage students to slow down and reflect before coming to conclusions. When discussing an issue, the teacher can ask students first, *"Is the issue clear? What do you need to know to settle it? What would someone who disagreed with you say?"* Students should be encouraged to continually reformulate the issue in light of new information. They should be encouraged to see how the first statement of the issue or problem is rarely best (that is, most accurate, clear, and complete) and that they are in a better position to settle a question *after* they have developed as clear a formulation as possible.

When discussing an issue, teachers can have students ask themselves such questions as, *"Do I understand the issue? Do I know how to settle it? Have I stated it fairly? (Does my formulation assume one answer is correct? Would everyone involved accept this as a fair and accurate statement of the issue?) Are the words* clear? Do I have to analyze any concepts? Do I know when the key terms apply and don't apply? Do I clearly understand how they apply to this case? Does this question ask something about facts, or about the meanings of words? Am I evaluating anything? What? Why? What criteria should I use in the evaluation? What facts are relevant? How can I get the evidence I need? How would the facts be gathered? What would researchers have to do to conduct such a study? What problems would they face? How could those obstacles be surmounted?"

When a claim is unclear, the class can discuss such questions as, "How can we know whether or not this is true? What would it be like for this claim to be true? False? Do we clearly understand the difference? What evidence would count for it? Against it? Are any concepts (words or phrases) unclear? What does this claim assume? What does this claim imply? What does its opposite imply? Is there a clearer way to word this claim? Is there a more accurate way to word it? Can it be rephrased? Do the different ways of putting it say the same thing? Why would someone agree with this claim? Disagree?"

This strategy provides a way of remodelling lessons that focus on "Fact/ Opinion," or which have vague passages of text.

To encourage students to distinguish fact from interpretation, for example, the teacher could use questions like the following: Does this description stick to the facts, or is reasoning or response included? Is this something that can be directly seen, or would you have to interpret what you saw to arrive at this statement? Is this how anyone would describe the situation, or would someone else see it differently? What alternative descriptions or explanations are there? Students could then examine the assumptions, inferences, and theories underlying the alternatives.

Lesson plans in which the strategy is used

S-14 Clarifying and Analyzing the Meanings of Words or Phrases

Principle: Critical, independent thinking requires clarity of thought. A clear thinker understands concepts and knows what kind of evidence is required to justify applying a word or phrase to a situation. The ability to supply a definition is not proof of understanding. One must be able to supply clear, obvious examples and use the idea appropriately. In contrast, for an unclear thinker, words float through the mind unattached to clear, specific, concrete cases. Distinct concepts are confused. Often the only criterion for the application of a term is that the case in question "seems like" an example. Irrelevant associations are confused with what are necessary parts of the idea (e.g., "Love involves flowers and candlelight.") Unclear thinkers lack independence of thought because they lack the ability to analyze a concept, and so critique its use.

73

Application: There are a number of techniques the teacher can use for analyzing concepts. Rather than simply asking students what a word or phrase means, or asking them for a definition, the teacher can use one of the techniques mentioned below.

When introducing concepts, paraphrasing is often helpful for relating the new term (word or phrase) to ideas students already understand. The teacher can also supply a range of examples, allowing students to add to the list.

When introducing or discussing a concept that is not within students' experience, the teacher can use analogies which relate the idea to one with which students are familiar. Students could then compare the ideas.

When discussing words or phrases with which students are familiar, we suggest that teachers have students discuss clear examples of the concept, examples of its opposite (or examples which are clearly not instances of the concept), and examples for which neither the word or its opposite are completely accurate (borderline cases). Have students compare the facts relevant to deciding when the term and its opposite apply. Students could also discuss the implications of the concept and why people make a distinction between it and its opposite. *"Give me examples of X and the opposite of X. Why is this an X? What is it about this that makes you call it an X? What are you saying about it when you call it that? Why would someone use this expression? Why would someone want to bring it to people's attention? What are the practical consequences of calling it that? How do we feel about or treat X's? Why?"* *(Do the same for the opposite.)* When discussing examples, always start with the clearest, most obvious, indisputable cases and opposite cases. Only when those have been examined at length move to the more problematic, controversial, difficult, or borderline examples. *"Why is this case different from the others? Why do you kind of want to call it X? Why do you hesitate to call it X? What can we call this case?"*

When clarifying a concept expressed by a phrase rather than a single word, discuss cases in which the phrase applies, instead of merely discussing the individual words. For example, if clarifying the idea of a 'just law,' though a general discussion of 'justice' may be helpful, the more specific idea *'just law'* should be discussed and contrasted with its opposite.

For ideas that commonly have a lot of irrelevant associations, the teacher can have students distinguish those associations which are logically related to the concept, from those which are not. Have the class brainstorm ideas associated with the term under discussion. *(What do you think of when you think of school?)* Then ask the students if they can imagine using the term for situations lacking this or that listed idea. *(If teachers and students gathered in a building to study, but there were no blackboard or desks, is it a school?)* Students may see that many of their associations are not part of the concept. They are left with a clearer understanding of what is relevant to the concept and will be less tempted to confuse mere association with it.

Whenever a text or discussion uses one term in more than one sense, the teacher can ask students to state how it is being used in each case or have students paraphrase sentences in which they occur. Then the teacher can ask students to generate examples in which one, both, or neither meaning of the term applies. For example, students could distinguish ordinary from scientific concepts of work and energy. The class could rephrase such seeming absurdities as "This solid table isn't solid," into "This table that I can't pass my hand through actually has lots of empty spaces in it."

When a text confuses two distinct ideas, students can clarify them. Students can distinguish ideas by discussing the different applications and implications of the concepts. Students could rewrite passages, making them clearer. For example, a social studies text explains how 'consensus' means that everyone in the group has to agree to the decisions. The teachers' notes then suggest discussion of an example wherein a group of children have to make a decision, so they vote, and the majority gets its way. The example, though intended to illustrate the idea of consensus, misses the point and confuses the concepts 'consensus' and 'majority rule.' The class could compare the two ideas, and so distinguish them. *"What did the text say 'consensus' means? What example does it give? Is this an example of everyone having to agree? What is the difference? How could the example be changed to illustrate the term?"* The class may then try to understand and evaluate consensus.

Lesson plans in which the strategy is used

S-15 Developing Criteria for Evaluation: Clarifying Values and Standards

Principle: Critical thinkers realize that expressing mere preference does not substitute for evaluating something. Awareness of the process or components of evaluating facilitates thoughtful and fairminded evaluation. This process requires the development and use of criteria or standards of evaluation, or making standards or criteria explicit. Critical thinkers are aware of the values on which they base their judgments. They have clarified them and understand *why* they are values.

When developing criteria, critical thinkers should understand the object and purpose of the evaluation, and what function the thing being evaluated is supposed to serve. Critical thinkers take into consideration different points of view when attempting to evaluate something.

Application: Whenever students are evaluating something — an object, action, policy, solution, belief — the teacher can ask students what they are evaluating, the purpose of the evaluation, and the criteria they used. Criteria for evaluating an object usually presuppose a purpose of the object. With practice, students can see the importance of developing clear criteria and applying them consistently. When discussing criteria as a class or in groups, rational discussion, clarity, and fairmindedness are usually more important than reaching consensus.

The class could discuss questions like the following: *What are we evaluating? Why? Why do we need an X? Name or describe some good X's versus bad X's. Why are these good and those bad? What are the differences? Given these reasons or differences, can we generalize and list criteria? Can we describe what to look for when judging an X? What features does an X need to have? Why?*

Much of Language Arts instruction can be viewed as developing and clarifying criteria for evaluating writing. Students should continually evaluate written material and discuss their criteria. Specific grammatical points should be explained in terms of the values they support (such as clarity or vividness).

Students could relate the evaluation of governments to their perspectives on the purposes and functions of governments. During discussions in which they evaluate specific actions or policies of some government, they could relate their evaluations to this discussion of criteria and underlying values.

Lesson plans in which the strategy is used

S-16 Evaluating the Credibility of Sources of Information

Principle: Critical thinkers recognize the importance of using reliable sources of information when formulating conclusions. They give less weight to sources which either lack a track record of honesty, contradict each other on key questions, are not in a position to know, or have a vested interest in influencing belief. Critical thinkers recognize when there is more than one reasonable position to be taken on an issue; they compare alternative sources of information, noting areas of agreement; they analyze questions to determine whether or not the source is in a position to know; and they gather further information where sources disagree. They recognize obstacles to gathering accurate and pertinent information. They realize that preconception, for example, influences observation — that we often see only what we expect to see and fail to notice things we aren't looking for.

Application: When the class is discussing an issue about which people disagree, the teacher can encourage students to check a variety of sources supporting different points of view. This strategy can be used in history and news lessons.

The class can discuss the relevance of a source's past dependability, how to determine whether a source is in a position to know, and how motives should be taken into account when determining whether a source of information is credible. The teacher can ask the following questions: *Is this person in a position to know? What would someone need, to be in a position to know? Was this person there? Could he have directly seen or heard, or would he have to have reasoned to what he claims to know? What do we know about this person's expertise and experience? What experience would you need to have to be an expert? What must you have studied? What does he claim about this issue? Where did he get his information? Is there reason to doubt him? Has he been reliable in the past? Does he have anything to gain by convincing others? Who commissioned this report? Why?*

To more fully explore the idea of expertise with respect to a particular topic, the teacher could ask, *"What subjects, perspectives, theories, what kinds of details, what sorts of analyses would someone need knowledge of, in order to develop a complete and fairminded view of this subject?"* (For example, if the subject is a political conflict, an expert would need to know the historical background of the groups, their cultures, religions and world views — including, for example, how each group sees itself and the others, how much diversity is within each group — the geography of the area, the economic system or systems under which the groups live, etc.)

Finally, the teacher can use examples from the students' personal experience (e.g., trying to determine who started an argument) and encourage students to recognize the ways in which their own motivations can affect their interpretations and descriptions of events.

Lesson plans in which the strategy is used

S-17 Questioning Deeply: Raising and Pursuing Root or Significant Questions

Principle: Critical thinkers can pursue an issue in depth, covering germane aspects in an extended process of thought or discussion. When reading a passage, they look for issues and concepts underlying the claims expressed. They come to their own understanding of the details they learn, placing them in the larger framework of the subject and their overall perspective. They contemplate the significant issues and questions underlying subjects or problems studied. They can move between basic underlying ideas and specific details. When pursuing a line of thought, they are not continually dragged off subject. They use important issues to organize their thought and are not bound by the organization given by another. Nor are they unduly influenced by the language of another. If they find that a set of categories or distinctions is more appropriate than that suggested by another, they will use it. Recognizing that categories serve human purposes, they use those categories which best serve their purpose at the time. They are not limited by accepted ways of doing things. They evaluate both goals and how to achieve them.

Application: Each of the various subject areas has been developed to clarify and settle questions peculiar to itself. The teacher can use such questions to organize and unify details covered in the subject. Perhaps more important are basic questions everyone faces about what people are like, the nature of right and wrong, how we know things, and so on. Both general and subject-specific basic questions should be repeatedly raised and discussed at length.

Texts fail to develop this trait of pursuing root questions by presenting preformulated conclusions, categories, solutions, and ideals, by failing to raise crucial or thought-provoking issues (and so avoiding them), by suggesting a too-limited discussion of them, by mixing questions relevant to different issues or by pursuing their objectives in a confusing way. To rectify these problems, teachers need to provide opportunities for students to come to their own conclusions, construct their own categories, devise their own solutions, and formulate their own ideals. They need to raise thought-provoking issues, allow extended discussion of them and keep the discussion focussed, so that different issues are identified and appropriately addressed. The students, in turn, need to be clear about the objectives and to see themselves as accomplishing them in a fruitful way.

The class can begin exploration of an important topic, concept, or issue not discussed in any one place in their texts by looking for references to it. They can then read and discuss all pertinent passages, and pose questions to guide further research using other resources, and share their findings. Each student could then write an essay pulling the ideas together.

Rather than asking students to place objects into pre-existing categories, for instance, the teacher can encourage students to form their own categories. Students can then discuss the reasons they had for forming each category. When different students have used different sets of categories to form groups, the teacher can ask such questions as: *When would this set of categories be most useful? When would that set be best? Why would someone else make different groupings?*

What main concepts (distinctions, categories) are used in this subject? Why? Why is this distinction more important in this field than that one?

When a class discusses rules, institutions, activities, or ideals, the teacher can facilitate a discussion of their purposes, importance, or value. Students should be encouraged to see institutions, for example, as a creation of people, designed to fulfill certain functions, not as something that is "just there." They will be in a better position, when they are adults, to see that it fulfills its goals. Or, for another example, ideals will be better understood as requiring specific kinds of actions, instead of being left as mere vague slogans, if the class examines their value.

When the text avoids important issues related to or underlying the object of study, the teacher or students could raise them and discuss them at length. Students can go through the assigned material, and possibly other resources, using the chosen issue or issues to organize the details, for example, making a chart or issue map. Socratic questioning, it should be noted, typically raises root issues. (See the section on Socratic discussion in chapter 3 "Global Strategies.")

When a lesson does raise important questions but has too few and scattered questions, the teacher can pull out, rearrange, and add to the relevant questions, integrating them into an extended and focussed, rather than fragmented, discussion. Students can begin study with one or more significant questions and list relevant details as they read.

Lesson plans in which the strategy is used

S-18 Analyzing or Evaluating Arguments, Interpretations, Beliefs, or Theories

Principle: Rather than carelessly agreeing or disagreeing with a line of reasoning based on their preconceptions of what is true, critical thinkers use analytic tools to understand it and determine its relative strengths and weaknesses. When analyzing arguments, critical thinkers recognize the importance of asking for reasons and considering alternative views. They are especially sensitive to possible strengths of arguments that they disagree with, recognizing the tendency of humans to ignore, oversimplify, distort, or otherwise unfairly dismiss them. Critical thinkers analyze questions and place conflicting arguments, interpretations, and theories in opposition to one another, as a means of highlighting key concepts, assumptions, implications, etc.

When giving or being given an interpretation, critical thinkers, recognizing the difference between evidence and interpretation, explore the assumptions on which it is based, and propose and evaluate alternative interpretations for their relative strength. Autonomous thinkers consider competing theories and develop their own theories.

Application: Often texts claim to have students analyze and evaluate arguments, when all they have them do is state preferences and locate factual claims, with very limited discussion. They fail to teach most techniques for analyzing and evaluating arguments. Texts that do address aspects of argument critique tend to teach such skills and insights in isolation, and fail to mention them when appropriate and useful. (See "Text Treatment of Critical Thinking and Argumentation," in the chapter, "Thinking Critically About Teaching: From Didactic to Critical Teaching".)

Instead of simply asking students why they agree or disagree with a line of reasoning, students should be encouraged to place competing arguments, interpretations, or theories in opposition to one another. Ask, *"What reasons are given? What would someone who disagreed with this argument say?"* Students should be encouraged to argue back and forth, and modify their positions in light of the strengths of others' positions. Students can become better able to evaluate reasoning by familiarizing themselves with, and practicing, specific analytic techniques, such as making assumptions explicit and evaluating them; clarifying issues, conclusions, values, and words, developing criteria for evaluation; recognizing contradictions; distinguishing relevant from irrelevant facts; evaluating evidence; and exploring implications. (See strategies addressing these skills.) After extended discussion, have students state their final positions. Encourage them to qualify their claims appropriately.

When learning scientific theories, students should be encouraged to describe or develop their own theories and compare them with those presented in their texts. Students can compare the relative explanatory and predictive powers of various theories, whenever possible testing the predictions with experiments.

Lesson plans in which the strategy is used

S-19 Generating or Assessing Solutions

Principle: Critical problem-solvers use everything available to them to find the best solution they can. They evaluate solutions, not independently of, but in relation to one another (since 'best' implies a comparison). They take the time to formulate problems clearly, accurately, and fairly, rather than offering a sloppy, half-baked description and then immediately leaping to a solution. They examine the causes of the problem at length. They have reflected on such questions as, "What makes some solutions better than others? What does the solution to this problem require? What solutions have been tried for this and similar problems? With what results?" But alternative solutions are often not given, they must be generated or thought-up. Critical thinkers must be creative thinkers as well, generating possible solutions in order to find the best one. Very often a problem persists, not because we can't tell which available solution is best but because the best solution has not yet been made available — no one has thought it up yet. Therefore, although critical thinkers use all available information relevant to their problems, including the results of solutions others have used in similar situations, they are flexible and imaginative, willing to try any good idea whether it has been done before or not.

Fairminded thinkers take into account the interests of everyone affected by the problem and proposed solutions. They are more committed to finding the best solution than to getting their way. They approach problems realistically.

Application: The best way to develop insight into problem-solving is to solve problems. If problems arise in the class — for example, if discussions degenerate into shouting matches — students should be assisted in developing and instituting their own solutions. If the first attempt fails or causes other problems, students should consider why and try again. Thus, they can learn the practical difficulties involved in discovering and implementing a workable solution.

We recommend first that the teacher have students state the problem, if that has not been done. Students should explore the causes at length, exploring and evaluating multiple perspectives. Encourage them to integrate the strong points within each view. As the process of exploring solutions proceeds, students may find it useful to reformulate the description of the problem.

Rather than simply asking students if a given solution is good, the teacher could encourage an extended discussion of such questions as, *"Does this solve the* problem? How? What other solutions can you think of? What are their advantages and disadvantages? Are we missing any relevant facts? (Is there anything we need to find out before we can decide which solution is best?) What are the criteria for judging solutions in this case? (How will we know if a solution is a good one?) Why do people/have people behaved in the ways that cause the problem? How do the solutions compare with each other? Why? What are some bad ways of trying to solve the problem? What is wrong with them? Do any of these solutions ignore someone's legitimate concerns or needs? How could the various needs be incorporated? If this fact about the situation were different, would it change our choice of solutions? Why or why not?"

Fiction often provides opportunities for analysis of problems and evaluation of solutions. Texts' treatments are often too brief, superficial, and unrealistic.

History texts often provide opportunities for use of this strategy when they describe problems people or government attempted to solve, for instance, by passing new laws. Students can evaluate the text's statement of the problem and its causes, evaluate the solution tried, and propose and evaluate alternatives. Students should be encouraged to explore the beliefs underlying various choices of solutions. (For instance, ask, *"Why do conservatives favor this solution and liberals that one? What does each claim causes the problem? What does each perspective assume? What sort of evidence would support each perspective? What other perspectives can there be? Can the perspectives be reconciled? What is your perspective on this problem? Why?"*)

When presenting problem-solving lessons or activities, texts tend to provide lists of problem-solving steps which unnecessarily limit the process. For example, texts rarely encourage students to consider how others solved or tried to solve the same or a similar problem. They generally make "describing the problem" step one, without having students reformulate their descriptions after further examination.

Social studies texts provide innumerable opportunities for exploring crucial problems. *"What problems do we have in our country or part of the country? Why? Who is involved in this? Who contributes? How? Why? Who's affected? How? Why? What should be done? Why? Why not do it? What could go wrong? What do other people think should be done? Why? How can we find out more about the causes of this? How can we find out what different people want? Can the wants be reconciled? How? Why not? What compromises are in order?"*

What does this passage say was the problem? The cause? Explain the cause. What other explanations are there? Evaluate the explanations. What else was part of the cause? What was the solution tried? (Action, law, set of laws, policy, amendment, etc.) What were the effects? Who was affected? Did it have the desired effects? Undesirable effects? What should have been done differently, or what should we do now to rectify the problems that solution caused? Do we need the law now?

Lesson plans in which the strategy is used

S-20 Analyzing or Evaluating Actions and Policies

Principle: Critical thinking involves more than an analysis of clearly formulated instances of reasoning; it includes analysis of behavior or policy and a recognition of the reasoning that behavior or policy presupposes. When evaluating the behavior of themselves and others, critical thinkers are conscious of the standards they use, so that these, too, can become objects of evaluation. Critical thinkers are especially concerned with the consequences of actions and recognize these as fundamental to the standards for assessing both behavior and policy.

Critical thinkers base their evaluations of behavior on assumptions to which they have rationally assented. They have reflected on such root questions as: What makes some actions right, others wrong? What rights do people have? How can I know when someone's rights are being violated? Why respect people's rights? Why be good? Should I live according to rules? If so, what rules? If not, how should I decide what to do? What policies should be established and why? What are governments supposed to do? What shouldn't they do?

Application: The teacher can encourage students to raise ethical questions about actions and policies of themselves and others. Students can become more comfortable with the process of evaluating if they are given a number of opportunities to consider the following kinds of questions: *Why did x do this? What reasons were given? Were they the real reasons? Why do you think so? What are the probable consequences of these actions? How would you feel if someone acted this way toward you? Why? What reasons were your evaluations based on? Might someone else use a different standard to evaluate? Why? Do you think the action was fair, smart, etc.? Why or why not?*

Too often history texts fail to have students evaluate the behavior and policies about which they read. Texts often assume that people's stated reasons were their real reasons. Sometimes texts describe behavior inconsistent with the stated intentions, yet fail to have students discuss these inconsistencies. *"Why did that group or government say they took this action? What did they do? What result did they say they wanted? What results did it actually have? Who was helped? Hurt? Why? Is the stated reason consistent with that behavior? Was the reason they gave their real reason? Why do you think so?"*

Students should evaluate the behavior of important people of the past. Such evaluation can be enhanced by having interested students report on the long-term consequences of past actions and policies. Future citizens of a democracy need to develop their own sense of how leaders and countries should and shouldn't behave.

Lesson plans in which the strategy is used

S-21 Reading Critically: Clarifying or Critiquing Texts

Principle: Critical thinkers read with a healthy skepticism. But they do not doubt or deny until they understand. They clarify before they judge. They realize that everyone is capable of making mistakes and being wrong, including authors of textbooks. They also realize that, since everyone has a point of view, everyone sometimes leaves out some relevant information. No two authors would write the same book or write from exactly the same perspective. Therefore, critical readers recognize that reading a book is reading one limited perspective on a subject and that more can be learned by considering other perspectives. Critical readers ask themselves questions as they read, wonder about the implications of, reasons for, examples of, and meaning and truth of the material. They do not approach written material as a collection of sentences, but as a whole, trying out various interpretations until one fits all of the work, rather than ignoring or distorting statements that don't fit their interpretation.

Application: Students should feel free to raise questions about materials they read. When a text is ambiguous, vague, or misleading, teachers can raise such questions as, *"What does this passage say? What does it imply? Assume? Is it clear? Does it contradict anything you know or suspect to be true? How do you know? How could you find out? What might someone who disagreed with it say? Does the text leave out relevant information? Does it favor one perspective? Which? Why do you suppose it was written this way? How could we rewrite this passage to make it clearer, fairer, or more accurate?"*

In Language Arts, rather than simply using recall questions at the end of fictional selections, have students describe the plot. Furthermore, don't forget that students should continually evaluate what they read.

Students can evaluate unit, chapter, section titles and headings in their texts. *"What is the main point in this passage? What details does it give? What ideas do those details support, elaborate on, justify? Is the heading accurate? Misleading? Could you suggest a better heading?"*

Often passages which attempt to instill belief in important American ideals are too vague to mean more than the idea that our ideals are important. Such passages could be reread slowly with much discussion. Such passages typically say that the ideals are important or precious, that people from other countries wish they had them or come here to enjoy them, that we all have a responsibility to preserve them, and so on.

The class could discuss questions like the following: *Why is this right important? How is this supposed to help people? Does not having this right hurt people? How? Why? Why would someone try to prevent people from voting or speaking out? How could they? Have you ever denied someone the right to speak or be heard? Why? Were you justified? Why or why not? What should you have done? Why would* someone want to find out how people voted? Why is this right precious? Why are these rights emphasized? Do you have other rights? Why doesn't the text (or Constitution) say that you have the right to eat pickles? What are the differences between that right and those mentioned? Does everyone believe in this or want this? How do you know? Have you ever heard anyone say that tyranny is the best kind of government, or free speech is bad? Why? Is there a basic idea behind all of these rights? Why does the text say people have this responsibility? How, exactly, does this help our country? Why do some people not do this? What does it require of you? And how do you do that? Is it easy or hard? What else does it mean you should do?*

The teacher could make copies of passages from several sample texts which cover the same material and have students compare and critique them.

Students can discuss their interpretations of what they read. Have them compare their paraphrases and interpretations.

Lesson plans in which the strategy is used

S-22 Listening Critically: The Art of Silent Dialogue

Principle: Critical thinkers realize that listening can be done passively and uncritically or actively and critically. They know that it is easy to misunderstand what is said by another and difficult to integrate another's thinking into our own. Compare speaking and listening. When we speak, we need only keep track of our own ideas, arranging them in some order, expressing thoughts with which we are intimately familiar: our own. But listening is more complex. We must take the words of another and translate them into ideas that make sense to us. We have not had the experiences of the speakers. We are not on the inside of their point of view. We can't anticipate, as they can themselves, where their thoughts are leading them. We must continually interpret what others say within the confines of our experiences. We must find a way to enter into their points of view, shift our minds to follow their trains of thought.

What all of this means is that we need to learn how to listen actively and critically. We need to recognize that listening is an art involving skills that we can develop only with time and practice. We need to learn, for example, that to listen and learn from what we are hearing, we need to learn to ask key questions that enable us to locate ourselves in the thought of another. We must practice asking questions like the following: "I'm not sure I understand you when you say ..., could you explain that further?" "Could you give me an example or illustration of this?"

"Would you also say ...?" "Let me see if I understand you. What you are saying is .... Is that right?" "How do you respond to this objection?" Critical readers ask questions as they read and use those questions to orient themselves to what an author is saying. Critical listeners ask questions as they listen to orient themselves to what a speaker is saying: Why does she say that? What examples could I give to illustrate that point? What is the main point? How does this detail relate? Is she using this word as I would, or somewhat differently? These highly skilled and activated processes are crucial to learning. We need to heighten student awareness of and practice in them as often as we can.

Application: The first and best way to teach critical listening is to model it. It is necessary that we listen to what students say actively and constructively, demonstrating the patience and skill necessary to understand them. We should not casually assume that what they say is clear. We should not pass by their expressions too quickly. Students rarely take seriously their own meanings. They rarely listen to themselves. They rarely realize the need to elaborate or exemplify their own thoughts. And we are often in a position to help them to do so with a facilitating question that results from close, enquiring listening.

Secondly, students rarely listen carefully to what other students have to say. They rarely take each other seriously. We can facilitate this process with questioning interventions. We can say things like: "Joel, did you follow what Dianne said? Could you put what she said in your own words?" Or we can say, "Richard, could you give us an example from your own experience of what Jane has said? Has anything like that ever happened to you?"

The success of Socratic questioning and class discussion depends upon close and critical listening. Many assignments are understood or misunderstood through word of mouth. We need to take the occasion of making an assignment an occasion for testing and encouraging critical listening. In this way, we will get better work from students, because in learning how to listen critically to what we are asking them to do, they will gain a clearer grasp of what that is, and hence do a better job in doing it. Students often do an assignment poorly, because they never clearly understood it in the first place.

Lesson plans in which the strategy is used

S-23 Making Interdisciplinary Connections

Principle: Although in some ways it is convenient to divide knowledge up into disciplines, the divisions are not absolute. Critical thinkers don't allow the somewhat arbitrary distinctions between academic subjects to control their thinking. When considering issues which transcend subjects, they bring relevant concepts, knowledge and insights from many subjects to the analysis. They make use of insights into one subject to inform their understanding of other subjects. There are always connections between subjects (language and logic; history, geography, psychology, anthropology, physiology; politics, geography, science, ecology; math, science, economics). To understand, say, reasons for the American Revolution (historical question), insights from technology, geography, economics, philosophy, etc., can fruitfully apply.

Application: Any time another subject is relevant to the object of discussion, those insights can be used and integrated. Some teachers allot time for coverage of topics in different subjects so that the topic is examined from the perspective of several subjects. Study of the news can combine with nearly every subject — language arts, social studies, math, geography, science, health, etc.

Socratic questioning can be used to make subject connections clear. The teacher can use discussion of students' issues and problems to show the importance of bringing insights from many subjects to bear.

Students could compare how data is gathered and used in different subjects, for example, scientific studies and public opinion polls.

The class could evaluate writing in their texts from a literary or composition standpoint. *"Given what you know about good writing, is this passage well written? Organized? Interesting? Why or why not? How can it be improved? Is the quote used evocative? To the point? How does it illustrate or enhance the point made?"*

Students can evaluate the psychological, sociological, or historical accuracy or sophistication of fiction and biography.

Lesson plans in which the strategy is used

S-24 Practicing Socratic Discussion: Clarifying and Questioning Beliefs, Theories, or Perspectives

Principle: Critical thinkers are nothing, if not questioners. The ability to question and probe deeply, to get down to root ideas, to get beneath the mere appearance of things, is at the very heart of the activity. And, as questioners, they have many different kinds of questions and moves available and can follow up their questions appropriately. They can use questioning techniques, not to make others look stupid, but to learn what they think, helping them develop their ideas, or as a prelude to evaluating them. When confronted with a new idea, they want to understand it, to relate it to their experience, and to determine its implications, consequences, and value. They can fruitfully uncover the structure of their own and others' perspectives. Probing questions are the tools by which these goals are reached.

Furthermore, critical thinkers are comfortable being questioned. They don't become offended, confused, or intimidated. They welcome good questions as an opportunity to develop a line of thought.

Application: Students, then, should develop the ability to go beyond the basic what and why questions that are found in their native questioning impulses. To do this, they need to discover a variety of ways to put questions which probe the logic of what they are reading, hearing, writing, or thinking. They need to learn how to probe for and question assumptions, judgments, inferences, apparent contradictions, or inconsistencies. They need to learn how to question the relevance of what is presented, the evidence for and against what is said, the way concepts are used, the implications of positions taken. Not only do we need to question students, we also need to have them question each other and themselves.

Classroom instruction and activities, therefore, should stimulate the student to question and help make the students comfortable when questioned, so that the questioning process is increasingly valued and mastered. Questioning should be introduced in such a way that students come to see it as an effective way to get at the heart of matters and to understand things from different points of view. It should not be used to embarrass or negate students. It should be part of an inquiry into issues of significance in an atmosphere of mutual support and cooperation. We therefore recommend that teachers cultivate a habit of wondering about the reasoning behind students' beliefs and translating their musings into questions.

The teacher should model Socratic questioning techniques and use them often. Any thought-provoking questions can start a Socratic discussion. To follow up responses, use questions like the following: *Why? If that is so, what follows? Are you assuming that...? How do you know that? Is the point that you are making that... or, ...? For example? Is this an example of what you mean..., or this,...? Can I summarize your point as...? What is your reason for saying that? What do you mean when using this word? Is it possible that...? Are there other ways of looking at it? How else could we view this matter?* (For more questions, see the section on Socratic discussion in the chapter, "Global Strategies: Beyond Subject Matter Teaching.")

To develop students' abilities to use Socratic questioning, the teacher could present an idea or passage to students and have them brainstorm possible questions. For instance, they could think of questions to ask story or historical characters, a famous person or personal hero, on a particular subject. Students can practice questioning in pairs, trading the roles of questioner and questioned. The teacher may provide lists of possible initial questions and perhaps some follow-up questions. Students could also be allowed to continue their discussions another day, after they've had time to think of more questions. As students practice Socratic questioning, see it modeled, and learn the language, skills, and insights of critical thinking, their mastery of questioning techniques will increase.

The direction and structure of a Socratic discussion can be made clearer by periodically summarizing and rephrasing the main points made or by distinguishing the perspectives expressed. *"We began with this question. Some of you said ____, others ____. These arguments were given .... Joan recommended that we distinguish X from Y. We've reached an impasse on X because we can't agree about two contradictory assumptions,___ and ____. We decided we would need to find out _____. So let's take up Y."*

87

To practice exploring the idea of illuminating and probing Socratic questioning, students could read and evaluate different kinds of interviews, categorizing the questions asked. They could then list probing follow-up questions that weren't asked, and share their lists.

Lesson plans in which the strategy is used

S-25 Reasoning Dialogically: Comparing Perspectives, Interpretations, or Theories

Principle: Dialogical thinking refers to thinking that involves a dialogue or extended exchange between different points of view, cognitive domains, or frames of reference. Whenever we consider concepts or issues deeply, we naturally explore their connections to other ideas and issues within different domains or points of view. Critical thinkers need to be able to engage in fruitful, exploratory dialogue, proposing ideas, probing their roots, considering subject matter insights and evidence, testing ideas, and moving between various points of view. When we think, we often engage in dialogue, either inwardly or aloud with others. We need to integrate critical thinking skills into that dialogue so that it is as fruitful as possible. Socratic questioning is one form of dialogical thinking.

Application: By routinely raising root questions and root ideas in a classroom setting, multiple points of view get expressed and the thinking proceeds, not in a predictable or straightforward direction, but in a criss-crossing, back-and-forth movement. We continually encourage the students to explore how what they think about x relates to what they think about y and z. This necessarily requires that students' thinking moves back and forth between their own basic ideas and those being presented by the other students, between their own ideas and those expressed in a book or story, between their own thinking and their own experience, between ideas within one domain and those in another, in short, between any two perspectives. This dialogical process will sometimes become dialectical. Some ideas will clash or be inconsistent with others.

Texts come close to teaching dialogical thinking by having students discuss perspectives other than that presented by their texts. Yet such discussion is simply tacked on; it is not integrated with the rest of the material. Thus, the ideas are merely juxtaposed, not synthesized. Rather than separate activities or discussions about different perspectives, the teacher can have students move back and forth between points of view. *"What do the environmentalists want? Why? Factory owners? Why? Workers? Why? Why do the environmentalists think the factory owners are wrong? How could/do the factory owners respond to that? ... What beliefs do the sides have in common? How would ecologists look at this dispute? Economists? Anthropologists?"*

Lesson plans in which the strategy is used

S-26 Reasoning Dialectically: Evaluating Perspectives, Interpretations, or Theories

Principle: Dialectical thinking refers to dialogical thinking conducted in order to test the strengths and weaknesses of opposing points of view. Court trials and debates are dialectical in form and intention. They pit idea against idea, reasoning against counter-reasoning in order to get at the truth of a matter. As soon as we begin to explore ideas, we find that some clash or are inconsistent with others. If we are to integrate our thinking, we need to assess which of the conflicting ideas we will provisionally accept and which we shall provisionally reject, or which parts of the views are strong and which weak, or how the views can be reconciled. Students need to develop dialectical reasoning skills, so that their thinking not only moves comfortably between divergent points of view or lines of thought, but also makes some assessments in light of the relative strengths and weaknesses of the evidence or reasoning presented. Hence, when thinking dialectically, critical thinkers can use critical micro-skills appropriately.

Application: Dialectical thinking can be practiced whenever two conflicting points of view, arguments, or conclusions are under discussion. Stories and history lessons provide many opportunities. Dialectical exchange between students in science classes enables students to discover and appropriately amend their preconceptions about the physical world.

The teacher could have proponents of conflicting views argue their positions and have others evaluate them. A dialogical discussion could be taped for later analysis and evaluation. Or the teacher could inject evaluative questions into dialogical discussion. *"Was that reason a good one? Why or why not? Does the other view have a good objection to that reason? What? And the answer to that objection? Does each side use language appropriately and consistently? To what evidence does each side appeal? Is the evidence from both sides relevant? Questionable, or acceptable? Compare the sources each side cites for its evidence. How can we know which of these conflicting assumptions is best? Is there a way of reconciling these views? The evidence? What is this side right about? The other side? Which of these views is strongest? Why?"*

Lesson plans in which the strategy is used

S-27 Comparing and Contrasting Ideals with Actual Practice

Principle: Self-improvement and social improvement are presupposed values of critical thinking. Critical thinking, therefore, requires an effort to see ourselves and others accurately. This requires recognizing gaps between facts and ideals. The fairminded thinker values truth and consistency and, hence, works to minimize these gaps. The confusion of facts with ideals prevents us from moving closer to achieving our ideals. A critical education strives to highlight discrepancies between facts and ideals, and proposes and evaluates methods for minimizing them. This strategy is intimately connected with "developing intellectual good faith."

Application: Since, when discussing our society, many texts consistently confuse ideals with facts, the teacher can use them as objects of analysis. Ask, *"Is this a fact or an ideal? Are things always this way, or is this statement an expression of what people are trying to achieve? Are these ideals yours? Why or why not? How have people attempted to achieve this ideal? When did they not meet the ideal? Why? What problems did they have? Why? How can we better achieve these ideals?"* Students could rewrite misleading portions of text, making them more accurate.

Sometimes this strategy could take the form of *avoiding oversimplification*. For example, when considering the idea that Americans are free to choose the work or jobs they want, the teacher could ask, *"Can Americans choose any job they want? Always? What, besides choice, might affect what job someone has or gets? Would someone who looked like a bum be hired as a salesman? Does this mean they don't have this freedom? Why or why not? What if there aren't enough openings for some kind of work? How can this claim be made more accurate?"*

The teacher can facilitate a general discussion of the value of achieving consistency of thought and action. Ask, *"Have you ever thought something was true about yourself but acted in a way that was inconsistent with your ideal? Did you see yourself differently then? Did you make efforts to change the behavior? Is it good to have accurate beliefs about yourself and your country? Why? Can anyone think of ways to be more consistent? Why is it often hard to be honest about yourself and the groups you belong to? Is it worth the pain?"*

Sometimes texts foster this confusion in students by asking questions to which most people want to answer yes, for example: Do you like to help others? Do you listen to what other people have to say? Do you share things? Since none of us always adheres to our principles (though few like to admit it) you might consider rephrasing such questions. For example, ask, *"When have you enjoyed helping someone? When not? Why? Did you have to help that person? When is it hard to listen to what someone else has to say? Why? Have you ever not wanted to share something? Should you have? Why or why not? If you didn't share, why didn't you?"*

Obviously, the more realistic are our ideals, the closer we can come to achieving them: therefore, any text's attempt to encourage unrealistic ideals should be remodelled. For example, rather than assuming that everyone should always do everything they can for everyone anytime, allow students to express a range of views on such virtues as generosity.

90

When discussing a departure from ideals or theory, have students analyze and evaluate it. Students could write an essay in which they focus on one such point. *"How is this supposed to work in theory? Why? What result is that supposed to have? Why is that considered good? How does this really work? Why? What incorrect assumption is made in the theory? What reasons are there for accepting this as it is? For trying to make it closer to the idea? Is the way we actually do this justified? Why or why not? If it isn't justified, how can we correct it?"*

Lesson plans in which the strategy is used

S-28 Thinking Precisely About Thinking: Using Critical Vocabulary

Principle: An essential requirement of critical thinking is the ability to think about thinking, to engage in what is sometimes called 'metacognition.' One possible definition of critical thinking is the art of thinking about your thinking while you're thinking in order to make your thinking better: more clear, more accurate, more fair. It is precisely at the level of "thinking about thinking" that most critical thinking stands in contrast to uncritical thinking. The analytical vocabulary in the English language (such terms as 'assume,' 'infer,' 'conclude,' 'criteria,' 'point of view,' 'relevance,' 'issue,' 'elaborate,' 'ambiguous,' 'objection,' 'support,' 'bias,' 'justify,' 'perspective,' 'contradiction,' 'credibility,' 'evidence,' 'interpret,' 'distinguish') enables us to think more precisely about our thinking. We are in a better position to assess reasoning (our own, as well as that of others) when we can use analytic vocabulary with accuracy and ease.

Application: Since most language is acquired by hearing words used in context, teachers should try to make critical terms part of their working vocabulary.

When students are reasoning or discussing the reasoning of others, the teacher can encourage them to use critical vocabulary. New words are most easily learned and remembered when they are clearly useful.

When introducing a term, the teacher can speak in pairs of sentences: first, using the critical vocabulary, then, rephrasing the sentence without the new term, e.g., *"What facts are relevant to this issue? What facts ought we to consider in deciding this issue? What kinds of information do we need?"* The teacher can also rephrase students' statements to incorporate the vocabulary.

When conducting discussions, participating students could be encouraged to explain the role of their remarks in the discussion: supporting or raising an objection to a conclusion, distinguishing concepts or issues, questioning relevance, etc. *"Why were you raising that point here? Are you supporting a view, or ...?"*

Students could look up and discuss sets of related critical vocabulary words, and discuss relationships among them, when each can be used, and for what purposes.

S-29 Noting Significant Similarities and Differences

Principle: Critical thinkers strive to treat similar things similarly and different things differently. Uncritical thinkers, on the other hand, often miss significant similarities and differences. Things superficially similar are often significantly different. Things superficially different are often essentially the same. It is only by developing our observational and reasoning skills to a high point that we become sensitized to significant similarities and differences. As we develop this sensitivity, it influences how we experience, how we describe, how we categorize, and how we reason about things. We become more careful and discriminating in our use of words and phrases. We hesitate before we accept this or that analogy or comparison.

We recognize the purposes of the comparisons we make. We recognize that purposes govern the act of comparing and determine its scope and limits. The hierarchy of categories biologists, for instance, use to classify living things reflects biological judgment regarding which kinds of similarities and differences between species are the most important biologically and which shed the most light on how each organism is structured and how it operates. To the zoologist, the similarities whales have to horses is considered more important than their similarities to fish. The differences between whales and fish are considered more significant than those between whales and horses.

Application: Texts often call on students to compare and contrast two or more things — ideas, phenomena, etc. Yet these activities rarely have a serious purpose. Merely listing similarities and differences has little value in itself. Rather than encouraging students to make such lists, these activities should be proposed in a context which narrows the range of pertinent comparisons and requires some use be made of them in pursuit of some specific goal. For example, if comparing and contrasting two cultures, students should use their understanding to illuminate the relationship between them, perhaps to explain factors contributing to conflict or war. Thus, only those points which shed light on the particular problem need be mentioned, and each point has implications to be drawn out and integrated into a broader picture.

"What does this remind you of? Why? How is it similar? Different? What does it tell us about our topic? How useful is that comparison? Can anyone think of an even more useful comparison?"

S-30 Examining or Evaluating Assumptions

Principle: We are in a better position to evaluate any reasoning or behavior when all of the elements of that reasoning or behavior are made explicit. We base both our reasoning and our behavior on beliefs we take for granted. We are often unaware of these assumptions. It is only by recognizing them that we can evaluate them. Critical thinkers have a passion for truth and for accepting the strongest reasoning. Thus, they have the intellectual courage to seek out and reject false assumptions. They realize that everyone makes some questionable assumptions. They are willing to question, and have others question, even their own most cherished assumptions. They consider alternative assumptions. They base their acceptance or rejection of assumptions on their rational scrutiny of them. They hold questionable assumptions with an appropriate degree of tentativeness. Independent thinkers evaluate assumptions for themselves, and do not simply accept the assumptions of others, even those assumptions made by everyone they know.

Application: Teachers should encourage students to make assumptions explicit as often as possible — assumptions made in what they read or hear and assumptions they make. Teachers should ask questions that elicit the implicit elements of students' claims. Although it is valuable practice to have students make good assumptions explicit, it is especially important when assumptions are questionable. The teacher might ask, *"If this was the evidence, and this the conclusion, what was assumed?"*

There are no rules for determining when to have students evaluate assumptions. Students should feel free to question and discuss any assumptions they suspect are questionable or false. Students should also evaluate good assumptions. Doing so gives them a contrast with poor assumptions.

The following are some of the probing questions teachers may use when a class discusses the worth of an assumption: *Why do people (did this person) make this assumption? Have you ever made this assumption? What could be assumed instead? Is this belief true? Sometimes true? Seldom true? Always false? (Ask for examples.) Can you think of reasons for this belief? Against it? What, if anything, can we conclude about this assumption? What would we need to find out to be able to judge it? How would someone who makes this assumption act?*

Lesson plans in which the strategy is used

S-31 Distinguishing Relevant From Irrelevant Facts

Principle: Critical thinking requires sensitivity to the distinction between those facts that are relevant to an issue and those which are not. Critical thinkers focus their attention on relevant facts and do not let irrelevant considerations affect their conclusions. Furthermore, they recognize that a fact is only relevant or irrelevant in relation to an issue. Information relevant to one problem may not be relevant to another.

Application: When discussing an issue, solution to a problem, or when giving reasons for a conclusion, students can practice limiting their remarks to facts which are germane to that issue, problem, or conclusion. Often students assume that all information given has to be used to solve a problem. Life does not sort relevant from irrelevant information for us. Teachers can encourage students to make a case for the pertinence of their remarks, and help them see when their remarks are irrelevant. *"How would this fact affect our conclusion? If it were false, would we have to change our conclusion? Why or why not? What is the connection?"*

Students could read a chapter of text or story with one or more issues in mind and note relevant details. Students could then share and discuss their lists. Students can then discover that sometimes they must *argue* for the relevance of a particular fact to an issue.

Another technique for developing students' sensitivity to relevance is to change an issue slightly and have students compare what was relevant to the first issue to what is relevant to the second.

Students who disagree about the relevance of a particular point to the issue discussed, should be encouraged to argue its potential relevance, and probe the beliefs underlying their disagreement.

Lesson plans in which the strategy is used

S-32 Making Plausible Inferences, Predictions, or Interpretations

Principle: Thinking critically involves the ability to reach sound conclusions based on observation and information. Critical thinkers distinguish their observations from their conclusions. They look beyond the facts, to see what those facts imply. They know what the concepts they use imply. They also distinguish cases in which they can only guess from cases in which they can safely conclude. Critical thinkers recognize their tendency to make inferences that support their own egocentric or sociocentric world views and are therefore especially careful to evaluate inferences they make when their interests or desires are involved. Remember, every interpretation is based on inference, and we interpret every situation we are in.

Application: Teachers can ask students to make inferences based on a wide variety of statements and actions. Students, for example, can make inferences from story titles and pictures, story characters' statements and actions, as well as their fellow students' statements and actions. They can then argue for their inferences or interpretations. Students should be encouraged to distinguish their observations from inferences, and sound inferences from unsound inferences, guesses, etc.

Sometimes texts will describe details yet fail to make or have students make plausible inferences from them. The class could discuss such passages. Or groups of students might suggest possible inferences which the class as a whole could then discuss and evaluate.

Teachers can have students give examples, from their experience, of inferring incorrectly and encourage them to recognize situations in which they are most susceptible to uncritical thought. The class can discuss ways in which they can successfully minimize the effects of irrationality in their thought.

Science instruction all too often provides the "correct" inferences to be made from experiments or observations rather than having students propose their own. Sometimes science texts encourage poor inferences given the observation cited. Though the conclusion is correct, students should note that the experiment alone did not prove it and should discuss other evidence supporting it.

Lesson plans in which the strategy is used

S-33 Evaluating Evidence and Alleged Facts

Principle: Critical thinkers can take their reasoning apart in order to examine and evaluate its components. They know on what evidence they base their conclusions. They realize that unstated, unknown reasons can be neither communicated nor critiqued. They can insightfully discuss evidence relevant to the issue or conclusions they consider. Not everything offered as evidence should be accepted. Evidence and factual claims should be scrutinized and evaluated. Evidence can be complete or incomplete, acceptable, questionable, or false.

Application: When asking students to come to conclusions, the teacher should ask for their reasons. *"How do you know? Why do you think so? What evidence do you have?"* etc. When the reasons students supply are incomplete, the teacher may want to ask a series of probing questions to elicit a fuller explanation of student reasoning. *"What other evidence do you have? How do you know your information is correct? What assumptions are you making? Do you have reason to think your assumptions are true?"* etc.

When discussing their interpretations of written material, students should routinely be asked to show specifically where in the book or passage they get that interpretation. The sentence or passage can then be clarified and discussed and the student's interpretation better understood and evaluated. *"On what evidence is this conclusion based? Where did we get the evidence? Is the source reliable? How could we find out what other evidence exists? What evidence supports opposing views? Is the evidence sufficient? Does another view account for this evidence?"*

Lesson plans in which the strategy is used

S-34 Recognizing Contradictions

Principle: Consistency is a fundamental — some would say the *defining* — ideal of critical thinkers. They strive to remove contradictions from their beliefs, and are wary of contradictions in others. As would-be fairminded thinkers they strive to judge like cases in a like manner.

Perhaps the most difficult form of consistency to achieve is that between word and deed. Self-serving double standards are one of the most common problems in human life. Children are in some sense aware of the importance of consistency ("Why don't I get to do what they get to do?"). They are frustrated by double standards, yet are given little help in getting insight into them and dealing with them.

Critical thinkers can pinpoint specifically where opposing arguments or views contradict each other, distinguishing the contradictions from compatible beliefs, thus focussing their analyses of conflicting views.

Application: When discussing conflicting lines of reasoning, inconsistent versions of the same story, or egocentric reasoning or behavior, the teacher can encourage students to practice recognizing contradictions. *"What does x say? What does y say? Could both claims be true? Why or why not? If one is true, must the other be false? Is this behavior consistent with these beliefs or values? Where, exactly, do these views contradict each other? On what do they agree?"*

Sometimes fiction illustrates contradictions between what people say and what they do. The teacher could use questions like the following: *What did they say? What did they do? Are the two consistent or contradictory? Why do you say so? What behavior would have been consistent with their words? What words would have been consistent with their behavior?*

History texts often confuse stated reasons with reasons implied by behavior. They will often repeat the noble justification that, say, a particular group ruled another group for its own good, when they in fact exploited them and did irreparable harm. Students could discuss such examples.

When arguing opposing views, students should be encouraged to find points of agreement and specify points of dispute or contradiction. *"What is it about that view that you think is false? Do you accept this claim? That one? On what question or claim does your disagreement turn? What, exactly, is it in this view that you doubt or disagree with?"*

The class can explore possible ways to reconcile apparent contradictions. *"How could someone hold both of these views? How might someone argue for their compatibility?"*

Lesson plans in which the strategy is used

S-35 Exploring Implications and Consequences

Principle: Critical thinkers can take statements, recognize their implications (i.e., if x is true, then y must also be true) and develop a fuller, more complete understanding of their meaning. They realize that to accept a statement one must also accept its implications. They can explore both implications and consequences at length. When considering beliefs that relate to actions or policies, critical thinkers assess the consequences of acting on those beliefs.

Application: The teacher can ask students to state the implications of material in student texts, especially when the text materials lack clarity. The process can help students better understand the meaning of a passage. *"What does this imply/mean? If this is true, what else must be true? What were, or would be, the consequences of this action, policy, solution? How do you know? Why wouldn't this happen instead? Are the consequences desirable? Why or why not?"*

The teacher can suggest, or have students suggest, changes in stories, and then ask students to state the implications of these changes and comment on how they affect the meaning of the story.

Teachers can have students explore the implications and consequences of their own beliefs. During dialogical exchanges, students can compare the implications of ideas from different perspectives and the consequences of accepting each perspective. *"How would someone who believes this act? What result would that have?"*

Lesson plans in which the strategy is used

When texts teach a skill or concept, they describe how to use it (and when and why), but the practice is drill: Perform this operation on, or apply this distinction to, the items below. (Of the sentences below, rewrite those that are run-ons. What is X percent of Y? Put your results in the form of a bar graph using the following headings .... Locate N on the map on page 63.) Even when students can produce the correct results and repeat the explanations, they don't necessarily understand the functions and purposes of the skills and concepts, and so fail to use or apply them spontaneously when appropriate.

Remodelling Language Arts Lessons

Introduction

Language arts, as a domain of learning, principally covers the study of literature and the arts of reading and writing. All three areas — literature, reading and writing — deal with the art of conceptualizing and representing *in language* how people live and might live their lives. All three are significantly concerned with gaining command of language and expression. Of course, there is no command of language separate from command of thought and no command of thought without command of language.

Very few students will ever publish novels, poems, or short stories, but presumably all should develop insight into what can be learned from literature. Students should develop a sense of the art involved in writing a story and, hence, of putting experiences into words. At bottom is the need everyone has to make sense of human life. This requires command of our own ideas, which requires command over the words in which we express them.

In words and ideas there is power — power to understand and describe, to take apart and put together, to create systems of beliefs and multiple conceptions of life. Literature displays this power, and reading apprehends it. Students lack insight into these processes. Few have command of the language they use or a sense of how to gain that command. Not having a command of their own language, they typically struggle when called upon to read literature. They often find reading and writing frustrating and unrewarding. And worse, they rarely see the value of achieving such command. Literature seems a frill, something artificial, irrelevant, and bookish, outside of the important matters of life. Reading, except in its most elementary form, seems expendable as a means of learning. Writing is often viewed as a painful bore and, when attempted, reduced to something approaching stream-of-consciousness verbalization.

The task of turning students around, stimulating them to cultivate a new and different conception of literature, of reading, and of writing, is a profound challenge. If we value students thinking for themselves, we cannot ignore, we must meet, this challenge. If a basic goal of

English classes is to instill lifelong reading, we must seriously confront why most students have little or no interest in literature. We need to think seriously about the life-world in which they live: the music they listen to, the TV programs and movies they watch, the desires they follow, the frustrations they experience, the values they live for.

Most teachers can probably enumerate the most common features and recurring themes of, say, students' favorite movies: danger, excitement, fun, sex, romance, rock music, car chases, exploding planets, hideous creatures, mayhem, stereotypes, cardboard characters, and so on. The lyrics and values of most popular music are equally accessible, expressing as they do an exciting, fast-moving, sentimentalized, superficial world of cool-looking, athletic, sultry bodies. Much student talk consists in slang. Though sometimes vivid it is more often vague, imprecise, and superficial. Most quality literature seems dull to students in comparison.

Good English instruction must respect and challenge student's attitudes. Ignoring student preferences doesn't alter those preferences. Students must assess for themselves the relative worth of popular entertainment and quality works. Students need opportunities to scrutinize and evaluate the forms of entertainment they prefer. They need to assess the messages they receive from them, the conceptions of life they presuppose, and the values they manifest. As instruction is now designed, students typically ignore what they hear, read, and reiterate in school work and activity. They may follow the teacher's request to explain why a particular classic has lasted many generations, but this ritual performance has little influence on students' real attitudes. Critical thinking can help encourage students to refine their tastes, and we should encourage it with this end in mind. Nevertheless, under no conditions should we try to force or order students to say what they don't believe. A well-reasoned, if wrong-headed, rejection of Shakespeare is better than mindless praise of him.

The Ideal English Student

In addition to the need to enter sympathetically into the life-world of our students, appreciating how and why they think and act as they do, we must also have a clear conception of what changes we are hoping to cultivate in them. We must have a clear sense of the ideals we are striving for as teachers. Consider language itself and the way in which an ideal student might approach it. We want students to be sensitive to their language, striving to understand it and use it thoughtfully, accurately, and clearly. We want them to become autonomous thinkers and so command rather than be commanded by language.

As Critical Reader

Critical readers of literature approach literature as an opportunity to live within anothers' world or experience, to consider someone else's view of human nature, relationships, and problems. Critical readers familiarize themselves with different uses of language to enhance their understanding of and appreciation of literature. They choose to read literature because they recognize its worth. They can intelligently discuss it with others, considering the interpretations of others as they support their own.

Critical readers approach a piece of nonfiction with a view to entering a silent dialogue with the author. They realize they must actively reconstruct the author's meaning. They read because there is much that they know they do not know, much to experience that they have not experienced. Thus, critical readers do not simply pass their eyes over the words with the intention of filling their memories. They question, they organize, they interpret, they synthesize, they digest what they read. They question, not only what was said, but also what was implied or presupposed. They organize the details, not only around key ideas in the work, but also around their own key ideas. They not only interpret, they recognize their interpretations *as interpretation*, and consider alternative interpretations. Recognizing their interpretations as such, they revise and refine their interpretations. They do not simply accept or reject; they work to make ideas their own, accepting what makes most sense, rejecting what is ill-thought-out, distorted, and false, fitting their new understanding into their existing frameworks of thought.

As Critical Writer

Command of reading and command of writing go hand-in-hand. All of the understanding, attitudes, and skills we have just explored have parallels in writing. When writing, critical writers recognize the challenge of putting their ideas and experiences into words. They recognize that inwardly many of our ideas are a jumble, some supporting and some contradicting other ideas, some vague, some clear, some true, some false, some expressing insights, some reflecting prejudices and mindless conformity. Because critical writers recognize that they only partially understand and only partially command their own ideas and experiences, they recognize a double difficulty in making those ideas and experiences accessible to others.

As readers they recognize they must *actively* reconstruct an author's meaning; as writers they recognize the parallel need to *actively* construct their own as well as the probable meanings of their readers. In short, critical writers engage in parallel tasks in writing to the ones in reading. Both are challenging. Both organize, engage, and develop the mind. Both require the full and heightened involvement of critical and creative thought.

As Critical Listener

The most difficult condition in which to learn is in that of a listener. It is normal and natural for people to become passive when listening, to leave to the speaker the responsibility to express and clarify, to organize and exemplify, to develop and conclude. The art of becoming a critical listener is therefore the hardest and the last art that students develop. Of course, most students never develop this art. Most students remain passive and impressionistic in their listening throughout their lives.

Yet this need not be the case. If students can come to grasp the nature of critical reading and writing, they can also grasp the nature of critical listening. Once again, each of the understandings, attitudes, and skills of reading and writing have parallels in listening. There is the same challenge to sort out, to analyze, to consider possible interpretations, the same need to ask questions, to raise possible objections, to probe assumptions, to trace implications. As listeners we must follow the path of another person's thought. Listening is every bit as dialogical as reading and writing. Furthermore, we cannot go back over the words of the speaker as we can in reading.

What is more, our students face a special problem in listening to a teacher, for if they listen so as to take seriously what is being said, they may appear to their peers to be playing up to the teacher, or foolish, if they seem to say a wrong or dumb thing. Student peer groups expect students to listen with casual indifference, even with passive disdain. To expect students to become active classroom listeners is, therefore, to expect them to rise above the domination of the peer group. This is very difficult for most students.

The ideal English student, as you can see, is quite like the ideal learner in other areas of learning, in that critical reading, writing, and listening are required in virtually all subject areas. Yet the language arts are more central to education than perhaps any other area. Without command of one's native language, no significant learning can take place. Even other domains of learning must utilize this command. The ideal English student should therefore come close to being the ideal learner, and while helping our students to gain command of reading, writing, and listening we should see ourselves as laying the foundation for all thought and learning.

Ideal Instruction

Considering the ideal reader, writer, and listener paves the way for a brief overview of ideal instruction. In each case, we should utilize our understanding of the ideal as a model to move toward, as an organizer for our behavior, not as an empty or unrealistic dream. Reading, writing, and listening, as critical thinking activities, help to organize and develop learning. Each is based on a recognition that if we actively probe and analyze, dialogue and digest, question and synthesize, we will begin to grasp and follow alternative schemes of meaning and belief. The world of Charles Dickens is not the same world as that of George Eliot, nor are either the same world as that of Hemingway or Faulkner. Similarly, each of us lives in a somewhat different world. Each of us has somewhat different ideas, goals, values, and experiences. Each of us constructs somewhat different meanings to live by. In ideal instruction, we want students to discover and understand different worlds so that they can better understand and develop their own. We want them to struggle to understand the meanings of others so they can better understand their own meanings.

Unfortunately, most texts do not have a unified approach to this goal. They are often a patchwork, as if constructed by a checklist mentality, as if each act of learning were independent of the one that precedes or follows it. Texts typically lack a global concept of literature, language, reading, writing, and listening. Even grammar is treated as a separate, unconnected set of rules and regulations.

This is not what we want, and this is not how we should design our instruction. Rather, we should look for opportunities to tie dimensions of language arts instruction together. There is no reason for treating any dimension of language arts instruction as unconnected to the rest. Thus far, we have talked about reading, writing, listening, and literature as ways of coming to terms with the constructing and organizing of meanings. We can now use this central concept to show how one can tie grammar to the rest of language arts instruction, for clearly grammar itself can be understood as an organized system for expressing meanings. Each "subject" of each sentence, after all, represents a focus for the expression of meaning, something that we are thinking or talking about. Each "predicate" represents what is said about, the meaning we are attributing to, the subject. All adjectives and adverbs are ways of qualifying or rendering more precise the meanings we express in subjects and predicates. By the same token, each sentence we write has some sort of meaningful relationship to the sentences that precede and follow it. The same principle holds for the paragraphs we write. In each paragraph, there must be some unifying thing that we are talking about and something that we are saying about it.

To put this another way, at each level of language arts instruction, we should aim at helping the student gain insight into the idea that there is a "logic" to the language arts. This is a key insight that builds upon the idea of constructing and organizing meanings; it makes even more clear how we can tie all of the language arts together. It reminds us that there are established uses for all facets and dimensions of language, and that the reasons behind these uses can be made intelligible. Basic grammar has a logic to it, and that logic can be understood. Individual words and phrases also have a logic to them, and, therefore, they too can be understood. When we look into language use with a sense that there is intelligible structure to be understood, our efforts are rewarded. Unfortunately, we face a special obstacle in accomplishing this purpose.

Typically, students treat the meanings of words as "subjective" and "mysterious." I have my meanings of words, and you have your meanings of them. On this view, problems of meaning are settled by asking people for their personal definitions. What do *you* mean by 'love,' 'hate,' 'democracy,' 'friendship,' etc.? Each of us is then expected to come forward with a personal definition. *My* definition of love is this.... *My* definition of friendship is that....

If we are to persuade students that it is possible to use words precisely, we must demonstrate to them that all of the words in the language have established uses with established *implications* that they must learn to respect. For example, consider the words 'rise,' 'arise,' 'spring,' 'originate,' 'derive,' 'flow,' 'issue,' 'emanate,' and 'stem.' They cannot be used in any way one pleases, with a merely personal definition in mind. Each of them has different implications in use:

> 'Rise' and 'arise' both imply a coming into being, action, notice, etc., but 'rise' carries an added implication of ascent (empires *rise* and fall) and 'arise' is often used to indicate causal relationship (accidents *arise* from carelessness); 'spring' implies sudden emergence (weeds *sprang* up in the garden); 'originate' is used in indicating a definite source, beginning, or prime cause (psychoanalysis *originated* with Freud); 'derive' implies a proceeding or developing from something else that is the source (this word *derives* from the Latin) 'flow' suggests a streaming from a source like water ("Praise God, from whom all blessings *flow*"); 'issue' suggests emergence through an outlet (not a word *issued* from his lips); 'emanate' implies the flowing forth from a source of something that is non-material or intangible (rays of light *emanating* from the sun); 'stem' implies outgrowth as from a root or a main stalk (modern detective fiction *stems* from Poe).

Or consider the words 'contract,' 'shrink,' 'condense,' 'compress,' and 'deflate.' Each of them, too, has definite implications in use:

> 'Contract' implies a drawing together of surface or parts and a resultant decrease in size, bulk, or extent; to 'shrink' is to contract so as to be short of the normal or required length, amount, extent, etc. (those shirts have *shrunk*); 'condense' suggests reduction of something into a more compact or more dense form without loss of essential content (*condensed* milk); to 'compress is to press or squeeze into a more compact, orderly form (a lifetime's work *compressed* into one volume); 'deflate' implies a reduction in size or bulk by the removal of air, gas, or in extended use, anything insubstantial (to *deflate* a balloon, one's ego, etc.)

There is a parallel insight necessary for understanding how to arrange sentences in logical relationships to each other. Our language provides a wide variety of adverbial phrases that can make connecting our sentences together easier. Here, as above, students need to learn and respect this established logic.

Group I

Connectives	How they are used	Examples
besides what's more furthermore in addition	To add another thought.	Two postal cards are often more effective than one letter. *Besides*, they are cheaper.
for example for instance in other words	To add an illustration or explanation.	There is no such thing as an "unlucky number." *In other words*, this idea is pure superstition.

Group II

in fact as a matter of fact	To connect an idea with another one.	Last week I was ill, *in fact*, I had to stay in bed until Monday.
therefore consequently accordingly	To connect an idea with another one that follows from it.	The President vetoed the bill. *Consequently*, it never became a law.

Group III

of course to be sure though	To grant an exception or limitation.	He said he would study all day. I doubt it, *though*.
still however on the other hand nevertheless rather	To connect two contrasting ideas.	I like painting; *however*, I can't understand modern art.

Group IV

first next finally meanwhile later afterwards nearby eventually above beyond in front	To arrange ideas in order, time, or space.	*First*, drink some fruit juice. *Next*, have a bowl of soup. Then eat the meat. *Finally*, have some pie and coffee.
in short in brief to sum up in summary in conclusion	To sum up several ideas.	Scientists say that we should eat food that has all the proteins, fats, and vitamins we need. *In short*, they recommend a balanced diet.

104

Common Problems With Texts

A critical thinking approach to language arts instruction, with its emphasis on helping students understand the *logic* of what they study, can provide a strong unifying force in all of the basic dimensions of the language arts curriculum: reading, writing, language, grammar, and appreciation of literature. Unfortunately, it is rare to find this unifying stress in most language arts textbooks. As a result, the emphases in reading, writing, language, grammar, and literature do not "add-up" in the minds of students. They don't recognize common denominators between reading and writing. They don't grasp how words in language have established uses and so can be used precisely or imprecisely, clearly or vaguely. Their lack of understanding of the logic of language in turn undermines their clarity of thought when reading and writing.

By the same token, grammar seems to students to be nothing more than an arbitrary set of rules. Typically, texts take a didactic approach. They introduce principles or concepts, then provide drills. Specific skills are often torn from their proper contexts and practiced merely for the sake of practice. Yet, without context, skills have little or no meaning. An occasional simple reiteration of basic purposes or ideas is insufficient. Students need to see for themselves when, how, and why each skill is used specifically as it is.

Texts rarely even mention that most crucial distinction: well vs. poorly written. Students rarely, if ever, evaluate what they read. Students do not explore their standards for evaluating written material, or distinguish for themselves when a written work is clear or unclear, engaging or dull, profound or superficial, realistic or unrealistic, and so on.

Texts occasionally have a short lesson or activity on describing plot, identifying theme, and finding the main point. But students are rarely, if ever, called upon to describe the plots of selections, for example. Yet these basic concepts are worthy of frequent discussion.

Unfortunately, texts seldom have students examine work for themselves, discovering strengths and flaws, distinguishing main points from details, exploring the use of various techniques, formulating their conceptions of theses, plots, and themes. Texts occasionally have lessons on "identifying the main point" or on "plot." These ideas are not taught often nor integrated into reading lessons.

Some questions to raise about the logic of language and grammar

Keeping in mind the idea that language and grammar are, on the whole, logical, we should ask questions that help students discover this.

"What is a sentence? How is it different from a group of words? What is a paragraph? How is it different from a group of sentences? What are words for? What do they do? How? How are words alike? Different? How many - what different - kinds of words are there? How is each used? Why are some ways of using a word right and others wrong? What different kinds of sentences are there? When and how should each be used? Why follow the rules of grammar? How does punctuation help the reader? How does knowing about grammar help me write? Read? When do I need to know this? How should I use this? How does knowing this help me as a writer? A reader? Why and how do different types of writing differ? What do they have in common?"

Some questions to raise about the logic of literature

Stories have their own logic. Events don't just happen. They make sense within the meanings and thinking of their authors. When we ask a question, there should be method to it. The questions should lead students to discover how to come to terms with the logic of the story. In every case, we should have students support their answers by reference to passages in the story. It is not their particular answers that are of greatest importance, but rather how they support their answers with reasons and references to the story.

What happened? Why? What is the author trying to convey? Why is this important? What is the main character like? How do you know? What parts of the book gave you that idea? What has shaped the main character? How has this person shaped others? Why do the characters experience their worlds as they do? How do those experiences relate to my experience or to those of people around me? How realistic are the characters? How consistent? If they aren't (realistic, consistent) why not? Is it a flaw in the work, or does it serve some purpose? What conflicts occur in the story? What is the nature of this conflict? What is its deeper meaning? What relationship does it have to my life? What meaning does that conflict have for the character? For me? Though the world, society, lifestyle or characters are obviously different than what I know, what does this work tell me about my world, society, life, character and the characters of those around me? What needs, desires, and ideas govern these characters? Can I identify with them? Should I? How does the view presented in this work relate to my view? To what extent do I accept the conception of humanity and society present or implicit in this work? To what extent or in what way is it misleading? How does it relate to conceptions I've found in other works? How good is this work?

Some questions to raise about the logic of persuasive writing

Persuasive writing has a straightforward logic. In it, an author attempts to describe some dimension of real life and hopes to persuade us to take it seriously. We, as readers, need to grasp what is being said and judge whether it does make sense.

What parts of this work do I seem to understand? What parts don't I understand? What, exactly, is the author trying to say? Why? How does the author support what he is saying with reasons, evidence, or experiences? What examples can I think of to further illuminate these ideas? What counter-examples can be cited? What might the author say about my counter-examples? What are the basic parts of this work? How are the pieces organized? Which claims or ideas support which other claims or ideas? What beliefs does this claim presuppose? What does it imply? What are the consequences of believing or doing as the author says? What kind of writing is this? How has the writer attempted to achieve his purpose? Given that this is what I think he means, how does this claim fit in? Could he mean this instead? Which of these interpretations makes more sense? How does he know what he claims to know? Have I good reason to accept his claims? Doubt them? How could I check, or better evaluate what he says? How are such questions settled, or such claims evaluated? What deeper meaning does this work have? What criticisms can I make? What has he left out? Distorted? How does he address his opponents? Has he been fair to his opponents? Does his evidence support exactly the conclusions he draws? If not, am I sure I understand his conclusions and his evidence? Where did he get his evidence? How should I evaluate it? What has he left unexplained? What would he say about it? Of all the ideas or concepts, which does he take to be the most fundamental or basic? How does he use these concepts? To what other concepts are they related? How does his use of concepts relate to mine and to that of others? Should he have used other concepts instead? How can I reconcile what he has said with what others have said?

Some questions to ask while writing

Writing has a logic. Good substance poorly arranged loses most of its value. Whatever the principle of order chosen, thought must progress from somewhere to somewhere else. It must follow a definite direction, not ramble aimlessly. In the entire piece, as well as in in section and paragraph, ideally, each sentence should have a place of its own, and a place so plainly its own that it could not be shifted to another place without losing coherence. Remember, disorderly thinking produces disorderly writing, and, conversely, orderly thinking produces orderly writing:

What do I want to communicate? Why? What am I talking about? What do I want to say about it? What else do I want to say about it, and why? What else do I know or think about this? How is what I am saying like and unlike what others have said? What am I sure of? What questions do I have? What must I qualify? How can I divide my ideas into intelligible parts? What are the relationships between the parts? How can I show those relationships? How does this detail fit in? How does that claim illuminate my main point? What form of expression best gets this idea across? Would the reader accept this? What questions would the reader have? How can I answer those questions? If I word it this way, would the reader understand it the way I intended? How can I clarify my meaning? How could someone judge this idea or claim? How can it be supported? How would others refute it? Which of those criticisms should I take into account? How can I reconcile the criticisms with my ideas? How should I change what I've said? Will the support seem to the reader to justify the conclusion? Should I change the conclusion, or beef up the support? What counter-examples or problems would occur to the reader here? What do I want to say about them? How am I interpreting my sources? How would someone else interpret them? How can I adjust or support my interpretation?What implications do I want the reader to draw? How can I help the reader see that I mean this and not that? Which of all of the things I'm saying is the most important? How will the reader know which is most important? Why is this detail important? Have I assumed the reader knows something he may not know?

Conclusion

As a teacher of the language arts, it is essential that you develop for yourself a clear sense of the logic of language and of the unity of the language arts. If you model the insight that every dimension of language and literature makes sense, can be figured out, can be brought under our command, can be made useful to us, your students will be much more apt to make this same discovery for themselves. Remember that students are not used to unifying what they are studying. They are, rather, used to fragmented learning. They are used to forgetting, for everything to begin anew, for everything to be self-contained.

Furthermore, they are not used to clear and precise language usage. They are usually satisfied with any words that occur to them to say or write. They are unfamiliar with good writing. Disciplined thinking is something foreign to their life and being. Therefore, don't expect the shift from a didactic approach ("The teacher tells us and we repeat it back") to a critical one ("We figure it out for ourselves and integrate it into our own thinking") to occur quickly and painlessly.

Expect a slow transition. Expect the students to experience many frustrations along the way. Expect progress to come by degrees over an extended period of time. Commit yourself to the long view, to what Matthew Arnold called "the extreme slowness of things," and you will have the attitude necessary for success. Teaching in a critical manner with a critical spirit is a global transformation. Global transformations take a long time to achieve, but their effect is then often permanent. And that is what we want — students who learn to use language clearly and precisely for the rest of their lives, students who listen and read critically for the rest of their lives, students who become critical and creative persons for the rest of their lives.

Vitalizing Vapid Vocabulary

by Diane McCurdy, Ursuline High
School, Santa Rosa, CA

Objectives of the remodelled plan

The students will:
- have an increased understanding of words in their functional context through extended analysis
- think independently by making their own logical deductions of word meanings from their roots
- prepare for SAT examinations

Standard Approach

Every week students are given 10-50 words from an alphabetically arranged vocabulary book. They are to memorize spelling, meaning, and sometimes part of speech. At the end of the week, students are given an orally administered written quiz or a matching type ditto.

Critique

All English teachers are stuck with this repetitive, ritual rubric of vocabulary presentation. Memorization being the lowest form of learning, the weekly quizzes can be as tedious for the teacher as they are for the student. Whenever the spelling test type of format is adopted, cheating is rampant. Words studied out of context have little relevancy.

Strategies used to remodel

S-14 clarifying and analyzing the meanings of words or phrases
S-1   thinking independently
S-29 noting significant similarities and differences

Remodelled Lesson Plan S-14

Ten words from the vocabulary lists are put on the chalkboard. Derivations and stems are discussed. "Do you recognize any parts of words? Can you figure out what they might mean, or what they have something to do with?" After the etymologies have been discussed and verified in dictionaries, students can discuss contexts for using the words. "When would this word be used? Why? For what purpose?" Students are then assigned to write a logical, flowing paragraph of about two hundred words using the target ten words. Cheating is eliminated. **S-1**

editor's note: When making vocabulary lists, give students a group of related words, rather than randomly chosen, or alphabetically grouped words. Have students brainstorm, use dictionaries and thesauruses to list synonyms and other related words. Discussion and writing, then, can focus on distinguishing synonyms and exploring relationships between related concepts. "When would this word be used? What do these words have in common? What other words could we add to this group? When might any of these synonyms do equally well? When would this but not that be most appropriate, accurate, etc.? **S-29** Would you apply these two words to the same thing? Ever, often, never? Would two people who were arguing use them for the same thing? What other words are similar or have related meanings? Do any of these words imply any of the others?"

It should not be assumed that there is a universal standard for how fast teachers should proceed with the task of remodelling their lesson plans. A slow but steady evolutionary process is much more desirable than a rush job across the board.

Vocabulary

by Laura Racine, Gifted Education
Department, Wyandotte Special
Education Cooperative, Kansas City, KS

Objectives of the remodelled lesson

The students will:
- become more motivated to learn new words
- develop a disposition to investigate the significance of a word and its application
- clarify words by incorporating vocabulary terms into their experiences through Socratic discussion
- employ all thinking capacities in the attainment of new vocabulary
- apply new terms appropriately in real situations

Standard Approach

The student's task is to learn vocabulary terms. The words are presented with suggested systems for remembering their meanings. Visualization and imaging are modeled by the teacher. Sensory learning techniques are used. Students are invited to share their own techniques for learning vocabulary terms by presenting a new word not included in the list to the class. The teacher encourages the learner to incorporate the new terms into the learner's experiential world.

Critique

One of the blocks to vocabulary acquisition seems to be motivation. Learning new words is dull and dreary fare; in fact, the common approach to vocabulary learning is memorization through mundane methods. As a result, the student's underlying attitudes toward learning a list of words and their uses do not produce energy nor high-level interest. The student typically responds in habitual patterns, by not integrating the new concepts with life experience.

But creative thinking techniques can be employed to enliven this process. If the learner can go beyond recall to discover insights about the words and even develop a personal connection to their significance, they will be more likely to retain the new knowledge. However, the terms must be more than manipulated, even if the perspective is new and unique. Real comprehension must be undertaken. Using critical thinking principles will enrich the student's experience as an active participant in the learning process as well as promote understanding and retention of concepts.

111

I chose to remodel a lesson with content not readily considered in terms of the critical thinking philosophy. I wished to experiment with the concept in an adverse circumstance.

Strategies used to remodel

S-14 clarifying and analyzing the meanings of words or phrases
S-35 exploring implications and consequences
S-4 exploring thoughts underlying feelings and feelings underlying thoughts
S-24 practicing Socratic discussion: clarifying and questioning beliefs, theories, or perspectives
S-23 making interdisciplinary connection

Remodelled Lesson Plan *S-14*

The lesson could be organized to move from the molecular level to the molar level, then back to the molecular level for review. In this manner, the learner can experience the *gestalt*, through expanding understanding of content as well as experiencing helpful potent learning tactics.

The vocabulary list could be presented to the learner in a variety of formats (individual lists, overhead projectors, or chalkboards).

The List
meretricious
deleterious
milieu
cacophony
euphemism
collegial
bellicose
malaise
sacrosanct
concomitant

Before approaching the list, the students could be provided with or invited to supply action words that stimulate the mind to be open to new experiences. A list might be compiled:

embellish
transform
magnify
stimulate
manipulate

What images do these words conjure in the learner's experience?

The teacher can encourage the student to express thoughts and feelings, indicating no convergent nor "right" response, but accepting all responses equally. The learner's confidence in thinking independently can be elevated as the students share common reactions and as the class members are asked to explain and elucidate their reactions. Through this dialogical process, students may gain insights. One "Aha" experience fuels another. As students share and question — What do you mean exactly by 'open-mindedness'? — they are pushed to clarify and define ideas. **S-14** At this introductory anticipation level of the lesson, the learner may have to explore the implications of each: Is there a value overtone to the act of manipulating? **S-35** Is it too mystical in a classroom setting to think about transformations?

The teacher can encourage retention of the vocabulary terms: What do you need to do to connect the word 'collegial' to your experiential realm? **S-14** What techniques work for you? Are you aware of techniques used by famous achievers that enabled them to be productive? What was Mozart's composition technique? How did Einstein experience his ideas?

If the class is exploring the word 'collegial,' a dictionary definition might be provided, after students share their own understandings of the term. In committing to a definition, the process may become more personal, thus more meaningful. As the class members share their perceptions they may touch upon the connotative significance of the word. Further delving may encourage clarification of their ideas. This is an opportunity to address the feelings underlying definitions. Experiences of individual learners will begin to have meaning. Personal reactions to the word should be bounced off the dictionary meaning. **S-4** "Can anyone improve upon Mr. Webster's position? What does Funk & Wagnall's say?"

The students may choose which of the remaining words the class will explore together. The questions can be directed from learner to learner, while the teacher participates as a student, generating ideas. The leader's role would involve policing the "I don't know" responses, encouraging deeper exploration and more accurate identification. "What occurs to you? What impression do you have? Why? What else do you think? What words are related? How? How are they different? When do you think people use this word? For what kinds of purposes?" **S-24**

At some point, a solution or definition must be accepted by individual learners and the group as a whole. Generating potential solutions to the choices of definitions is perhaps the most germane principle of the lesson. A student might ponder, "How might the word 'concomitant' be used in the math classroom, in music, in the world of syntax or semantics? How might a minister use the word sacrosanct? What professionals rely on euphemisms to ensure congruity and security in their careers?" **S-23**

The students can select a word remaining on the list, or find a new word to present to the class. Integrating the terms into the learner's repertoire is the ultimate goal.

Encourage the student's active and critical participation. Their contributions need to be defensible. Learners need to feel ownership and exercise control over the concepts presented.

Concepts you tie to your experience are translatable to reality.

"The Dream Keeper"

by Odessa Cleveland, North Hollywood High School Zoo Magnet, North Hollywood, CA

Objectives of the remodelled plan

The students will:

- interpret the poem "The Dream Keeper," by Langston Hughes
- assess the practicality of dreams
- discuss the use of created words for poem and figures of speech used

Standard Approach

The teacher reads the poem aloud. Students listen. Students read the poem silently. Then a volunteer reads the poem aloud. The poem's main theme deals with dreams that need to be protected, because if they are not, they can be broken. Langston Hughes, the author, repeatedly says that dreams are valuable.

Most of the questions under comprehension probe interpretive understanding. One question requires a literal understanding: "To whom is the poem addressed?"

Critique

Questions in the original lesson require students to understand the meaning of dream keeper. Other questions are concerned with understanding and recognizing figures of speech: "the too-rough fingers/ Of the world." There are no questions dealing with a discussion of the dream keeper not fulfilling dreams. If students are given a chance to discuss the opposite side of this view, then they will start to recognize that poetry can be appreciated more for its conciseness and literary beauty.

Strategies used to remodel

S-21 reading critically: clarifying or critiquing texts
S-17 questioning deeply: raising and pursuing root or significant questions

Remodelled Lesson Plan S-21

The definition of 'dream keeper' should be brainstormed on the board for extension. From selected choices made by students, they should be able to clarify the poet's meaning of the words 'dream keeper' and to determine whether the pronoun 'me' refers to *anyone* with a dream.

For further exploration, ask questions like the following: Have you ever had a dream that you tried to make a reality? How do you deal with disappointment and frustration? Are dreams of any use? Do they ever help us? Why do illusions and delusions enter dreams? **S-17**

What two ideas are combined in each of these terms: cloud-cloth; heart melodies? What do they evoke? Could the poet have used different words and still had the same effect? Try out different possible substitute words.

Of course, during and after the discussion and note taking, questions should be encouraged. Afterwards, review and have students write a paragraph discussing whether dreams are useful, or on whether they agree or disagree with the poet's theme.

When texts teach a skill or concept, they describe how to use it (and when and why), but the practice is drill: Perform this operation on, or apply this distinction to, the items below. (Of the sentences below, rewrite those that are run-ons. What is X percent of Y? Put your results in the form of a bar graph using the following headings .... Locate N on the map on page 63.) Even when students can produce the correct results and repeat the explanations, they don't necessarily understand the functions and purposes of the skills and concepts, and so fail to use or apply them spontaneously when appropriate.

The Quest for the Tragic Hero

by June Tinkhauser, Baldwin High
School, Baldwin, NY

Objectives of the remodelled plan

The students will:
- research to review previously learned concepts and deeply question their application
- clarify and assess their beliefs about the tragic hero in *Macbeth*
- understand how a classical model works through the ages

Standard Approach

At the conclusion of the play *Macbeth*, it is of interest to see how some of the classical applications of Aristotle's *Poetics* can apply to Elizabethan drama (in this case, Macbeth, and later to modern drama as with Arthur Miller and Maxwell Anderson.) After discussing Aristotle's notes on aspects of comedy and tragedy, the teacher zeros in on the concept of the Tragic Hero, a character, mortal, yet towering over others, who goes from good to bad fortune as a result of a fatal flaw in his or her character. Lots of good Greek terms apply here: hubris, anagnorisis, catharsis. The teacher illustrates the concept of the Tragic Hero by drawing, or having a student draw, an architectural column on the board, adding a chink into the side of the column which ultimately spreads, undermining the column, causing it to fall. An analogy is drawn between the column and the Tragic Hero and Shakespeare's Macbeth.

Critique

This lesson, the teacher's own, is satisfying in some respects. Students are able to see a classical ideal operating in an Elizabethan context and should see this further developed when we read Miller's *Death of a Salesman*. But students have difficulty seeing Macbeth, a bloody, murdering tyrant as a good man gone bad. Exegesis is offered from the text, but it's the "Blood will have blood," that sticks.

Strategies used to remodel

S-17 questioning deeply: raising and pursuing root or significant questions
S-1 thinking independently
S-13 clarifying issues, conclusions, or beliefs

Remodelled Lesson Plan

Let's not trash the whole lesson. The column concept is a good, graphic illustration, but perhaps students could do their own research on Aristotle's Poetics, since this is probably not their first introduction to the Tragic Hero. (They have studied other Shakespearean plays.)

Then have that artistic student draw that column and ask students to make the connections to the Tragic Hero, eliciting vocabulary: tragic flaw, peripetia, anagnorisis, catharsis if possible. If not, hubris and catharsis are probably the most useful. *S-17*

Now the quest for the Tragic Hero in Macbeth. Students will suggest Macduff, Malcolm, Banquo, Duncan and possibly Macbeth and Lady Macbeth. *S-1* For the next day, ask students to be prepared to role-play each of these characters, presenting their case for status as Tragic Hero. The teacher acts as facilitator, asking questions if necessary to clarify connections to the classical model. "Would you call this character 'towering'? How so? More so than another? What was his or her tragic flaw? How is it exhibited?" *S-13*

Students can decide who makes the best case; the teacher again asks what convinced them. When students ask about *the* Tragic Hero, the teacher might tell them the Jean Kerr anecdote about her son who was playing Adam in a play about the Garden of Eden. One day he returned home, dejected. When asked why, he said, "The snake has all the lines."

"Who, then, has the best lines in Macbeth?" No doubt about it, students can now consider and accept Macbeth as the Tragic Hero, and also realize the applications to many characters in literature and in life.

> *Everyone learning to deepen her critical thinking skills and dispositions comes to insights over time. We certainly can enrich and enhance this process, even help it to move at a faster pace, but only in a qualified way. Time to assimilate and grow is essential.*

"Harrison Bergeron"

by Brenda McEvoy, Healdsburg High
School, Healdsburg, CA

Objectives of the remodelled plan

The students will:

- analyze the concepts 'equality' and 'justice'
- evaluate the policies of the government depicted in the story
- analyze and critique the author's perspective
- use critical vocabulary while analyzing the story

Standard Approach

Kurt Vonnegut's satirical short story is about a future American society in which all people are made equal in every respect by making people wear handicaps; the graceful or athletic must wear weights; the intelligent must wear devices in their ears which transmit a sharp noise every twenty seconds, making sustained thought impossible; the beautiful must wear masks. Fourteen year old Harrison is stronger, more handsome, and more intelligent than anyone else; he wears the most handicaps. His parents watch on television as he rebels, tears off his devices, and declares himself Emperor by right of his extraordinary abilities. He challenges a group of ballerinas to join his rebellion. One does, and he removes her handicaps and dances with her. The woman in charge of handicaps appears and shoots the rebels, ending the brief moment of rebellion. Harrison's average mother and intelligent but handicapped father immediately forget what they have seen. Texts ask recall questions, have students describe the society depicted, and state the theme of the story.

Critique

This lesson was selected because the text makes so little use of a story which deals with ideas of immediate concern to adolescents: the concepts of equality and justice, and the idea of adult authoritarianism towards teen-agers. The text does not offer students an opportunity to practice critical thought.

Strategies used to remodel

S-14 clarifying and analyzing the meanings of words or phrases
S-20 analyzing or evaluating actions or policies
S-19 generating or assessing solutions

S-25 reasoning dialogically: comparing perspectives, interpretations, or theories
S-21 reading critically: clarifying or critiquing texts
S-28 thinking precisely about thinking: using critical vocabulary

Remodelled Lesson Plan

Before reading the story, students could discuss the concept of equality. "What does it mean as a legal concept? What does it mean as a social concept? Why?" The discussion might be started by the teacher giving an example of equality, or lack of it, and then having the students explain why they agree or disagree with the example. The discussion could continue with students supplying further examples and analyzing them. **S-14**

After reading the story, the students could discuss Vonnegut's future society and discriminate between equality and justice. Was this society actually equal? Consider the people who imposed and enforced the handicapping. Were they equal? Compare that society's concept of equality with the concept meant in the American ideals of equality. **S-14** In this story does equality promote justice? Why or why not? Cite evidence from the text. **S-20**

If the students decide that Harrison lived in an unjust society, a written assignment might follow a brainstorming session on how a society could be remodelled to include both the concepts of equality and justice. **S-19**

After working with the content issues, the students could analyze the story itself. What statement is the author making in this satire? How do you know? How does he make his point? What would be the opposing point of view? What arguments could be used to support the opposing view? Explain the reasoning behind the handicapping system. Who would most want it? Why? **S-25** What effects does the system of handicapping have? What, exactly, is wrong with the society described? Does it seem right to you? What is wrong with how that society interprets the ideal of equality? Does this society bear any resemblance to ours? In what ways? Is Vonnegut trying to say something to us? What? Do you agree with the author's point of view? Why or why not? **S-21**

Critical thinking vocabulary could be integrated into the discussion sessions. "What *evidence* do you have for the point of view? What *inferences* can be drawn about the author's beliefs from reading this story? What *conclusion* can you reach after weighing the evidence? What is *implied* by Vonnegut's choice of satire as a means of expression?" **S-28**

The Crucible

by Sheree Shown, Vintage High School, Napa, CA

Objectives of the remodelled plan

The students will:
- pursue root questions raised in the play *The Crucible*
- analyze characters by exploring thoughts, feelings, and actions

Standard Approach

In this play, *The Crucible* by Arthur Miller, many characters have been accused of witchcraft by first one, and then several young girls of Puritan Salem. The girls have suffered mysterious "fits," hallucinations, and visions before the public. One man, John Proctor is finally singled out by the leader of the girls, Abigail, as the cause of their suffering. John and Abigail had a brief affair earlier, but John had put an end to it for the sake of his marriage, believing his soul to be forever damned for the encounter. At the end of the play, Proctor refuses to confess to any crime, and is hanged with several dozen others as a "witch."

Students have read the text of the play and have gone through several discussions and worksheets concerning the various characters in it. Students are told to write a three page paper analyzing one character through his actions, and in so doing, find a theme for the novel. Background for the paper comes from class discussions and journal entries.

Critique

Although the original lesson asks students to analyze, the assignment asks them to do this on their own, without any formal structure to go by. Papers received in the past have been marginal, lacking depth and focus. The lesson places blinders on the students, in that they examine only one character without any relation to another, yet it is the interaction of the characters that produces conflict and brings the theme into focus.

Strategies used to remodel

S-21 reading critically: clarifying or critiquing texts
S-17 questioning deeply: raising and pursuing root or significant questions
S-4 exploring thoughts underlying feelings and feelings underlying thoughts
S-32 making plausible inferences, predictions, or interpretations
S-20 analyzing or evaluating actions or policies
S-8 developing intellectual perseverance

Remodelled Lesson Plan *S-21*

As an introduction to this paper, students will have become familiar with the terms 'motivation,' 'conflict,' and 'theme' through various group exercises and discussions. In a large class discussion, students will be asked "Have you ever become jealous? Have you ever wanted something you could not have? Can a person be totally honest all of the time? What does it mean to be a good person? When has the truth hurt you? When has a lie hurt you?" **S-17**

Students will examine these question both orally and in informal "free-writing" that is ungraded and shared voluntarily. Next, students will be asked to fill in a small chart on three characters they feel comfortable analyzing: **S-4**

character   predominant emotions   3 major actions   possible motivation   result

They will then break up into small groups of three to five and share their work, discussing the similarities and differences they found. These cooperative groups will report their findings to the class. Students will be asked at this point to choose one character for their papers. Groups will be organized by the character selected.

Each group will build a "resource map" to be used as a study resource aide for their individual papers. The resource map consists of six "cells," or categories:

portrait of character and physical description;
descriptive words with clarification;
quotes from the character which show an aspect of personality;
quotations about the character and their sources;
a motto the character might choose to live by and at least three metaphors
   for the character; **S-32**
major actions of the character, possible motivations, and the results of
   those actions; **S-20**

Each student shall be responsible for at least one cell on the map, but it would be the responsibility of the group as a *whole* to complete the task and evaluate it.

When complete (one week), the groups share their work. All maps would be tacked up in the room and discussed. Only now would students be given the actual writing assignment on character analysis. Students would be free to use not only their own resource map, but others as well, to complete their essay. Thus, students would be familiar with the material, have a means of organizing it, and have the resources necessary to feel confident of their information. **S-8**

To Kill a Mockingbird

by Janis Key, Vintage High School,
Napa, CA

Objectives of the remodelled plan

The students will:

- recognize their own sociocentricity by discussing school cliques
- examine the nature, causes, and consequences of their assumptions about other groups
- develop intellectual courage by examining social pressure to agree with one's group
- understand stereotypes and be able to identify examples in their own lives
- transfer insight into their sociocentricity to that described in the novel

Standard Approach——————————

To prepare students for *To Kill a Mockingbird*, a novel of social injustice in the South during the Depression, background information is given in a lecture covering the author, Harper Lee, and facts about the Depression. Students should be aware of the quasi-autobiographical nature of the novel, references such as FDR, blue eagle, WPA, and John Dewey, as well as the social and economic climate in the South during the Depression.

Critique

This novel presents an excellent opportunity for students to explore stereotypes and prejudice while examining their own sociocentricity. Although background information enhances the understanding of the novel, students have a deeper understanding of the issues presented in this novel and the relevance of these issues in their own lives by sharing a more active role in the gathering and evaluation of the information. The background information will be more meaningful if presented after students are engaged in the above issues and if they play an active role in gathering that information.

Strategies used to remodel

S-2   developing insight into egocentricity or sociocentricity
S-3   exercising fairmindedness
S-4   exploring thoughts underlying feelings and feelings underlying thoughts
S-35 exploring implications and consequences
S-6   developing intellectual courage
S-11 comparing analogous situations: transferring insights to new contexts

Remodelled Lesson Plan S-2

Students are to bring to class a definition and an example of stereotype.

In small self-selected groups, students identify the social groups at Vintage High School. They list several characteristics and several values of each group. Students discuss the following questions. To which group do you belong? Which other groups do you or would you associate with? Which groups would you never associate with and why? What characteristics or values do these groups have that conflict with yours? Do those groups feel the same way about your group? Explain. **S-3** Why does each group hold these views of the other? Why do you have these feelings about different groups? **S-4**

A representative from each group shares the group's observations and conclusions with the entire class.

The class discusses the implications of these observations and conclusions. "What happens when people make these kinds of assumptions about others? What are the positive and negative consequences of identifying yourself with a particular group and excluding yourself from other groups? **S-35** What forms of group identification are legitimate? Which are unjustified? Why do people make such unjustified distinctions? Why is it hard to express attitudes that conflict with those of your group? How do group members respond to dissent? Why? How do you feel about those who disagree with the rest of the group? How does the group members' response make the dissenters feel? Why?" **S-6**

Then, as background preparation for reading, students could do their own research about the Depression and the South, sharing their results.

editor's note: When the book is finished, students can discuss the social class distinctions made in it: What groups of people are covered in this book? (Townspeople, Blacks, people like the Cunninghams, the Ewells.) "What are Aunt Alexandra's distinctions, and attitudes about others? Why did she feel this way about each group? Was she fair? Why or why not? What were Jem and Scout's theories on class distinctions? Why did they come up with these theories? Why did the theories make some sense to them? How reasonable were they? Where did they miss the mark? Where does Boo fit in? Would he have been treated differently if he had been from another class?" **S-2**

Students can compare the social distinctions in the book to those of their school. "How are the social distinctions made at school like and unlike those in the book?" The class can take specific points made in the two sets of discussions, and see if they apply to the other context. (For example, if, when discussing the book, students note that people in the book were born into their classes, they could discuss whether they chose their groups.) Students can discuss the consequences of the differences between the two "societies," and the justification of the social systems and the kinds of behavior it allows and even encourages. **S-11**

The Grapes of Wrath

by Janis Key, Vintage High School,
Napa, CA

Objectives of the remodelled plan
The students will:
- apply insights into dust-bowl refugees to other groups
- recognize unfounded beliefs they may have about the homeless
- explore significant similarities and differences between the situation in *The Grapes of Wrath* and that of the homeless, Mexican migratory farm workers, or immigrants
- clarify the meanings of tolerance and concern for humanity and apply them to the situation of the homeless
- develop insight into sociocentricity by examining attitudes toward and treatment of oppressed peoples

Standard Approach

> After the students finish reading *The Grapes of Wrath*, a novel by John Steinbeck about the Okie migration to California during the 1930's and the difficulties they encountered, students discuss the development of the following themes in the novel: toleration, concern for humanity, social reform, and survival. As the discussion progresses, the teacher writes important ideas on the board under each theme heading and students copy these for use in a paper or essay exam.

Critique

Although this lesson provides an opportunity for students to begin to consider the major issues present in the novel and explore how they are developed, there is no opportunity to draw conclusions about these issues or to identify them independently. There is also the likelihood that only a few students will participate in the discussion. Students are not asked to examine the lack of tolerance in their society or in themselves, nor are they asked to find relevance in the novel to their own society and times.

Strategies used to remodel
S-11 comparing analogous situations: transferring insights to new contexts
S-2 developing insight into egocentricity or sociocentricity
S-35 exploring implications and consequences
S-1 thinking independently
S-29 noting significant similarities and differences
S-23 making interdisciplinary connections

Remodelled Lesson Plan *S-11*

The students individually list the qualities and characteristics of the homeless. "What do you assume a homeless person is like?" Students share items on their lists to generate a class list on the board. If some students disagree with an item, it is checked and reasons for the disagreement are voiced. The students are asked, "Where did you get these assumptions? Is there good reason to question them? How could these claims be verified or disproven? What characteristics listed on the board are positive or negative? Why? Why do people react in these ways?" **S-2**

Students read two articles on the homeless, such as, "What Can Be Done?" Tom Mathews, *Newsweek*, 3/21/88 and "The Homeless and Their Children," Jonathan Kozol, *The New Yorker*, 1/25/88.

In small groups, students discuss the answers to the following questions as well as asking questions of their own: What does this situation imply for the future of these people, particularly the children? **S-35** Have you changed any of your ideas about the homeless or possible solutions to the problem? What led you to do so? Students, in their groups, discuss the situation of the homeless, create a new list of characteristics and qualities and develop possible solutions. **S-1**

Students discuss the similarities and differences between the problems of the Okies in *The Grapes of Wrath* and those of the homeless in America today. "In what ways are these two groups alike? Unlike? What do the differences imply? Does this difference effect conclusions or judgments about them? How? Why?" **S-29**

Individual writing assignment: Compare and contrast the situation of the Okies in *The Grapes of Wrath* to that of the homeless today. Examine particularly the attitudes toward these groups by outsiders and the causes of the situations. **S-2** If you think Steinbeck offered a solution to the problems of the Okies, discuss whether or not that solution would work for the homeless. Use specific examples from the articles and the novel.

editor's note: What kinds of things about the dust-bowlers did Californians dislike (ridicule, resent)? What other people are disliked (ridiculed, resented) for similar reasons? Why do people respond to others these ways? How did negative images help rationalize the ways they were treated? **S-2**

An even closer comparison can be made between dust-bowl refugees and Mexican migratory farm workers. Some students might research this group. The class can compare problems each group faced, and attitudes others have toward them. **S-29**

Another set of comparable groups would be the various waves of immigrants coming to the U.S., throughout its history. Perhaps social studies classes could be coordinated with this unit. Such a project could have the added benefit of exploring more long-range consequences of attitudes and policies. "What problems did this group face? How did they respond? What images did others here have of them? Why? What was done about their problems? What results did that have?" **S-23**

"Charles"

Objectives of the remodelled plan

The students will:
- compare the short story to other genres through writing and Socratic discussion
- probe the motives for a character's actions
- evaluate a story
- discuss the effect knowing the ending has on the experience of reading a story
- explore consequences of adding another character or changing the setting

Standard Approach

> This lesson is based on "Charles," a short story by Shirley Jackson, which is frequently anthologized in literature texts at this level. The story concerns a boy named Laurie, who starts kindergarten and comes home each day to tell stories about a bad boy in class named Charles. The end of the story reveals that there is no child in the class named Charles, and implies that Laurie was describing himself. Students respond to such questions as, "Why did Laurie make up the stories about Charles?"

Critique

Short stories are commonly studied in high school, but in-depth analysis is rare. A format used in many classrooms involves reading the story, discussing the story, answering factual questions, learning new vocabulary and perhaps writing about some aspect of the story. This method is tedious for both the teacher and the students. Students know what to expect when the lesson begins, realize that not much is expected of them intellectually and become bored or lose interest. New texts do include questions beyond the factual and comprehension level, but teachers who embrace the principles of critical thinking can even go beyond this and use the short story form to clarify students' thinking and challenge them academically.

By the time students reach this level, they no doubt have been exposed to the short story form many times and often with the elements of the short story such as setting, character, plot, point of view, and theme. If these elements are presented as definitions, separate from the genre itself, they not only lose meaning, but give students the mistaken idea that literature involves formulas. As with any specialized terminology, we use these terms to discuss the subject (fiction) clearly and insightfully. The usual lackluster approach places students in a passive role and preempts discovery which involves real learning.

Standard lessons often miss the point of stories, and include little discussion of the themes or significant issues raised in them.

Strategies used to remodel

S-1   thinking independently
S-29 noting significant similarities and differences
S-35 exploring implications and consequences
S-21 critical reading: clarifying or critiquing text
S-24 practicing Socratic discussion: clarifying and questioning beliefs, theories, or perspectives

Remodelled Lesson Plan

The short story form S-29

Teachers who teach literature critically will invite students to generate the definition and elements of the short story. **S-1** Open a unit on the short story by having the students work in pairs and respond to questions like the following in writing:

List some characteristics of short stories besides their length.

Compare short stories to novels. Do not consider the facts of specific plots. List differences and similarities *in general.*

Compare the short story form to poetry.

Compare the short story form to plays.

After students have completed their lists, regroup them into groups of 4-6 and have them compare notes. Ask them to combine their answers into a paragraph or more describing the form of the short story and using the ideas on their lists. Then ask a representative from each group to read their answers. At this point, the teacher can clarify any points the students may be confused about or rephrase some of their terms to fit the traditional elements. For example, if students say that stories must have people in them, then the teacher could remind them that some stories involve animals and that a general term for all of them is 'characters.'

"Charles"

The next part of the lesson will involve the short story the teacher has chosen to study. The teacher should select stories carefully, since different stories provide different opportunities for analysis. Teachers should clarify in their own minds what the possible themes of the story are. Even though I will be using "Charles" as an example, the method will work for any story.

If the class needs help describing the plot, this could be done as a class facilitated by the teacher, or in small groups. Or, students who have that skill can model it (in pairs or small groups) for those who don't. Later, the other students can practice, guided by the first. **S-1**

In order to practice discussing the entire story, students could rank incidents according to their importance. What was the outcome of each incident? Identify the emotional reactions of the characters involved. **S-35**

To take advantage of the twist in this particular story, you might ask, "What did you think was going on? What was Laurie's attitude towards Charles? Now that you know the end, why do you think he had that attitude? Discuss the mother's reaction.

"Why did Laurie do those things? Make up Charles? Do you think he believed in Charles? Evaluate Laurie. Evaluate this story. Is it readable, interesting? Would you recommend it? Why or why not? Was it realistic, or did the characters seem phony?" **S-21**

Another activity that could be done after reading the story involves having students think about the concept of truth or evading responsibility. Students could participate in a large group discussion which addresses the following questions:

Do you always tell the truth?

Under what conditions would you lie? Why did Laurie lie?

In your opinion, is lying ever necessary?

Do all people receive the same message from the same statements, i.e., do some see lies where others see truth? Give examples.

Can something be totally true or totally false? Give examples. **S-24**

Stories with surprises can be fruitfully read a second time, and discussed with questions like the following: How is reading the story different this time, that is, now that you know the ending? How was the author able to keep the secret? Now that you know the ending, were there hints and clues that you missed before, that foreshadow the ending? Did you enjoy the story more the first or second time?

As a writing exercise for closure, students could be asked to think about the themes of the story and then write about a minor theme that has not been discussed in class. Students would be expected to provide support from the text for their ideas.

Macro-practice is almost always more important than micro-drill. We need to be continually vigilant against the misguided tendency to fragment, atomize, mechanize, and proceduralize thinking.

"Spring and Fall"

Joan F. Barry, Staff Development
Specialist, Green Bay Area Public
Schools, Green Bay, WI

Objectives of the remodelled plan

The students will:

- brainstorm a reference list of words which describe thought
- understand the universality of the experience expressed in the poem (the nature of loss, the process of mourning)
- compare Hopkins's poem to modern music and ads
- understand the distinction between emotional responses that fit the experience, and sentimentality
- develop hypotheses about the purpose and nature of poetry

Standard Approach

The focal point of the lesson is the universality of sorrow and loss, and the distinction between emotional responses that are fitting and sentimental responses that are self-indulgent. The author's attention is on a young girl, Margaret, who is mourning the loss of summer and that season's abundance. It is fall; the leaves are dying and dropping from the trees. It is a time of loss, of death. The poem is the author's silent conversation with Margaret as he watches her. He advises that, as she grows older, she will not be moved by such turns of nature. Her heart will grow callous; perhaps because it will need to in order to survive. She will have more serious tragedies to mourn over. For the first nine lines, the author laments over the loss of innocence that the passing of time brings to each of us. Margaret's tender heart seems to be admirable.

In line ten, however, the author makes a dramatic shift in point of view. Hopkins makes the case that all pity is self-pity; all mourning, self-mourning. No matter what the catalyst, no matter what the event in the outside world (loss of summer, disappointment in work or love, or loss of a loved one) what we really mourn for is ourselves. The author now seems to believe Margaret's emotions are sentimental, silly, and self-indulgent.

I begin the lesson by reading the poem aloud to the class. I then ask clarification questions to determine the author's literal meaning. ("What is Margaret watching? What is the meaning of 'Goldengrove,' 'wanwood,' 'leafmeal'?") I ask student to summarize lines 1 through 9. Then, I point out the shift in point of view and "give" them the author's interpretation of loss, sorrow, and mourning. That is, I tell them (in a didactic approach) the author's point of view: "All pity is self pity, all mourning, self-mourning." I then cite the text and critical essays for support of my claim. I point out that, like many human emotions, the author is of two minds in his reaction to Margaret. He both admires her innocence and respect for life, and, at the same time, believes that her mourning reflects self-pity and self-indulgence. Her emotions, therefore, are silly and sentimental even while they are admirable and he envies them.

I further point out how the genré of poetry makes possible the expression of conflicting simultaneous emotions. The precision of poetic language makes the expression of universal emotions possible. The beauty of the poetic expression makes possible the reflection of intense, conflicting emotions.

Critique

The obvious flaw in the scholastically dominant approach to teaching this poem is that it does not let the students discover for themselves. It does not allow them to undergo the struggle and the joy of discovery that is inherent in an appreciation for and excitement over the study of poetry.

Because the teacher, as the "knower of truth" about the poetic experience, interprets the experience for them, they are denied the intellectual stimulation of discovery. In addition, I have limited the group's interpretation of the poem, because I have supplied the "right" answer up front. Thus, not only has the individual student's thinking been stifled, but the group is denied the synergistic response to the beauty of the poem.

The remodelled lesson plan is student-centered rather than content and teacher-centered. It replaces the scholastically dominant theory of knowledge, learning, and literacy with the emerging critical theory of knowledge, learning, and literacy.

Strategies used to remodel
S-9 developing confidence in reason
S-1 thinking independently
S-12 developing one's perspective: creating or exploring beliefs, arguments, or theories
S-17 questioning deeply: raising and pursuing root or significant questions
S-15 developing criteria for evaluation: clarifying values and standards
S-29 noting significant similarities and differences

Remodelled Lesson Plan S-9

The lesson is divided into five parts. Part one occurs before the students see the poem. We brainstorm thinking. I ask them to think of any words that describe thinking. I write them on the board. A class member records them on paper. We adhere to all the rules of brainstorming. We record everything everyone says without making judgments and without editorializing. The recorder records exactly, asking only for repeats if he or she does not hear or understand. We work for a prescribed period of time. After the list is complete, we sep-

130

arate cognitive and affective thinking strategies to create two lists. I then ask for additions to the lists. The final lists are displayed in large print on easels visible to all members of the class as we complete the remainder of the unit.

The students complete part two of the unit individually. I give them a written copy of the poem that is divided into couplets, and one sestet. The right half of the page is blank, leaving room for student responses. I ask them to record one question and one comment about each of the couplets. This activity takes approximately twenty minutes. **S-1**

Part three involves sharing questions and comments. Since students have had an opportunity to record their questions and comments, I call on folks at random. As a question is given, I repeat the question and wait for students to suggest answers. All questions are handled first. Then comments are shared and a discussion ensues. If someone from the group does not ask about or comment on the author's shift in point of view at line 10, I will ask the group about it. It is likely that the question *will* emerge from the group. Also, if no one poses the question of the author's feelings about and attitude toward Margaret's emotional response, I will pose it. Again, it is likely that the issue will surface from the group. "What is the poet's response to Margaret's attitude? Does he approve of her? Why do you say so? What is the poet trying to say? What's the difference between being emotional and being sentimental? How can you tell which one applies to a particular response? **S-12**

This is the point where we will spend some time talking about the nature of poetry and the poetic expression. This discussion will continue as we get involved in the next day's assignment. **S-17**

Part four of the unit asks the students to bring examples to class of modern poetry in any of its modern forms: written, as lyrics in music, in advertising. As a group we will compare and contrast the feelings expressed and the style of expression. "Is one poetry and the other not? How do we define poetry? Is one form of expression more valuable than another? How do we determine the value of poetry? **S-15** Does one reflect a higher level of thinking than another?" **S-29**

Each student will given a five minute oral report on a poem of choice, reading the selection, then responding to the assigned questions. After five minutes, the class will spend ten minutes reacting. This exercise will be completed while the class remains seated in a circle. The purpose of the exercise is not to arrive at conclusions or right and wrong answers, but to involve the group in the joy of inquiry.

The final part of the unit, part five, asks the students to do projects of their choice, capitalizing on their own skills and talents. The only guideline is that the project must deal with loss. Students can do another oral report, a paper, an artistic illustration (painting, sculpture, pencil sketch,) they can write their own poem or song, or create another kind of project. The project must deal in some way with loss and personal response to loss. *S-12*

The students are evaluated on their five-minute oral reports, and on their final projects. The brainstorming and sharing of questions and comments is not graded, but serves as the interest generator for the reports and final projects.

We learn how to learn by learning, think by thinking, judge by judging, analyze by anlyzing; not by reading, hearing, and reproducing principles guiding these activities, but by using those principles. There is no point in trying to think for our students.

Testing for Thinking: *The Outsiders*

Objectives of the remodelled plan
The *teacher* will:
- recognize weak testing methods
- identify student assumptions about subject mastery
- develop new techniques for short quiz questions which require critical thinking
- restructure test questions to allow students to take and defend positions on novels read
- modify tests to include critical vocabulary

Standard Approach

Testing methods in the middle grades may take a variety of forms: true/false, objective, multiple choice, and essay. Most teachers agree that the essay form is best educationally. Close on the heels of this statement is the reality a workload of 150 students or more imposes. Teachers simply do not have the time to grade essay exams whenever they need an evaluation of a student's progress. Sometimes a teacher only wants to confirm that a student has done the reading. In these situations, the recall test is a common tool. In a five to ten question quiz, the student will be asked to supply facts from the literature, often including such questions as: Where did Mercy leave her necklace in Chapter Six? What was Harold's adopted brother-in-law's step son's name? How much did Sabella pay for her new condo?

For a model, we have used the book, *The Outsiders* by S. E. Hinton.

For the first chapter, a test might include the following questions:

- What were the two gangs called? (Greasers and Socs)
- What do you know about the gangs? How?
- Who were Ponyboy's two brothers? (Soda and Darry)
- Which group did Ponyboy belong to? (Greasers)
- Where was Ponyboy coming from at the start of the chapter? (movies)
- What did the Socs do to him on the way home? (cut his hair, assaulted him)
- Who was described as the "real character" of the Greaser gang? (Dally)

Critique

Recall quizzes do test the reader's ability to regurgitate information from the reading. But they do something more insidious as well. They give the students two messages. First, that the point of reading a novel, play, or short story is to memorize the facts presented therein. In this way, students are almost discouraged from ruminating on the *ideas* of the book. Instead they are using valuable reflection time to commit the nuts and bolts information to memory. The second questionable thing about recall exams is that they give students the notion that if they master the facts, they have mastered the book. Most teachers have experienced reading nothing but information recall in response to an essay question that specifically asked for synthesis, evaluation, or other higher level skills. At the very least, recall tests, if they must be given, should stick with the key facts, and events, and not ask for randomly selected details.

Other modes of testing present problems as well. One may construct sophisticated true/ false statements, but the test has a 50% guess factor. Multiple choice questions also have the potential for critical composition, but they take some time to compose and the potential for cheating is great if the test is reused. They also limit the responses of the students, who may have some genuine insights to convey about the book.

Strategies used to remodel

S-29 noting significant similarities and differences
S-32 making plausible inferences, predictions, or interpretations
S-30 examining or evaluating assumptions
S-17 questioning deeply: raising and pursuing root or significant questions
S-20 evaluating actions or policies
S-21 reading critically: clarifying or critiquing texts
S-35 exploring implications or consequences
S-4 exploring thoughts underlying feelings and feelings underlying thought

Remodelled Lesson Plan

For teachers interested in moving away from the recall test, we offer a variation which gives students the opportunity to use their thinking skills. If you ask students to keep the responses brief, a few words or one sentence, grading will not be difficult. Below is a sample of questions and possible answers.

• State two ways in which Ponyboy differs from his brother, Soda. (Pony reads and seems more interested in school; Pony's younger; Pony behaves like a brother, but Soda acts like a father.) **S-29**

• What can you infer about the emotional state of Pony at the opening of the book. (Happy, reflective — thinking about his brothers; he's a bit anxious about walking alone.) **S-32**

• Both of the gangs introduced in Chapter One are guilty of oversimplification. Give examples from each gang. (Socs think all Greasers are dirty, rough, stupid. Greasers think all Socs are rich snobs, aren't cool, fight without justification.) **S-30**

• Speculate on the *reasons* that these two groups exist (difference of social class; macho tendencies; makes them feel grown-up; makes them feel close). **S-17**

• Characterize the relationship between Pony and Soda in three *different* ways (parental, siblings, adoring, blind, overprotective). **S-32**

• Do you think the attitude toward women expressed by the Greasers is fair? Why/why not? (No, they call their girls broads and admire the Socs' girls. It's contradictory. No, they criticize them harshly. Yes, Greaser girls are just as misguided as the boys are.) **S-20**

• What factors led to conflict? Who bears primary responsibility for this event and why? **S-20**

This quiz requires students to use critical thinking skills to answer the questions. If the teacher uses this type of quiz frequently, students will develop the habit of reading and reflecting on the concepts presented.

If you wish, students may exchange papers and grade the quizzes. Various answers are volunteered by students. The teacher can then ask, "Does anyone have an answer that differs from those we have discussed?" The teacher may ask for the reasoning behind the answer to determine if credit will be given. Discussion may result. The process of giving and grading a quiz such as this deepens understanding for the whole class. Quizes given later in the book can have students evaluate characterization for consistency or realism.

Having students write a short description of the plot requires more than recall, since students have to select the most pertinent details to recall and describe. Requiring students to describe plots of everything they read develops the concept of plot much better than the standard method of teaching the concept in a few lessons over the course of the year.

Episode Analysis S-21

Another method of testing, which also could be used instead of the rote quiz is moving away from the question format altogether. At a Language Arts conference, Dr. Robert Calfee of Stanford University presented some critical analysis methods from Project Read. One of these, termed "Episode Analysis" is a preprinted page which could be used as a testing device. It is set up like this: **S-35**

Problem	**Emotional Response**	**Action**	**Outcome**

The students are expected to fill in each category. If the outcome is as yet unknown, then instruct the student to predict the outcome. For example:

Pony gets attacked by the Socs	Scared	Pony gets cut	Resentment against the Socs builds

The teacher may have students analyze more than one episode analysis.
An alternative format might be: **S-4**

Event/Situation	**Emotion**	**Assumption**

If the students have had exposure to critical vocabulary, the teacher could compose a quiz which asks students to list some assumptions made by the characters. **S-30**

Any improvement on the recall test will produce a more stimulating and interesting test to grade. Because students are given the opportunity to think in ways which motivate them to be inventive, teachers may even gain insight into material they have taught many times.

Writing Argumentative Essays

Objectives of the remodelled plan

The students will:
- develop their perspectives through dialectical exchange, writing, and argument analysis and evaluation
- clarify issues and key words
- evaluate evidence
- practice critical thought by writing and revising argumentative essays

Standard Approach

Students pick an issue or position and find reasons to support their conclusions. Sometimes students are told to state and refute opposing arguments. They research their topics, noting facts supporting their positions. Sometimes texts introduce fallacies and a bit of logic as preparation. Students write an argumentative essay, defending their positions.

Critique

Though this handbook mainly focuses on incorporating critical thinking into other lessons, lessons specifically on critical thinking can also be useful. Generally, texts' treatment of argumentation suffer from many serious flaws and misunderstandings, display fuzziness of thought, misuse terms, and lack critical insight. As a whole, texts downplay evaluation of reasoning. (Where mentioned or suggested, they give little guidance and often use confusing language). They rarely suggest evaluating the relevance of support to conclusions.

Texts mainly focus on how to defend opinions, not how to shape them more reasonably. Though they address the importance of giving reasons for beliefs, they often neglect the importance of considering opposing views, or strengthening one's reasoning by weeding out or altering unjustified beliefs. Presenting good reasons, though valuable, is only half of a discussion. The standard approach allows reactions that are too often impressionistic and based on prejudice or lack of understanding.

Rather than teaching argument analysis and evaluation, texts generally have students attempt to distinguish fact from opinion. Though the motive of having students distinguish *questionable* from *acceptable* claims is worthwhile, the usual approach does not accomplish this purpose. It produces an unquestioning attitude of acceptance for statements that *seem* factual, though factual (empirical) claims are not necessarily reliable, and students can't necessarily tell if so-called facts are true. Facts, when used in an argument, may not be complete or relevant. Since statements students are called on to judge as opinions are given without context, students cannot rationally judge whether they are mere whim or can be well defended. Rather than using the fact/opinion distinction, students can distinguish questionable from acceptable claims and fact from interpretation and judgment.

This remodel illustrates a way of orchestrating cognitive strategies to reason dialectically.

Strategies used to remodel

S-26 reasoning dialectically: evaluating perspectives, interpretations, or theories
S-12 developing one's perspective: creating or exploring beliefs, arguments, or theories
S-28 thinking precisely about thinking: using critical vocabulary
S-31 distinguishing relevant from irrelevant facts
S-34 recognizing contradictions
S-18 analyzing or evaluating arguments, interpretations, beliefs, or theories
S-3 exercising fairmindedness
S-13 clarifying issues, conclusions, or beliefs
S-15 developing criteria for evaluation: clarifying values and standards
S-14 clarifying and analyzing the meanings of words or phrases
S-16 evaluating the credibility of sources of information
S-33 evaluating evidence and alleged facts

Remodelled Lesson Plan *S-26*

Introduction

We have written these lessons as a unified unit culminating in a well-thought-out argumentative essay. Similar units, repeated over the course of the year, can greatly improve both reasoning and its expression.

Class discussions can be used to introduce and clarify aspects of critical thought through the analysis and improvement of two opposing arguments selected as models. The models should address the same issue from different perspectives, be fairly strong, but require some improvement. Small group discussions allow students to develop and clarify their positions on issues of their choice, and argue between opposing views.

For their essay and discussion groups topics, students could brainstorm issues of interest to them. Each group must share an issue about which group members disagree. The issues from which they choose should not be questions of mere preference but should call for reasoned judgment.

Each student then picks an issue and writes an essay. Students should state their positions and support them with their best reasons. This is the first draft of their argumentative essays. **S-12**

Beginning Argument Analysis **S-28**

The teacher might develop students' use of critical vocabulary by having them rephrase the model arguments into explicit premises, assumptions, and conclusions. To have students identify the conclusion of each model, ask, "What is the *conclusion*? What is the point of the argument? What statement is this argument trying to convince you to believe? Is the conclusion stated or implied?" Then ask, "What reasons are given? Is the reasoning complete, or is there a hidden claim, or *assumption*?"

Students could then begin to analyze and evaluate the arguments in a class discussion. You could have them give reasons for their evaluations, or guide discussion with questions like the following: "Does it present evidence? What? Are the claims clear? What do they mean? Could they mean something else? Are they *ambiguous*? Questionable? Complete? What is left out? Is this reason *relevant* — should it affect our conclusion? Why or why not? **S-31**

To help students pinpoint the conflict between the model arguments, you might ask, "Do these reasoners disagree about the facts? (Which facts?) Their interpretations of the facts? (On what theories do they base their interpretations?) Do they disagree about values? About how to realize those values? About which of two values is most important?" **S-34**

Students could suggest ways to make each argument stronger. The teacher may also model improving the arguments and their expression during this and future class discussions. **S-18**

When assigning discussion groups, emphasize the importance of listening carefully and openmindedly to other arguments. Students can take notes on, and include, opposing views in their essays. Students should argue their positions (that is, give reasons to convince the others to adopt their conclusions). The groups could note assumptions, pinpoint contradictions, and look for strengths and weaknesses in the arguments given. Each group could recap the main points of their discussion to the entire class. Encourage the groups to find some points of agreement.

You may want to have students argue each other's positions. **S-3** Students can then evaluate each other's presentations of their arguments.

Have students rewrite their papers.

Clarification

Another lesson could be used to develop students' ability to clarify issues and concepts, again using the model arguments previously mentioned. How would this arguer state the issue? The other arguer? How could we state the issue in words both sides would accept? How could this issue be settled? What concepts do we need to clarify? Is something being evaluated? (What? Why? What standards are most appropriately applied?) **S-13**

The teacher can have students identify the key terms in the model arguments. Ask students to describe examples to which the key words or phrases in the model arguments would properly apply. Then ask for examples of their opposites. Also ask what phrase could apply to both kinds of cases. Students should then discuss features common to each kind of case, and make the standards they use to judge such cases explicit. **S-15** Why is this a case of X? What does the word imply? Why does this arguer characterize the situation as X? **S-14**

Then each group can meet again to clarify the key claims and terms from their discussion groups. Have students distinguish those terms which all agree apply from disputed terms. They should then clarify the disputed terms or claims by using examples of terms, opposites, and other cases. The standards used for applying the terms or claims should be clarified, the facts required to justify evaluations made explicit.

Evaluating Claims and Evidence

You may want to focus the next section directly on distinguishing claims which need further support from those which are acceptable without further support. You may use questions like the following: Does anyone know whether or not this is true? How do you know? Is there reason to doubt this statement? Why or why not? Accept it? What would support it Undermine it? **S-13** Stress that one can't judge truth or reasonableness of a claim from its form or appearance. A statement alone doesn't tell us how much or little thought, or what quality of thought produced it.

For each model, students can evaluate the evidence cited by considering questions like the following: Where did this information come from? How could the source know this? Is this source reliable? (Do they have a good track record? Anything to lose or gain? Are they in a position to know?) **S-16** Is this evidence relevant? Is relevant evidence left out? **S-31** Would that evidence require the reasoner to change the conclusion? Why or why not? **S-33**

Students can then expand and revise their essays. They should give their new positions and arguments, supporting claims which require support. Stress that the strongest arguments take the strengths of other points of view into account. **S-12**

Students could trade their papers with other members of their groups. Students can comment on the papers requesting clarification or evidence, pointing out where the relevance of claims is unclear, or facts or assumptions are questionable, and correcting distortions of opposing points of view. Students can use the comments when revising their essays.

The teacher could have students write group papers, instead of individual papers giving all sides of the disagreement and clarifying points of disagreement.

Judgment is best developed, not when told what, how, and why, to judge, but by repeatedly judging and then assessing those judgments.

Interview on Ethics

Objectives of the remodelled plan

The students will:

- examine aspects of the interview process
- engage in Socratic discussion regarding ethics
- identify belief systems and generate interview questions
- practice Socratic discussion by conducting interviews
- evaluate interviews

Standard Approach

Texts address the design of interview questions, i.e., what types of questions can be asked to elicit the desired information, for example, biographical. They also recommend how the interview can be written up in one of two desired formats, question and answer, or in this case, biographical essay or story format, which allows the student more creative embellishment.

Some questions considered in this lesson might be: "What were you like as a child? What was it like to grow up in such-and-such a time period? How were you similar to or different from other children?"

Critique

A lesson on interviewing can be a valuable teaching tool in that students learn a variety of questioning techniques and engage in extended discussion with people outside their peer group. A well-formulated lesson provides an opportunity for students to ask clarifying and probing questions, listen actively, and organize and synthesize what they hear.

A common lesson, the biographical interview, is an interesting choice because of its biographical concentration which is "safe" territory for interviewing, especially at this level. Most people will supply information about their past with little provocation. This type of questioning would surely elicit responses that would give students enough information to formulate a history for biographical background, but would probably give little understanding of the person being interviewed. It is too likely to elicit a simple chronology. The student would have collected a number of interesting facts or stories, but any deeper insight would be gained only by inference. Such lessons assume a didactic theory of knowledge and thought in which one needs only discover details. A critical approach would focus on the *structure* of anothers' ideas — how beliefs are linked to each other, how some beliefs are more basic, how individual beliefs form a system, how systems of belief differ.

The following remodelled lesson plan focuses on the belief systems of those being interviewed, which would not only challenge the student presenting the questions but would also allow the interviewee to give a more thoughtful and introspective interview. To illustrate, we've chosen ethics as a topic. Furthermore, the student will begin to think critically about how belief systems are formed, how they differ, and how such systems affect our daily judgment.

Strategies used to remodel

S-22 listening critically: the art of silent dialogue
S-29 noting significant similarities and differences
S-24 practicing Socratic discussion: clarifying and questioning beliefs, theories, or perspectives
S-12 developing ones perspective: creating or exploring beliefs, arguments, or theories
S-8 developing intellectual perseverance
S-15 developing criteria for evaluation: clarifying values and standards

Remodelled Lesson Plan S-22 ───────

Introduction

The teacher can begin this lesson by asking how an interview differs from ordinary conversation. (A conversation with an individual is unstructured; may take several turns and cover any number of topics; is two-way since usually — or, at least, ideally — both participants offer their ideas. One may have a vague objective in mind like, "Getting to know Mr. Williams." Interviews are more structured insofar as they begin with a prescribed set of questions; are one-way, insofar as *one* participant answers, the other asks; often have a narrower purpose.) **S-29**

Then, ask the students to think of different types of interviews. They may offer such responses as these: college interviews, job interviews, celebrity interviews, or interviews which probe the position of those running for elected office. Some of these interviews have specific objectives: Would this person perform well at our university? Would this person be qualified for the position? Would this person represent the people of the community on the city council?

The teacher could then assign cooperative groups the task of composing questions that would accomplish these tasks. Afterwards, one person of the group could serve as the interviewer (admissions director, employer, newspaper reporter) and another as the interviewee. The mock interviews should be conducted in front of the entire class. When the interview is over, the class should critique the process by pointing out which questions provided the best information and adding any questions that were left out.

Students could study some printed interviews, evaluate them, and formulate probing questions and follow-up questions which could have been asked. **S-21**

By now the class has begun to think about the interview process. They have witnessed a few models and have had some experience composing questions. They also will have seen how the type of questions asked depends on the objective of the interview.

Preparation for the interview

To introduce the students to their interview assignment, the teacher may ask students to consider how many different points of view on questions of right and wrong are represented in the class. Someone could take notes on the following Socratic discussion, or it could be taped.

Ask, "How do you know when something is right or wrong? When is it hard to tell what's right? Why do people do wrong? When do you blame people for doing something wrong? Not blame them? When did you first learn right from wrong? How? What do your beliefs assume about human nature? How does this assumption affect how you act? How you judge others? Should people have their own ideas of right and wrong, or should they accept the judgment of authorities? Can you think of something that would be wrong in one instance and right in another? Can you think of something that is absolutely wrong, regardless of the circumstances?" **S-12** The teacher could then ask the students to frame more specific questions about what they believe. **S-24**

Recap the main points made in the above discussion. The idea of organized belief systems can now be raised. The class could group the responses by similarities among the perspectives. Ask students to think about which views expressed by the others most resemble their own and which differ most from their own. Have them try to characterize the similarities and differences among these perspectives, distinguishing major from minor differences. **S-29**

By now the students have begun to identify their own belief systems and are now ready to begin the interview assignment. They can begin by thinking about how the questions will be framed for a "Belief System Interview." Suggest that they use some of the questions previously posed: How do you know when something is right or wrong? When did you first learn right from wrong? Did someone teach you?

The students should know that a good interviewer will ask clarifying questions like, "What exactly do you mean by that? Can you give me an example? How would you respond to this idea (give an opposing view)? What led you to that belief?" etc.

Next, the students can frame more questions. The entire class may work on this project and then choose the best of the lot. By practicing on other students first, students may better develop a sense of good follow-up questions.

Assign the interview. You may want students to tape record the interview (with permission of the interviewee). Or you may want them to develop note-taking skills and record the responses that way. The class could evaluate various ways of presenting their interviews.

Students could show their work to the interviewees for confirmation and further clarification, and then revise their reports. **S-8**

When the interviews have been shared, the class can relate points made in them to the previous discussions by comparing the perspectives expressed in them with their own, and evaluating the questions raised.

If the teacher wishes to repeat the lesson, other topics which interest students and lend themselves to analysis could be chosen:

Religion How would you define 'religion'? Do religions have anything in common? If so, what? How do religious authorities decide what is right/wrong? Can a person know right from wrong without religion? How? Are all religions equal? If not, why not? How much does religion affect what you believe? Does a person have to accept religious laws without question? Why or why not?

Prejudice How is it defined? Does it exist in our community, school, home? When were you first aware of prejudice? Why do you think prejudice exists? How could we solve some of our race problems?

Sex Education What should sex education consist of? At what age should it be taught? When did you first learn about sex? Was this a good way to get information? Should birth control be taught? Why/why not? What issues are most relevant for sex education today? Can you think of ways of discouraging teenage pregnancies?

The interview process requires careful preparation in the classroom with specific instructor intervention regarding the types of questions asked, as well as the process of clarifying information. The students not only learn to examine their own beliefs, they learn to analyze the types of questions asked, consider conflicting opinions, and evaluate the answers given. The value in this lesson is not only the interview process, but the critical evaluation of the topic. The students gain confidence in their critical thinking skills and enjoy the process as well.

> *When the powerful tools of critical thinking are used merely at the service of egocentrism, sociocentrism, or ethnocentrism, then genuine communication and discussion end, and people relate to one another in fundamentally manipulative, even if intellectual, ways.*

"A Modest Proposal"

by June Tinkhauser, Baldwin High
School, Baldwin, NY

Objectives of the remodelled plan

The students will:
- infer the motivation for writing "A Modest Proposal"
- recognize the importance of point of view
- see how satire uses shock and irony to promote change
- read critically as they analyze the structure of Swift's Modest Proposal

Standard Approach

"A Modest Proposal" is a good introduction to the works of Jonathan Swift in any British Literature survey course. The usual procedure involves dramatic oral reading or playing a well-read recording. Historical background on the English-Irish situation that precipitates the proposal is explained, and students write Modest Proposals of their own.

Critique

The original is a dry lesson in the "what" of Swift's Modest Proposal. The why and how, the juice of this absurd piece of persuasion is lost.

Strategies used to remodel

S-33 evaluating evidence and alleged facts
S-32 making plausible inferences, predictions, or interpretations
S-21 reading critically: clarifying or critiquing texts
S-23 making interdisciplinary connections
S-12 developing one's perspective: creating or exploring beliefs, arguments, or theories

Remodelled Lesson Plan

In Literary Satire, a senior English elective, we have remodelled this lesson as follows: We start with the student, then go to Swift. We ask students to make a list of serious problems that really bother them and that they would like to change. Then we read the proposal aloud in class. Next, we analyze structure of the proposal. The dialogue runs something like this:

How do we begin?

Student: State the problem.

Is it a real problem? How do we know?

Student: The problem is clearly stated and supported by facts and figures.

Facts? Figures? How do you know these are facts and figures? **S-33**

Student: They seem plausible. It coincides with what we know about the Irish situation then and now.

Now?

Student: Well, maybe not exactly, but that's what the situation is all about in Northern Ireland. Belfast and all that.

Do we all agree on this? Remember Mayor Koch came back confused. He said recently that England was the peace-keeper, not the oppressor. But then later, he changed his mind. Why was that? **S-32**

Student: He remembered the large number of voters in NYC of Irish background.

Mmmm. In Satire is it important to remember where your writer is coming from?

Student: Not just in Satire.

Why?

Student: As you say, — Where you're coming from is where you'll be trying to take me.

OK, that's Part I. (Writes on board: **State the Problem** *(legitimate). What's next on Swift's agenda? Let's look at the text.* **S-21**

Student: Then he drops it on you. His proposal.

Is it modest? (Writes on board: **State your solution.** *Then adds, Outrageous!')*

Student: Are you kidding? It's outrageous: Selling the babies like a commodity!

Is his tone reasonable or outrageous?

Student: It sounds reasonable; that's what's so outrageous.

How does he make it seem reasonable? **S-21**

Student: More facts and figures.

So facts are not always facts? Figures, not always figures? Liars figure; figures lie, says this English teacher. That's point of view, too.

What's Swift's next step? Is this an exercise in fatuity?

Student: Stupidity?

No, but close to the same thing. Look it up.

Student: (Hopefully) Negative. Satire has a serious purpose: to change things.

Let's stay with this .... What does Swift want to change? Why? **S-21**

Student: England's predatory policies regarding Ireland.

Student: Swift was Anglo-Irish, sympathetic to the Irish.

Let's keep our perspective about this. What's the year here?

Student: It's right here: 1729.

What's going on in the world in the 1730's? The new world?

Student: Colonization. Before our revolution.

So the attitude at that time was that colonies exist solely to accommodate the Mother country? **S-23**

Student: But we rebelled and Ireland is still at it.

OK, Back to our proposal. What's all this italics? "Let no man talk to me of other expedients ...." etc. Plausible? **S-21**

Student: Sounds like what he really wants the English and Irish to do to solve their problem. But he says it negatively.

Why does he do this? **S-32**

Student: Because people tend to reject common sense.

Example? **S-12**

Student: Like us with pollution, race relations, nuclear warfare, etc. So Swift resorts to absurdity and irony to give us a kick in the head.

(Teacher writes on the board: Part III Reject Valid Solutions)

Student: Don't forget facts and figures, but these should make sense.

Swift does something interesting at the end. What does he claim?

Student: It's like a Letter to the Editor — "I'm just a good citizen with nothing to gain, just trying to help his country."

(Teacher writes on board: Part IV Deny Self-Advantage.)

What do you think people thought about this "Letter to the Editor"? Did they take it seriously? Would you? **S-32**

Student: (Varied replies.) People who know Swift's game would recognize the satire. Others tend to believe anything they see in print.

OK, that's the spirit of "A Modest Proposal"; Pair up — two heads can be sharper than one, share your problem sheet, dream up solutions absurd and realistic, don't forget facts and figures (absurd and realistic), deny the realistic and tout the absurd, deny self-advantage and write your own Modest Proposal using our structure.

It should not be assumed that there is a universal standard for how fast teachers should proceed with the task of remodelling their lesson plans. A slow but steady evolutionary process is much more desirable than a rush job across the board.

"Clothe the Naked"

by June Tinkhauser, Baldwin High
School, Baldwin, NY

Objectives of the remodelled plan
The students will:
* read critically as they go beyond plot line and the state theme
* make judgments and inferences based on dialogue, writing techniques, and actions
* empathize with situations beyond most students' experience
* test their own responses to the handicapped

Standard Approach

Students are asked to read and take notes on Dorothy Parker's short story, "Clothe the Naked." The usual aspects are discussed: setting, characters, characterization, conflict, theme, stated in the introduction as "Heartbreak in a new suit of clothes." The author's background and relationship to the story, as well as her reputation as a satirical writer are also worth exploring.

Critique

This approach oversimplifies what this teacher feels is a trenchant commentary on values: people who are reputed to do good and those who really do. An opportunity to view the world through the sensitivities of the handicapped is also missed.

Strategies used to remodel
S-21 reading critically: clarifying or critiquing texts
S-4 exploring thoughts underlying feelings and feelings underlying thoughts
S-33 evaluating evidence and alleged facts
S-32 making plausible inferences, predictions, or interpretations
S-1 thinking independently

Remodelled Lesson Plan S-21

The remodelled lesson picks up where the traditional lesson leaves off in an effort to explore Dorothy Parker's "slice of life" in a small southern town.

> *Let's focus on Mrs. Delabarre Ewing. Why do you think Dorothy Parker chose a name like that?* **S-4**

Student: Maybe she was based on an actual character.

With that name?

Student: A name's a name; what's the big deal?

How does it sound to you? What does the name suggest? Connotation, remember? S-4

Student: Well, she sounds important.

Is she?

Student: Well, it says here, "Mrs. Ewing was a personage in the town. When she visited Richmond or when she returned from viewing the azalea gardens, the newspapers always printed that fact."

Important fact, eh?

Student: It's a small town sooo ...

OK, Let's find out more about Mrs. Ewing. What does the text say about her sense of "noble obligation"?

Student: Reads "She was a woman rigorously conscious of her noble obligation; she was prominent on the Community Chest committee and it was she who planned and engineered (!) the annual Bridge Drive to raise funds for planting salvia around the cannon in front of D. A. R. headquarters."

Big deal, eh?

Student: What's Salvia? What's D. A. R.?

Let's look these up.

Student: So she's a do-gooder.

Is that bad?

Student: No. but she thinks she's hot stuff; so good and generous as she tells Big Lannie.

Big Lannie, Dorothy Parker calls her.

Student: Yes, she is physically big and big-hearted.

How do we know that? S-33

Student: The way she gives up everything to take care of her blind grandchild.

You believe this? On what evidence? S-33

Student: She quits her jobs, makes ends meet as best she can, makes Raymond feel good about himself so he feels he's really contributing to the family.

Now, how does Big Lannie feel about Mrs. Ewing? S-32

Student: Says right here: "It was Mrs. Ewing ...."

Mmmm, read that last part over. What does that mean? S-32

Student: Mrs. Ewing doesn't need prayers or intercessions, she's directly connected.

What did Mrs. Ewing do for Lannie?

Student: She took Lannie back as her laundress.

Why did she do this? Because she was soft-hearted? "A regular little old easy mark," as she says?

Student: Maybe. But it also says Lannie was an excellent worker and Mrs. Ewing was very fussy.

So maybe Mrs. Ewing is not as kindhearted, altruistic and philanthropic as she says she is?

Student: (Hopefully) Yes, but don't forget she gives Lannie clothes for Raymond.

Good point. Let's role play this scene. We need Lannie, Mrs. Ewing, and a director. It begins past middle, page 95.

(Students play the scene, depending on their point of view: humble Lannie, generous Mrs. Ewing, or humble Lannie, haughty Mrs. Ewing

Let's look at the dialogue here, What do you make of all of those "she saids"? Notice Parker does the same thing on page 94. **S-32**

Student: Various answers

Mmmm. How does this "he/she said" change this statement? "He dates her for her great personality,' he said."

or

"'The test was easy, she said.' (She's the brightest girl in the class.)"

Student: In those examples, it means that's what he/she said, but it's not so; it's not so; it's sarcastic.

An indication of verbal irony, perhaps?

(By this time students have had it with delving and they want to know what actually happens to Raymond in that tricky final scene.)

Student: What did happen to Raymond? Did a dog attack him? Or what?

OK, let's role play again: You are Raymond. What kind of kid are you? What's your mood? "His anticipation was like honey in his mouth." What do you do? Let's go down the stairs. You're blind, remember. **S-1**

Student director, following the text, takes over ...

Student: Turn your face "to the gentle air." Guide yourself by the fence. Call out to the folks "so that he would hear gay calls in return, he laughed so that laughter would answer him." (You) hear it.

What is it? (Audience, cued by teacher, laughs derisively.) What happens? Raymond, show us. Remember, you are blind. You rely heavily on other senses. OK, Raymond, drag yourself home.

What has Raymond discovered? About life? About what is means to be poor and handicapped? Does it matter that he's black? **S-32**

Student: Why did they laugh? Who were "they" anyway?

See Parker's last line. Visualize Raymond's appearance after a prolonged absence in Mr. Ewing's coat. What kind of coat is it? An over-sized, long, tail coat from the over-generous Mrs. Ewing, eh?

Student: (Responses will probably range from classmates' sarcasm and mocking laughter in response to a wrong or naive answer, to a friend's callous response to your emotional outpouring to some students' response when "special students" try to navigate their way across the commons to the snickers of some of the student body.)

All the various strategies explained in the handbook are couched in terms of behaviors. The principles express and describe a variety of behaviors of the 'ideal' critical thinker; they become applications to lessons when teachers canvass their lesson plans to find appropriate places where those behaviors can be fostered. The practice we recommend helps guard against teachers using these strategies as recipes or formulas, since in each case good judgment is required in the application process.

Remodelling Social Studies

Introduction

The major problem to overcome in remodelling social studies units and lessons is that of transforming didactic instruction within one point of view into dialogical instruction within multiple points of view. As teachers, we should see ourselves not as dispensers of absolute truth nor as proponents of relativity, but as careful reflective seekers after truth, a search in which we are inviting our students to participate. We need continually to remind ourselves that each person responds to social issues from one of a variety of mutually inconsistent points of view. Each point of view rests on assumptions about human nature. Presenting one point of view as the truth limits our understanding of issues. Practice in entering into and coming to understand divergent points of view, on the other hand, heightens our grasp of the real problems of our lives. Children, in their everyday lives, already face the kinds of issues studied in social studies and are engaged in developing sets of assumptions on questions like the following:

> What does it mean to belong to a group? What rights and responsibilities do I have? Does it matter if others do not approve of me? Is it worthwhile to be good? What is most important to me? How am I like and unlike others? Whom should I trust? Who are my friends and enemies? What are people like? What am I like? How do I fit in with others? What are my rights and responsibilities? What are others' rights and responsibilities?

Humans live in a world of humanly constructed meanings. There is always more than one way to conceptualize human behavior. Humans create points of view, ideologies, and philosophies that often conflict with each other. Students need to understand the implications of this crucial fact: that all accounts of human behavior are expressed within a point of view, that it is not possible to cover all the facts in any account of what happened, that each account stresses some facts over others, that when an account is given (by a teacher, student, or textbook author), the point of view in which it is given should be identified and, where possible, alternative points of view considered, and finally, that points of view need to be critically analyzed and assessed.

Adults, as well as children, tend to assume the truth of their own unexamined points of view. People often unfairly discredit or misinterpret ideas based on assumptions which differ from their own. In order to address social issues critically, students must continually evaluate their beliefs by contrasting them with opposing beliefs. From the beginning, social studies instruction should encourage dialogical thinking, that is, the fairminded discussion of a variety of points of view and their underlying beliefs. Of course, this emphasis on the diversity of human perspectives should not be covered in such a way as to imply that all points of view are equally valid. Rather, students should learn to value critical thinking skills as tools to help them distinguish truth from falsity, insight from prejudice, accurate conception from misconception.

Dialogical experience in which students begin to use critical vocabulary to sharpen their thinking and their sense of logic, is crucial. Words and phrases like 'claims,' 'assumes,' 'implies,' 'supports,' 'is evidence for,' 'is inconsistent with,' 'is relevant to' should be integrated into such discussions. Formulating their own views of historical events and social issues should enable students to synthesize data from divergent sources and to grasp important ideas. Too often, students are asked to recall details with no synthesis, no organizing ideas, and no distinction between details and basic ideas or between facts and common U.S. interpretations of them.

Students certainly need opportunities to explicitly learn basic principles of social analysis, but more importantly, they need opportunities to apply them to real and imagined cases, and to develop insight into social analysis. They especially need to come to terms with the pitfalls of human social analyses, to recognize the ease with which we mask self-interest or egocentric desires with social scientific language. In any case, for any particular instance of social judgment or reasoning, students should learn the art of distinguishing *perspectives on the world* from *facts* (which provide the specific information or occasion for a particular social judgment). In learning to discriminate these dimensions of social reasoning, we learn how to focus our minds on a variety of questions at issue.

As people, students have an undeniable right to develop their own social perspective — whether conservative or liberal, whether optimistic or pessimistic — but they should be able to analyze the perspective they do use, compare it accurately with other perspectives, and scrutinize the facts they conceptualize and judge in the social domain with the same care required in any other domain of knowledge. They should, in other words, become as adept in using critical thinking principles in the social domain as we expect them to be in scientific domains of learning.

Traditional lessons cover several important subjects within social studies: politics, economics, history, anthropology, and geography. Critical education in social studies focuses on basic questions in each subject, and prepares students for their future economic, political, and social roles.

Some Common Problems with Social Studies Texts

- End-of-chapter questions often ask for recall of a random selection of details and key facts or ideas. Often the answers are found in the text in bold or otherwise emphasized type. Thus, students need not even understand the question, let alone the answer, to complete their assignments.
- Timelines, maps, charts and graphs are presented and read as mere drill rather than as aids to understanding deeper issues.
- There is rarely adequate emphasis on extending insights to analogous situations in other times and places.

- Although the texts treat diversity of opinion as necessary, beliefs are not presented as subject to examination or critique. Students are encouraged to accept that others have different beliefs but are not encouraged to understand why. Yet it is by understanding *why* others think as they do that students can profit from considering other points of view. The text writers' emphasis on simple tolerance serves to end discussion, whereas students should learn to consider judgments as subject to rational assessment.

- Students are not encouraged to recognize and combat their own natural ethnocentricity. Texts encourage ethnocentricity in many ways. They often present American ideals as uniquely American when, in fact, every nation shares at least some of them. Although beliefs about the state of the world and about how to achieve ideals vary greatly, the American version of these is often treated as universal or self-evident. Students should learn not to confuse their limited perspective with universal belief. Ethnocentricity is reflected in word choices that assume an American or Western European perspective. Cultures are described as isolated rather than as isolated from Europe. Christian missionaries are described as spreading or teaching religion rather than Christianity. Cultures are evaluated as modern according to their similarity to our culture. In addition, texts often assume, imply, or clearly state that most of the world would prefer to be just like us. The American way of life and policies, according to the world view implied in standard texts, is the pinnacle of human achievement and presents the best human life has to offer. That others might believe the same of their own cultures is rarely mentioned or considered.

- Texts often wantonly omit crucial concepts, relationships, and details. For example, in discussing the opening of trade relations between Japan and the U.S., one text failed to mention why the Japanese had cut off relations with the West. Another text passed over fossil fuels and atomic energy in two sentences.

- Most texts treat important subjects superficially. There seems to be more concern for the outward appearance of things than for their underlying dynamics. Many texts also tend to approach the heart of the matter and then stop short. Topics are introduced, treated briefly, and dropped. History, for instance, is presented as merely a series of events. Texts often describe events briefly but seldom mention how people perceived them, why they accepted or resisted them, or what ideas and assumptions influenced them. Texts often cover different political systems by mentioning the titles of political offices. Most discussions of religion reflect the same superficiality. Texts emphasize names of deities, rituals, and practices. But beliefs are not explored in depth; the inner life is ignored, the personal dimension omitted.

- In many instances, texts encourage student passivity by providing all the answers. After lengthy map skills units, students are asked to apply those skills to answer simple questions. However, they are not held accountable for providing the answers on their own. Texts usually err by asking questions students should be able to answer on their own, and then immediately providing the answer. Once students understand the system, they know that they don't have to stop and think for themselves, because the text will do it for them in the next sentence.

- Graphs and charts are treated in the same manner. Students practice reading maps in their texts for reasons provided by those texts. They are not required to determine for themselves what questions a map can answer, what sort of map is required, or how to find it. Map reading practice could be used to develop students' confidence in their abilities to reason and learn for themselves, but typically isn't.

153

- Chart assignments can be remodelled to provide more thought-provoking work on students' parts by adding headings regarding implications, consequences, or justifications and by having students compare and argue for their particular ways of filling the charts out.
- Although the rich selections of appendices is convenient for the students, they are discouraged from discovering where to find information on their own. In real life, problems are not solved by referring to a handy chart neatly put into a book of information on the subject. In fact few, if any, complex issues are resolved by perusing one book. Instead we ought to be teaching students to decide what kind of information is necessary and how to figure out a way to get it. In addition, many of the appendices are neatly correlated, designed and labeled to answer precisely those questions asked in the text. Students therefore do not develop strategies they need to transfer their knowledge to the issues, problems, and questions they will have as adults.
- Texts often emphasize the ideal or theoretical models of government, economic systems, and institutions without exploring real (hidden) sources of power and change. The difficulty and complexity of problems are alluded to or even mentioned, but without exploring the complexity. Furthermore, texts typically do not separate ideals from the way a system might really operate in a given situation.
- Explanations are often abstract and lack detail or connection to that which they explain, leaving students with a vague understanding. Texts fail to answer such questions as: *How* did this bring about that? What was going on in people's minds? Why? How did that relate to the rest of society? Why is this valued? Without context, the little bits have little meaning and therefore, if remembered at all, serve no function and cannot be recalled for use.

Subject-Specific Problems

There are somewhat different problems which emerge in each of the areas of social studies. It is important to identify them:

History
- Primary sources, when used or referred to at all, are not examined as sources of information or as explications of important attitudes and beliefs which shaped events. Their assessment is not discussed, nor are influences which shape that assessment. Texts fail to mention, for example, that most history was written by victors of wars and by the few educated people. Much information about other points of view has been lost. Most selections from primary sources are trivial narratives.
- History texts state problems and perceived problems of the past, give the solutions attempted, and mention results. Students don't evaluate them *as solutions.* They don't look at what others did about the same problem, nor do they analyze causes or evaluate solutions for themselves. We recommend that teachers ask, "To what extent and in what ways did the action solve the problem? Fail to solve it? Create new problems?" Students could argue for their own solutions.
- When discussing causes of historical events, texts present the U.S. interpretation as though it were fact. Thus, students gain little or no insight into historical reasoning.
- When texts present negative information on the U.S., they don't encourage students to explore the consequences or implications of it.

Politics

- Traditional lessons seldom discuss the difficulty of being a good citizen (e.g., assessing candidates and propositions before voting), nor do they discuss the positive aspects of dissent, i.e., the need to have a wide-ranging open market of ideas.
- Texts tend to make unfair comparisons, such as comparing the *ideal* of governments of the U.S. and its allies to the *real* Soviet government.
- Important ideals, such as freedom of speech, are taught as mere slogans. Students read, recall, and repeat vague justifications for ideals rather than deepen their understanding of them and of the difficulty in achieving them. In effect, such ideas are taught as though they were facts on the order of the date a treaty was signed.
- Texts often confuse facts with ideals and genuine patriotism with show of patriotism or false patriotism. The first confusion discourages us from seeing ourselves, others, and the world accurately; we often don't see the gap between how we want to be and how we are. The second encourages us to reject constructive criticism.

Economics

- Texts assume a capitalist perspective on economics, and texts generally contrast ideal capitalism with real socialism.
- Texts cover economic systems superficially, neglecting serious and in-depth coverage of *how* they are supposed to work (e.g., in our system, people must make rational choices as consumers, employers, and voters).

Anthropology

- Cultural differences are often reduced to holidays and foods rather than values, perspectives, and more significant customs, giving students little more than a superficial impression of this field.

Geography

- Texts more often use maps to show such trivialities as travelers' and explorers' routes than to illuminate the history and culture of the place shown and the lives of the people who actually live there.

What ties many of these criticisms together and points to their correction is the understanding that study of each subject should teach students how to reason in that subject, and this requires that students learn how to synthesize their insights into each subject to better understand their world. The standard didactic approach, with its emphasis on giving students as much information as possible, neglects this crucial task. Even those texts which attempt to teach geographical or historical reasoning do so occasionally, rather than systematically. By conceptualizing education primarily as passing data to students, texts present *products* of reasoning. A critical approach, emphasizing root questions and independent thought, on the other hand, helps students get a handle on the facts and ideas and offers students crucial tools for thinking through the problems they will face throughout their lives.

Students need assignments that challenge their ability to assess actual political behavior. Such assignments will, of course, produce divergent conclusions by students in accordance with the state of their present leanings. And don't forget that student thinking, speaking, and writing should be graded not on some authoritative set of substantive answers, but rather on the clarity, cogency, and intellectual rigor of what they produce. All students should be expected to learn the art of social and political analysis — the art of subjecting political behavior and public policies to critical assessment — based on an analysis of important relevant facts and on consideration of reasoning within alternative political viewpoints.

Some Recommendations for Action

Students in social studies, regardless of level, should be expected to begin to take responsibility for their own learning. This means that the student must develop the art of independent thinking and study and cultivate intellectual and study skills. This includes the ability to critique the text one is using, discovering how to learn from even a poor text. And since it is not reasonable to expect the classroom teacher to remodel the format of a textbook, the teacher must choose how to use the text as given.

Discussions and activities should be designed or remodelled by the teacher to develop the students' use of critical reading, writing, speaking, and listening. Furthermore, students should begin to get a sense of the interconnecting fields of knowledge within social studies, and the wealth of connections between these fields and others, such as math, science, and language arts. The students should not be expected to memorize a large quantity of unrelated facts, but rather to think in terms of interconnected domains of human life and experience. This includes identifying and evaluating various viewpoints; gathering and organizing information for interpretation; distinguishing facts from ideals, interpretations, and judgments; recognizing relationships and patterns; and applying insights to current events and problems.

Students should repeatedly be encouraged to identify the perspective of their texts, imagine or research other perspectives, and compare and evaluate them. This means, among other things, that words like 'conservatism' and 'liberalism,' the 'right' and 'left,' must become more than vague jargon; they must be recognized as names of different ways of thinking about human behavior in the world. Students need experience actually thinking within diverse political perspectives. No perspective, not even one called 'moderate,' should be presented as *the* correct one. By the same token, we should be careful not to lead the students to believe that all perspectives are equally justified or that important insights are equally found in all points of view. Beware especially of the misleading idea that the truth always lies in the middle of two extremes. We should continually encourage and stimulate our students to think and never do their thinking for them. We should, above all, teach, not preach.

History

History lessons should show students how to reason historically and why historical reasoning is necessary to understanding the present and to making rational decisions regarding the future. To learn to reason historically, students must discuss issues dialogically, generating and assessing multiple interpretations of events they study. This requires students to distinguish facts from interpretations. It also requires that they develop a point of view of their own.

• Dates are useful not so much as things-in-themselves, but as markers placing events in relation to each other and within context (historical, political, anthropological, technological, etc.). To reason with respect to history, we need to orient ourselves to events in relation to each other. So when you come across particular dates, you might ask the students to discuss in pairs what events came before and after it and to consider the significance of this sequence. They might consider the possible implications of different conceivable sequences. Suppose dynamite had been invented 50 years earlier. What are some possible consequences of that?

- Why is this date given in the text? What dates are the most significant according to the text? To us? To others? Notice that many dates significant to other groups, such as to Native Americans, are not mentioned. All dates that are mentioned result from a value judgment about the significance of that date.

Economics

When reasoning economically, Americans reason not only from a capitalist perspective, but also as liberals, conservatives, optimists, or pessimists. Lessons on economics should stress not only *how* our system is supposed to work but also how liberals, conservatives, etc. tend to interpret the same facts differently. Students should routinely consider questions like the following: "What can I learn from a conservative or liberal reading of these events? What facts support a conservative interpretation?" They should also have an opportunity to imagine alternative economic systems and alternative incentives, other than money, to motivate human work. Students should analyze and evaluate their own present and future participation in the economy by exploring reasoning and values underlying particular actions, and the consequences of those actions.

Some Key Questions in Subject Areas

Instruction for each subject should be designed to highlight the basic or root questions of that subject and help students learn how to reason within each field. To help you move away from the didactic, memorization-oriented approach found in most texts, we have listed below some basic questions, to suggest what sort of background issues could be used to unify and organize instruction. We have made no attempt to provide a comprehensive list. Consider the questions as suggestions only. In most cases, some translation or specific follow-up questions would be necessary before they could be posed to students.

History

Why are things the way they are now? What happened in the past? Why? What was it like to live then? How has it influenced us now? What kinds of historical events are most significant? How do I learn what happened in the past? How do I reconcile conflicting accounts? How can actions of the past best be understood? Evaluated? How does study of the past help me understand present situations and problems? To understand this present-day problem, what sort of historical background do I need, and how can I find and assess it? Is there progress? Is the world getting better? Worse? Always the same? Do people shape their times or do the times shape people?

Anthropology

Why do you think people have different cultures? What shapes culture? How do cultures change? How have you been influenced by our culture? By ideas in movies and T.V? How does culture influence people? What assumptions underlie my culture? Others' cultures? To what extent are values universal? Which of our values do you think are universal? To what extent do values vary between cultures? Within cultures? How can cultures be categorized? What are some key differences between cultures that have writing and those who don't? What are the implications and consequences of those differences? How might a liberal critique our culture? A socialist? Is each culture so unique and self-contained, and so thoroughly defining of reality, that cultures cannot be compared or evaluated? How is your peer group like a culture? How are cultures like and unlike other kinds of groups?

Geography

How do people adapt to where they live? What kinds of geographical features influence people the most? How? How do people change their environment? What effects do different changes have? How can uses of land be evaluated? How can we distinguish geographical from cultural influences? (Are Swedes hardy as a result of their geography or as a result of their cultural values?) Which geographical features in our area are the most significant? Does our climate influence our motivation? How so? Would you be different if you had been raised in the desert? Explain how. Why is it important to know what various countries export? What does that tell us about that country, its relationships to other countries, its problems, its strengths?

Politics

What kinds of governments are there? What is government for? What is my government like? What are other governments like? How did they come to be that way? Who has power? Who should have power? What ways can power be used? How is our system designed to prevent abuse of power? To what extent is that design successful? What assumptions underlie various forms of government? What assumptions underlie ours? On what values are they theoretically based? What values are actually held? How is the design of this government supposed to achieve ideals? To what extent should a country's political and economic interests determine its foreign relations? To what extent should such ideals as justice and self-determination influence foreign policy decisions? Take a particular policy and analyze the possible effects of vested interests. How can governments be evaluated? How much should governments do to solve political, social, economic, etc., problems?

Economics

What kinds of economic decisions do you make? What kinds will you make in the future? On what should you base those decisions? How should you decide where your money goes? When you spend money, what are you telling manufacturers? How is a family like an economic system? What kinds of economies are there? In this economy, who makes what kinds of decisions? What values underlie this economy? What does this economic system assume about people and their relationship to their work — assume about why people work? According to proponents of this economic system, who should receive the greatest rewards? Why? Who should recieve fewer rewards? How can economic systems be evaluated? What problems are there in our economy according to liberals? Conservatives? Socialists? What features of our economy are capitalistic? Socialistic? Communistic? How does ideal capitalism (socialism) work? In what ways do we depart from ideal capitalism? Are these departures justified? What kinds of things are most important to produce? Why? What kinds of things are less important? Why?

Unifying Social Studies Instruction

Although it makes sense to say that someone is reasoning historically, anthropologically, geographically, etc., it does not make the same sense to say that someone is reasoning socio-scientifically. There is no *one* way to put all of these fields together. Yet, understanding the interrelationships between each field and being able to integrate insights gained from each field is crucial to social studies. We need to recognize the need for students to develop their own unique perspective on social events and arrangements. This requires that questions regarding the interrelationships between the fields covered in social studies be frequently raised and that lessons be designed to require students to apply ideas from various fields to one topic or problem. Keep in mind the following questions:

What are people like? How do people come to be the way they are? How does society shape the individual? How does the individual shape society? Why do people disagree? Where do people get their points of view? Where do I get my point of view? Are some people more important than others? How do people and groups of people solve problems? How can we evaluate solutions? What are our biggest problems? What has caused them? How should we approach them? What are the relationships between politics, economics, culture, history, and geography? How do each of these influence the rest? How does the economy of country X influence its political decisions? How does the geography of this area affect its economy? How is spending money like voting? How can governments, cultures, and economic systems be evaluated? Could you have totalitarian capitalism? Democratic communism? Are humans subject to laws and, hence, ultimately predictable?

In raising these questions beware the tendency to assume a "correct" answer from our social conditioning as Americans, especially on issues dealing with socialism or communism. Remember, we, like all peoples, have biases and prejudices. Our own view of the world must be critically analyzed and questioned.

Try to keep in mind that it takes a long time to develop a person's *thinking*. Our thinking is connected with every other dimension of us. All of our students enter our classes with many "mindless" beliefs, ideas which they have unconsciously picked up from T.V., movies, small talk, family background, and peer groups. Rarely have they been encouraged to think for themselves. Thinking their way through these beliefs takes time. We therefore need to proceed with a great deal of patience. We need to accept small payoffs in the beginning. We need to expect many confusions to arise. We must not despair in our role as cultivators of independent critical thought. In time, students will develop new modes of thinking. In time they will become more clear, more accurate, more logical, more open-minded — if only we stick to our commitment to nurture these abilities. The social studies provide us with an exciting opportunity, since they deal with issues central to our lives and well-being. It is not easy to shift the classroom from a didactic-memorization model, but, if we are willing to pay the price of definite commitment, it can be done.

International Trade

Objectives of the remodelled plan

The students will:
- discuss and evaluate international trade decisions and policies
- develop intellectual good faith and courage by comparing ideal capitalism with practice, and evaluating departures from ideals

Standard Approach———

This lesson explains that the real world is far more complex than the example of two countries and two goods. The students investigate a nation's situation when it has a positive balance of trade and when it has negative balance of trade.

Critique

This lesson does not necessarily call for suspending judgement or distinguishing facts from ideals. The student does not look critically at international trade. The lesson does not challenge the student to look at the interdependence of trade among nations. The economy of developing countries is not a part of our students' experience and therefore they are unaware of the implications and the consequences of trading with us as a nation. Students need to explore implications and consequences on all levels of economic prosperity.

Strategies used to remodel

S-20 analyzing or evaluating actions or policies
S-3 exercising fairmindedness
S-27 comparing and contrasting ideals with actual practice
S-6 developing intellectual courage
S-35 exploring implications and consequences
S-7 developing intellectual good faith or integrity

Remodelled Lesson Plan *S-20* ———

When discussing trade, encourage students to research and reflect the meaning of "trade" from different countries' perspectives (i.e. 1st world, 2nd world, 3rd world and 4th world countries). Have the class discuss the effects of positive balance of trade in developing countries. **S-3** What is the trade policy of the U. S.? Is it consistent with the principles of free enterprise? **S-27** Do you agree with our policies? Why or why not? **S-6** How might a short term positive balance of trade in developed countries negatively affect longer term trade interests? What are some signs of interdependence which call us away from a short term or narrowly pragmatic perspective on trade? **S-35**

In small groups first, and then in a report given to the class, students can research news reports, and discuss key questions. "What values beyond immediate self interest call us to recognize our linkage with other nations? Why? What is our action in relation to our trade policy? Why was this done? Is our trade policy consistent? Explain." **S-27**

editor's note: To guide research, have students find news articles in which disputes regarding international trade are covered or analyzed. Some students could trace back long-term consequences of trade policy decisions made a decade or more ago. "What is (was) the issue in this case? What sides are being taken? What reasons given? What principles or goals are behind each position? What results did each side give for the policies considered? Which consequences are most plausible? Why? **S-35** Which of these older cases bear most resemblance to which current cases? What was done? What were the results? Were they desirable? What should be done now? **S-20** How does capitalistic theory address international trade issues? In what ways do we depart from the theory? **S-7** Do we favor trade with some nations for political rather than economic reasons? Why? What countries do we refuse to trade with? Why? Is this wise? Why or why not? Can this sort of behavior be reconciled with belief in capitalism? Why or why not?" **S-6**

> *The reader should keep in mind the connection between the principles and applications, on the one hand, and the character traits of a fairminded critical thinker, on the other. Our aim, once again, is not a set of disjointed skills, but an integrated, committed, thinking person.*

Free Enterprise

by Phyllis V. Walters, Redwood
Academy, Santa Rosa, CA

Objectives of the remodelled plan
The students will:
- evaluate their participation in the economy
- develop and discuss criteria for evaluating an economic system
- discuss and evaluate the major economic systems of the world
- develop an appreciation for our natural resources as well as for human resources
- generate and assess economic systems

Standard Approach───

> This lesson covers the following points: discussion of how nations answer the three basic economic questions — *1)* What goods and services are to be produced? *2)* How should goods and services be produced? *3)* For whom should goods and services be produced? — and then follow the answers to the economic system which is established. Capitalism, in its pure form, is described as having private enterprise, the right of property, profit motive, competition, and the freedom of choice. Students interview owners of private businesses regarding the benefits of private enterprise. The advantages and disadvantages of competition in business are discussed. Socialism and communism are briefly discussed as alternative systems chosen by certain countries. Students role play workers in a variety of jobs in the three main economic systems and their freedoms or lack of them.

Critique

This lesson misses the opportunity to have students focus on the importance of their contributions to their economic system and how they easily abuse their freedoms. The material isn't related directly to the students' lives, nor does it promote insight into each peoples' egocentricity when viewing the workings of their economy or when deciding how to use resources.

Strategies used to remodel
S-15 developing criteria for evaluation: clarifying values and standards
S-20 analyzing or evaluating actions or policies
S-35 exploring implications and consequences
S-17 questioning deeply: raising and pursuing root or significant questions
S-27 comparing and contrasting ideals with actual practice
S-19 generating or assessing solutions

Remodelled Lesson Plan S-15

Identify the basic meaning of 'capital.' When discussing what, how, and for whom goods and services should be provided, ask, "What goods and/or services do you personally produce? Would you prefer to go on errands on foot, on bicycle, or in a car? Which is most time efficient? Which is most efficient in saving capital resources? Which is most important to you — saving energy, gas, time, or money? Is it important to you to have freedom to choose to drive, walk, or ride your bike? Would you rather someone else decide that for you? If you work 8 hours do you receive more pay from your employer than one the same age who works two hours? Should you? Why? Should your grandparent receive the same pay for 8 hours of work as you do for 8 hours of work? In the past, when you have had the choice of how to spend money, how have you used it? Do you spend it wisely? Why or why not? **S-20** What does it mean to spend your money wisely? Unwisely? Given the principle of supply and demand, what are the consequences for the economy of spending money unwisely?" **S-35**

Explore the resources that we have to produce the goods and services that our country needs. Ask, "What resources other than money do you have? If you have been allowed to choose how to spend your time, have you often wasted it? Do you still want the freedom to decide how to spend your money, time, energy even though you sometimes waste it? Why? If you over-spend your money, your time, and your energy, how do you get more? What resources does our country have? What other resources must we have to use natural resources? If we are given the freedom to produce goods and services, will we over-spend or waste our resources? Is freedom worth it?" **S-17**

When role playing leader/worker of the economic system, ask, "Who is important in this system? Why? Should they receive in proportion to what they put in? Why? How can we decide which people put more in to it? Why? What jobs or professions, do you think, get more money than they deserve? Why? Less than they deserve? How could this be changed?" **S-27**

Students can redesign and discuss their present systems. Ask, "How do we evaluate this system? What is our checklist? Do we need to redesign our system? How would you implement those changes? Are your changes in everyone's best interest? Who might object? Why? How would you respond?" **S-19**

The teacher should emphasize than an economic system is only as good as those who are implementing it. The system depends on our usage of resources.

The Energy Crisis

by Susan Dembitz, Miranda, CA

Objectives of the remodelled plan

The students will:
• practice dialogical thinking while examining opposing viewpoints regarding energy
• examine the assumptions of opposing positions on energy and the environment
• make inferences about what current policy should address
• assess evidence for positions taken in the energy versus environment dispute
• practice dialectical thinking and listening critically by evaluating the views
• make interdisciplinary connections between economic, political, and ethical problems

Standard Approach

The text provides a good summary introduction to the events and issues of the energy crisis. The paragraph on page 692 explains that Nixon's support for Israel during the Yom Kippur War led to the gasoline shortage of 1973-74. On page 723 the text briefly outlines the history of oil pricing up to 1973, describes OPEC, and outlines Nixon's energy proposals. On pages 728-30 is a summary of the energy problem, the EPA, problems with coal and the nuclear industry, and the conflict between energy needs and environmental concerns. In the Section Review, students are asked to *1)* identify or explain EPA, acid rain, strip-mining, Three Mile Island, Shah Mohammad Reza Palevi and *2)* show how environmental and energy concerns collided.

Critique

The Energy Crisis will be more comprehensible to students when it is taught as a unit. In this text, the students need to consult three different sections to do this. Carter's political problems need to be treated separately. The energy material provides an ideal springboard for students to test their intuitive grasp of economics and its interrelation with politics in dealing with a group of topics which are still very much at issue now. It also provides an avenue for discussing important moral and ethical issues which the text begins to address.

Strategies used to remodel

S-25 reasoning dialogically: comparing perspectives, interpretations, or theories
S-11 comparing analogous situations: transferring insights to new contexts
S-32 making plausible inferences, predictions, or interpretations
S-35 exploring implications and consequences
S-23 making interdisciplinary connections
S-30 examining or evaluating assumptions
S-33 evaluating evidence and alleged facts

S-26 reasoning dialectically: evaluating perspectives, interpretations, or theories
S-16 evaluating the credibility of sources of information
S-22 listening critically: the art of silent dialogue

Remodelled Lesson Plan S-25

Understand Economics

Use a series of questions to draw out students' understanding of basic laws of supply and demand, and the extension of this to the energy crisis. **S-11** Help them see the connection between shortages and price hikes, and how the price of energy is a component of all other prices. **S-32** Indicate how rising prices promotes conservation. **S-35**

Discuss Energy S-23

Divide the class into groups to collect information and prepare arguments about the various forms of energy used and researched, and economic, environmental, and political problems. Students should be preparing to discuss the trade-offs between producing energy economically and protecting the environment. Students should be alerted to examine the assumptions of the opposing viewpoints and the evidence, and then to examine current policy recommendations and explore the implications of policies. Students could consider questions like the following:

What problems are caused by our need for energy? How do energy suppliers define the problems? Environmentalists? Consumers? What are the environmental problems? Economic problems? Political problems? What kinds of solutions does this group propose? That one? What assumptions does each group make? Compare these assumptions. Why do they make these assumptions? Are the assumptions compatible or contradictory? Why? **S-30** What values and interests does each group bring to their thinking about the issue? What further problems could be caused by each group's proposed solutions? What problems do the other groups claim would be caused? Based on what evidence? Where did the evidence come from? What evidence do you accept? Why? **S-33** What implications do those facts have? What do you think should be done? Why? How? How would industrialists, environmentalists, and consumers respond? **S-26**

Then each team can prepare a panel discussion to present to the rest of the class. Students not discussing can evaluate the arguments. "Why did this person take that position? What evidence was used to support it? Where did this information come from? Which of these contradictory sources should we believe? Who is in a better position to know? Who might lie? Who should we accept? Why? **S-16** What did this position leave out?" **S-22**

editor's note: Have students begin this unit by using the table of contents and index in their texts to find all references to energy. Students can read those references, share them with each other, and synthesize the points made throughout the text. Students can then brainstorm questions to guide their research. At the end of the unit, students could critique or rewrite relevant sections of their text.

Oil

Objectives of the remodelled plan

The students will:

- explore the significance of oil in various respects, discovering interdisciplinary connections
- consider the implications and consequences of oil possession and use on different countries and from a variety of perspectives

Standard Approach

Texts generally state that petroleum oil is the most important mineral deposit of our century, that we can find where the largest deposits of oil are located, or what percentage of the world's energy supply is derived from oil at any point in history. One text considers the effect of oil on Saudi Arabians: a farmer may now be in the oil business, a poor family may now be rich, and this family's son may now be able to go to college. Some texts mention OPEC and the energy crisis of the 1970's.

Critique

Oil makes a good topic, due to its economic, political, and environmental significance. Students should explore the implications and effects of widespread use of oil. Study of oil provides background information crucial for understanding domestic politics, international relations, economics, and environmental concerns, and is a good example of the overlap of these areas.

Students are *told* that oil is an important mineral, rather than being allowed to come to that conclusion on their own by exploring its significance. There is no discussion of perspective; students do not sort out different attitudes on oil use and how to meet energy needs.

Strategies used to remodel

S-23 making interdisciplinary connections
S-1   thinking independently
S-13 clarifying issues, conclusions, or beliefs
S-35 exploring implications and consequences
S-17 questioning deeply: raising and pursuing root or significant questions
S-25 reasoning dialogically: comparing perspectives, interpretations, or theories
S-5   developing intellectual humility and suspending judgment

Remodelled Lesson Plan

This topic provides an opportunity for students to research various aspects — oil location and available amounts, the effect of oil on oil-rich developing countries, oil as an international point of contention, environmental concerns. **S-23** Students can share their findings when relevant in the discussion. Ask them what fields of study they have to pursue to learn about oil and its effects on people. **S-1**

Why is oil important to people? Would everyone agree? Who might not? Would people have agreed with you in 1800? 1600? BC? 1900? Find times in history where the importance of oil changed. Why did it change? **S-13**

To explore the significance of owning oil, have the students consider Saudi Arabia. Would all Saudis agree about the importance of oil? How about the newly rich? The old rich? The poor? The rulers? The religious leaders? Why is oil so important to Saudi Arabia? How has it affected their culture? Find other countries which have been affected by oil to that extent. Look at countries with a great deal of oil as well as those with very little oil. **S-17**

Have students discuss differences in oil use among several countries and discuss the causes for and implications of these differences. Why does this country use so much (so little) oil? And why is that? How does that affect that country? Its citizens? Its relationships to other countries? **S-35**

What reasons are there to lessen or end our dependence on oil? What reasons are there against doing so? What problems does use of oil cause? Who is affected? How? Who is helped? Harmed? Who would be hurt if we changed to using other kinds of energy? How could everyone's needs be met? How would you solve the problems caused by extensive use of oil? **S-25**

How has oil affected our foreign policy? Which oil rich countries are our friends? Enemies? Neither? Why? How should we treat countries that supply us with oil? What if they want to cut us off? **S-35**

Why did I focus on oil in this lesson? What do you think my purpose was? Why do you think so? What are some significant questions surrounding oil? How could we research them? **S-5**

There is no one 'right' remodel. Many different improvements are possible.

167

Maps

Objectives of the remodelled plan

The students will:
- analyze the concept of a map
- discuss the purposes for maps
- explain why symbols are used on maps, and why particular symbols may have been chosen
- think independently in order to make maps
- practice independent thought by using maps to understand the countries they study

Standard Approach

> The following skills are generally covered in materials regarding maps: latitude/longitude calculations, identification of different kinds of maps, and calculations of scale and elevation. The other main topic covered is the problem of making a flat map to represent a globe; several different world map projections and their limitations are explained.

Critique

Texts provide little on the concept of maps and map theory. There is no adequate development of the concepts 'map' or 'model.' Students are *told* about a map's legend, and the symbols locating specifics on the map, but are not asked to consider why symbols need to be used, or why the particular symbols were chosen. They do not evaluate choice of symbols. Map projections are presented without any opportunity for independent thinking; they are just listed with their good and bad qualities.

There is no discussion as to how to choose maps for particular purposes, nor are students offered any atlas skills. It is more important for students to be able to find and use the kinds of maps they need for particular purposes, and to be able to read new kinds of maps, than to or simply locate listed places on a given map.

Strategies used to remodel

S-9 developing confidence in reason
S-14 clarifying and analyzing the meanings of words or phrases
S-1 thinking independently
S-19 generating or assessing solutions
S-15 developing criteria for evaluation: clarifying values and standards

Remodelled Lesson Plan S-9

You might begin by first asking students what a model is. Ask them to make a list of all the different kinds of models they can think of. "What do these models have in common?" The students might say they represent something, they have to be a certain size, they look like something else, etc. Ask students what a model of the Earth is called. They may say map or globe. Look at a variety of maps with the class. (Street map, map for tourists, celestial map, floor plan.) Ask them what they notice. "What does each represent? What is each used for? What do the maps have in common? Why? How does this particular difference serve the function of the map, or arise from the nature of the place and from features it represents? Compare maps to verbal descriptions. Why do you think we use symbols on maps? Why has someone chosen these particular symbols?" **S-14**

Ask students how they would go about making a map of the world. "What are some of the problems we might run into? What would you want to consider when making a flat representation of a sphere? Look at different kinds of maps of Earth. Are they all the same? How are they different? Make your own map of the Earth. Compare it with those of other students. What can you learn from looking at all of the maps?" **S-1**

You may want to have students use art time to make maps of countries, states, towns, their school, their bedrooms. "Which maps will have which features? Why? How do you decide? Where should you put each feature? How far away from other features? How can you make clear what each represents? What do you want your map to show? What purposes could it serve?" **S-19**

Make a personal atlas yourself, and a classroom atlas as a group. Which maps belong in which atlas? How did you decide? What were you assuming that led you to make that decision? **S-15**

Have students write test questions and answer keys (on copies of various kinds of maps) and select some for a map-use test. **S-1**

Fostering independent thought throughout the year **S-1**

When discussing specific countries and periods of history, have students read and discuss population distribution, physical, political, linguistic, and land use maps before reading their texts. They could also discuss such things as trade routes and difficulty or ease of travel, noting what other groups are nearby, etc.

Whenever they are about to use a map to pursue a question or problem, first ask them what kind of map they need, and how and where to find it.

Natural Resources

Objectives of the remodelled plan
The students will:
- clarify the concept of natural resource and the values underlying the concept
- explore the implications and consequences of having natural resources, including using, misusing, and not using them
- consider what it means to be successful as a country

Standard Approach

Most of the information is presented in map form, with the main emphasis on the location of various resources.

One text offered a short discussion on conservation, and several offered alternative forms of energy and the concept of energy itself as a natural resource. One text was interested in the role natural resources play in the formation of a world leader, emphasizing that, although nature gave us rich natural resources, we had to use them well to become productive and powerful.

Critique

It is less important for students to know who has what than it is for them to learn how to find such information when they need it, and to understand the implications of having and not having or using and not using various natural resources. Additionally, examples covered in the book should be used as opportunities for discussion of deeper issues, especially as they relate to ecology, geology, economics, politics, anthropology, technology, and history.

The implications of various mineral deposits and other natural resources on history and culture are inadequately drawn out. There is far too much emphasis on who has what, and too little on how and why people use their resources, and on the long term effects. Few implications are brought out concerning modern forms of energy. Using resources is assumed to be what all intelligent nations do to get ahead, and no other view is examined or evaluated.

Claims that "Nature gave us bountiful resources" could be explored and compared to another point of view — that nature didn't give them to us. They were here, and we got them because we came here and took them.

Strategies used to remodel
S-14 clarifying and analyzing the meanings of words or phrases
S-15 developing criteria for evaluation: clarifying values and standards
S-1 thinking independently
S-21 reading critically: clarifying or critiquing texts
S-9 developing confidence in reason

Remodelled Lesson Plan

Students could begin by analyzing the key concept. "What kinds of things are called natural resources? What aren't? Why? What qualifies something as a natural resource? *S-15* What are natural resources used for? Why is this important to know about? *S-14*

How could we find out who has what resources? What role have natural resources played in history? How could we find out? *S-1*

"What effects does our use of natural resources have? How can we find out? What does 'use wisely' mean? As opposed to what? How can use of resources be evaluated?" For each example, ask, "Why would this be called wise? Unwise? Why was this done? Not done? In what ways do we 'use them wisely'? How do we not? How has our use of resources hurt us? Why have we done this? Why does (name a country) export rather than use (name a resource)?" (Discuss at length.) *S-15*

"Why have we made more use of natural resources than developing countries have or did? Who should control how natural resources will be used? Why? Who does now?

Ask, "What is progress? What issues involve this concept?" If the text uses the concept 'success,' students could develop a concept of success as it applies to a country and a means of evaluation. Then they can discuss what fits this ideal. "How did the book attribute success? Why? Do those things go with success?" *S-14*

Continue probing into the assumptions of the text. "What does it mean to say that 'Nature gave us these resources?' What does it assume? Imply? How else could we describe why we have the resources we do? What does that assume? Imply? Why did the text choose that way of speaking?" *S-21*

To develop students' confidence in their ability to think independently, the teacher could have them study resource maps and predict areas of conflict, whenever they are about to study an area or country *S-9*

It is better to use one clearly understood strategy than to attempt to use more than you clearly understand.

War

Objectives of the remodelled plan

The students will:
- discuss the consequences of technology on war
- discuss the moral implications of war, evaluating actions and policies

Standard Approach

When covering wars, texts often mention the technology available or which developed during each war. Texts provide explanations of the causes and results of wars covered.

Critique

Connections are rarely made between the technology of war and the outcomes. There are few discussions of war strategies, or the social changes that occur after them. Some texts point out that technology changes war. One does not get the sense from most texts that people are involved in war, and that war affects people. The students are not given any indication of what war is like for any of the parties. Students don't discuss the moral implications of certain kinds of weapon technology, like nerve gas, germ warfare, nuclear missiles, and napalm. Students miss the opportunity to think independently about how to avoid World War III. They do not consider the ways in which we wage war and how that has changed over time, partly as a result of technology. Students do not consider the significant question of ethics of war or causes of war.

Strategies used to remodel

S-35 exploring implications and consequences
S-20 analyzing or evaluating actions or policies
S-10 refining generalizations and avoiding oversimplifications
S-17 questioning deeply: raising and pursuing root or significant questions

Remodelled Lesson Plan

Students could develop more insight into the effects of technology on war by discussions like the following: Consider a medieval war and discuss the technology that was available. How did the technology affect the way the war was fought and the effects it had? Now compare that with a 19th Century war. **S-35**

How do humans wage war? Why? What are some ways we could use technology to avoid war? Why do you think this would prevent war? How might technological advances cause war?

Is it morally acceptable to do whatever it takes to win a war? Why or why not? What weapons or techniques of war are unjustified? (Students could discuss biological warfare, defoliation, etc.) **S-20** What might be some exceptions? Why are they exceptions? **S-10** Write a code of honor for yourself that includes wartime behavior toward the enemy. Think about this in terms of types of weapons, targets, when to wage war, who to protect, etc.

Other discussion on war include pursuing questions like the following: Why are there wars? Is there one sort of cause, or many kinds of causes of wars? (Have students consider specific examples and possible counter-examples.) Does anyone think war is good? Why do many people believe war is necessary? What would people have to do to stop war? What kinds of effects do wars have on the people involved in them? **S-17**

What kinds of wars are there? What are the differences between fighting wars in your own country and fighting wars elsewhere?

When, if ever, is going to war justified? Are all parties responsible for being in a war? Can you think of a war that was clearly only one side's fault? When, if ever, is violence justified? **S-20**

> *Teachers who don't learn how to use basic critical thinking principles to critique and remodel their own lesson plans probably won't be able to implement someone else's effectively. Providing teachers with the scaffolding for carrying out the process for themselves, and examples of its application, opens the door for continuing development of critical thinking skills and insights.*

Surveys

by Laura K. Racine Gifted Education Department, Wyandotte Special Education Cooperative, Kansas City, KS

Objectives of the remodelled plan

The students will:

- formulate and clarify the specific questions about which they want information
- analyze their word choices through dialectical reasoning and critical listening
- write clear answer choices to the survey questions
- specify clearly the significance of each answer choice
- format the survey coherently and efficiently
- develop greater precision of thought and expression

Standard Approach

Gifted learners often question statistical results of polls and surveys, discounting or embracing results as they line up with their own particular positions. In order to gain some insight into the process of collecting data which will yield statistical results we might design a survey from start to statistical end. The students' designs would include a question, a series of possible choices to answer the questions, a defined target population, a plan for recording results, a method and means of satisfactorily interpreting the results of the survey statistically.

Critique

Survey writing is highly specific and detailed work, dependent upon clarity of purpose and expression. Survey questions provide fertile ground for imprecise and biased language. Gifted adolescents who typically approach planning globally rather than with a step-wise system tend to be rather poor authors of sound surveys.

Analysis of the semantics, syntax, and connotative correlations of language which can yield insightful results are just that —"inciteful" — to the students. They detest being deterred from their purpose for petty analysis chores. The frustration level soars when they are prevented from asking their confusing and inadequate questions in an unsystematic way. The lesson design is not specific to the task of survey writing nor statistical analysis, nor its interpretation. It is perhaps too large a chunk even for gifted learners, however driving the urge to know the bubble-gum preference of their pals.

Focussing primarily on selecting the question which will most accurately elicit the desired data as content for this lesson may minimize the incidence of the survey results being affected by misunderstood meaning of terms and different frames of reference.

The guidelines of the original lesson are not specific to the type of learning that the students desire. The experience would not have been either appropriate or useful to learners. The lesson has little affect on the learners' experiential interchange with the data they wish to obtain.

Strategies used to remodel

S-13 clarifying issues, conclusions, or beliefs
S-14 clarifying and analyzing the meanings of words or phrases
S-12 developing one's perspective: creating or exploring beliefs, arguments, or theories
S-30 examining or evaluating assumptions
S-32 making plausible inferences, predictions, or interpretations
S-22 listening critically: the art of silent dialogue
S-28 thinking precisely about thinking: using critical vocabulary
S-18 analyzing or evaluating arguments, interpretations, beliefs, or theories
S-10 refining generalizations and avoiding oversimplifications
S-26 reasoning dialectically: evaluating perspectives, interpretations, or theories
S-8 developing intellectual perseverance

Remodelled Lesson Plan *S-13*

The focus of this lesson is to enable learners to discover the root question about which they want information. The facilitator could suggest that the students "play with" the issues and ideas of their subjects. Students can order components of their topics, evaluating their relevance to their interests and purposes. Becoming acquainted with the root question should enable the learners to order and specify the issues germane to formulating their formal questions. The learners can discuss their interests with the facilitator, "What data do you wish to obtain? From whom do you want this information? How else could you phrase the question? Which most precisely specifies what you mean? Why do you want to know this? What will it tell you?"

Clarifying their intent to classmates in discussion will cause them to clarify terms and to generate examples in order to answer the questions for clarification that will arise. The learners would be encouraged to manipulate words in order to gauge the appropriate language to form their questions. **S-14** In the process of trying out ideas in give and take questioning of their peers, they would explore implications and consequences of their choices. The results of the practice time could move the learners to new questions in which they had a higher level of interest. **S-12**

In the practice sessions, the students share the ideas through questions and reply. Oversimplified answers would require clarification and more profound response. Assumptions would be exposed and examined as students discover them in each other's work. **S-30**

Discussion of the inferences that could be drawn from answer choices would be important as rough drafts are shared. **S-32** "Does this mean that if ..., then? Could that lead to the assumption that ...? Are you meaning to infer ...?

175

John, please tell Jim how you perceive this question. **S-22** Jane, how accurate is John? What can you change or rearrange with the language of your question, Jane, so that John catches your meaning more precisely? What does this answer imply? Is that what you want to imply?" **S-28**

Because the students' topics have some significance for them, there may be some personal attachment to their verbiage. When disagreements over meaning arise, they will have to evaluate the arguments presented against them. Other class members can also evaluate the quality of arguments based on their perspectives. **S-18**

The teacher's goal is for the students to catch one another's simplification errors, and for one learner to help another clarify ideas. "Could that term be interpreted in another way? **S-10** Doesn't that imply ...? What is the cause and effect relationship as you interpret it?" **S-28**

As students question each other, changing positions, they will experience the fallacies, assumptions, lack of clarity, incompleteness and bias in the writing of others, elucidating some of their own frailties.

The dialectical thinking that ensues may encourage questions like: Is this what you really intend to ask? Do you need question three? Does it add data that is relevant to your question? What does choice C on question 4 contribute to the information you want to obtain? **S-26**

Students ultimately must assume the responsible role of author, evaluating arguments, making decisions, and committing their ideas to paper.

The focus upon manipulating statistics in the original lesson caused the students to be frustrated. They did not have the skills with which to formulate an adequate survey question. Therefore, the goal of statistical analysis was never attained. To solve this problem, the survey lesson will succumb to a bit of megalomania and graduate to the status of survey unit, billed accordingly in the syllabus, to build to a full survey experience. Building the unit in this molecular style should provide more experiential opportunities, the goal is to ultimately bring the learners to a better understanding of themselves. **S-8**

editor's note: To prepare for the unit, students could collect and analyze opinion poll questions from newspapers.

> *One does not learn about critical thinking by memorizing a definition or set of distinctions.*

The Cold War

Objectives of the remodelled plan
The students will:
- practice intellectual courage by considering the Cold War from multiple perspectives
- develop intellectual good faith by applying the same standards to the U.S. and U.S.S.R.
- raise and clarify questions regarding particular Cold War incidents

Standard Approach

> Texts trace the rise of hostilities between our government and that of the Soviet Union. They generally mention Soviet expansion in Europe, the Berlin Wall, the Cuban Missile Crisis, The Warsaw Pact and NATO, Soviet support of revolutionaries throughout the world, and U.S. aid to non-communist countries.
>
> The U.S.S.R. forces countries to become communist and puts communist leaders in power, while the U.S. fights to keep countries from becoming communist by supplying food, money, and help to fight communism. Since the communists use poverty to incite communist revolutions, the U.S. gives assistance to improve those conditions and thus strengthen the country against communism.

Critique

Predictably, treatment of the Cold War is generally biased. In each case covered, they want to oppress, we want to free; they take over or interfere with, we offer aid and assistance; their friends are dictatorships and tyrannies, ours are democracies. Students are given little or no idea of how other perspectives conceptualize the Cold War or the superpowers. Students should come to understand how others see us and the world, and come to their own conclusions on specific events. Every country's foreign policy can stand some improvement. Ours is no exception.

This entire remodel helps students develop intellectual courage and integrity.

Strategies used to remodel
S-6 developing intellectual courage
S-7 developing intellectual good faith or integrity
S-21 critical reading: clarifying or critiquing text
S-25 reasoning dialogically: comparing perspectives, interpretations, or theories
S-13 clarifying issues, conclusions, or beliefs
S-12 developing one's perspective: creating or exploring beliefs, arguments, or theories
S-20 evaluating actions or policies
S-11 comparing analogous situations: transferring insights to new contexts
S-26 reasoning dialectically: evaluating perspectives, interpretations, or theories

Remodelled Lesson Plan S-6

Ask students to read whatever their text has on the subject of the Cold War. Have them clarify and critique their texts with questions like the following: "What does the text say about the Cold War? Whose fault is it? What assumptions are made in the text? As this text is written, is there a clear 'good guy' and a clear 'bad guy?' From what perspective is this text written? How can you tell? What is the point of view presented in the text? What must the authors believe to present this point of view? What else might a person think? How could the text be written to reflect another point of view? How would a text written from a Soviet perspective present similar material? What would such a perspective assume? *S-25* What other points of view are possible?" Students could pick two paragraphs to rewrite from another point of view. *S-21*

Ask, "How does the U.S. government distinguish countries — what categories are used? Why? What categories does the U.S.S.R. use? Why? How are the U.S. and the U.S.S.R. different in their foreign policies? What do U.S. and U.S.S.R. foreign policies and perspectives have in common? How should foreign policy be evaluated? Do countries have the right to involve themselves in how other countries are run? Why or why not? If they do, when? In what ways?" *S-20*

Have students (or groups of students) focus on one incident or conflict at a time, list the parties involved, and discuss each. "What happened? What reasons were given? How could we figure out if those were the real reasons? What should have been done?" The class could compare two or more similar incidents and responses to them. *S-29* Students should be encouraged to apply the same standards to each country. ("Do any differences between these two situations warrant different evaluations of these actions?") *S-7*

Have students raise questions the text doesn't answer. Ask questions to help the students to refine their questions: "Why do you raise that question? Why does that seem significant to you? What would this answer imply? How could this question be settled? What points of view need to be considered?" *S-13*

Students could locate Vietnam and Afghanistan on maps and compare the two wars. *S-29* Students could interview adults regarding their views about the war in Vietnam. Students could begin with such questions as, "What did you think of the war then? Why? What did you think of those who disagreed with you? Have your views changed? Why?" Have them probe the interviewees' responses. Students could then discuss the views they collected. *S-25*

Students could also research news accounts of the war and anti-war protest. What, if anything, was settled? What issues remain?

Organize a conference on whether we should increase aggressions in Vietnam (1968) or pull out (or something else altogether). Each student can take a particular perspective from which to argue. Have the student conduct a similar meeting about a current issue. *S-11*

Have groups of three students take turns arguing from three different perspectives in a dialectical discussion regarding a dispute between the U.S. and the U.S.S.R. mentioned in the text. They could trade positions and thus argue each side. Have the students evaluate the arguments they have generated. *S-26*

China

Objectives of the remodelled plan

The students will:
- evaluate evidence for the approximate age of a culture
- recognize ethnocentrism in others, in themselves, and in the text
- transfer insight into aspects of Chinese history to analogous situations
- analyze the teachings of Confucius and Lao-Tzu

Standard Approach

China is described as the oldest culture, with a civilization reaching back for at least 3,500 years. China is described as an ethnocentric society, basically due to its isolation throughout history. Some texts mentioned the various dynasties, sometimes briefly discussing one or two. One text focused on Shih Huang Ti, an early ruler. China of the Chou dynasty is compared to ancient Egypt. The climates and populations of China and the United States are compared. Recent Chinese history is mentioned: the Opium War with Great Britain, the revolt of the Emperor's army in 1911 and the underlying causes, the conflict between Chiang Kai-Shek of the Nationalist Party and Mao Tse-tung of the Communist party, including Japan's invasion of China and Mao's system of social control in which community is more important than the family. Most texts mention the Wall and its purpose.

Nearly every text includes a section on Confucius. Some texts also mention Lao-tzu (the founder of Taoism) and contrast his views with those of Confucius.

Suggested activities include: fact recall (reading a timeline of the dynasties), defining vocabulary words, and map reading (listing bordering countries and areas of high population density).

Critique

Study of ancient China provides an example of an old and powerful culture very different from ours. It is also a case of an area that mainly had only one big power, unlike much of Mediterranean history. Furthermore, since China was strong, understanding its influence on East Asia is necessary to understanding East Asia. But the main value of study of any country and time is to develop students' ability to think historically and anthropologically and to begin to have them consider whatever basic historical forces, events, and aspects of culture are mentioned in their texts.

Texts generally emphasize details. Chapters are largely filled with fact after fact, with little or no analysis. Analyses that are given are generally too brief and often too superficial to mean much to students. For example, they may explain the break in economic linkage between China and Russia in one sentence, giving as the reason the Soviets' sudden departure from China.

Often, end-of-chapter questions demand little more than simple recall. "What are China's natural barriers? What is loess? How is it formed?" Timelines and map activities merely require students to read them. Students do not discuss the implications of what they see. Often, questions imply the desired answer such as in the following example: "Do we even try to cultivate slopes as the Chinese do? Why or why not?"

One text dealt effectively with the Mongol invasion, giving a detailed and reasonable explanation, but ended the section with the implication that it was insignificant that the Mongols had invaded and were ruling China, since they had acquired many Chinese customs. Students could compare this case with invasion by those of alien culture and/or discuss whether it made a difference, and of what sort.

By emphasizing *Chinese* ethnocentrism, and ignoring American ethnocentrism, many texts inadvertently support student ethnocentrism. One activity had students reflect on ways in which our pro-American bias shows in the media. Another asked students to look at a China-centered map and a U.S.-centered map, and infer attitudes from these. Such activities can be extended with in-depth discussion of why people have these attitudes and various ways ethnocentricity is manifested.

Brief study of the philosophers can provide insight into the culture, as well as opportunity for dialectical thought. Such discussion requires going beyond paraphrase, and into discussion of the ideas; whether compatible with each other, evaluating them, or probing contradictions between or among others.

Strategies used to remodel

S-9 developing confidence in reason
S-33 evaluating evidence and alleged facts
S-13 clarifying issues, conclusions, or beliefs
S-11 comparing analogous situations: transferring insights to new contexts
S-20 analyzing or evaluating actions or policies
S-2 developing insight into egocentricity or sociocentricity
S-18 analyzing or evaluating arguments, interpretations, beliefs, or theories
S-26 reasoning dialectically: evaluating perspectives, interpretations, or theories

Remodelled Lesson Plan

You could begin by asking students (or having them write as a homework assignment) what they know about China. Throughout the lesson, students could make a timeline, with periods and events in China above, the Mid-east and Europe below. Students can look at various kinds of maps, list their observations, and make inferences regarding the significance of what they find. **S-9**

Then have them read their texts, and ask for the main points covered. "What does the text say? Why did it mention these points? What is the most important thing to learn from this chapter? Is there anything you want to know about? How could you find out?"

To develop students' insight into anthropological reasoning and clarify the claims regarding China's age, you could ask, "How do we know how old a culture is? What kinds of things would we find in China to illustrate that China has the oldest culture? Why would these show us how old China is? How would they show us how old Chinese culture is compared to other cultures? *S-33* Is it significant that Chinese culture is so old? Why? Would it be more significant to the Chinese or to us? Why do you think so?" *S-13*

What would you need to do in order to understand Chinese history and culture? Compare Chinese history, culture and ideas with other countries In what ways was China ahead of Europe? Behind?

Students can compare any wars mentioned in their texts to other wars they have discussed. "Who started this war? What motivated them? What would you say caused this war? Why did that occur? What wars that you know about are like this one? In what ways? In what ways are they different? Is there anything you know about that other war that you can apply to understanding this war? What? What does that tell you about this war? What that you know about this war can you apply to better understand other wars you know something about?" *S-11*

• What was it like to live near the place the Wall is, before the Wall was built? What motivated the building of the Wall? What effects did the Wall have on the society? What was it like to build it? *S-20*

• Why does this text discuss China's ethnocentrism? What evidence do they have of it? What explanation do they give? What reasons have they for feeling superior? How do you think the Chinese thought of other people? How do you think they thought of themselves? *S-2*

• What have we learned about Asia? How could we characterize China's relationship to the rest of Asia?

If the text mentions Confucius and Lao-tzu, students could analyze their ideas with questions like the following: What did each say? What do you think they meant? Have you thought or heard similar ideas? What would they agree about? Disagree about? If you lived your life according to Confucius, how would you live? How would your study of Confucius affect how you live your life? Lao-tzu? What is Confucius' basic idea? Lao-tzu's? What specific differences are there between these two thinkers? Can their insights be reconciled? Why are they important? *S-18* Students could write a dialectical discussion between followers of Confucius and Lao-tzu, and evaluate it. *S-26*

Every trivial lesson you abandon leaves more time to stimulate critical thinking.

181

The Railroad Business

by Susan Dembitz, Miranda, Ca

Objectives of the remodelled plan

The students will:
- exercise fairmindedness when discussing 19th Century viewpoints of fear of standard time
- practice critical reading while evaluating the arguments presented in an interview with Vanderbilt
- practice dialogical thinking by conducting their own interviews
- explore the implications and consequences of new forms of business organization

Standard Approach

> This topic is discussed in parts of two separate chapters. In the first, the text explains the need for improved transportation, the enormous expansion of track mileage, the reasons for and process of adopting standard time and standard gauge, and the development of trusts as a way to limit competition. There are also brief vignettes of John D. Rockefeller, J. Pierpont Morgan, and Andrew Carnegie. In the second chapter, the Interstate Commerce act of 1887 and the Sherman Antitrust Act are each given half a page.

Critique

In the Section Review, students are asked to:

1) identify or explain certain people and concepts (which they need only look up in the text).

2) find out how the railroads and the public benefitted from land grants, standard time, and standard gauge. (This is good, because it introduces the concept of differing viewpoints, but doesn't go far enough.)

3) explain how a dozen big sugar companies might have formed a trust and why. (This is good critical thinking because it asks students to transfer an idea to a new context, to develop insight, and to exercise fairmindedness by putting themselves in the place of sugar company executives and understanding their motives.)

4) describe how companies had become more impersonal and inhuman. (This question could lead to a good discussion of feelings and differences between life in the 19th Century and now, but needs more development.)

5) explain how wealth accumulated by Morgan and Carnegie benefitted the public. (This question sidesteps the whole issue of the ethics of trusts. This area is dealt with very superficially in the succeeding chapter.)

The text calls the great 19ᵗʰ Century entrepreneurs the "Go-Getters," and characterizes them flatteringly: J. P. Morgan is a "man of culture," and "an amazing organizer;" Andrew Carnegie is "intelligent" and "responsible for the spread of the free public library." The political and social effects of their actions on the working class and on the rest of American society is barely touched on. Vanderbilt and his famous "Public be damned" remark is not mentioned at all.

In the later chapter on politics, the ICC Act is summarized as the first attempt by Congress to regulate big business. In the description of the Sherman Antitrust Act mentions how big companies and monopolies affected small businesses and farmers, and of how ineffective the Act was until Teddy Roosevelt become president. These laws could be used as spring boards to discuss social problems caused by the "Go-Getters."

Strategies used to remodel

S-24 practicing Socratic discussion: clarifying and questioning beliefs, theories, or perspectives
S-3 exercising fairmindedness
S-21 reading critically: clarifying or critiquing texts
S-18 analyzing or evaluating arguments, interpretations, beliefs, or theories
S-25 reasoning dialogically: comparing perspectives, interpretations, or theories
S-35 exploring implications and consequences
S-19 generating or assessing solutions

Remodelled Lesson Plan S-24

Use Socratic questioning to compare the 19ᵗʰ Century viewpoint (perhaps some students will agree with it!) to the modern one on time zones. Use the sentence from the text, "This was a sensible plan, but it took a long time to convince everybody that they ought to tamper with God's time." Relate this to differing contemporary effects of religion on society. Get students to put themselves in the place of rural Americans afraid to change "God's time." **S-3**

Give students Vanderbilt's interview and read it aloud, explaining any difficult language.

"The Public Be --!"

AN OPINION BY THE RAILROAD CRŒSUS ON MATTERS THAT GREATLY INTEREST THE PUBLIC.

Mr. Vanderbilt, in an interview with a Chicago reporter yesterday, expressed himself with unusual freedom, and made some statements that will naturally be read with interest. He said:

The roads are not run for the benefit of the "dear public." That cry is all nonsense. They are built by men who invest their money and expect to get a fair percentage on the same. Freight rates have been altogether too low and the roads have seen that it was the best policy to get together, arrive at an amicable understanding and transact their business on business principles; that is, they will not do business for nothing. I consider that it is an excellent thing to have the rates controlled by the Commissioners who are selected by the roads, but I don't believe in those State Railroad Commissioners. They are usually ignorant persons who have to be bought up by the railroads if any legislation favorable to the road is desired. The idea of having the roads under the control of any set or sets of State Commissioners is nonsense. No cast iron rules which any State may adopt will do for all roads which run through it. The Government should appoint a National Board of Railroad Commissioners, men capable to fill the office, who understand the business, and who will adopt rules of a flexible nature, and who will do all that is possible to encourage the building of roads and not repress it.

In reply to the question as to whether the "limited express" was run to accommodate the public he said:

"The public be --. What does the public care for the railroads except to get as much out of them for as small a consideration as possible? I don't take any stock in this silly nonsense about working for anybody's good but our own, because we are not. When we make a move we do it because it is our interest to do so, not because we expect to do somebody else some good. Of course, we like to do everything possible for the benefit of humanity in general, but when we do we first see that we are benefitting ourselves. Railroads are not run on sentiment, but on business principles and to pay, and I don't mean to be egotistic when I say that the roads which I have had anything to do with have generally paid pretty well."

"What do you think of this anti-monopoly movement?"

"It is a movement inspired by a set of fools and blackmailers. To be sure, there are some men interested in it whose motives are good, if their sense is not. When I want to buy up any politician, I always find the anti-monopolists the most purchasable. They don't come so high."

Use this and the text to lead a Socratic discussion examining the assumptions of the "Go-Getters" in general and evaluating Vanderbilt's arguments. During this discussion, encourage students to reread the interview, and have them quote it to back up their points. "Where does he say that? How do you interpret that statement?" *S-21*

"Explain Vanderbilt's view. What conclusions did he come to? What reasons does he give for each? Are any words or phrases unclear? (What attitudes and behaviors would he accept as *capable* and *flexible?*) Evaluate his reasoning. (For each point, ask,) Should you doubt or accept this claim? Why? What would opponents say? Why? What do you think of the attitudes expressed? Why?" *S-18*

Then evaluate the actions and policies that resulted from railroad expansion. Divide students into pairs or small groups to practice dialogical thinking. In each group Mr. Vanderbilt (and his advisor) would face questioners or opponents. *S-25*

Finally, the teacher could lead the class as a whole in a discussion of the consequences of rapid business expansion in the late 19ᵗʰ Century. "What were the results of this? And what did that lead to? Why? How did these people respond? Those? Why? What positive and negative affects did this have on our world today? **S-35** What should have been done differently? Why? What should we do now? Why?" **S-19**

    editor's note: Have students compare the image of Vanderbilt in their text with that which they get from reading the interview. **S-21**

    What rights and responsibilities do big business owners have? Why? **S-24**

> *To think critically about issues we must be able to consider the strengths and weaknesses of opposing points of view. Since critical thinkers value fairmindedness, they feel that it is especially important that they entertain positions with which they disagree.*

Nigeria

Objectives of the remodelled plan

The students will:
- explore reasons for British colonization of Nigeria and evaluate it
- explore its consequences
- construct the perspectives of different people involved
- discuss causes for Nigeria's present problems, thus practicing historical reasoning

Standard Approach

Some texts introduce the history of Nigeria tracing British colonialism. After the Boer wars, the British moved north into Central Africa, including Nigeria. After WWII, most of Africa was independent. Nigeria, in particular, gained its freedom in 1960, deciding to keep the name given them by the British. Along with other former British colonies, Nigeria joined the Commonwealth of Nations. When the British took over, Nigeria was a land of various different groups with quite different ways of life and languages. They were very hard to hold together in one nation. Their civil war between 1967 and 1970 brought the West and East together. Even today there are communication problems in Nigeria, due to their many languages and customs. In addition, the discovery of oil in Nigeria in 1958 brought changes such as big cities, traffic jams, clogged harbors, limited telephones and gas stations, and housing shortages. Nigeria's problems are hard to solve.

Critique

Study of Nigeria can illustrate how understanding the history of a place is necessary to intelligently discussing its present problems. Here, the original cultures and groups and their differences, colonialism, developing countries and their relationships to developed countries are key elements.

Typically, texts stick to the bare facts, (though once able to feed itself, Nigeria must now import much of its food; Nigerians decided to keep the name 'Nigeria;' Nigeria had a civil war) with little or no explanation of reasons, causes, implications, or evaluations. Many of the details approach deeper issues, but they are not adequately explored or explained.

The concept of colonialism is seriously underdeveloped. The world views and attitudes that allowed and justified colonialism, the reasons underlying it, its effects on culture and development are ignored. Some texts do not really discuss colonization much at all, especially not the

186

opinions of the colonized, except to say that everyone would rather be free like we are. Students are not asked to consider why. Little attempt is made to understand the differences between the many points of view represented in this slice of history. For example, what of the British who were appalled at colonialism, or the tribes and individuals in Africa who welcomed British and western ways? One can't understand colonialism without understanding events and social structures in colonizing powers that supported it.

The fact is offered in one of the texts that Nigeria used to produce nearly all of its food, but now is forced to import much of it. Although the book acknowledges that this is a serious concern, it did not refer to any causes of this situation. The text did not draw out any of the implications if this trend continues, how to reverse this trend, or how it could have been avoided. The students are not invited to wonder how egocentrism, sociocentrism, or differing points of view and culture might have helped to cause this problem and interfere with its solution. Nor do students consider the ways other countries interfere with developing countries' attempts to improve. Nigeria is treated in isolation from the rest of the world.

Texts generally confuse development and modernization with becoming like the U.S., thus failing to recognize the potential variety of forms of development and progress. Other countries must learn from us; we have little to learn from them.

Strategies used to remodel

S-32 making plausible inferences, predictions, or interpretations
S-1 thinking independently
S-35 exploring implications and consequences
S-12 developing one's perspective: creating or exploring beliefs, arguments, or theories
S-15 developing criteria for evaluation: clarifying values and standards
S-20 analyzing or evaluating actions or policies
S-8 developing intellectual perseverance

Remodelled Lesson Plan ——————————

Students could begin by looking at physical, political, and linguistic maps of Africa and West Africa, describing observations, and making inferences. **S-32** When students have read the material, they could do a timeline of events in Africa and Europe.

Interested students could research Nigeria, other colonies, and the colonizing countries, before this section is covered. They could report to the rest of the class during discussion. At the very least, English history of the time should be studied or reviewed, in order to provide background for understanding colonialism. "What do we know of England at the time? How powerful was England? Why? What does this tell us about why England had colonies? What did England get from its colonies? How did it treat its colonies? Why?" **S-17**

Students could compare West African cultures with Great Britain and other European countries.

Who drew Nigeria's boundaries? Would Africans have drawn the same boundaries? What have been long term effects of the way Europeans drew boundaries in West Africa?

How did the British characterize West Africans and colonization? What different kinds of English people were in Africa? Why? What kinds of relationships did they have with native Africans? What reasons did the British government give justifying colonization? How about the Nigerians? Why did the British colonize this area? What different groups might have had opinions on this subject in the U.K.? In Nigeria? Elsewhere? Did England have the right to rule? Should the English have done anything differently? *S-20*

Why did Nigeria gain independence? Compare this to other examples of colonies gaining independence.

What problems does Nigeria face? What are the causes? What features of Nigeria have most influenced its history? What historical facts influence Nigeria presently? Why is Nigeria not producing enough food? *S-1* What has changed? Why? Should other people be worried about this problem? What will happen if this trend continues? How can this be avoided? What would you advise the Nigerians to do? What would happen then? *S-35* Is this what you really want to happen? What would a solution require? With what kinds of knowledge are experts from here and Europe most needed? African experts most needed? Whose knowledge has been most relied on? What kinds of knowledge has been lost?

Why are some countries at a subsistence level? Why is farming poor, medical care scarce, health education poor, and income so low? Should a country want to change this? Why? Why might they? Why wouldn't they? Who might want things to change? Who might not? Does anyone benefit from this situation? What could keep a country from changing when they want to? What could make them change against their will?

Ask students to describe the standard of living in Nigeria. Is it the same for everybody? How many different kinds of living situations can you think of? What was life like before the British arrived, during the British rule, and in the independent Nigeria (at the beginning and now)? When was the quality of life best? In what ways? In what ways worse? For whom? Were other times better for other people? Who? Why do you think so? What are you assuming when you say that life is better? In what ways? In what ways worse? When is it better? When is it better for poor people? When is it better for rich people? Is this true everywhere, in any country, in any culture? *S-12* Have students develop criteria for classifying living arrangements in terms of subsistence, developing economies, and industrial economies. *S-15*

What were the long-range affects of colonialism on Nigeria? Do you think colonialism was justified? What, if anything, should the British have done differently? **S-20** Discussion of colonialism could be extended by having students discuss whether any group of people has the right to rule over others. The issue can be raised, and students reminded of this chapter, whenever relevant during the course of the year. **S-17**

To more fully explore the idea of historical thinking with respect to Nigeria, the teacher could ask, "What perspectives would we need to study in order to develop a complete and fairminded view of Nigerian history? (Different Nigerian groups/cultures, pro- and anti-Western Nigerians, pro- and anti-colonial British.) How would one gain expertise on Nigeria? **S-8**

"Be aware of the hidden curriculum in all schools. If teachers ask only factual questions that test memory and recall, students assume that this is the most important aspect of learning. If principals spend more time focusing on administrative concerns, discipline, or standardized test scores, teachers also assume these aspects of school are the most important." Greensboro Handbook

Economic Systems

Objectives of the remodelled plan

The students will:

- compare and evaluate economic ideals and practices of the U.S. and U.S.S.R.
- examine assumptions underlying economic systems
- compare our attitudes about the U.S.S.R. with our attitudes about similar systems, systems like ours, and completely different systems

Standard Approach

The students are told that, although the U.S. and the U.S.S.R. have similarly good resources, their economies are quite different. The U.S. is characterized by individuals deciding how to spend their money, while in the U.S.S.R. the government decides or commands what shall be produced, and controls land, farms, factories, and industry. Prices in the U.S. are governed by supply and demand, while the Soviet government may set prices to discourage the purchase of certain items. The market economy shows producers that Americans want many consumer goods for their own use. In our free enterprise system, people choose jobs and careers, what to buy, sell, and produce, what to pay and charge. Businesses are run for profit. In the U.S.S.R. many of these decisions are made by the government, not by each individual.

One text offers a chart to show the number of hours a worker in the U.S. and the U.S.S.R. would have to work in order to earn enough to purchase various luxury items. Salaries in the U.S.S.R. are lower than those in the U.S., yet education and skills are rewarded with money, housing, good meats, and cosmetics. The U.S. government does play a role in the U.S. economy, but only to protect consumers and oversee trade with other countries. The government in the U.S. also functions as a buyer/consumer, as a market itself. If our government does anything more directive, it is usually because enough people request help. We take for granted a lifestyle that is only available to the rich in other countries.

Critique

Students studying lessons like this need to grasp how capitalism is supposed to work, the mechanics of it, the view of man and economics on which it is based, and how to evaluate departures from those ideals. They should come to understand communism and how it is supposed to work, what conception and ideals underlie it, and how to evaluate departures therefrom. Texts give abstract principles but little sense of how capitalism is supposed to work and what is required to keep it going; for example, rational consumers and employers, and a government which is neutral toward particular businesses and which prevents businessmen from abusing each other or the public.

The comparison of the two systems is rife with ethnocentricity. It is also full of misleading information. Sometimes texts almost make it sound as though each American individually designs the economy. There is no mention of the factors that inhibit millions of people from participating freely and equally, or other factors in our society which conflict or interfere with ideal capitalism. There is little opportunity for independent thought, as students are told what values and aspirations to have. Students do not have an opportunity to begin to consider different American viewpoints regarding economic problems we face. The texts present only two positions, two choices, us and the good life, or them and oppression. There is little attempt to treat the concept of communism as a communist, or even a neutral party, would. Although one text acknowledged that the U.S.S.R. offers its citizens free education, medical care, and vacations, nothing else was said supporting the ideals or practices of the U.S.S.R.

Strategies used to remodel

S-6 developing intellectual courage
S-1 thinking independently
S-29 noting significant similarities and differences
S-30 examining or evaluating assumptions
S-27 comparing and contrasting ideals with actual practice
S-10 refining generalizations and avoiding oversimplifications
S-25 reasoning dialogically: comparing perspectives, interpretations, or theories
S-3 exercising fairmindedness
S-2 developing insight into egocentricity or sociocentricity
S-35 exploring implications and consequences

Remodelled Lesson Plan S-6

Capitalism

When students have read their texts, they can discuss the negative opinion of the U.S. toward the U.S.S.R. and the negative opinion of the U.S.S.R. toward the U.S. and compare the countries. How is their government different from ours? Their economy? Their industry? **S-1** Students can then begin in-depth analysis of capitalism.

What are the goals of capitalism? For owners? For workers? For consumers? Do these goals conflict? How does the system address the conflict? On what assumptions about people is this system based? What does this system assume about why people work, produce, and create? What evidence is relevant to settling that question? What is your position? Why? **S-30** How is a capitalist economy supposed to provide the best goods and services for the best prices? Why would this system have that result? What does this system assume about how people decide which goods and services to use? What employees to hire? How should these decisions be made?

Now that the ideal system has been set out, students can begin to distinguish actual practice from those ideals. How is our government supposed to protect consumers? From whom? What would producers do? Why? What are some possible economic choices individuals make? What kinds of decisions can your parents make? Not make? **S-10** How do people make economic decisions? How do they decide which brand of a particular product to buy? What role does advertising play in our system? What role should it play? What kinds of forces, factors, attitudes, and habits interfere with the free working of market forces? Do Americans decide what job to take, how much they will be paid? How do individuals help to decide? What are the limitations of our freedom to decide issues for ourselves? Are these deviations from ideal capitalism good, or should they be prevented? If so, how? What interferes with Americans' freedom to determine their careers? **S-27**

Emphasize that no country has a pure version of any economic system. You could talk about some of the aspects of socialism in our economy. You might mention (or have students mention) Social Security, Medicare, or note that government-controlled postal and passenger rail services in the U.S. are further examples of aspects of socialism in our economy. Ask, "In what ways are these 'socialist' in nature?" **S-10**

A written assignment here might be: Explain the goals of capitalism. Consider such things as: fairness, and whether the goals are easy or hard to achieve.

Have students "play capitalist" in a genuinely free market economy, to discover such ideas as supply and demand, etc. They could then discuss and compare their experiences with real situations (e.g., students are given capital and resources to start with).

Socialism

You might list the essential features of socialism for clarity, including some of the benefits that socialism ideally provides, such as comprehensive health care, free education through university level, guaranteed employment, etc. **S-3** For example, ask, "What might be some implications of the features of socialism? How are the services, such as free medical care, paid for? **S-35** What would life be like for a person living under socialism? How would it be different from capitalism? The same? Where is socialism practiced? What are some of the goals and ideals of socialism? What do you think of them?"

When examining our own system, we saw how the form of capitalism we have departs from ideal capitalism. What do you think is true for the Soviets? What evidence do you have for your answer? Where could we get information like this? What do we have to watch for in our information? How could our negative feelings for the U.S.S.R. influence the information we find? **S-16** Why are there unions in some socialist countries? What problems do socialist countries face? Is the U.S.S.R., for example, a classless society? What would be some examples of how class distinctions persist in the Soviet Union? Why? **S-27**

Comparison of the Economic Systems

What problems does each system face? What sort of people does each system claim to reward the most? Actually reward? What sort of people do you think should be rewarded most? Why? What sort of a society would that produce? How could such a system be implemented? **S-1**

What can make each system go wrong? Do you approve of the goals? Have they been achieved? To what extent? Why or why not? **S-27**

How can we find American opinions on other systems of economies and governments? Devise a method to measure American opinion. (Through media or by surveying adults.) Show this information on a chart or graph. Why do most Americans disapprove of communism and socialism so strongly? Notice how we feel about the U.S.S.R. itself. How does this compare to how we feel about countries with systems similar to the U.S.S.R., more similar to us, completely different from both? Who do we like best? Least? How would the U.S.S.R. probably make a scale? Who might they like most and least? Why? How can you explain these differences? **S-2**

Several concluding activities could now tie the lesson together. One would be to assign students to role play defenders and critics of both systems. They could compare the assumptions, basic concepts, and values of each. **S-25**

A written assignment might be given as follows: "People who emigrate from the U.S.S.R. to the U.S. sometimes have difficulty adjusting to our economic system. Could you predict what some of those difficulties might be and why it could be hard for them to adapt?" (The assignment could be reversed for an American taking up residence in the Soviet Union.) **S-3**

Students could write analyses and assessments of their texts.

The highest development of intelligence and conscience creates a natural marriage between the two. Each is distinctly limited without the other. Each requires special attention in the light of the other.

The Constitution

Objectives of the remodelled plan

The students will:

- learn some functions of the three branches of U. S. government
- clarify claims in their texts by exploring root issues regarding government and the distribution of power in our government
- compare ideals of the Constitution with actual practice
- develop criteria for evaluating political candidates
- through Socratic questioning, understand the reasons for and assumptions underlying rights guaranteed under the Bill of Rights
- develop their perspectives on human rights, and functions and limits of government
- transfer insight into the Constitution to current events

Standard Approach

The history of the Constitution, as well as some of its present day applications, is presented. Main themes and concepts are explained such as federalism, separation of powers, judicial review, the Bill of Rights, how a bill becomes law, and democracy. Students are asked to consider the role of these concepts in current American politics. Typical end-of-chapter questions are, "Why did our leaders call the constitutional convention? What were the four main compromises? What were the main arguments for the opponents and the supporters?" Other questions ask for explanation and evaluation, such as,"What is meant by the statement 'The government is you'? Do you agree with the statement? State your reasons." Vocabulary enrichment involves having the students look up words and put them into sentences.

Critique

We chose this lesson because understanding the Constitution is crucial to citizenship in a democracy. Students should explore the ideas underlying important aspects of our government: how it is supposed to work, why it was structured the way it was, how the structure is supposed to preserve citizens' rights, how it could fail to do so, and why rights are important to preserve. Critical education demands clear and well-developed understanding of these points. When understanding is superficial or vague, hidden agendas and mere associations guide thought and behavior. Slogans substitute for reasons, prejudices for thought. Citizens become willing to accept the appearance of freedom, equality under the law, and democracy, rather than insisting on their realization.

The greatest flaw with the standard approach is its lack of depth; not nearly enough time is given to fostering understanding of this important document. The relative importance of different material should be reflected in the text space given and time spent on it. Spending insufficient time on such important ideas leads texts to treat them superficially or vaguely. Students have little opportunity to understand key ideas fully, see the whole picture, appreciate reasons for important parts of the Constitution, or develop their perspectives on government, human relations, and how to preserve their rights.

Texts generally ask too few questions, have little extended discussion, and ask too many questions which are trivial, or simple recall. Some of the suggested explanations and answers are generally sorely incomplete, vague, confusing, or fail to answer the questions. To simply tell students that our government's system of checks and balances helps protect people's freedom does little to help students understand that system or how it is supposed to work.

Important explanations are undeveloped, fail to probe the reasons. Texts offer abstract and unclear explanations, and then merely require students to reiterate them. Often the answers to the end-of-chapter questions are tagged by bold face in the text. Students are encouraged to substitute reiteration for understanding; to accept apparently unconnected answers as adequate explanations, for example, that the right to trial was thought important because it was denied by the British.

Similarly, regarding the Bill of Rights, texts fail to answer the important questions: Why did people think these rights should be written down? What is the advantage? Why write them into the Constitution? Does writing them into the Constitution guarantee they won't be violated? Crucial questions and connections are left unanswered. Neither texts nor students clarify the various Constitutional rights, leaving them in the realm of empty slogans.

Strategies used to remodel

S-21 reading critically: clarifying or critiquing texts
S-17 questioning deeply: raising and pursuing root or significant questions
S-7 developing intellectual good faith or integrity
S-27 comparing and contrasting ideals with actual practice
S-15 developing criteria for evaluation: clarifying values and standards
S-19 generating or assessing solutions
S-24 practicing Socratic discussion: clarifying and questioning beliefs, theories, or perspectives
S-13 clarifying issues, conclusions, or beliefs
S-30 examining or evaluating assumptions
S-12 developing one's perspective: creating or exploring beliefs, arguments, or theories
S-26 reasoning dialectically: evaluating perspectives, interpretations, or theories
S-14 clarifying and analyzing the meanings of words or phrases
S-35 exploring implications or consequences
S-11 comparing analogous situations: transferring insights to new contexts

Remodelled Lesson Plan

Introduction to the Constitution

When the passages about the Constitution and whatever portions of the document students can read have been read, allow students a chance to get the "big picture," by asking, "What is this document for? What is its purpose? What basic points does it cover?" (It defines the three branches of Federal Government, describes how offices are filled, lists duties of and limits on each branch.) You might read the Preamble to the students and discuss it with them. The class could analyze portions of the Constitution in depth. You could then tell the students about some of the details left out of their texts. Students could reiterate the veto and override process, and discuss what protection it gives. **S-21**

Separation of Powers, and Checks and Balances **S-17**

Discussion of the previous point can lead into a discussion of the separation of powers and checks and balances. To probe these ideas in depth, thereby making the reasons for our system of government clearer, you could ask, "Have you ever been in a situation where someone had too much power or abused power? Why was that a problem? How could the problem be solved? How did the authors of the Constitution try to solve it? Why not give all of the power to one branch, say, the Executive? Why can't the President declare war? Why have each branch have some power over the others, rather than giving each branch complete control over its duties? What does the text say in answer to this question? What does its answer mean? How could concentrating power lead to loss of people's rights? **S-21** Make up an example which shows how a system like this could prevent abuse of power. This separation of powers and system of checks and balances is the ideal. What could make it go wrong? How could the President start a war without Congressional approval? Has this ever happened? Should it ever happen? **S-7** Why or why not? Make up an example of how it could go wrong. (Using the checks and balances unfairly, or not using them at all.) Why would that be bad? **S-27** What has to happen to make it work right? What should we look for in our leaders? What sort of people should be chosen? (e.g., when voting for President, voters should consider who the candidate would appoint to important offices or whether the candidate is a good judge of character. Perhaps members of Congress who abuse or fail to use checks on the President should be reconsidered.) **S-15**

The class could also relate some of the above ideas to a specific historical or current issue regarding abuse of power or charges of abuse of power. The students could also try to come up with alternative solutions to the problem of abuse of power and compare their solutions with those in the Constitution. **S-19**

The Bill of Rights **S-24**

Students could generate a list of the rights covered. To foster in-depth understanding of the meaning and importance of the Bill of Rights, the teacher could conduct a Socratic discussion clarifying and analyzing each right with questions like the following: What does this right mean? What does it say people should be allowed to do? How could it be violated or denied? **S-13** Why might people try to take it away? How important is it? Why? Why would not having this right be bad? How would it hurt the individual? Society? Are there exceptions to this right? Should there be these exceptions? Why or why not? **S-17**

The class could also discuss the underlying ideas and assumptions behind the Bill of Rights, especially the First Amendment rights. (The importance of following conscience, especially regarding political and religious beliefs; the belief that when everyone can discuss their ideas and consider all alternatives, the best ideas will prevail or compromise can be reached; people who do no wrong shouldn't have to be afraid of their government; even people who do wrong have rights; trials in which both sides argue before a jury of impartial citizens will best render justice; government has an obligation to be fair to citizens and not make arbitrary or unjust laws; etc.) **S-30** You might ask, "Why did some people want these rights written down? What are the advantages? Are there disadvantages? Are there important rights omitted? Should they be added to the Constitution? Why or why not?"

For this activity, the teacher could split the class into groups, each of which could discuss one or two rights. One member of each group could then report to the rest of the class.

Human Rights Throughout the World S-12

The class could also discuss these rights with respect to people all over the world, and so begin to forge their own perspectives on international politics, human nature, and the role of the U. S. as a world power. Ask, "Do you think everyone all over the world should have these rights? Why or why not?" (You may need to point out that not every country has these rights: In some countries you can be put in jail for disagreeing with your government leaders, even if you don't advocate violence; you can be taken by the police or soldiers, kept, tortured and even killed without ever having a trial; you can be arrested for practicing your religion or for not following the rules of the official religion; etc.) Students could then talk about what, if anything, our government should do about these countries. How should we treat such countries? Should we give them aid or withhold it? What kind of aid? Should we tell them we want them to change, or is it none of our business? What if most of the people of the country voted for the leaders that do these things? If people want to escape these countries, should we let them move here and become citizens? Why do some Americans object to this idea? **S-7** Teachers familiar with the U.N. Declaration of Human Rights could mention it here. If students express different points of view, the teacher could conduct a dialectical exchange by having students defend their views, clarify key concepts, explore assumptions, and note where the perspectives conflict. **S-26** As always in such a discussion, encourage students to listen carefully to, and note strengths in, perspectives with which they disagree.

Purposes and Limits of Government S-17

The lesson could also be used for a discussion probing the purposes and limits of government and deepening students' understanding of government and our Constitution. The Preamble could be re-read to initiate discussion.

197

The following questions could be used to develop an analogy with, say, student government, if the school or class has one: Why do we have student government? What does it do? Are you glad there is student government? Why or why not? Why did the writers of the Constitution believe they had to start a government? Do you agree with them? Why or why not? What does government provide for us? (The class could use a list of Federal Departments to generate some ideas.) How could we have these things without government, or why couldn't we have them without government? What is our government *not* supposed to do? Why?

Students could discuss the concepts 'fair' and 'unfair laws,' or 'just' and 'unjust laws,' with questions like the following: Give me examples of unjust laws. (Discuss each at length — Does everyone agree it is unjust? Why is it unjust?) Why was each made? What justification was given for each law? Then students might summarize the differences between just and unjust laws. *S-14*

Students could compare possible reactions to unjust laws, and the consequences of these reactions. Encourage them to include examples in their discussion. You may use questions like the following: What can people do when their laws are unjust here? Elsewhere? What have different people done? What happened next? Why? *S-35* Students could compare alternatives and their results, for both the individuals and countries. *S-19* Do people have the right to break unjust laws? Why or why not? When? Under what circumstances? If a government has many unjust laws, should other governments do anything about it, or is it none of their business? Why? What, if anything, should be done? What might the people in the unjust government say? Would they think of themselves as unjust? Should we help governments that seem to us to be unjust? *S-12*

Current Events *S-11*

The lesson could also be linked to a unit on the news. The class, or groups of students who could report to the class, could find newspaper articles about major bills being debated or passed, Supreme Court decisions, a Cabinet or Supreme Court nomination, or debates on foreign affairs. The class could outline both sides of the issue, pinpoint the relevant part of the Constitution, and discuss the implications of different possible outcomes. If the issue revolves around interpreting the Constitution, the class could discuss why there is no agreed-upon interpretation. Students could also distinguish aspects of the issue involving the Constitution from aspects which have become part of our government but are not set out in the Constitution.

Remodelling Science Lessons

Introduction

The scientific approach is a very powerful way to know the world. Science provides us with two particular areas of knowledge: one is the kinds of thinking which scientists use to find answers to questions — science process; and the other is the answers themselves — science content. As science teachers, we would like to help our students develop a deep and critical understanding of both of these areas of knowledge. But what is a critical understanding of science process and content?

Rather than tackle the critical approach to science education headlong, let us begin by understanding what a critical approach *is not*. Too often science teaching over-emphasizes narrow mastery of the conventional explanations and techniques of established science. Sometimes this means asking students literally to memorize facts, definitions, diagrams, and so forth. At other times, students are asked to paraphrase a wide array of standard information and explanations and answer standard questions in the physical sciences, life science, or earth science. Many textbooks emphasize preparing students to answer questions like the following, all of which are paraphrased from high school science texts.

- What are the three kinds of volcanoes and how are they formed?
- What are the details of the Kreb's Cycle?
- What are the three parts of a transformer? What kind of electricity does a transformer use?
- How are antibiotics produced? Do antibiotics cure all diseases?
- What are the bonding orbitals on the carbon atom in the methane molecule?

In addition to this kind of content knowledge, high school science teaching often stresses a certain kind of problem solving. We could call the problems to be solved "textbook problems." Most science teachers will quickly recognize textbook problems: problems about balancing equations, calculating an equivalent resistance, figuring out the proportion of second-generation roses which will be pink. The necessary data, and no more, is given in the problem. The method for solving the problem is given in the chapter in the textbook. Whether these problems are easy or hard for students, they represent an approach which asks students to master a standard technique by practicing on several similar problems.

There are good reasons for teaching this kind of content and textbook problem solving in high school science classes. Some of this information is interesting and helpful to students. Some textbook problems help students understand aspects of science. However, mastery of this kind of information alone does not constitute the most powerful approach to science education. Teaching for a critical understanding of science involves additional elements. Let us go on and see what these elements are.

Science education should help students understand how scientists establish their scientific beliefs. In other words, how have scientists learned the knowledge of the world which we want students to learn? Through exploration of this question, students come to a more fully informed understanding of how the very involved and beautiful explanations of professional science have developed. They begin to see that science does not arise in some impersonal way from experiments, but that human thought, in both logical and intuitive forms, plays as important a role as experimental data. In this way, they see that scientific understanding is often powerful, but also fallible. Thus, they become more critically aware "consumers" of the claims made in the name of science which we can read about in the newspapers every day. Understanding scientific thought deeply rather than superficially, they will be less inclined to take psuedo science as real science. But perhaps even more importantly, students develop an attitude of intellectual autonomy, the sense that they too can interpret their world through their own clear observation and critical thought. One attribute of critical thinkers is that they exercise independent thought and recognize that at times it is possible to come to an understanding of the world independent of authorities. Science education should combat the widespread belief that "It's someone else who does and understands science."

One important way to teach students how scientists establish their knowledge is to allow students to investigate actual questions in the laboratory. Many typical laboratory manuals, however, take all the initiative out of the "investigation" by presenting a detailed list of procedures to be followed, the steps to take in thinking about observations, even what the student should observe and conclude. Thus, the lab work is not true investigation, and the steps taken and results found mean little to students. To learn from a laboratory investigation, the students should understand its purpose, have some opportunity to plan the approach, and interpret data or observations. Of course, teachers play an important role in student inquiry through their guidance and structuring, but students can be given the responsibility for designing parts of investigations and interpreting their own data. Some of the remodelled lessons which follow point out ways to do this. In general, students can determine what data they need; design their own data tables; conduct experiments; think about their own interpretation of their data; and discuss their interpretations with classmates who might agree or disagree.

This is a key point in a critical approach to student inquiry: scientific thinking is not a matter of running through a set of steps called "the scientific method." Rather, it is a kind of thinking in which we move back and forth between questions, answers to those questions, and experiments which test those answers. "What do I think about this? If that's so, what will happen when I try ...? Why didn't this come out the way I expected?" In this process, we engage many of the attributes and skills of critical thinking. We must not make snap judgements, we must pose questions clearly, we must see the implications of ideas clearly, we must listen as someone comes to a different interpretation from ours.

Science textbooks usually devote a few pages to a general discussion of "the scientific method." One of the problems with this approach is that there is no one method which all scientists follow. For instance, the work of a theoretical physicist who speculates about the fundamental nature of matter is different than that of the ornithologist trying to understand the behavior of birds. The physicist relies heavily on abstract mathematics, logical considerations, and even a sense of aesthetics, while ornithologists observe the natural environment very carefully and try to find a pattern in their observations. So these two scientists use a very different set of "tools" in their work. As another example, some scientists do experiments, but not all do. Chemists can go into the lab and try a reaction in a variety of conditions; in this way they can test a theory about reactions. But evolutionary biologists can not see what would have evolved if the situation had been different; they can only look at various kinds of evidence left behind by what has already happened. So these two scientists must work in different ways, with one able to perform experiments in the laboratory and the other unable to experiment but forced to rely on historical data.

Science is more than ways of thinking, however. Science includes a vast array of interlocking factual information, concepts, and theories which provide us with one particular way of understanding ourselves and the world. In this introduction, we will discuss two key features of a critical approach to teaching science content. First, that a critical understanding of science content emphasizes understanding of the fundamental ideas of science and their relationships, rather than shallow understanding of lots of material. Second, that teaching for a deep understanding must include the recognition that students come to our classes with already well-established intuitive ideas about many areas of science.

The debate about coverage versus depth is old. While there may be reasons to emphasize a brief treatment of many science subjects, advocates of the critical approach to science teaching argue that students will understand science better and become better thinkers generally, if they come to a deeper understanding of the central ideas of science. Since it takes time for students to grasp the implications of ideas and to see the connections between various scientific concepts and explanations, we must spend more time on selected material.

It is beyond the scope of this introduction to outline the most important ideas in high school science. We encourage you to review your own teaching to assure yourself that you are providing students the time and experience they need to reach a deep understanding of the ideas central to the science you teach. If we discuss one particular example, though, it will help us understand the point. In high school biology, students are introduced to the basic principles of plant growth. They are introduced to a long list of ideas like chloroplasts, photosynthesis, light reaction, dark reactions, and so forth. They learn about stomata, roots, the cambrium. After all this, try asking them the following simple question. "There is a one-thousand pound oak tree outside the window. Where did that thousand pounds of stuff come from?" I have tried this question on many of my students. Several other teachers I know have also, and we all find the same thing; many students don't know that the raw materials to make a tree are basically water from the ground and carbon dioxide from the air. Though we have taught the details of photosynthesis to some degree, we have failed to help many students understand one of the most basic concepts about plants. When we try to teach for a critical understanding, we should pay more attention to the deep ideas and try not to lose the forest for the trees.

Our second point involves the preconceptions that students have concerning the science topics we teach. Science educators must recognize that students of all ages have their own ideas about the world around us. From our earliest years on, we develop ideas about the growth of plants, the motions of pendulums, how birds can fly, and many other everyday experiences. These pre-conceptions play a very strong role when we teach for the deep understanding implied by a critical approach to science education. It is not enough to present the established knowledge of science. Every science teacher has experienced giving a clear and articulate explanation only to find, with a sinking feeling, that her or his students did not "get it." Reading or listening to an explanation is not enough to replace the students' original beliefs. The *Proceedings of the International Seminar on Misconceptions in Science and Mathematics* gives an example of a child who was presented with evidence about electrical current flow which was incompatible with the child's preconceptions. In response to a demonstration, the child replied, "Maybe that's the case here, but if you come home with me you'll see it's different there."* A critical approach to teaching science content recognizes that students must first articulate their own beliefs if they are to modify them in the light of their school experiences. Science teaching must begin by helping students to clarify and state their preconceptions so that students can go on to develop the deeper, more accurate understanding which is the goal of the critical approach to science education. Some of the remodelled lessons which follow suggest ways in which this might be accomplished.

As you think about the critical approach to science teaching, keep these things in mind. We must try to emphasize the fundamental ideas rather than a myriad of factual detail. We must try to emphasize a flexible understanding of science concepts and problem solving rather than just drill and practice to master some standard explanations and problems. And finally, we must help students understand how scientists answer questions through both experiment and thought.

---

* Hugh Helm & Joseph Novak, "A Framework for Conceptual Change with Special Reference to Misconception," Presented at the International Seminar on Misconceptions in Science and Mathematics, Cornell University, Ithaca, NY, 1983.

Titration

Objectives of the remodelled plan

The students will:
- learn the technique of titration and some of its applications
- think independently by clarifying their results
- transfer insights and make interdisciplinary connections by discussing applications of key concepts

Standard Approach

Students will obtain samples of standard acid and base solutions of unknown concentration from the teacher and follow the procedure outlined in the laboratory manual, to determine the concentration of the base. At least three trials should be done, and reasons stated in the discussion section of the laboratory report, for variations in results among the three trials.

Critique

This lesson fails to take advantage of the information and mis-information which students already possess regarding the roles of acids and bases in the world around them and in their own bodies. The process of titration has numerous applications in pure science and industry. These applications and their importance should be brought out.

Strategies used to remodel

S-1   thinking independently
S-11 comparing analogous situations: transferring insights to new contexts
S-23 making interdisciplinary connections
S-9   developing confidence in reason

Remodelled Lesson Plan

Students will be encouraged to tell what they think the word "neutralization" means and will, after discussion of the various interpretations of this term, be presented with the process from the point of view of the chemist. Relationships between volume and molarity of acids and bases and the titration process will be explained. Students will proceed to the laboratory where the process of titrating a sample of a solution of sodium hydroxide of unknown concentration will be demonstrated. Students will carry out the appropriate calculations to determine the concentration of the unknown solution. Class results will be presented, in the form of a table, on the chalkboard, and reasons for variations will be discussed so that the method may be clarified. **S-1**

Students will be asked to name substances which they are likely to encounter on a day-to-day basis which would lend themselves to the titration process. **S-11** Possibilities would include household ammonia, vinegar, lemon and lime juices, etc. A discussion of a variety of indicators which might be used with these substances should be postponed, as it would only complicate matters.

Students will be asked to bring substances from home which might be titrated to determine their acid or base concentration. Care must be taken that, when these substances are titrated, they are properly diluted.

A discussion of the application of the titration process to medicine and industry will serve to relate this laboratory exercise to other branches of science. **S-23**

editor's note: Have students describe what happens when they are conducting their tests, explain why the procedure is as it is, and explain how they make their calculations and why. "What, exactly are you doing? Why? What effect will that have? What are these liquids doing in there during this process? Why use this? Why have that control? What would happen if we ...? How might that affect our results? Why? What does this information tell you? What do you need to know? What numbers do you need? Why? What equation are you using? Why? Which numbers go where? Why?" Etc. **S-9**

> *Teachers who can formulate and articulate what attitudes and behaviors they are trying to foster, why they are important, and how they foster them in their classrooms, are more likely to be able to create an appropriate atmosphere and to structure classroom activities that lead to good student thinking.*

The Nervous System

Objectives of the remodelled plan
The students will:
- learn the parts of the nervous system and their functions
- think independently and share what they know about the parts of the nervous system
- relate this knowledge to diseases of the nervous system
- predict results of breakdown of parts of the nervous system

Standard Approach

Students will locate the terms describing the parts of the human nervous system in their text and record the terms in the proper spaces on the worksheets distributed at the beginning of class. In addition, students will be asked to write, in their own words, a description of the function of each of the parts of the nervous system which they have located.

Critique

This lesson does not attempt to relate the names and functions of the parts of the human nervous system to the health of the students. No attempt is made to incorporate information which is vital to the students regarding acute and chronic diseases of the nervous system or the effects of substances, both controlled and uncontrolled, on the nervous system.

Strategies used to remodel
S-1 thinking independently
S-23 making interdisciplinary connections
S-32 making plausible inferences, predictions, or interpretations

Remodelled Lesson Plan

Students will be asked to label as many of the parts of the nervous system as they can without making use of their textbooks. Discussion will then be carried out, with sharing of information until all of the key parts of the nervous system are labeled on the drawings with which they have been supplied. Using their texts only as much as necessary, students will, working in small groups, prepare a list of functions of each of the parts of the nervous system which they have labeled. **S-1**

Information will then be gathered from the group regarding diseases of the nervous system with which the students might be familiar through contact with patients. Information will be presented regarding the similarities and differences among these diseases. There will also be a brief discussion of diseases such as polio with which the students have had little or no contact.

Students will be encouraged to bring to school clippings and articles from magazines regarding diseases and injuries to the nervous system. These will be shared orally for discussion and comment. In addition, a film will be shown, at a later date, describing the effects of drugs and alcohol on the nervous system. At all times, an attempt will be made to be consistent in the use of the proper terminology for the parts of the nervous system, in order to reinforce the learning which took place on the first day. **S-23**

editor's note: To allow further opportunity for independent reasoning, students could predict what would happen to someone who suffered a breakdown of each of the parts of the nervous system which they have named and labeled, before being informed of such diseases. "If this has this function, what would happen if it no longer functioned fully or at all? Why do you say so? What would that be like for the victim?" Students' predictions could then be compared with the diseases discussed. **S-32**

Follow up brainstorming sessions with discussion of the items listed — categorizing, evaluating, analyzing, comparing, ordering, etc.

Scientific Reasoning: Do Snails See?

Objectives of the remodelled plan

The students will:
- develop confidence in their ability to reason scientifically
- propose experiments to provide evidence on the key question
- clarify, through discussion, that the interpretation of experiments are based on assumptions
- develop intellectual humility by examining their preconceptions

Standard Approach

Many standard biology texts devote a very large proportion of their effort to descriptive information. They tell the student how an organism is classified, how it's put together, how it all works. The standard approach to discussing the mollusks, for instance, is to talk about "mollusks with one shell" and to use the snail as a particular example. Generally, a text devotes about one page to the snail. In that page, students read about the evolution of the snail, they see a diagram of its structure and a brief description of "how the snail works." Among many other statements, there is always a statement to the effect that land snails have eyes on the tips of two tentacles.

Critique

Instruction in the life sciences emphasizes information on the processes and physiology of cells and organisms. Too often, however, we forget that science education should also include experience with the ways in which scientists establish this information. An understanding of the ways of science is important for two reasons. First, as students grow in their ability to understand how scientific ideas are established, they become more critically informed "consumers" of scientific knowledge. They learn that scientific knowledge is established by people more-or-less like themselves. They also learn that scientific knowledge does not come with an ironclad guarantee that it is "correct." Second, by learning the ways of science, students will begin to be able to transfer those same skills to experiences they encounter in their own everyday lives. They begin to develop the attitudes and skills needed to become intellectually more autonomous and to come to their own understanding of the world based on their own experience and critical thought.

Another problem with the discussions of "scientific method" found in texts is that they are often rather abstract. Students usually cannot make much sense of these kinds of discussions. They can memorize a list of steps, but they often cannot apply these steps in particular actual situations. As with all of our teaching, we must give students practice applying general, abstract ideas to particular situations. For that reason, this remodelled discussion focuses on helping students understand how scientists go about answering questions like "Can snails see?"

Strategies used to remodel

S-9　developing confidence in reason
S-5　developing intellectual humility and suspending judgment
S-30　examining or evaluating assumptions
S-33　evaluating evidence and alleged facts
S-13　clarifying issues, conclusions, or beliefs
S-3　exercising fairmindedness

Remodelled Lesson Plan *S-9*

We could start this lesson with a discussion of snails and their behavior in order to bring out students' preconceptions. **S-5** "Do you believe snails can see? What makes you believe this? Are you certain? Why or why not?" Often, students express a range of opinions of the "sightedness" of snails. Some of the reasons for their beliefs could be called "theoretical." For example, some students say that all animals have eyes, therefore snails must have eyes. Others say that those stalks on snails heads look like eyes so they must be eyes. Other students have reasons for their beliefs which could be called "experimental" in the sense that they are based on observational evidence. Examples of this might be the fact that snails are active at night, when it it dark, so they must be able to tell light from dark. All these reasons provide a context for students to practice many of the critical thinking skills like examining assumptions and evidence. We can help our students practice these skills by asking questions like the following? "Can you be sure they are eyes just because they look like eyes? Are you sure that all animals have eyes? **S-30** Snails do come out at night, but that might be because it is cooler out. If that were so, could you still be sure that they were telling light from dark?" **S-33**

After questioning students about their present beliefs and reasons we turn to "experimental" ways to explore these ideas. It would be ideal if students could actually observe snails in the classroom as they test their ideas, but discussion may be the only possibility. To have students clarify this scientific conclusion, we could start by asking, "What would be the difference in the snails' behavior if they could see or if they couldn't see?" Perhaps a student would respond that snails would back away from a bright light. We could ask "Would shining a flashlight at a snail and observing its behavior *prove* that the snail either could, or couldn't see? Could other explanations be consistent with that evidence?" **S-13** Depending on the particular responses which students made, you might suggest *1)* that the light bulb also is hot, and that might be what the snail sensed; *2)* that the light might not be bright enough to affect snails; *3)* that snails might *like* bright lights and might have moved toward the light. While some of these possibilities seem a little far-fetched, they do illustrate that experimental proof in science is complex, and that the implications of an experiment depend on assumptions.

Discussions of this sort also give students practice in listening to the arguments of others. **S-3** Through this kind of discussion, we can help students to critically examine how they, and scientists in general, might establish reasons for holding their beliefs. In this way, students can come to see scientific knowledge as the result of thought and evidence working together, and they will also begin to understand that evidence is *interpreted* in order to arrive at knowledge. Scientific knowledge does not arise unambiguously out of experiments.

School time is too precious to spend any sizeable portion of it on random facts. The world, after all, is filled with an infinite number of facts. No one can learn more than an infinitesimal portion of them. Though we need facts and information, there is no reason why we cannot gain facts as part of the process of learning how to think.

Inferences and the Structure of Atoms

Objectives of the remodelled plan

The students will:
- think more precisely about thinking by developing a concept of 'inference' distinguished from evidence
- practice making and assessing inferences in everyday contexts
- practice making inferences in the specific context of the Marsden Rutherford experiment on atomic structure

Standard Approach

> Texts often introduce the idea of the atom in a straight-forward way. The ideas of the Greeks are discussed briefly and Dalton's atomic theory is presented along with a brief review of the kinds of evidence which led Dalton to these ideas. The general structure of the atom is presented by making some statements about protons, neutrons, and electrons and their location in the atom. The experiments of Marsden and Rutherford in which gold foil was bombarded with a beam of alpha particles are described. The implications of this experiment are discussed through statements like the following: "To everyone's surprise, a very small fraction of the alpha particles bounced back. Rutherford proposed that the mass of the atom and the positive charge are concentrated in a small region. He called this region the nucleus. He thought of the rest of the atom as more or less empty space."

Critique

This standard approach is straightforward and may be appropriate as a simple introduction to the basic structure of the atom. The approach is direct and it is easy for students to master, at a simple level at least, the names of the three basic subatomic particles, their properties, and their locations inside the atom.

This chapter could, however, be expanded to teach students something about *inferring* as a general thinking skill. In addition, students could be exposed to the idea that our picture of the atom is not a picture in the literal sense at all, but is an inference based on experimental data like Marsden's and Rutherford's along with theoretical ideas like the nature of electrical forces and so forth. In the remodelling discussion, we will discuss some ways in which the material of this chapter could be used to teach about inferences.

Strategies used to remodel

S-28 thinking precisely about thinking: using critical vocabulary
S-32 making plausible inferences, predictions, or interpretations
S-33 evaluating evidence and alleged facts
S-18 analyzing or evaluating arguments, interpretations, beliefs, or theories
S-13 clarifying issues, conclusions, or beliefs

Remodelled Lesson Plan S-28

You might begin teaching about inferences through a class discussion, like the examples which follow, of inferences in everyday settings.

"In everyday life, we think many things are true from very simple things, like, 'my dog is standing outside the door' to very complex things like 'the world is built of very tiny things called atoms.' Have you ever stopped to think about how you know what is true?

"We think some things are true because we believe that we have direct evidence. For instance, you might see your dog standing outside the door and so you know that he is there. You know because you can see him. But we also believe things are true even though we do not have such clear or direct evidence. Suppose you are in your house and you hear a scratching noise coming from the front door. Just as before, you might believe that it is true that your dog is standing at the door. But this time, the evidence is different; you don't actually see him, but the sound you hear makes you think he is at the front door. You might think this because you can't think of any better explanation for the noise. So you think it is your dog. We call this process 'making an inference.' An inference is something we believe to be true based on some evidence.

"We can not be sure of the truth of all of our inferences. But some inferences are better than others. In our dog example, for instance, if we hear his chain rattling and hear him barking and scratching we could be pretty sure that it is him outside the door. We could say we are pretty sure about this inference. If, on the other hand, all we heard was some scratching, we might sill infer he was out there, but this time inference is less sound. It could be we are hearing some other animal, perhaps a raccoon.

"Sometimes we get so used to making a particular inference that we do not even realize that we are inferring. If every time we hear scratching at the door we find out that it is our dog, we just take for granted that scratching means our dog is out there. We get used to taking the scratching as direct evidence that our dog is there. Many of the 'facts' of science are really inferences, but we are so used to them that we do not consider them any longer to be inferences, we often just take them for truth. But it is important to remember that things like the details of atoms are really inferences from evidence and not something we have observed directly."

After this general introduction, students could review their general sense of the process of inference by answering the following questions. There are sever-

211

al possible answers to some of these questions. This reinforces the idea that when we make inferences, we can not be sure of the truth of our inferences, even when we have considered the evidence rationally.

1. While sitting in a sunlit room, you notice that the direct sunlight has quit coming through the window. What are the different things you might infer?

2. A few minutes after the sunlight quit coming through the window, you could observe drops of water falling from the sky. Does this provide any additional evidence for your inference? **S-32**

3. Can you be sure that what you have inferred is true? Why or why not? What additional evidence would support or undermine your inference? **S-18**

    Students could then be asked to describe other everyday examples of inferring.

    Now that your students understand some general ideas about inferences, you can apply this understanding to the subject of this chapter, the basic structure of the atom, and especially to the evidence of Marsden and Rutherford. The following questions are helpful:

1. We say the atom is made of a very small positively charged nucleus and negatively charged electrons which exist outside of the nucleus. Some evidence relating to the discovery of the nucleus was provided by the experiments of Marsden and Rutherford when they shot alpha particles at a gold foil. Briefly, what is that evidence?

2. After reviewing this evidence, would you say that scientists have directly observed the nucleus or have they inferred that it was there? **S-33**

3. Can you think of any other explanation that might account for their results? **S-32**

4. Explain whether or not their evidence shows that atoms of the different elements all have the same basic structure of a positive nucleus surrounded by negative electrons. **S-33**

5. Summing up, would you say that we know the basic structure of atoms for sure from their experiments with alpha particles and gold foil? **S-13**

    After students have learned more about atoms, they could discuss other evidence which supports the idea.

"It does no good to know the right answer, if you don't know what it means."
quote from a student

Ectothermy

by Carol R. Gontang, Mountain View
High School, Mountain View, CA

Objectives of the remodelled plan

The students will:
- ask and clarify a question and propose a hypothesis
- generate and assess lab procedures to settle the question
- organize and evaluate their data
- make inferences from their results
- deeply question scientific reasoning by exploring the relative significance of various zoological classifications
- modify hypotheses, if necessary, to fit data
- examine and correct their original misconceptions

Standard Approach

Students are given a set of instructions to perform the experiment of counting breaths a goldfish takes in various temperatures. The instructions provide background information and direct the students' thinking about the problem. The procedure is provided in detail. Students are told how to graph the results. Students are called upon to make a hypothesis, collect data, and come to a conclusion.

Critique

This experiment, like most others in high school lab books, is intended to confirm a concept that has already been presented to students. Since students know this, it often leads to more confusion. High school students often have firmly-held beliefs that are based upon their own limited experience, and these ideas are not easily broadened. They tend to interpret the results of experiments in light of these limited ideas and not to look for the application of new ideas. If these students are negligent in their reading and thinking (as many students are) they will assume that the experiment is confirming their preconceived notions and will interpret data in this way. In this case, the fundamental difference between endotherms and ectotherms is the idea that may be missed unless the student is actively involved in both the design and the analysis of the experiment.

Strategies used to remodel

S-1 thinking independently
S-29 noting significant similarities and differences
S-17 questioning deeply: raising and pursuing root or significant questions
S-19 generating or assessing solutions
S-32 making plausible inferences, predictions, or interpretations
S-5 developing intellectual humility and suspending judgment

Remodelled Lesson Plan

Day one

In small groups, students could be asked to brainstorm what they know about fish for three minutes. This list is shared and put on the board. Next, they are asked to brainstorm what they know about cold-bloodedness versus warm-bloodedness, and this list is also put on the board. **S-1**

Next, each team of students is given a goldfish to observe for five minutes. The fish is in a beaker of water. Some beakers are set in larger bowls containing warm water, and some in ice chips. Students are asked to write down as many observations as possible about the fish and its surroundings. Students are asked to report their observations and "warm" teams and "cold" teams compare what they saw. One inevitable observation is that the fish in warm water were breathing faster than the fish in cold water. The teacher could focus the discussion on this fact and on the idea of metabolism. Other observations, like increased movement in warm water could be related to this. **S-29**

The teacher asks the class to think about a good scientific question or two that could be asked about this situation. This discussion should include discussion of what is meant in science by a good question. "Can we test this question? How? Why ask this? What value does the answer have?" **S-17** Through questioning, the students can also be reminded that data involving a larger number of fish will be more reliable than data only involving one or two fish, so the entire class should follow the same procedure and combine data.

In small groups, students can decide upon a procedure to propose to the class. Each group can then present its proposal, and the class can decide upon which one to follow. "Would this procedure answer our question? Would the results be accurate? What, exactly are we looking for?" **S-19**

Day two

Students follow the procedure decided upon on day one, and collect data.

Day three

Data from the various teams is combined on the board, and the meaning of the data is discussed. "What did we find? What does it mean? What can we infer from these results?" **S-32** This discussion should now focus upon the idea of endothermy and ectothermy, and the difference between the way the fish responded and the way a mammal or bird would respond in a similar situation. "Are mammals affected the same way? What accounts for the difference? How? Why?"**S-29**

The data is likely to involve the variables of temperature and breathing rate, and the teams can be given time in groups to review graphing techniques. The remainder of the time on day three can be given to the groups to organize their notes and start work on their lab papers. The paper can be a group product.

editor's note: Students could review their original brainstormed ideas, evaluate them, and discuss possible connections between the items they mentioned and their experiments. "Does this point have any connection to our study? What? Why? How sure can we be of this? How could we find out for sure?" **S-5**

How important is the distinction between warm and cold-blooded animals? Why? What distinctions are more important to zoologists? Why? Less important? Why? Students can examine charts showing biological classifications, and explore possible reasons for the hierarchy of distinctions. (For example, vertebrates versus invertebrates is a more basic and therefore more important distinction than that studied in this lab.) **S-17**

Did any categorizations surprise you? Do zoologists group together animals that seem very different? Which? How can we find out why they are grouped this way? (For example, students may be surprised at some of the animals considered rodents. They could look the term up in a glossary, dictionary, encyclopedia, or text index, and speculate on the significance of the category.) **S-17**

> *We learn how to learn by learning, think by thinking, judge by judging, analyze by anlyzing; not by reading, hearing, and reproducing principles guiding these activities, but by using those principles. There is no point in trying to think for our students.*

Periodic Trends in the Elements

Objectives of the remodelled plan

The students will:
- predict trends of some important atomic characteristics
- give reasons for their predictions, engaging in dialogical discussion of them
- check the accuracy of their predictions against explanations given in their texts

Standard Approach

Many chemistry texts approach the idea of "chemical periodicity" in a similar way. They begin with a brief review of the historical work of Mendeleev. They say that he listed the elements in order of atomic number and then was able to note periodic occurrence of particular chemical properties. These texts then go on to present the modern periodic table. They explain the particular form the periodic table takes, by referring to the electron populations of the various atomic orbitals. These texts also explain several different characteristics of atoms including atomic radius, ionization energy, electron affinity, chemical reactivity, and others in terms of the electronic configuration of the atoms and their location on the periodic table.

Critique

The standard approach raises two questions. First, the content represented by this approach to the topic of chemical periodicity is complicated and abstract. Students must master several fundamental concepts in order to understand the underlying causes for the periodicity of many atomic properties. These concepts include atomic orbitals, especially the energies and spatial distributions of electrons in the various orbitals. Attentive and motivated high school students can state definitions, facts, and some standard explanations about these kinds of topics. When approached with a somewhat new situation, however, these same students often give evidence of not clearly understanding these topics. Are the broad goals of high school science education well served by teaching material which is so abstract that it may be beyond the understanding of our better students? The usual answer is that those students who go on to college chemistry will need this background. In our view, there is some basis to this. High school science teachers must weigh the question of how much of their teaching is justified only by the preparation of their students for future study. It is also our view, however, that a clear understanding of the fundamental ideas of science serves the needs of all students, regardless of their future plans by helping them understand and retain the essence of important scientific concepts. For these reasons, we caution teachers to think carefully about their emphasis on the many details which could be included under the topic "chemical periodicity."

Our second point concerns the depth of understanding which students develop from the standard approach to chemical periodicity. Texts often cover a wide range of atomic characteristics, including atomic radius, ionization energy, electron affinity, chemical reactivity, ionic size, electronegativity and others. We must ask, however, how well students understand the *fundamental concepts* which explain the trends we can observe across the periodic table. Our students give us evidence of their level of real understanding when we observe how they study for this chapter. We often see their periodic tables marked up with arrows indicating that the ionization energy goes up as we go to the right on the table along with arrows indicating that the atomic radius goes down, and so forth. While these are important facts to a practicing chemist, what we really want is for our students to understand *why* these trends are observed. It's really more important for them to understand the *why* of all these trends, than to know the direction of each trend. For this reason, our remodel focuses on strategies for helping students understand the important concepts underlying chemical periodicity rather than on learning the trends in the properties themselves.

In general, we think that it is a good strategy to emphasize mastery of a few fundamental ideas rather than emphasizing knowledge of the detailed information which practicing scientists use in their work. As a basic strategy in teaching periodicity, we suggest that you emphasize understanding and applying the fundamental concepts of energies and sizes of orbitals. You can do this by using activities which require students to make predictions of the various periodic properties like atomic size, ionization energy, and so forth. In this way, you do two things. First, when students predict these trends, they pay more attention to the basic ideas themselves than to the direction of the particular trends. This helps students learn the basic ideas and it also gives them insight into how science can be seen as the sum of a relatively few basic ideas. Second, asking students to make predictions is one of the bast ways for you to check their understanding of basic ideas. By listening to them explain how they arrived at their predictions, you can get an accurate sense of their understanding.

First, you should consider for yourself what the basic ideas of this chapter are. All the trends mentioned in the standard approach to chemical periodicity can be predicted on the basis of three fundamental ideas: *1)* for a given principal quantum number, the energies of the electrons with that principal quantum number are lowered if the nuclear charge is increased; *2)* for a given principal quantum number, the electrons are pulled closer to the nucleus as the nuclear charge is increased; and *3)* as the principal quantum number is increased, both the energy and distance of the electron from the nucleus increase. This effect can overpower the opposite effect of greater nuclear charge. The first two of these ideas can be explained simply in terms of greater nuclear attraction. The third idea is more difficult to explain, since it is the result of a feature of quantum mechanics overpowering the effect of greater nuclear attraction. The point of this remodelling discussion, however, is not to analyze the three fundamental ideas in detail. We are demonstrating that it is possible to list the few basic ideas of a chapter and then to review them with students so that they can practice using the basic ideas to make predictions.

Strategies used to remodel
S-25 reasoning dialogically: comparing perspectives, interpretations, or theories
S-32 making plausible inferences, predictions, or interpretations

Remodelled Lesson Plan S-25

You should present your own form of the basic ideas to your students, and then present them with some challenges. "Can any of you use these ideas to predict how the size of atoms will change as we go across a row of the periodic table? Down a column? **S-32** What are your reasons for this prediction?" Encourage students to argue with each other, trying to justify their positions. Through these kinds of questions, you will help your students think about the basic ideas. You will also encourage them to look at the graphs and tables in the text with more curiosity, since they will be trying to find the information to prove whether the class's predictions were accurate. "Can anyone find a graph or table in the chapter which will let us check the accuracy of these predictions?" This simple technique encourages them to be more active processors of information. Having made predictions, the correct answers and explanations will mean more to them than if they are given from the start.

In the same way you can ask them to predict some of the other trends such as ionization energy. **S-32** While we do hope that their predictions will be accurate, keep in mind that it's the spirit of thoughtful prediction you are encouraging. In this way, topics like periodic trends can be used to encourage thoughtful exploration of basic ideas, rather than mastery of detailed information which remains unconnected in students' minds and is often misapplied later.

Teachers need time to reflect upon and discuss ideas, they need opportunities to try out and practice new strategies, to begin to change their own attitudes and behaviors in order to change those of their students, to observe themselves and their colleagues — and then they need more time to reflect upon and internalize these concepts.

Snell's Law: Designing Labs

Objectives of the remodelled plan

The students will:
- design a laboratory procedure for taking data to provide an answer to a question, thus developing confidence in using reasoning to solve problems
- provide an answer which is justified by reasoning from their own observations

Standard Approach

Many laboratory manuals introduce the index of refraction of a substance by defining it as "the ratio of the speed of light in a vacuum to its speed in the substance." These lab manuals might then state that "All indices of refraction are greater than one," and "The index of refraction is also obtained from Snell's Law, which states that the ratio of the sine of the angle of incidence to the sine of the angle of refraction is a constant for all angles of incidence." They may also state that "If a ray enters a more dense optical medium obliquely, it is bent toward the normal." A typical approach would be to give two objectives to students: *1)* measure angles of incidence and refraction; and *2)* calculate the index of refraction of glass using Snell's Law. Many manuals give a step-by-step procedure, a data table, directions for calculations, and several questions for interpreting the data. Students will sometimes be able to find the answers to some of these questions in the introductory paragraph for this activity.

Critique

One problem with this standard approach, from the point of view of encouraging critical thinking, is that students are directed to perform a series of measurements *without* first conceiving a question or planning a strategy. The point of the activity unfolds only through the questions in the "Conclusions" part of the activity, which is located at the end of the activity. The problem with this design is that students are asked to engage in a series of measurements which have no apparent relationship to any particular question. This "cookbook" approach to laboratory instruction is very common in commercial lab manuals, and this particular case gives us a good example in which to discuss an alternative approach. In addition, by asking students to copy a particular data table (for which a model is given in the text), no chance is given for the students to invent a way to organize the data they are about to take. Again, this strategy removes another opportunity for students to organize their own approach to answering a question. The remodelled discussion will focus on this lab as an example of a general approach to lab procedures designed by the students with substantial teacher direction. We will call this process "directed student-invention" of labs.

Another problem, perhaps related to the first, is that the three questions posed by the manual are actually answered in the introductory paragraph. This reinforces the attitude that there is nothing really to be learned by actually investigating in the lab.

This activity also gives us the chance to raise the question of the *appropriateness* of particular science concepts for high school students. Refraction is an interesting and important characteristic of light. The quantitative, trigonometric expression of Snell's Law is one way of looking at refraction, but this quantitative expression may well mask the more fundamental qualitative understanding students should develop. For instance, what is the physical meaning of the statement that "All indices of refraction are greater than one?" Of course this means that light travels slower through any material than it does through a vacuum. But the manual does not make this clear, nor does it cause the student to think about this.

The major change needed in this lesson is to reduce the cookbook style in which directions are given by the lab manual. This can be done by asking the students to "invent" the lab without the use of the lab manual. Of course it would be foolish to ask students to invent their labs with no help; after all, many bright people have worked over a long period of time to understand the science we now teach in schools, and we certainly cannot expect our students to invent everything they are to learn or do. But students can consider certain kinds of questions and, with their teachers' guidance, design a way to find answers which are based on their own analysis of data they take in lab. It is often necessary to ask questions which are simple enough for students to really understand what the question means and design a procedure to find an answer. This necessity can be viewed as a "blessing in disguise," since it encourages us to limit the concepts to ones which students can understand and investigate in a deep and critical way.

Strategies used to remodel
S-9   developing confidence in reason
S-19   generating or assessing solutions
S-11   comparing analogous situations: transferring insights to new contexts

Remodelled Lesson Plan S-9

The basic approach to "student-designed" labs is to pose a question in an intriguing way and then guide the class, through an interactive discussion, to a procedure for settling it. Clearly, if you ask students to invent something, you may get a wide range of inventions, or in this case, a wide range of possible laboratory procedures. While there are pros and cons to various approaches, we suggest you guide the students' thinking and discussion sufficiently that the class as a whole converges to a common procedure. Moreover, a skillful teacher can guide the class to an approach he or she knows will work. Often, this procedure could be the one that the lab manual has suggested. But the important point is that the students will become more aware of the actual question to which they are trying to find an answer, and they will have a better understanding of the reasons for the particular procedure they will use.

One practical technique for using this approach is for you to discuss with the class possible approaches to the lab while you make a record of the class's conclusions on the overhead projector. In many cases, it is useful to have this discussion the day preceding lab day. The use of the overhead has two advantages. First, you have the ability to shape the written record. You can reject or accept ideas, reword ideas, and generally control the discussion. Second, the notes (including drawings, ideas for tables and graphs, etc.) can be projected the next day to help students remember what they are to do, what kind of table to make, and so forth. **S-19** Since the record was made during class discussion, it is familiar to students and they will tend to feel a kind of psychological ownership of the procedure they are following. **S-9**

A variation of the Snell's Law lab discussed here is ideally suited to this technique of teacher-directed student invention. The full trigonometric expression of Snell's Law is probably too obscure for most students to investigate, but a simpler qualitative sense of the law is appropriate for student investigation without use of cookbook-like instructions. The question for investigation could be posed by having students experiment with familiar demonstrations like viewing a coin in the bottom of a cup first empty and then filled with water, or observing a straight rod inserted into a container of water. Both these demonstrations give the teacher a chance to ask how light is bent as it passes into or out of transparent media. We are not suggesting that most students could deal with this question productively without some help, and this is one of the points where you must give some information or help, but not too much. One approach is to stick two large pins or nails into a board and ask the class where you would have to put your eye along the surface of the board to make the more distant pin appear to lie behind the closer pin. Of course they will respond that you eye should go on a straight line drawn through the location of the two pins. But what does this prove? Perhaps it will not be immediately obvious to your students, but this simple observation shows that light from both pins travels in a straight line to your eye. That is why you cannot see the one pin in its location behind the other.

With some classes you could now give them their own setups and tell them to view the two pins through a rectangular piece of glass. With rather able students, it will be sufficient to tell them that they can now invent a way to answer the question generated during the demonstration. You may want to have them experiment a bit then have a whole-class discussion. In this way the class as a whole can understand how the simple setup they have can be used to answer the question. Depending on the class and your judgment of their abilities and needs, you could provide more or less direction until the class understood that they could take the data they need to answer the question. Your instructions would then be to take data, in this case, they would probably make some line drawings of a few locations of the block and glass and the resulting "sight line" of the two pins as the light emerged, refracted, through the glass. Your instruction could include the requirement for students to provide an answer to the question with justification by using the data which they have collected. As a nice wrap-up they could try to explain why the coin became visible over the edge of the cup when water was added. *S-11*

A teacher committed to teaching for critical thinking must think beyond compartmentalized subject matter teaching to ends and objectives that transcend subject matter classification. To teach for critical thinking is, first of all, to create an environment that is conducive to critical thinking.

The Wave-Particle Theory of Light

Objectives of the remodelled plan
The students will:
- explore and clarify the nature of models and the use of model in science through discussion
- note significant similarities and differences between models and what they represent
- develop confidence in reason by proposing a model to explain a physical observation
- interpret an observation with light in terms of the wave model of light

Standard Approach————————————

> In introducing the electromagnetic spectrum, texts will mention the wave-par-
> ticle theory of light. Students are told that if they look at a distant light source
> through a pinhole in a card, the pattern of light they observe is larger than the
> actual size of the pinhole. They are told that this "strange effect can be explained
> if light is thought of as a series of waves." They are then told that other kinds of
> experiments give different results. These experiments show that light "always
> transfers energy in the form of small particles." The students are told that these
> light particles are called photons. The passage concludes by saying the *wave-
> particle theory of light* is the name of the theory that results from combining
> these two different kinds of experimental results.

Critique

This brief passage raises several questions: how models are used in science; why diffraction through a pinhole indicates that light acts like a wave; what "transfers energy in the form of small particles" means; what it means for light to act as a wave in some experiments and as a particle in others. Most of these issues cannot be dealt with successfully in a brief introductory passage. (In fact, such passages suggest considering whether these issues should be addressed this briefly if the result is to raise issues which students cannot understand.) It is possible, though, to help students understand the role of *models* in science and, for this reason, this remodelling discussion will focus on the use of models in science.

Strategies used to remodel
S-14 clarifying and analyzing the meanings of words or phrases
S-29 noting significant similarities and differences
S-9 developing confidence in reason
S-32 making plausible inferences, predictions, or interpretations

Remodelled Lesson Plan

The discussion could begin by raising the issue of models in general. The most familiar use of the word 'model' to students is probably as in 'model airplane,' a small representation of a larger object. The following questions will help students discover some features of models. "How is a model airplane like an actual airplane? How is it different? What does a model of an airplane enable you to do? What kinds of things does a real airplane do that a model cannot do?" Through these kinds of questions, we try to help students clarify their own thinking about this simple kind of model. **S-14**

Next, we could introduce models which are more abstract than simple model airplanes. Most students have had experience with some kind of map, and we will use this to extend the idea of a model. After reminding the students about road maps, perhaps by showing them a road map of your state as an example, you could ask them to think of the ways in which this map is a model and how this map model differs from an airplane model. "Is the map a complete picture of your state? Could you use the map to find out everything you might want to know about your state?" These kinds of questions will help students understand that a map is a useful representation of some aspects of your state in which people might be interested. The map is not a complete, accurate representation of every aspect of your state, but it does help us understand and use the road system. We would probably make a different kind of map if we wanted to understand how the hills and mountains of the state worked to form river systems, for instance. The following kinds of questions will encourage students to explore the usefulness of maps. "What does this road map tell us? What does it help us do? Is this map a miniature model of our state? Are there things in our state which aren't shown on this map? Why are these things left off?" The point of these questions, and many other possible questions, is that maps (or models in general) are not complete representations but are designed to help us understand some particular aspect of the thing we are studying. **S-29**

In the case of maps, we make a small model of a large object. In much of science we do the opposite — we make a large model of small things like atoms, for instance. But these models in science have many of the same features of the models and maps we have been discussing.

Sometimes in our science teaching, we can describe something or let students experience it directly and then ask students to invent some kind of model. For example, after watching a drop of ink slowly diffuse through a glass of water, students could try to invent the best model they can to explain what they saw. **S-9**

In the case of a model for light, we can let students observe diffraction through a pinhole, as the original lesson points out. The students can also be shown pictures of water waves bending around objects — breakwaters in a harbor, for instance. You could ask, "If light acted like these kinds of waves, what would we expect to see when light travels through pinholes and into our eyes?" **S-32**

Through questions like this, you can lead students to understand possible implications of the pinhole in the card activity mentioned in the original text passage. In this way we can begin to help students understand what it means to say "lights acts like a wave" or that "we can use a wave model of light."

The text goes on to mention the particle model for light. Unfortunately, the evidence leading to this model is much more difficult to observe and interpret. We cannot present this evidence to students. In this remodelling discussion, we have, however, seen an approach which helps students understand what models are and how they are used in science. We have also taken a brief look at some of the evidence which is best interpreted thorough the wave model of light.

Your first remodels should use those skills or insights clearest to you. Other principles can be integrated as they become clear.

Newton's Second Law

Objectives of the remodelled plan

The students will:

• make plausible predictions about motions of objects
• analyze their experiences regarding motions of objects
• clarify the concepts of force, friction, and mass through discussions and questions about common experiences

Standard Approach

Texts often approach teaching Newton's Second Law of Motion by using examples of frictionless surfaces, such as a hockey puck on ice. They then state that experiments in such situations have shown that doubling the force will double the acceleration. Some texts introduce the mass of an object as the ratio between the force and acceleration, and provide a summary of Newton's Second Law: "When a force is applied to an object, the object accelerates in the direction of the applied force. The acceleration is greater when the force is greater. The acceleration is less when the mass of the object is greater."

Critique

Newton's Second Law is very difficult for students to understand, since it apparently contradicts many of our everyday experiences. For instance, frictional forces are so much a part of everyday life that students rarely have the opportunity to experience frictionless motions. The text misses an important opportunity for students to come to terms with this aspect of their experiences. Also, the definition of 'mass' as force divided by acceleration is much too abstract to be of use to students at this level.

This lesson gives us the chance to raise the question of the *appropriateness* of presenting particular science concepts to high school students. It is appropriate for these students to try to understand the motion of objects in terms of their own experience and in terms of the ideas of scientists who have studied motion. Newton's Laws, though, present a highly abstract and condensed way of understanding motion. Many of the important aspects of Newton's Laws are often not apparent in everyday life, and therefore, students' preconceptions about motion are often quite at odds with the abstractions of Newton's Laws. Briefly, what are some of the preconceptions students have which apparently contradict Newton's Laws?

The First Law states, "Objects move in a straight line at constant speed unless a force is acting on them." Since everyday motions are always subject to forces, especially frictional forces, children are without the kinds of experience which would enable them to have "experienced" the First Law. As a different example, many students think that if a stone whirled overhead in a circle on a string is released, the stone will follow a kind of curved path (when viewed from above). Their preconceptions on this kind of motion are entirely at odds with the prediction of the First Law that the stone will follow a straight line.

The Second Law deals with the relationship between force, *mass*, and *acceleration*. Again, this presents difficulty for students, since our everyday experience leads us to see motions in terms of force, *weight*, and *speed*. Based on everyday experience, most students believe that the harder you push something, the faster it goes. We develop these preconceptions from experiences like pushing heavy objects across the floor. While the confusion of weight for mass is not a relatively important issue for students, the spirit of the Second Law is lost when we relate forces to *speeds* rather than to *accelerations*.

Strategies used to remodel

S-12 developing one's perspective: creating or exploring beliefs, arguments, or theories
S-1   thinking independently
S-14 clarifying and analyzing the meanings of words or phrases

Remodelled Lesson Plan *S-12*

We begin remodelling this lesson by changing its goal somewhat. Instead of trying to teach Newton's Laws, we try to do two things: *1)* we try to help students articulate their preconceptions about the motion of objects; and *2)* we try to challenge students in a way which encourages them to modify their understanding to arrive at a more powerful, all-encompassing view of their experiences, thus developing their perspectives. If we can accomplish these goals, we will help prepare them for a critical understanding of the abstract statement of Newton's Laws later in their education.

As an example, let us begin with the relationship between force ("pushes and pulls" to students) and motion. We could have students consider two extreme situations: pushing a car along a road and pushing an object over a very smooth, frictionless surface. (Use a situation your students might have experienced like a frozen lake, an air hockey table, sliding on a smooth or wet floor, etc.) "What happens when we stop pushing? Why?" *S-1* Through questions like this, we are trying to challenge one characteristic preconception which is that something moving requires a continuing force. Our strategy is to cause students to consider the difference between high-friction and low-friction situations. Also have them consider the force required *1)* to *stop* moving objects, and *2)* to change their direction. Through this strategy, we hope that students will see changing motion (in speed or direction) as the result of external force acting on the object. This is one of the difficult points in Newton's Laws for beginners.

Another major point in Newton's Second Law is the mass of an object. While the texts' definition of mass as "the ratio of force to acceleration" is technically correct, it is not an appropriate definition for students at this level. At this age, students should learn science by considering concrete ideas. While force and, to some extent, acceleration are concepts with which students have direct experience, the idea of a *ratio* of these quantities is too abstract for students to understand in a critical sense. It is probably better to refer to the mass of an object as "the amount of matter." Students often confuse the *mass* of an object with the *frictional force* associated with moving it. Big objects, like pianos, are difficult to move around due to friction. It is, however, surprisingly easy to move a small boat weighing about as much as a piano, since the frictional force opposing the motion of a boat in the water is very small. Through questions involving large objects and small objects, along with high- and low-friction situations, we can clarify students' understanding of mass of objects. *S-14*

Ask students, "Why is it harder to move objects on rough surfaces than smooth or slippery surfaces? Why is it harder to start an object moving on a smooth surface, than it is to *keep* it moving? Why is it harder to stop a bulky object than one with less matter? A faster object than a slower one?" *S-1*

Macro-practice is almost always more important than micro-drill. We need to be continually vigilant against the misguided tendency to fragment, atomize, mechanize, and proceduralize thinking.

Photosynthesis: Designing Labs

by Carol R. Gontang, Mountain View
High School, Mountain View, CA

Objectives of the remodelled plan

The students will:

- ask good questions about observations they make
- form hypotheses concerning these questions
- generate and assess solutions by designing controlled experiments to test their hypotheses
- interpret their results through dialectical discussion
- modify their hypotheses, if necessary, to fit the data
- discuss at length the reason hypotheses are not "proven" by experiments
- correct their original misconceptions concerning plant metabolism based upon their experiments by recognizing contradictions

Standard Approach

Students are given a complete set of instructions concerning the setup of all parts of the experiment. They use the acid indicator bromthymol blue to see if plants left in light overnight take in carbon dioxide. Questions and hypotheses are provided by the manual. Students are asked to predict the results of the experiment based upon the hypotheses provided, and to make observations.

Critique

While students are collecting and interpreting data in the original lesson, they are missing out on an important thinking exercise by not being allowed to ask good questions and to design the experiment and control for each question themselves. The original lesson does not provide a discussion of the skill of asking a good question (in the scientific sense) or the importance of a model or hypothesis.

Like many "cookbook" style labs in high school science classes, this lab is presented after the students have been given the facts about photosynthesis, so that the experiment is not a true investigation, but is a confirmation of what the students have already been told. When experiments are presented this way, students tend to see results as "proof." The fact that in real science, experiments both begin and end with questions and hypotheses is lost when labs are presented this way. The traditional presentation gives students the idea that the objective in science is to prove a preconceived notion to be correct, and that to fail to do so means a bad experiment (and a bad grade). Students should also be encouraged to add other experiments, thus broadening and enriching their study.

Strategies used to remodel

S-5 developing intellectual humility and suspending judgment
S-32 making plausible inferences, predictions, or interpretations
S-10 refining generalizations and avoiding oversimplifications
S-19 generating or assessing solutions
S-9 developing confidence in reason
S-26 reasoning dialectically: evaluating perspectives, interpretations, or theories
S-34 recognizing contradictions
S-1 thinking independently

Remodelled Lesson Plan

The experiment could serve as an introduction to a unit on photosynthesis and respiration. Students have learned in earlier classes that plants "breathe in" carbon dioxide and give off oxygen, while animals do the reverse. Typically, however, they have not understood that plants also carry out aerobic respiration at the same time that they perform photosynthesis, and that this process goes on day and night.

Day One

To begin the investigation, the students could spend ten minutes in small groups brainstorming a list of all the things they know or assume about plants and photosynthesis. These lists could then be shared and put up on the board with no correction from the teacher. At the end of the lesson, students will return to the lists to see if their original views have been supported. **S-5**

In a demonstration, the teacher could show the students how to add carbon dioxide to water containing the acid/base indicator bromthymol blue, by adding drops of carbonated water or by bubbling his or her breath through the water with a soda straw. (The water-bromthymol blue mixture becomes yellow with the addition of CO_2.) A length of Elodea plant is added to the water in a test tube, and the tube is left in good light overnight.

Day Two

The next day, the water around the plant will have turned green or blue. The class could then be asked to discuss what this color change might mean. "How should we interpret this result? Why? How does that interpretation fit in with what we know?" **S-32** They could be asked how they can be sure that the plant caused the color change and not some other factor. This would lead to a discussion of the variables that may have played a part in the demonstration (plant, carbon dioxide, light, etc.) **S-10**

Students could next be given time in small groups to formulate questions about the effects of the variables, and to think of ways that they might use the demonstrated materials to try to answer their questions. "If the result might have been due to that, how could we test for it? How could we ensure that won't affect our results? How would it enter the picture? How could we eliminate it or keep it out?" **S-19** It is likely that students will ask what effect light had on the results, and that they will decide to try a similar set-up in the dark. They might also try a control with no plant, to ascertain that it was, in fact, the plant that caused the change; or leave a plant in water to which no carbon dioxide has been added (water is green or blue); or leave a tube with blue water and no plant; or put an airtight cover over the tube with a plant. Students' experiments are set up and left overnight. **S-9**

Day Three

The next day, students make observations and combine their data in a large group discussion. Through questioning, the teacher can guide the discussion to explore the results. The teacher invites hypotheses to explain the results.**S-32** It is important that the teacher asks for more than one hypothesis that would be consistent with the data, and then discusses which one might fit the data and background information best. "What might this show? What else could it show, instead? ... Which seems more plausible? Why? What do we know that should make us favor one explanation over another?" Students could argue with each other for their theories and argue against competing theories. **S-26**

Next, the teacher brings up the question of what a plant is doing in the dark when (as an earlier experiment indicated) photosynthesis is not going on. Students again devise experiments and controls to explore whether carbon dioxide is being used or given off at this time. **S-19**

Day Four

The results in this last set of experiments will show carbon dioxide being given off. Students can be asked to hypothesize about what type of process might produce carbon dioxide, and they can be reminded of how their own breath turned bromthymol blue to a yellow color. This discussion leads to the idea that plants perform cellular respiration just as animals do.

Finally, students review the lists they made at the beginning of the lesson to see if the lists need to be modified or expanded. "Is this statement consistent with what we've found? Do our results contradict this idea? Did our experiment prove this claim? Do we have sufficient evidence to judge this?" **S-34**

It is important that during the design sessions and the interpretation of the results the teacher avoids shutting off further discussion by telling students a particular interpretation of data is right or wrong. Instead, the teacher should respond to a student's proposed interpretation by inviting other students to respond to it. **S-1** Interpretations should be critiqued on the basis of whether they are consistent with the data, and not on the basis of whether the student has guessed a desired response correctly. **S-9**

Darwin: A Socratic Approach

by Joan C. Simons, Grimsley High
Schools, Greensboro, NC

Objectives of the remodelled plan
The students will:
- be introduced to the concepts of Darwinian evolution
- engage in analytical and evaluative thought in class discussion and writing

Standard Approach

I. The Darwin-Wallace Theory
   A. The planet is not static but changing
   B. Similar organisms have a similar ancestor
   C. Natural selection
      1. In every generation an enormous amount of variation occurs
      2. The individual best adapted to the environment is the one who will survive.
   D. Acquisition of traits through use and disuse, as well as adaptation
   E. The inheritance of acquired traits
II. The LaMarck Theory
   A. There exists in organisms a built-in drive toward perfection
   B. There is in nature a progression from simple and small (primitive) to large and complex (advanced) to man (perfection).
   C. There is frequent occurrence of spontaneous generation so that each organism represents a separate line of descent
   D. Organisms have the capacity to adapt to the environment, therefore they may acquire characteristics
   E. The inheritance of acquired traits
III. Using pictures of horse skulls and feet, discuss these theories as an explanation of these pictures
IV. Discuss the scientific problems of these theories in light of the students' knowledge of genetics.
V. Have the students write their own theory of evolution

Introductory note

In the fall of 1987, when my principal announced the organization of a committee to improve the teaching of critical thinking in the classroom, I made sure my name was on his list of volunteers. Finally, I thought, some administrator is interested in exciting teaching and good, lasting education for students. The result was the committee for Writing and Tactical Thinking Skills (WATTS). As direct outgrowth of my involvement with WATTS the above lesson on the introduction of Darwinian evolution was remodelled. This lesson was written and remodelled for a class of ninth and tenth grade, academically gifted students in Biology I.

Critique

This lesson plan is a basic lecture-class discussion format with the teacher acting as the primary information dispenser. This technique has the general disadvantage of encouraging student passivity rather than involvement. This format does not necessarily require thinking on the part of the students, let alone identification of thinking processes. While there is an opening for student discussion, thought-provoking questions would be a happy accident. One strength of this lesson is the attempt to urge students to tie this lesson into their knowledge of genetics. This lesson needs to identify what questions students should consider to improve their independent thinking skills as well as their content knowledge.

The Socratic lesson not only involved the students to a greater degree, but was more interesting for the teacher. The same basic information was covered as in Lesson I, but in such a way as to require greater student investment in the process. To obtain an overall view from an observer, read the evaluation included at the end of their paper. Notice that with the Socratic lesson, fewer students remained passive, and it resulted in more time on learning tasks for the entire class.

Strategies used to remodel

S-28 thinking precisely about thinking: using critical vocabulary
S-33 evaluating evidence and alleged facts
S-12 developing one's perspective: creating or exploring beliefs, arguments, or theories
S-17 questioning deeply: raising and pursuing root or significant questions
S-14 clarifying and analyzing the meanings of words or phrases

Remodelled Lesson Plan

Activity

I. The objectives of this lesson are three-fold:
 a) To reinforce your problem solving skills
 b) To help students determine what skills are used so that the process can be duplicated in the future
 c) To introduce the concept of evolution

II. On the board, when the students enter, are two drawings of the skulls (profile) and foot (front view)

 1. *Hyracotherium* and
 2. *Merychippus*

III. List answers to questions on board.

IV. Give the students five minutes to write their own explanation for the evolution of the horse.

Question

1. Can you interpret these drawings?
2. What do they appear to be?
3. Can you associate these drawings with anything that you are familiar with?
4. What thought processes are you using? **S-28**
5. Are you assessing all information available to you?
6. Where is that information coming from? **S-33**
7. How would you explain the changes in these drawings? You have five minutes to write your own explanation of the evolution of this animal. **S-12**

V.   "Now I will give you the theories of two men who have been very influential in the study of evolution" ... First, Darwin's theory.

    a)   the planet is not static but changing.

    b)   Similar organisms have a common ancestor

    c)   Natural selection

        1.   In every generation, an enormous amount of variation occurs

        2.   The individual best adapted to the environment is the one that will survive.

    d)   Acquisition of traits through use and disuse as well as adaptation

    e)   The inheritance of acquired traits.

The second man is a Frenchman, LaMarck. He has also been a major influence on evolutionary theory. LaMarck's Theory:

    a)   There exists in organisms a built-in drive toward perfection.

    b)   Therefore, there is a progression in nature from simple and small (primitive) to large and complex (advanced) to man (perfection).

    c)   There is a frequent occurrence of spontaneous generation so that each organism represents a separate line of descent.

    d)   Organisms have the capacity to adapt to the changes in the environment, therefore they may acquire characteristics.

    e)   The inheritance of acquired traits.

VI.   Write the name of the theory next to the explanations on the board.

VII. The major differences between the study of genetics and evolution are the concepts of direction and time.
Now try to associate these concepts with direction.

    VIII.

    IX.   For homework: Evaluate your theory with regard to acceptable scientific statements and rewrite it

8.   From where did Darwin draw this statement?

9.   On whose writings did Darwin base this statement?

10.   What constitutes biological success? **S-17 S-14**

11.   Who originated this theory?

12.   Which theory is most like your own?

13.   Which theory or part of a theory is most like the explanations on the board?

14.   What are some different concepts of time?

15.   Which direction of time is LaMarck concerned with?

16.   Darwin?

17.   Once again before we leave, list the critical thinking skills you have used today. **S-28**

Remodelling in Other Subjects

Introduction

This chapter contains a host of remodelled lessons from a variety of subjects demonstrating, among other things, that critical teaching strategies can be applied in all teaching situations. As always, we present these remodels not as perfect, but as plausible examples of how teachers can begin to reshape their instruction to encourage and cultivate critical thinking. As you read through them, you might consider how you might have critiqued and remodelled the original lessons. There are always a wide variety of ways in which we can exercise our independent thinking and decision-making while teaching for critical thinking. As critical thinkers we think for ourselves, thus our teaching reflects our uniqueness as persons. Our instruction is a creative as well as critical activity. Indeed we critique to create. We find fault only to improve. Critical thinking does not threaten; it excites us to think of new possibilities, new ways of encouraging our students to think for themselves, to become more responsible persons, and to put their own brain power into operation so that they can take control of their own learning. It is encouraging to see teachers in a variety of subjects remodelling and redesigning their own instruction. Within the next couple of years, exemplary remodels should be available for every subject and grade level.

Compound Interest

Objectives of the remodelled plan

The students will:

- be able to distinguish compounded interest, simple interest, and interest compounded continuously
- compare various institutions' investment programs by clarifying their claims, and refining generalizations
- custom tailor a financial plan for their own futures, distinguishing relevant from irrelevant factors

Standard Approach ─────────────────

Students will learn formulas for compound interest. They should be able to solve these equations with exponents and logarithms.

Critique

This lesson does not explain the difference in the various formulas nor when, why, or how to apply them. Using information pamphlets and ads from banks will also help students practice distinguishing relevant from irrelevant information. When students are setting up and working out equations, students should understand reasons for doing each step.

Strategies used to remodel

S-17 questioning deeply: raising and pursuing root or significant questions
S-13 clarifying issues, conclusions, or beliefs
S-10 refining generalizations and avoiding oversimplifications
S-31 distinguishing relevant from irrelevant facts

Remodelled Lesson Plan ─────────────

After the formulas for interest compounded continuously, daily, monthly, and simple interest are introduced, the students will be given examples that will not show a significant difference once the interests are calculated. They will then be asked why this worked in this manner. Have students explain in detail why the equations are set up as they are. When would one type of interest be more desirable than another? When would this kind of account be best? That? First have students guess, then do the calculations. **S-17**

Prior to the introduction of these formulas, the students will have been asked to gather information from five different banks/savings & loans. Discussion will then be stimulated by these questions which clarify the policies:

How do these institutions describe their method of calculation of interest? Are all these institutions offering similar plans? How are the plans different? Why are their plans different? What kinds of terms do they use? What do they mean? Are there special restrictions on these accounts? *S-13*

How could these various kinds of accounts apply to different personal situations? To what kind of individual would it apply and how? Are there factors that may change a particular situation? *S-10*

Next, on their own, the students would write a personal scenario of their lives ten years from now, briefly describing their lifestyles and incomes. They would explain what criteria they would use in selecting a bank. They would explain what factors in their lives are critical in their personal situation. *S-31*

To develop the next part of their papers, students must answer the following question. "In what ways would your association with this institution be advantageous to you?" For the last part of this paper students need to write a one page description of their future financial plan and on a second piece of paper they must back up their predictions with answers that have been derived from appropriate formulas. And finally, they should consider other options of investment. Would there be better ways to invest in their situations?

Lesson plan remodelling as a strategy for staff and curriculum development is not a simple one-shot approach. It requires patience and commitment. But it genuinely develops the critical thinking of teachers and puts them in a position to understand and help transform the curriculum into effective teaching and learning.

Using Percentages

by Susan Dembitz, Miranda, CA

Objectives of the remodelled plan

The students will:
- fulfill the objectives of the original plan
- distinguish relevant from irrelevant facts in word problems
- refine generalizations in the process of creating, analyzing, solving, and critiquing percentage problems

Standard Approach

Texts divide the work into small skills, and teach each one through examples and practice. It is easily adapted to the seven step lesson plan by using a few exercises for quiz material. Word problems are used in each lesson and in "applications" and "careers" lessons. The objectives are:

to change percents to decimals

to change decimals and fractions to percents

to solve problems using percents

to find a percent of a number

to find the percent one number is of another

to find a number given the percent of the number

to find commissions

to find total wages based on commission plus salary

to find the cost of an item if a discount is given

Critique

A major problem with this style of teaching is that students learn to use each algorithm, but still have difficulty understanding which one is appropriate in a given situation and what the answers mean. In addition, they don't learn to sort out relevant from irrelevant data because all the data given is relevant. They rarely examine their assumptions or understand that they are testing generalizations.

editor's note: Those who *understand* these mathematical relationships can always reconstruct and use them properly. Those who merely memorize and mindlessly apply formulas will more likely use the wrong formula, misuse it, or misinterpret the answer.

Strategies used to remodel

S-17 questioning deeply: raising and pursuing root or significant questions
S-31 distinguishing relevant from irrelevant facts
S-24 practicing Socratic discussion: clarifying and questioning beliefs, theories, or perspectives

Remodelled Lesson Plan S-17

The students will practice using: x percent of a equals b; commission equals rate times amount of sale; cost equals regular price minus discount; total price equals sum of individual prices plus tax; in many possible forms and combinations, by creating their own problems from newspaper and catalogue ads brought into the classroom. For data on commissions, the students will use data obtained if possible from a salesperson who visits the classroom and describes the use of percentage in their work.

The teacher will model the creation of problems, then students will choose materials, construct problems, solve them, and exchange with other students. As part of the process, the teacher will model Socratic questioning designed to clarify the problems, (especially having students explain the problems in words, for example, "For every dollar of the original price, they subtract ten cents") examine the assumptions, distinguish between relevant and irrelevant facts, and finally refine generalizations in the process of creating useful algorithms. "What question are you asking? What do you need to figure out? What information do you need? What information given here can you ignore? **S-31** How should you set up the equation? Why? What will this tell you? Does this answer make sense? Explain it in words. (Elicit complete explanations.) Would this equation work for any situation? Why or why not?" **S-24**

Students will be divided into groups to critique each others' formulations in the same fashion, while the teacher circulates through the classroom monitoring this activity.

Finally, the class will share generalizations gleaned from this process and each group will demonstrate its favorite problem to the whole class.

> *In order to think critically about issues we must first be able to state the issue clearly. The more completely, clearly, and accurately the issue is formulated, the easier and more helpful the discussion of its settlement.*

What is Spanish?

by Julia Epstein Kluger, Sinaloa Middle School, Novato, CA

Objectives of the remodelled plan

The students will:
- clarify ideas concerning that which is and is not Spanish
- develop a concept of the term 'Hispanic'

Standard Approach

The teacher asks the class to define the word 'Spanish'. Students generate a list of those meanings of Spanish. After the list is developed, each student is then asked to create a poster that illustrates some of the ideas from the list.

Critique

The concept of 'Spanish' has been greatly oversimplified to include anyone who speaks the language. Students need to be made aware of the distinction between that which is Spanish and comes from the country of Spain, and that which is Hispanic, or that which comes from a country in which Spanish is spoken. For example, many students confuse Spanish food with Mexican food. Similarly, a Spanish person, in their opinion, can be anyone who speaks the language, clearly limiting their awareness of the diversity in the Hispanic world.

Strategies used to remodel

S-14 clarifying and analyzing the meanings of words or phrases
S-29 noting significant similarities and differences
S-7 developing intellectual good faith or integrity

Remodelled Lesson Plan S-14

As an introduction, say to the class, "If I were to tell you that in Spain, a tortilla is made from eggs and potatoes, what would you think?" Through probing questions, explore with the class their ideas about what they think the word 'Spanish' means. Use maps, pictures, and other familiar images to help them clarify their ideas of what Spanish really means and how the term can be used in ways which are misleading, oversimplifying, or incorrect. If necessary, introduce the term 'Hispanic.' **S-29**

After the discussion, the teacher might ask, "How is what we have just discussed important to you now when you hear the word 'English'?" The connection here is irresistible. Ask, "Would you then call someone who speaks English and who lives in South Africa, 'English'? What would you think of someone who referred to you as 'English'? How would you feel? Why?" **S-7** The point should be well taken.

Finally, have the students write their own essay, "What is Spanish?"

In teaching for critical thinking in the strong sense, we are committed to teaching in such a way that children learn as soon and as completely as possible how to become responsible for their own thinking.

Queridos Amigos

by Julia Epstein Kluger, Sinaloa Middle
School, Novato, CA

Objectives of the remodelled plan
The students will:
- practice critical reading by posing questions as they read the introduction to their Spanish texts and analyzing words and phrases in it
- raise root questions regarding learning another language
- understand the difference between facts and ideals

Standard Approach

> Have students read the author's introduction to the text. Discuss the reasons for and advantages to studying Spanish. Ask the students if they agree and if they can think of any others. Assign students to write a paragraph explaining their reasons for studying Spanish.

Critique

Although the introduction does name many good reasons why students should study the language and even lists worthwhile objectives to pursue once we know the language, the basic assumption is that the students will, in fact, learn the language without any reference as to how they will learn it or what it really means to *know* the language. Furthermore, the authors use concepts like 'second language' and 'foreign language' without defining them. I believe that students need to be able to understand what they can expect from learning a language: What kind of commitment is involved? What are realistic goals? How will they use the language? Can you know a language and not be able to speak it?

Finally, the inspirational message that the authors are communicating to us seems to lack the necessary references to what the learner's responsibilities are. After reading the letter one might come away thinking that *the book* speaks Spanish as well!

Strategies used to remodel
S-21 reading critically: clarifying or critiquing texts
S-14 clarifying and analyzing the meanings of words or phrases
S-17 questioning deeply: raising and pursuing root or significant questions

Remodelled Lesson Plan *S-21*

Begin by having students read the introduction to themselves taking down any vocabulary or terms they may be unfamiliar with. Ask students to think as they read, posing questions based upon statements the authors make. Students can share their questions and discuss possible answers.

Clarify issues and identify unfamiliar words, terms, etc. Then ask the class to explain what they think the authors mean by a second language as opposed to a foreign language. "What do you think they mean? Would you use these expressions the way the authors do? Could you apply both of them in the same situation? Would the authors? Why do the authors use these expressions as they do? What point are they making? Is this a good way to make that point? Is it a worthwhile point to make?" *S-14*

Continue the discussion, and then ask questions regarding the methods used to learn a language. Students could examine the instructional methods of their texts. "What does it mean to *know* a language? What does it mean to *know* a culture? How did you learn your language? How long did it take? Was it easy or hard? Why? Will this experience be similar? Why or why not?" In addition to clarifying and raising root questions, the teacher might discuss the number of Americans who speak Spanish and the number of Hispanics who must learn English. Many exciting discussions can be developed from here that would require offering opinions, evaluating arguments, and discussing reasons for learning other languages. *S-17*

As a closing assignment, I would have students write their own introduction to the book based on the discussions in class.

Do not to spend too much time on the general formulations of what critical thinking is before moving to the level of particular strategies, since people tend to have trouble assimilating general concepts unless they are made accessible by concrete examples.

The Children of Sanchez

by John Lawrence Carolan Faculty
Ursuline High School, Santa Rosa, CA

Objectives of the remodelled plan

The students will:

- practice listening critically by discussing a movie
- evaluate possible turning points in the story
- examine their assumptions about Mexicans
- discuss the place of women in Hispanic society as developed in the movie and compare it to our culture

Standard Approach

First, the teacher points out the classic yet exaggerated nature of the movie (and book). Then he points out the fact that it is based on a true story. Then the students discuss the following aspects of the movie: The confusing story line and how that confusion was used to establish the tone of helplessness of Mexican urban poor; the tendency of Mexican society to be double-standard in nature, and the license this gives to the male head of the family; the matriarchal character of Mexican life, and how it falls apart without a mother in the family; therefore, the impossibility of (or incredible difficulty for) the Mexican woman to be liberated and independent; the characteristics of violence and discrimination that are similar between Mexican and American societies.

Homework of the lesson: That all students write a paragraph in Spanish talking about how winning the lottery changed the family's life. Students use this assignment to practice the newly learned past perfect tense.

Critique

There are two main problems with this lesson plan: *1)* It runs the risk of people generalizing and oversimplifying from what they see in the movie, as well as taking what they see at face value without examining the deeper implications and consequences of the events that took place. *2)* The lesson as planned does not force the students beyond an academic analysis of the movie itself, except finally to comparing cultures. There is no attempt to have the students examine their own personal, similar experiences.

Strategies used to remodel

S-22 listening critically: the art of silent dialogue
S-10 refining generalizations and avoiding oversimplifications
S-29 noting significant similarities and differences
S-34 recognizing contradictions
S-18 analyzing or evaluating arguments, interpretations, beliefs, or theories
S-5 developing intellectual humility and suspending judgment
S-30 examining or evaluating assumptions
S-17 questioning deeply: raising and pursuing root or significant questions
S-7 developing intellectual good faith or integrity
S-12 developing one's perspective: creating or exploring beliefs, arguments, or theories

Remodelled Lesson Plan S-22

First, discuss the movie itself and get beyond the literal events by asking the following questions: Was the movie difficult to follow? Why? Was the confusion resulting just from the point of view of the viewer, or was it perhaps a reflection of the confusion in the lives of the characters? **S-10**

What was the real source of confusion for the characters in the movie, especially for Consuelo? What virtue did the author depict in Consuelo that was stronger than in the other characters? **S-29** Why did her love for her father and his for her create a great contradiction? What would be the clearest statement of this contradiction? What beliefs and attitudes underlie or produce it? **S-34**

What was the apparent turning point for the movie? How many think this really *was* the turning point? What differences did winning the lottery make in their lives? Examining how everyone's life finally turned out at the end, what was the *real* turning point that changed the family's life? Why do you think so? What results did it have? Why was it more significant than this? That? Etc.? **S-18**

Second, discuss the assumptions and generalizations that we bring to the movie, that could keep us from seeing the gentleness and love that is the real theme and turning point.

What assumptions about Mexicans did we bring to the movie? What's your image of the typical poor Mexican family? (Discuss at length, making a list — laziness, macho, criminal, etc.) How did the movie re-enforce these assumptions? What specific events had you convinced you were right? Which of these assumptions were too simple? **S-5** What events did you see that were the result of different causes than you assumed? (For example, poverty was the real cause of lack of privacy which was in turn the cause of family violence and unrest.) **S-10** How could our assumptions be more accurate? **S-30**

What can we say about violence and poverty in general in the movie that is true in any society? How are the two related? Which begets which? Give some examples from the movie. Why is it hard to break this cycle? **S-17**

Third, students can compare our culture with Mexican culture.

We've just crossed the line into another culture. Let's talk about ours. When have you encountered contradictions similar to those depicted in the movie? **S-29**

When or how have you seen similar family violence? Poverty? Lack of privacy? Cultural entrapment? Is this all therefore proper just to minorities? **S-17**

Finally, what about the role of male and female? In the movie and Mexican culture? How about in ours? Are there similar problems? Are we more advanced here? Are we out of the woods yet? **S-7**

Homework: Write a paragraph in Spanish about the *real* turning point of the movie and its results. At the end, mention what you learned about life from the movie. **S-12**

The reader should keep in mind the connection between the principles and applications, on the one hand, and the character traits of a fairminded critical thinker, on the other. Our aim, once again, is not a set of disjointed skills, but an integrated, committed, thinking person.

Setting up and Typing a Table

by Barbara Johannes, Ursuline High
School, Santa Rosa, CA

Objectives of the remodelled plan

The students will:

- center a three-column table on an 8 1/2" x 11" sheet of paper
- develop confidence in their ability to reason their way through a difficult typing problem
- discuss which known facts are relevant to this task
- generate, test, and assess their own solutions to this problem

Standard Approach

1) Tell students that there are 66 vertical lines on an 8 1/2" x 11" sheet of paper.

2) Tell students that there are 85 horizontal spaces across that sheet of paper.

3) Teach the students how to count up the lines and spaces in the table and how to plug those numbers into the following formulas:

To find vertical starting line: (lines on paper) - (lines in problem) = (blank lines remaining); (blank lines) ÷ 2 = (vertical starting line).

To find left margin and tab settings: (spaces required) ÷ 2 = X; (horizontal center) - X = (left margin); (left margin) + (spaces for column 1) + (space between columns) = (first tab setting); (first tab) + (spaces for column 2) + (space between columns) = (second tab setting).

Critique

The lesson has an inherent problem since teachers lose 80% of their students at some point during the presentation. These students do not understand how the formulas work. Therefore, they do not remember the formulas, and each time they are faced with the job of typing a table, they do not remember how to do it. The students have not had the opportunity to think through the problem for themselves. They have not had the opportunity to go through given and previously learned facts, and use their own thinking process to solve the problem. As a result, many never do learn how to set up a table. They also do not learn that by working with information which they already know, they can figure out how to solve this table set up (and other) typing problems.

Strategies used to remodel

S-9   developing confidence in reason
S-11 comparing analogous situations: transferring insights to new contexts
S-31 distinguishing relevant from irrelevant facts
S-1   thinking independently
S-19 generating or assessing solutions
S-8   developing intellectual perseverance

Remodelled Lesson Plan S-9

When presenting the new typing problem of setting up a table, it would be important to brainstorm situations in which tables might be used, so that students could see the importance of learning how to do this task. Then it would be necessary to emphasize to students that there is more than one method which could be used to solve this problem of producing a vertically and horizontally centered table. Different typing books teach different methods, and they will come up with a variety of methods. Then write on the board all of the typing facts and information which they already know (lines and spaces on sheet of paper, center space, center line, how to center titles, how to set margins, etc.). They would then start to think of these facts in relation to the problem at hand. **S-11** Students would now start thinking about which of these facts might be relevant. "Which known facts are relevant to the solution of this problem and which are not? Why? How does that fact help?" **S-31** After this brainstorming and clarification process, students would team up into groups of two or three and use the information which has been generated to find a solution for the problem of setting up this table. **S-1**

The teams would test their solutions and then present them to the other teams. The students would discuss the advantages and disadvantages of the various solutions, point out problems to each other, stress good ideas, and so forth. They would then determine as a group, the best or most effective and efficient method or methods of solving this problem. "Which of these seems best? Why? Which is easiest to understand or remember?" **S-19**

The teacher would emphasize the key steps which students have followed and the fact that they have solved, on their own, the most difficult of typing problems. If they can set up a table correctly, they can set up any problem which they might encounter at the typewriter. This is a major accomplishment! **S-9**

editor's note: Students' initial solutions might not work. They should be allowed to try again after examining their mistakes and correcting for them. The class can then discuss the processes they used and problems they had, sharing the modes of reasoning with which they approached the problem. **S-8**

Composition at the Keyboard

by Cynthia Chauner-Niendorf, Ursuline
High School, Santa Rosa, CA

Objectives of the remodelled plan

The students will:

- discuss the consequences of using and failing to use standard business letter formats
- compose business letters for specific purposes at the keyboard
- evaluate each others' letters
- edit the rough draft and print out final copies in an appropriate business letter style

Standard Approach

Review the modified block and block business letter styles.

Discuss how productivity is improved by being able to compose and revise at the keyboard by *a)* speeding up correction of errors; *b)* eliminating manual re-typing; *c)* minimizing reduction in typing speed caused by "fear of making an error;" *d)* permitting "high speed" printing of final letter in "perfect copy"

Tell the students they may select any topic for their letter and that when they finish their first draft they are to revise it and then prepare the final copy.

Critique

This lesson does not involve the students in the preliminary process of getting from the idea for composition to the finished product. Typing students often do not relate their in-class production work to anything outside the classroom. This lesson fails to get the students thinking, but rather gives them somewhat of a rote exercise. Although the assignment is intended to give some creativity from its composition experience, it would be more effective if there were clearer and more specific guidelines for composition.

editor's note: By having students (first in groups, then the class as a whole) assess and correct the drafts, each student gains more insight into good business writing and editing of letters.

Strategies used to remodel

S-35 exploring implications and consequences
S-1 thinking independently
S-10 refining generalizations and avoiding oversimplifications
S-21 reading critically: clarifying or critiquing texts
S-8 developing intellectual perseverance

Remodelled Lesson Plan

When reviewing the letter styles, begin by asking the students to present the letter styles and formats by writing the basic features of block and modified block on the board. Then ask, "Why do you think we have letter formats? Why not just type letters any way we want? How would people receiving them react? What do people do with business letters? How do standardized formats help them file and refer to them?" *S-35*

By question instead of presentation by the teacher, ask, "Does the word processor improve productivity? How? Please give specific examples of how it speeds up error correction. What makes the word processor better than the typewriter? *S-1* Think of some jobs which could be better performed on a typewriter." *S-10*

Next, divide the students into four groups. Explain the assignment: We'd like to go on a class trip to Disneyland and we have some letters to write in planning that trip. Each group will brainstorm ideas, facts, pertinent questions to be asked, to whom will the letter be sent, for their particular aspect of the trip. *S-35* Brochures will be available for reference.

Group A — Transportation (bus/train)

Group B — Overnight Accommodations

Group C — Disneyland — Group Rates

Group D — Letter to parents of class members asking for parent chaperones

Each student takes notes of its group's ideas. One member of each group reports to the class the necessary components for a letter on their particular topic. The teacher can use this opportunity to question and bring out other points.

Then students would go back to their own machines and each compose a letter for their particular topic (saving their final version). This guarantees that all students must do some of their own work. *S-1*

When these letters are completed, the groups now get together and critique the letters of their group — re-editing and coming up with an improved version from the group. This is presented to the entire class for critique and final editing. Is this clear? Precise? To the point? Grammatically correct? Would it give the recipient a good impression of you? *S-21*

Students now update their versions to match the group's final version. Students would have specific addresses to use so that, in the case of transportation and hotels, the same letter would be written, with only the address information changing. In this manner, students have had the opportunity for small group work with some structure but lots of room for creativity and thinking. Students have 'hands-on experience' in the improved productivity using the word processor. The subject of a class trip to Disneyland would be academically less taxing while still getting the students to think objectively in the preliminary stages. Also the students are now transferring a typing lesson into the real world.

editor's note: Students could compare their first drafts with the final versions, noting specific improvements. *S-8*

Handling Stress Through Stretching

by Libby Stillman, Ursuline High School, Santa Rosa, CA

Objectives of the remodelled plan

The students will:

- explore thoughts and feelings which underlie experiences of stress
- learn the "Morning Stretch" as a means of relieving stress
- think independently by creating their own exercises

Standard Approach

The teacher will present a brief lecture emphasizing that "stretching" can help relieve the daily stresses we all experience. Examples of stress include: Alarm fails ... Car won't start ... Late to school ... Unprepared for class ... Low grade on test ... Term paper due ... Boyfriend doesn't call ... Mom and Dad have loud argument ... and so on. How does stress make you feel? What are the side effects of stress? Can stress make you physically sick? How does exercise relieve stress?" The teacher then demonstrates and teaches the "Morning Stretch," a simple series of yoga postures designed to massage the spine and relieve tension. Students will then try the stretch several times. Follow-up includes having students express how they feel after the series of postures and repeated daily participation for one or two weeks.

Critique

This lesson does not give the students an opportunity to discuss the meaning of the term "stress" nor to express their feelings on the subject as it relates to them personally. They are required to listen to a teacher explanation with teacher examples followed by some questions to stimulate some controlled thought. The demonstration by the teacher of the "Morning Stretch" is essential, though, since the students need to see what they will be doing.

Strategies used to remodel

S-4 exploring thoughts underlying feelings and feelings underlying thoughts
S-23 making interdisciplinary connections
S-1 thinking independently

Remodelled Lesson Plan

The class could begin by discussing the meaning of the word 'stress' with the teacher writing the definition on the chalkboard. The class could then be divided into small groups to discuss the stresses experienced personally by the students, and reasons for them. "Why do these things make you feel this way? How does your perception of a situation affect your feelings? How do feelings of stress affect your behavior? Your thinking? Why?" **S-4** The teacher should emphasize the questions in the original lesson plan by writing them on the chalkboard. Each group will contribute three stresses for the whole class to hear when the groups come together. The class will be asked to answer the questions above to emphasize the importance of exercise as a means of relieving daily stresses. "What does this tell us about the relationship between our bodies and how we think and feel? Do you know of any similar connections between mind and body?" **S-23**

After the demonstration of the "Morning Stretch" and student participation, the teacher can go a step further and ask each small group of students to design their own "stress relieving" series of stretches to be presented to the class during the two week unit. **S-1**

> *Though everyone is both egocentric and critical (or fairminded) to some extent, the purpose of education in critical thinking is to help students move away from egocentricity, toward increasingly critical thought.*

Soccer Tactics

by Joan M. West, Victorian Ministry of
Education, Australia

Objectives of the remodelled plan

The students will:
- participate in a previously planned fitness program specific to the requirements of soccer
- develop attacking and defensive strategies in soccer, thus thinking independently
- assess their solutions and actions
- develop and participate in modified games which will apply the devised strategies
- devise and participate in soccer ball skills practices

Standard Approach

Students analyze two specific aspects of the game of soccer — distance and player size — which affect the game outcome and hence influence strategy. In response to teacher-posed problems, small groups of students devise their own solutions within the limitations of their skill, fitness, rules of the game, and problem solving abilities.

Critique

This lesson is used to illustrate the "divergent" teaching style which is the *least* teacher-directed model discussed in one of the "classic" physical education instructional strategies texts. In the opening section of the lesson, pairs of students explore the implications of situations set up by the teacher. The students lose the chance to imagine their own situations, explain the problems which could occur, and devise possible strategies. By presenting the students with the two variables to be explored, this lesson misses a key step — that which provides the opportunity for students to discover the factors that they consider are important in the game outcome. From this point, small groups could design and try out strategies to either overcome or maximize these factors.

Strategies used to remodel

S-1 thinking independently
S-31 distinguishing relevant from irrelevant facts
S-19 generating or assessing solutions
S-20 analyzing or evaluating actions or policies

Remodelled Lesson Plan *S-1*

The lesson starts with a soccer-specific warm-up activity, devised in previous lessons by the students, which includes practice of dribbling, tackling, and passing in small groups. Students also pair up and then practice against other pairs. Discussion then follows in those small groups when students themselves identify and justify key factors which influence win-lose situations. *S-31*

Students devise and participate in practice situations for strategies which either overcome or maximize those variables. How, exactly, does this factor influence the game? Why? What problems can this cause? How? How could this problem be solved? What effect would that have? Which solution is best for which situation? *S-19*

This practice is followed by discussion in which the students assess the strategies' effectiveness. How did each proposed solution work? Which helped solve the problem? Did any create additional problems? Why? Which solution is best for which situations? *S-20*

When rule violations occur, in particular dangerous play, the teacher could direct the discussion to students' assessing the consequences of such behavior. Why did this happen? Why do players do this? What effect does this have? How can we all help prevent this from happening in the future? *S-20*

In closing the lesson, students and teacher could return to the original questions: Which factors influence the game outcome? What strategies can you use to maximize or minimize them? Students have the opportunity to explain the specific situations in which they identified key variables.

It should not be assumed that there is a universal standard for how fast teachers should proceed with the task of remodelling their lesson plans. A slow but steady evolutionary process is much more desirable than a rush job across the board.

I Didn't Want to Bother You

Martha De Leon, Clear Lake High
School, Lakeport, CA

Objectives of the remodelled plan

The students will:

- analyze and evaluate responses to the problem of fearing to ask for necessary explanations
- use analytical terms such as fairmindedness, reciprocity, and assumption
- develop an understanding about employer/employee work relationships
- probe the thoughts and feelings involved in fear of appearing stupid
- generate and assess strategies for overcoming this fear, thus developing intellectual courage

Standard Approach

This lesson focuses on the negative consequences of not asking questions when you don't know how to do a part of your job. Students read about Gary who didn't know how to refill his stapler. To solve his problem, he keeps taking staplers of co-workers while they are on their breaks. One co-worker, Henry, threatens to hit him.

Students write and discuss their answers to the following questions: What do you think the supervisor would say? What should Gary have done instead of taking staplers from co-workers? What have you done in situations like this?

Critique

The original lesson relates to one of the most basic premises of critical thinking — if there is a question or problem, one should critically analyze the possible solutions. The lesson as presented deals with not asking questions superficially and is too simplistic for high school students. It is boring, not capitalizing on the significance of critical thinking.

The three questions that were asked do encourage some critical thinking but not in depth. They require only a few words to answer. Students are also limited in their answers by the lines provided for them to write on.

editor's note: This lesson is typical in stressing the shoulds and shouldn'ts and completely neglecting reasons for improper behavior, and how to combat the powerful fear of embarrassment. Thus, this approach does not realistically address the root of the problem.

Strategies used to remodel

S-20 analyzing or evaluating actions or policies
S-17 questioning deeply: raising and pursuing root or significant questions
S-3 exercising fairmindedness
S-28 thinking precisely about thinking: using critical vocabulary
S-30 examining or evaluating assumptions
S-11 comparing analogous situations: transferring insights to new contexts
S-4 exploring thoughts underlying feelings and feelings underlying thoughts
S-6 developing intellectual courage
S-2 developing insight into egocentricity or sociocentricity
S-19 generating or assessing solutions

Remodelled Lesson Plan *S-20*

The teacher will give a brief statement about asking questions. The teacher will ask: Is it stupid to ask questions? What is being stupid? What is being smart? Can you be smart and stupid? **S-17**

At the end of this discussion, the teacher will have the students read the lesson "I Didn't Want to Bother You" excluding the questions at the end. The class will discuss the following questions: What else could Gary have done to solve his problem? Why did Henry react to Gary the way he did? Was Henry judging Gary in a negative way? How do you think Gary would feel if someone had taken his equipment? **S-3** Do you think he was being fairminded or demonstrating reciprocity? The supervisor assumed Gary knew how to fill the stapler. Was that a correct assumption? What is an assumption? **S-28** Why do you think he assumed Gary could complete that task? **S-30** How do you think other workers will treat Gary after they have learned of the way he dealt with the stapler problem? Do you think Gary's actions were smart? **S-20** Why or why not? Was Gary stealing? What reasons do you have for saying "Yes" or "No"? What does this tell us about the relationship between employer and employee? What do you think employers expect from their employees in the area of understanding the work expected of them? Have you ever experienced a situation that was similar to Gary's? **S-11**

editor's note: Students could also explore Gary's state of mind and the dynamics of fear of speaking up. "Why didn't Gary ask someone how to fill the stapler? How did he feel? Why? What was probably going on in his mind? Why? **S-4** Why is it so hard to do something you feel makes you look stupid? **S-6** How do people react to someone who doesn't know something they all know? Why? What other attitudes are like this? Why is this such a strong factor?" **S-2** Have students brainstorm and then evaluate ways to overcome such fears. "How can this problem be overcome? What should you do when you know you should ask or say something, but are afraid to look dumb? Would this suggestion work? For whom? For whom wouldn't this work? Why not? What might work for that person? Etc." **S-19**

Job Interview Questions

Martha De Leon, Clear Lake High
School, Lakeport, CA

Objectives of the remodelled plan

The students will:
- think independently by developing a list of common job interview questions
- answer common interview questions and assess the answers through Socratic discussion and critical listening
- practice interviewing for jobs

Standard Approach———————————

Students write answers to ten common job-interview questions. After reading further passages in their books, they then revise their answers.

Critique

The questions presented require some thought on the students' part, but the technique is boring. Students would get more out of the lesson by exploring and evaluating the questions and answers at length.

Strategies used to remodel

S-1   thinking independently
S-24 practicing Socratic discussion: clarifying and questioning beliefs, theories, or perspectives
S-22 listening critically: the art of silent dialogue
S-15 developing criteria for evaluation: clarifying values and standards
S-4   exploring thoughts underlying feelings and feelings underlying thoughts
S-29 noting significant similarities and differences

Remodelled Lesson Plan ———————————

The teacher will give a brief introduction on the objectives of the lesson. The students will discuss job interview questions that they have experienced in a job interview or what questions they think are appropriate for a job interview. **S-1** The teacher will list these questions on the board and ask the students what their answers would be to the questions on the board and develop a Socratic discussion in relation to the students' answers. What was your main point? Why did you say that? Did anyone answer this another way? What is an alternative answer? Why is this question important? Why was this question asked? What would a prospective employer think of that answer? Why? **S-24** As this discussion continues, the teacher can ask the students to evaluate the different answers. **S-22**

The students will break up into groups of two and practice interviewing and being interviewed. The last part of this lesson the teacher will video-tape students being interviewed for a job by a fellow classmate. The students will then evaluate the exercise. **S-22** The teacher can ask the following questions: Is this the best answer? What would be a better answer? Why is one answer better than another? **S-15** How did you feel as the person being interviewed? How did you feel as the interviewer? **S-4** What changes do you think you would make at your next job interview?

editor's note: The class could consider appropriate changes to the answers for different kinds of jobs (say, working with the public, versus working alone or with other employees.) What qualities would each kind of job require? Which of your own qualities, characteristics, and experiences would be important to emphasize for this job? For that one? Why? **S-29**

> *Despite the detail with which we have delineated the strategies, they should not be translated into mechanistic, step-by-step procedures. Keep the goal of the well-educated, fairminded critical thinker continually in mind.*

Five Minutes Late — So What?

Martha De Leon, Clear Lake High
School, Lakeport, CA

Objectives of the remodelled plan
The students will
- understand what production loss and overhead cost means
- develop an understanding of why being on time is important to employers
- explore other areas of life that require punctuality
- practice mathematically calculating production loss

Standard Approach

> The text explains how to calculate the loss to the company if one employee is five minutes late every day for one year. Students then examine a chart showing loss caused when one, five, ten, twenty-five, fifty, one-hundred, and five-hundred employees (at different hourly wages) are five minutes late. Students answer questions like the following: Ruth makes \$3.35/hour. How much does she cost her employer if she is five minutes late 255 days? How much would 10 employees who make \$5/hour cost their employer? If you and four others, at \$4.65/hour are late, do you think you will get a Christmas bonus? Why?

Critique

Calculation of wages lost should be related to individual students and personalized for more impact. The material jumps from one person to fifty and one-hundred people. The lesson becomes complicated for students who have difficulty with math skills and looses focus in the task of math rather than the understanding of the concept of being on time.

Strategies used to remodel
S-20 analyzing or evaluating actions or policies
S-3 exercising fairmindedness
S-28 thinking precisely about thinking: using critical vocabulary
S-2 developing insight into egocentricity or sociocentricity
S-26 reasoning dialectically: evaluating perspectives, interpretations, or theories

Remodelled Lesson Plan *S-20*

The students will read a revised version of "Five Minutes Late — So What?" ending with the sentence "Using the above formula ...." The teacher will direct the students to the sentence "Don't hassle me about five minutes — it's no big deal!" The class will discuss being on time. The teacher can ask why being on time is important, or if it is. Are there any other experiences in your life that have consequences for not being on time? If it's important to be on time to work, what about other areas of life? Is it important to be on time only for work? Ask the students to relate other situations requiring punctuality.

Discuss with the students the terms 'production loss' and 'overhead cost.' After reviewing the formula presented, give the students different numbers and have them calculate the loss in production. Discuss with the students their position as an employer who has an employee that is consistently late. **S-3**

editor's note: Have students explore the logic of an employers thinking regarding retention, promotion, and development of employees. "How do employers feel about consistently late workers? Why? How do they feel about consistently punctual workers? Why? How do employers interpret chronic lateness? **S-28** What are you telling the boss when you are consistently late?

• What qualities do employers look for in employees? Why? What do these qualities have in common? **S-3**

• Students could also discuss reasons people are late, and rationalizations they use, and examine those rationalizations at length. **S-2**

• Students could conduct dialectical discussions between an employer and late employee. **S-26**

• The lesson could end by having students brainstorm and then evaluate ways to ensure punctuality.

Follow up brainstorming sessions with discussion of the items listed — categorizing, evaluating, analyzing, comparing, ordering, etc.

Vincent van Gogh's *The Starry Night*

by Beverly Kjeldsen Ursuline High School, Santa Rosa, CA

Objectives of the remodelled plan

The students will:
- explore artistic aspects of *The Starry Night,* through Socratic discussion
- identify and understand the underlying structure of the painting
- explore the thoughts and feelings of the painter and the viewers

Standard Approach

The lesson begins with an explanation of what is going on in the painting. The instructor tells the students the different elements of design and principles of design that the artist uses (balance and counterbalance, etc.). The use of brush stroke is pointed out. Expressionism as a "style" is explained to the students through this painting, i.e., use of exaggeration of color and shape.

Critique

The original lesson plan is teacher directed. I would revise the entire plan using the Socratic method to explore the painting, the artist, and the style.

Strategies used to remodel

S-24 practicing Socratic discussion: clarifying and questioning beliefs, theories, or perspectives
S-4 exploring thoughts underlying feelings and feelings underlying thoughts
S-32 making plausible inferences, predictions, or interpretations

Remodelled Lesson Plan S-24

What colors are in the painting? How do these colors in this painting make you feel? Why? What parts or features of the painting give you those feelings? **S-4** Notice how these colors are applied to the canvas. (Heavy and short) What does this tell you about the artist? (Emotional) Would you call these colors intense? Why?

Notice the brush strokes. Which direction are they going? Why?

What is the lightest light? Why is it there? (The moon) What is the darkest dark? Why is it there? (The cypress tree)

Notice how small the village is compared to the night. Why?

Is this a religious painting? Why or why not? How do you think the artist felt as he painted this? Why? **S-32**

What is a complementary color? (Opposite ends of the color wheel.) Can you name them? (Red/green, blue/orange, yellow/purple) Where has van Gogh used them? (next to each other) Why? (for intensity)

How do you feel when you look at this painting? Why?

Words that can be introduced in context: *Helix:* a spiral which resembles a bed spring, as if wound around a cylinder. *Impasto:* Thick layers of pigment or paint, from the Italian word, impaste — to make into a paste. Paint applied with thick heavy brush strokes or palette knife. *Spiral:* a plane or curved line which moves outward encircling itself from a fixed center, either of a two- or three-dimensional nature. *Swirl:* to rotate, spin or whirl in a dizzying motion, as in a whirlpool.

> *What is remodelled today can be remodelled again. Treat no lesson plan as though it were beyond critique and improvement.*

What Is an American?

by Janet L. Williamson, Greensboro City Schools, Randleman, NC

Objectives of the remodelled plan
The students will:
- read critically by identifying and clarifying the central and supporting ideas
- evaluate arguments
- evaluate an analogy by examining significant similarities and differences
- evaluate the author's credibility

Standard Approach

An excerpt from "Letter from an American Farmer" is a standard section in both American social studies and literature textbooks. The typical textbook includes study questions such as "How does de Crevecoeur define an American? Compose a literary letter that describes a modern American."

The piece offers a generally glowing description of Americans (except those in the newest settlements who are more barbaric). He mentions that they are unlike Europeans because they are ethnically mixed, and live in a new place under a new government, free from having to pay tribute or tax to "either a despotic prince, a rich abbot, or a mighty lord." It describes differences among Americans inhabiting different regions.

Critique

These activities do not take full advantage of the possibilities of the lesson, which include dialogue about how credible the reader finds de Crevecoeur's ideas, how to analyze and evaluate his arguments, and identify and examine stated and unstated assumptions.

Strategies used to remodel
S-21 reading critically: clarifying or critiquing texts
S-18 analyzing or evaluating arguments, interpretations, beliefs, or theories
S-29 noting significant similarities and differences
S-16 evaluating the credibility of sources of information
S-2 developing insight into egocentricity or sociocentricity

Remodelled Lesson Plan *S-21*

You may introduce the unit by assigning a biographical report on de Crevecoeur, making sure the students understand that de Crevecoeur, who was born a Frenchman, was writing his essay about Americans from first-hand experience, but that experience had occurred many years before the essay was written.

After students have read the essay, you can guide them in a discussion to distinguish the main idea, recognize a possible contradiction in the text, and evaluate arguments. Sample questions include: What characteristics of Americans does the author delineate in the first paragraph? Does the author imply that these characteristics apply to all Americans? What, according to the author, causes diversity among Americans? What other factors might contribute to the diversity? (With these questions, make sure that students understand that de Crevecoeur mentions climate, government, religion, and types of employment as factors that lead to diversity. Other factors may include free will or determination of the individual.) In the last paragraph, the author brings together two disparate ideas, that Americans are similar in characteristics and that they are diverse. How does he reconcile these two ideas? Is his argument convincing? Why or why not? *S-18*

Next, ask students to locate the conclusion drawn in the first paragraph, "The American ought therefore to love this country much better than that wherein either he or his forefathers were born." Ask them to discuss what reasons he gives for his conclusions and if he is justified in reaching his conclusions.

Take de Crevecoeur's statement, "Men are like plants; the goodness and flavour of the fruit proceeds from the peculiar soil and exposition in which they grow," and use the following questions to analyze the analogy:

Consider the ways the items are similar and dissimilar. Decide if the similarities are significant and relevant to the purpose of the analogy. Why or why not? To what extent and in what ways does this seem true or false to you? *S-29*

(While these are open and dialogical questions, help the students to understand that the reasoning is based on the stated assumption that men are determined by external factors in the same way that a plant is determined by its environment. Students may examine ways in which the analogy (or the assumption) is not appropriate.)

de Crevecoeur based his generalizations about the men of the different geographical locations of the colonies on first hand experience. What factors can lead an observer to misrepresent, skew reality, or stereotype? *S-16* (Prejudice, selective attention or poor observation, writing from memory, applying causal reasoning inappropriately.)

In their discussion, students should consider the possible sociocentricity of de Crevecoeur's remarks. *S-2*

Risk/Benefit Assessment

by Lisa C. Quinn, Ursuline High School,
Santa Rosa, CA

Objectives of the remodelled plan

The students will:
- be introduced to the concept of risk/benefit assessment by making and assessing a risk oriented decision
- recognize that personal decisions are usually based on a combination of evidence and values
- evaluate evidence
- clarify values underlying their decisions
- compare other risk/benefit decisions that they may need to make, thus transferring insights to other contexts

Standard Approach———————

The students read a story about a mysterious disease that has been killing and disfiguring the members of a nearby community. The story presents the facts as they are "presently known," and "current" statistics. Some of the local doctors have been experimenting with a possible cure — injection of the disease. Following an outbreak of the disease in their neighborhood, the students are asked to independently decide whether or not they want to receive this injection. When everyone has made a decision, the teacher is to tally the "yes" and "no" answers, and lead a discussion of the possible reasons for the decisions which were made.

Critique

This lesson is a wonderful introduction to a decision making process or tool. It is a technique used by many industries today, but is seldom included in a high school text. Part of this lesson's effectiveness is due to the "real life" situation that it presents. Unfortunately, in an attempt to simplify the choices, generalizations are made and a wealth of material and approaches are eliminated. Students are limited to a choice between dying from the disease and dying from the injection, while any other options or results have been omitted. The students are asked to independently decide on a course of action, but in many cases the decisions are made without evaluating the validity, accuracy, and relevance of the data presented. In addition, the students have not considered the possible impact of feelings and other external factors (such as logistics, economics, politics, morality, or ethics). In many cases, this oversimplified version of historical information makes it difficult for students to relate to it, and they cannot extend these ideas to new contexts and situations.

Strategies used to remodel

S-33 evaluating evidence and alleged facts
S-19 generating or assessing solutions
S-31 distinguishing relevant from irrelevant facts
S-4 exploring thoughts underlying feelings and feelings underlying thoughts
S-15 developing criteria for evaluation: clarifying values and standards
S-11 comparing analogous situations: transferring insights to new contexts
S-29 noting significant similarities and differences
S-35 exploring implications and consequences

Remodelled Lesson Plan

The students can read the story, and then address specific questions. "What information was provided? Where did it come from? Can we accept it? Why or why not? **S-33** What are your options? What is your decision? Why?" **S-19** Once students have clarified their own perspectives, the class can begin a discussion. "What choices did you make? Why? What information is relevant? What is irrelevant? Are there other facts or factors that might affect your decision, which were not addressed in this story? **S-31** Is there a right or wrong choice? Why or why not? How do you feel about those who would choose differently? Why? What would you think of that? **S-4** What are the benefits of the options? (Responses can be probed for clarification and further development: Why is that important to you? What are you giving up? Why is what you choose more important to you that what you are giving up? Etc.) What are the risks? What values resulted in this choice? That one? Why do you hold these values? Do you reject the other values, or have you chosen the lesser of two evils?" **S-15**

When the specific topic has been completed, ask the students to identify decisions that they may have to make, which are also related to subject matter. Ask them to bring in current events or examples of issues that require similar decision making skills. **S-11**

editor's note: In what ways is this like the other decision? Unlike it? How do those similarities and differences effect making a decision in this new case? Why? **S-29**

• Encourage students to change the original story, and explore the implications of those changes: If this were the case, would that change your decision? Why? **S-35**

• Did the discussion lead you to change your mind? (If so, why?)

• If your spouse disagreed with your decision, would you change you mind? Why or why not?

The Catholic Bishop's Peace Pastoral

by Phyllis Bazzano, Cardinal Newman
High School, Santa Rosa, CA

Objectives of the remodelled plan
The students will:
- consider the topics of war, peace and nuclear weapons
- assess various forms of protest to solve the problem of nuclear weapons

Standard Approach

This lesson presents the American Catholic Bishop's Peace Pastoral of 1983 with its recommendations to the American government and the American people. The Bishops ask the question: Is a just war still possible in the face of nuclear threat?

The lesson presents two filmstrips, the first a parable on deterrence, the second on steps students their age can take to protest or make their viewpoints known.

The presentation of the filmstrips would be followed by a discussion of the material presented. The students would be expected to know the general contents of the peace pastoral from an historical perspective, as well as an understanding of the concepts of deterrence, first strike and the just war theory.

Critique

This lesson should start by allowing the students to voice their opinions and viewpoints on the subject of war and peace in the present time. It fails to use the opportunity to develop fairmindedness before any material is presented.

Strategies used to remodel
S-1 thinking independently
S-3 exercising fairmindedness
S-35 exploring implications and consequences
S-19 generating or assessing solutions
S-34 recognizing contradictions

Remodelled Lesson Plan

Day 1

Open discussion of war and peace, politics, and our country's policies, letting students voice their opinions. **S-1** To start discussion, I put three words and their definitions on the board: Deterrence, First Strike, Just War Theory.

The students are told to *suspend judgment* while listening carefully to one another's opinions of the issues. The discussion will help students to see their own narrowmindedness and foster an openness to see the others' viewpoints. Students can restate views to which they are opposed. **S-3**

Day 2

Filmstrip #1 is presented which shows a parable of a modern local neighborhood in which two families start feuding. They then begin to stockpile weapons to threaten the other family. Soon more and more of their budget goes into weapons and there is less money for food and other essentials. The discussion of the filmstrip would involve exploring implications and consequences of the two major world families stockpiling and practicing worldwide deterrence. What results does this policy have? How does it affect their "economies"? How does it affect them psychologically? (Probe and pursue responses. "And what is the result of *that?*")**S-35**

Day 3

Filmstrip #2 is presented showing some methods that young people might use to get their positions across. The discussion that follows would certainly include expressing their feelings regarding lawful and unlawful protests. "What do you think of this form of action? How effective is it? Why or why not? Is it right? Why or why not? (Could this type of behavior ever be justified? When? Why not? What should these people be doing instead?) What alternatives are there? Evaluate each for effectiveness and justifiability. **S-19**

Day 4

Their assignment is to write to their congressman, senator, or to the President of the United States. They are encouraged to express their honest opinions that, one hopes, have been altered or developed in some way after the three days of input and critical thinking. With luck, they will receive a response to their letters and will realize a sense of empowerment — that they do have a say in this democracy of ours.

editor's note: Pairs of students who disagree with each other could be given assignments to find points of agreement, and to pinpoint and clarify points of disagreement. "Find as many statements as you can about which you agree. What assumptions do you share, what facts do you both accept, what values do you have in common? What, exactly, do you disagree about? Put these points in the form of questions. What sort of question is each? Is it a question that turns on values or priorities, evidence, interpretation of the evidence?" **S-34**

Fallacies

by Michael Gonzalez, Teacher — Oral
Communications, St. Vincent High
School, Petaluma, CA

Objectives of the remodelled plan

The students will:
- gain insight into argument evaluation
- practice critical thinking by reading, evaluating, and rewriting arguments
- develop their critical thinking through question and answer exchanges, oral and written
- evaluate assumptions
- assess evidence, and sources of information

Standard Approach

The lesson was originally called "Fallacies in logic." It briefly describes six common fallacies. The lesson is taught with the assumption that if the students are able to name the root of the problem in the opponent's arguments, they are better equipped to counter it. The student is not always required to learn the Latin terms. The student is encouraged to have a mental shorthand for identifying logical fallacies. The six logical fallacies presented in the first lesson are: Appeal to authority (popularity, traditional wisdom). Provincialism, *Non sequitur,* Ambiguity, Slippery slope, and *Ad hominem.* Students are given a handout which contains passages with one or more fallacies of the type presented in class. The students are to name the fallacy in each example, and tell why they think their answer is correct.

Critique

The original lesson does not go far enough in making certain that the student is actually practicing critical thinking. The simple labeling of an argument as logical or fallacious does not in itself indicate critical, evaluative thinking. It does not develop the student's ability to re-construct and improve the argument. The lesson does not explain how merely being aware of the failures of logic makes students think more critically. The recognition of fallacies in arguments, whether one uses the proper Latin terms, English terms, or one's shorthand, does not indicate evaluation of the author as an authority or the reason for the *non-sequitur,* etc.

The recognition of fallacies is incomplete. How would the student write a logical argument on the same topic? How would the argument be written without the fallacy?

editor's note: This sort of approach has several negative results. *1)* Students don't distinguish justified from unjustified arguments of the same form. Thus, students tend to call all appeals to authority fallacious, etc., (especially when they disagree with the conclusion). *2)* Students find everyone else's fallacies, but not their own. *3)* Students tend to reject the whole argument, even when it has some strengths. *4)* Students often jump to the conclusion that, since the argument is fallacious, the conclusion must be false. All a judgment of fallacy tells you is that that particular argument doesn't make a strong case for the conclusion. This doesn't mean that no strong case can be made. As the author of this remodel points out, the standard approach to teaching fallacies neglects the crucial idea that every charge of fallacy can be countered, or the argument improved to avoid the error.

Strategies used to remodel

S-18 analyzing or evaluating arguments, interpretations, beliefs, or theories
S-30 examining or evaluating assumptions
S-16 evaluating the credibility of sources of information
S-33 evaluating evidence and alleged facts
S-28 thinking precisely about thinking: using critical vocabulary
S-12 developing one's perspective: creating or exploring beliefs, arguments, or theories

Remodelled Lesson Plan *S-18*

The teacher can present the six fallacies in logic as in the original lesson plan. The students could then give their own examples of fallacies. Since the teacher is not requiring the exact Latin terms, the translation of the definitions into examples can help students understand the fallacy in their own terms. In class discussion, students should be asked not only why the argument is fallacious, but also questions such as: What assumption is made? Is there a reason to accept it? Why or why not? When would it be safe to make assumptions like this? *S-30* What makes a source a good source? A questionable source? What kinds of reasons are there for questioning someone's evidence? (What if they weren't there? What if they have something to gain by lying, and those with nothing to gain or lose all disagree? How can we evaluate someone's track record?) *S-16* What makes an authority a good authority versus a poor authority? Is this evidence sufficient? Do we know if it's complete? Is it something that can be double-checked? How? *S-33* Can the claim be both true and false? Students should give more than one reason for their evaluation of the argument. Through this method, the teacher can introduce the practice of precise and critical thought. *S-28*

The re-construction of arguments can be introduced by the teacher through a series of questions such as: How could this person respond? How could this argument be improved? What evidence could be mentioned? Could the conclusion be rephrased to make this argument more reasonable? *S-12*

In order to take the recognition of fallacies one step further, the teacher will give the following assignment: The student will select an editorial from any newspaper or magazine and identify, evaluate, and reconstruct any example of the six fallacies studied.

270

Previewing Textbooks

by Susan G. Allen, Fort Osage High
School, Independence, MO

Objectives of the remodelled plan

The students will:
- engage in discussion about the importance of and advantages to previewing textbooks
- develop criteria for evaluating texts
- practice previewing and evaluating textbooks

Standard Approach

Students are given a description, taken from the *Encyclopedia Britannica*, of an unnamed animal and asked to draw a picture of the animal. From the confusion and frustration students experience, the teacher elicits that it would have been easier had they known what animal they were drawing. The teacher then asks if they preview before reading and transfers the lesson to previewing a textbook. A handout is used to elicit information about the class text and an assignment given to preview another text using the same form.

Critique

The basic idea of the original lesson is good and using the description to draw a picture is fun and effective. The point is ultimately lost, however. Students do not make the transfer to previewing a text, because critical thinking discussion is lacking. Students need to spend more time exploring the consequences of reading without previewing. The lesson is adequate on *how* to preview, but not *why*. Therefore, the students view previewing as a waste of time. The lesson does not help students develop criteria for evaluating textbooks or help them evaluate source credibility. The book survey worksheet, used to preview texts, is complete and effective.

editor's note: The reason for lack of transfer between the drawing activity and previewing textbooks is due more to the crucial dissimilarities between them. (Drawing is visual; reading, conceptual. Finding out what animal is meant is one simple, straightforward, discrete fact; previewing a textbook is a complex series of interrelated tasks, requires a deeper sort of understanding, cannot be proceduralized, and is more conceptual than factual.) Although the drawing activity addresses the importance of knowing something about "the whole" before digging into the parts, these two forms of this principle share little else.

Strategies used to remodel

S-11 comparing analogous situations: transferring insights to new contexts
S-16 evaluating the credibility of sources of information

S-15 developing criteria for evaluation: clarifying values and standards
S-21 reading critically: clarifying or critiquing texts

Remodelled Lesson Plan

After the animal description exercise, an extension is needed. The teacher could make two lists on the board of students' responses to advantages and disadvantages of knowing the animal before drawing. This discussion can lead to times when knowing some fact or having background would have led the person to make a different decision. (Why do you want to know where you're going when you get into a car with someone you don't know well? Is it helpful to know what type of problem you're working in math? Do you need to know if your theme is to be descriptive or expository in English?) **S-11**

Once the need to know is clearly established, questioning can be used to develop criteria for evaluating texts. When you choose a free-reading book, what do you look at? If you were choosing a textbook for ninth grade history (a class each of my students has had), what elements would you consider necessary? Important? What qualifications would you expect from the authors? Where do they get their information? Have they had other books published? In what subject areas? What reason do they give for writing this text? **S-16** What do they claim is unique about the text? Are those things important? Why or why not? What else would you look for? Why? What would that tell you? What distinguishes a good from a poor text? Why? How can you tell whether or not a text is a good one? How could you tell if the text lived up to the authors' claims about it? **S-15**

The class text should be previewed together in class so that students become accustomed to asking the questions as they preview. This gives the teacher an opportunity to clarify areas of confusion as well as check for understanding of the process. "Does the text favor one perspective? How can you tell? Why do you suppose this perspective was chosen? What does the author assume you know? Want to know? Is the author's writing style clear and direct or obtuse? Is the organization clear? Logical? How old is this information? Do the chapters build and depend on previously studied material, or can each be used in isolation? What are the major divisions of the book? What reference sections are there? What are they for? When would you need them? How will you use them?" **S-21**

The assignment to preview another text of their choice can then be made, followed by a class discussion the next day. "How has this process affected how you would use texts? Why?"

editor's note: "How does this text characterize the subject? Is this characterization accurate? What reasons does it give for studying the subject? Do those reasons make sense to you? Does the text cover the material in such a way as to help you achieve those goals?"

Stereotyping

Objectives of the remodelled plan

The students will:

- develop critical insight into the sociocentric phenomenon of stereotyping
- discuss the evidence for or against various stereotypes
- explore why stereotyping is so difficult a problem, due to its unconscious nature
- examine American media to determine the stereotyping common in the U.S.
- find out some of the stereotyping typical of their peer groups

Standard Approach

Many texts include discouraging stereotyping as part of their objectives. According to texts, stereotypes are negative and harmful beliefs about people usually based on false ideas about the ethnic groups to which they belong, or their gender. Texts mention common stereotypes and discourage students from using them.

Critique

One of the biggest obstacles to understanding people, and learning history, politics, sociology and psychology is oversimplification in the form of stereotyping. Texts address stereotypes in a category by themselves, rather than as one sort of poor reasoning. Stereotypes, like any beliefs, can be evaluated by examining *evidence*.

The standard approach is didactic in that students are informed that stereotyping is wrong, and so are unlikely to see themselves as engaging in it. Thus students do not discover their stereotypes, evaluate them, or evaluate their effects. Students should decide what, exactly, is wrong with stereotyping, by considering the evidence for and against conclusions of that nature. There is no hint that people might not be aware of stereotyping, that it may be unconscious, that people might not be able to admit that they do this. Students are not encouraged to explore how having a preconceived notion can affect perceptions.

Furthermore, texts unnecessarily restrict the concept, leaving out many common stereotyped notions — both positive and negative — of such people as: computer nerds, doctors, criminals, government officials, musicians and movie stars, blue collar workers, political radicals, yuppies, welfare recipients, etc.

By developing students' insight into sociocentricity and having them examine generalizations, this lesson helps students develop intellectual good faith.

Strategies used to remodel

S-7   developing intellectual good faith or integrity
S-2   developing insight into egocentricity or sociocentricity
S-10 refining generalizations and avoiding oversimplifications
S-9   developing confidence in reason
S-13 clarifying issues, conclusions, or beliefs
S-35 exploring implications and consequences
S-12 developing ones' perspective: creating or exploring beliefs, arguments, or theories
S-33 evaluating evidence and alleged facts

Remodelled Lesson Plan s-7

Consideration of this topic might begin with cliques and stereotypes students have of other students: How do you group or categorize the people you see around? Describe people in each group. How do you know so much about these people? On what evidence do you base your ideas? How do categories help us think about people? How can they mislead us? **S-10** How do you feel about the idea that others may have you classified? Why? **S-2**

To have students discuss the quality of evidence for and against their beliefs about those groups, ask: "What can and can't you say about groups of people? What evidence is needed to support this conclusion? That conclusion? What could account for that evidence? What evidence counts against it? **S-13** How can all of the evidence be accounted for?" **S-10**

Look at newspapers, news magazines, and popular culture for examples of stereotyping. Keep records of your findings. What do your findings say about our American perceptions? How might these perceptions affect the kinds of personal decisions we make? Decisions as a country? **S-35**

Students could discuss stereotypes presented on TV and in movies, and reasons for those portrayals. Have students name shows and movies. Ask, "What are the characters like? What types do they represent? Is anyone really like that? In what ways? In what ways are real people different?" **S-10**

Why do people generalize this way? Where do they get these ideas? Why do they keep them? Why is it hard to give up stereotyped notions? How could we combat this in ourselves? How do we know if our perceptions of others are accurate? **S-12**

Students could design a study or a poll to discover stereotypes held by their fellow students. What do we need to know? How can we get the information? What should we do first? Why? Then what? How can we be sure our information is accurate? How will we know when a person is being honest? How will we know if they are being honest with themselves? How could a person not be honest with himself? How would this complicate our study? How should we organize the information so that it is meaningful? **S-33**

Before studying a country or group of people, students could list ideas and images they associate with them. Later, students could critique those impressions in light of what they have learned. **S-2**

Human Treatment of Whales

by Noreen Miller, School District #12, Denver, CO & Lanai Wallin, Skyview Elementary, Denver, CO

Objectives of the remodelled plan

The students will:
- raise and pursue significant questions regarding our relationships with animals
- evaluate actions
- examine their assumptions through Socratic discussion

Standard Approach

This is a seatwork lesson on a newspaper article about four whales at Sea World who attacked their trainers — the trainers are suing. It is usually taught with emphasis on coding. That is, the students mark their copies of the article with an A for agree, D for disagree and I for interesting.

Critique

Although the usual manner of reading a newspaper article for an opinion is fast and efficient, it is a superficial approach to understanding belief systems. The lesson as stated would not establish why the students agree or disagree or the nature of the reasons for their thinking. The issues being raised need to be clarified, as do the assumptions underlying the students' beliefs. A seminar and dialogue using critical thinking would be more useful, as it would help students clarify their reasoning processes.

In the particular Socratic dialogue with fifteen students who had been trained in seminar techniques, some of the students also raised additional points such as: the people at Sea World are not well trained; these people should have studied the whales first; more research is needed; research under controlled conditions is different than field research; Sea World is run for profit.

Strategies used to remodel

S-17 questioning deeply: raising and pursuing root or significant questions
S-21 reading critically: clarifying or critiquing texts
S-20 analyzing or evaluating actions or policies
S-24 practicing Socratic discussion: clarifying and questioning beliefs, theories, or perspectives
S-18 analyzing or evaluating arguments, interpretations, beliefs, or theories

Remodelled Lesson Plan S-17 —————

Have the students read a newspaper article such as the one about four homicidal whales and their trainers. Ask them to think about the conflicts that are posed, both the obvious one and the more subtle ones, if they see any. Have them share the conflicts that they found. Then ask them to state in complete sentences the conflicts they discovered. Have them give their initial responses and reasons. **S-21**

Raise key questions, such as: "Who was responsible for what happened? Why? What should happen now?"

Discussion could move in the direction of more general and basic questions. "How do human beings relate to animals? What different relationships are there? What responsibilities, if any, do we have toward animals?" (Have students consider pets, stray animals, animals in zoos, in the wild, and animals that we eat.) Another question might be, "Is it necessary to conduct research on animals? If so, under what conditions can we accept such research? If not, what can we do instead of using animals for research?" **S-20**

Probe for further issues by asking questions such as, "Is it fair to put animals into captivity?" A possible student response could be, "No, because it makes them unhappy." The teacher could probe this answer in the following manner: "Are all animals in captivity unhappy? How can we as human beings know whether an animal is happy or unhappy? Do the needs of human beings ever take precedence over the happiness of animals?" **S-24**

After some discussion, ask the students to state some of the important issues that they have discovered. Write them on the board.

Begin to Socratically question the class as a whole about their responses to the issues raised. Probe them for the assumptions that underlie their belief systems by asking such questions as: "Do animals have rights? What is the status of a human being in comparison to an animal? Is it acceptable to confine animals just because it has been common practice to do so? Can humans kill and control animals without any negative consequences?" **S-24** By questioning students about the basis for their agreement or disagreement with a belief, they will gain practice in seeing their thought processes at work. They will better understand the reasons for their beliefs and the assumptions that underlie them. During the discussion, note related issues that are raised and come back to them later in the lesson or at another time.

When students disagree, encourage them to argue back and forth, trying to convince each other. Have students evaluate the arguments given. For example, you could ask, "Of all of the reasons given for (conclusion), which are the strongest? Weakest?" **S-18**

"Will There Always Be an England?"

Susan Allen, Fort Osage High School, Independence, MO

Objectives of the remodelled plan

The students will:

- exercise independent thought by identifying and clarifying the ideas and attitudes expressed in the video
- practice assessing solutions stated in the video
- practice making predictions
- clarify questions, points of view, and conclusions through Socratic discussion
- develop insight into sociocentricity by assessing their impressions of England

Standard Approach

Students watch a documentary discussing the postwar economic problems in Great Britain. They learn that the South holds all of the country's wealth and tradition with 90% of its people receiving a university education and 80% then able to find acceptable jobs. Conversely, the North has a population in which 45% are unemployed. Thus, two Englands, one rich and one poor, are developing.

Students are asked to list what they think of when they hear "England," "Great Britain," or "the British." The video is then shown, followed by a teacher-led discussion of the problems in Britain, the attitudes of the people, and possible solutions. The students then compare our country's problems to Britain's. This written assignment is then given: Agree or disagree with the following statement and support your answer. "To see the future of the United States, one has only to look at England."

Critique

I chose this lesson for its thought-provoking content and because it sets the tone for the entire semester of analyzing, evaluating, and comparing selections from British literature. It forces the students to analyze their present ideas about England and evaluate which are facts as opposed to stereotypes or vague generalities. By clarifying England's basic economic problems and comparing them to America's problems, students will suspend quick judgments and develop fuller and more accurate ideas.

Insufficient discussion and synthesis

The final writing assignment fosters some insight, but creative problem-solving is hampered by the lack of discussion in small groups. Students do not look at opposing points of view thoroughly and their insights are not synthesized before the writing assignment is given. Therefore, the writing assignment tends to produce opinions not based on analysis and evaluation.

Oversimplification

The students do not see this topic as relevant to their own lives. England is far away and we do not have those problems, so who cares? Their response is simply that England's government needs "to do something," and that the people need to take more initiative. There are no specific questions that force students to explore the underlying feelings and issues in order to evaluate the resulting problems.

Opportunity for fostering critical thought

The video is very factual about the problems and shows the sociocentricity of the Wickhamists. A more extended and detailed discussion could help students identify and grapple with the problems England faces. The lack of creativity in the British mind-set is shown when the man from Greece is able to establish a highly successful cake factory. Students can gain useful insight into sociocentricity by comparing his attitudes to that of the Wickhamists.

Strategies used to remodel

S-22 listening critically: the art of silent dialogue
S-5 developing intellectual humility and suspending judgment
S-1 thinking independently
S-15 developing criteria for evaluation: clarifying values and standards
S-25 reasoning dialogically: comparing perspectives, interpretations, or theories
S-2 developing insight into egocentricity or sociocentricity
S-11 comparing analogous situations: transferring insights to new contexts
S-19 generating or assessing solutions
S-24 practicing Socratic discussion: clarifying and questioning beliefs, theories, or perspectives

Remodelled Lesson Plan S-22

I have divided the remodelled lesson plan into four sections: *1)* Pre-discussion, *2)* Introduction of the video, *3)* Mid-discussion, and *4)* Conclusion of the video, discussion, and final assignment.

1. Pre-Discussion

Before viewing the video, students group themselves into units of four. They are asked the original question, "What do you think of when you hear the words 'England,' 'Britain,' or 'the British'?" After their lists are generated, ideas will be written on the board and discussed by the entire group. "How did you come to believe this? Do you *know* it or merely *think* that it's so? Why?" **S-5**

2. Introducing the Video S-1

Students will again group for discussion. What great nations do not exist anymore? Why? What happened economically? Socially? Militarily? What could have been done to prevent the fall of these nations? Choose one nation and write a paragraph for tomorrow explaining the criteria used to evaluate the nation's fall." Full group discussion the following day can identify the criteria necessary to evaluate the severity of national problems. *S-15*

3. Mid-discussion S-25

After showing approximately the first half of the video, which identifies the problem in England, explains the division between North and South, and interviews people from each area, students will again group for discussion. What assumptions about the North are made by the Wickhamists? Why do they make these assumptions? When have you made assumptions then changed your ideas after learning more information? What is your attitude toward the Wickhamists? Why? What response would they likely make? What is your attitude toward the teenage pregnancies in the North? How does the attitude of the Northerners toward teenage pregnancy compare to attitudes toward teenage pregnancy in the U.S.? Are the girls in the U.S. looking for the same things? What problems shown here were you unaware of? What has surprised you most so far? Why? What had you been assuming? Where did you get that idea? *S-2* What predictions can you make about where the video is going? Has the U.S. ever had a similar North/South division? What problems caused it? Are England's based on the same types of problems? Could the same problem occur in the U.S. today? *S-11*

4. Conclusion S-19

The rest of the video is then shown, and the students again group for discussion. "Which of your predictions were inaccurate? Why? *S-5* What solutions did the video offer?" An overnight assignment will then be made. Each student is to list a minimum of five solutions to England's problems.

The following day, a full group discussion will be used to synthesize ideas regarding the problems faced in England. "What are England's major problems? Why? Can you summarize the reasons for these problems? What must be done to reverse the process? Are outsiders, such as the Greek industrialist, necessary to reverse the process? What attitudes of the English hamper that reversal? How else could the Northerners help themselves? Are there other ways the Southerners can view industrialism? Must they? What parallels do you see between the U.S. and England? Can you give examples? What effects would (each solution) have on each country? What solutions do you see to England's problems? What effect would these solutions have? Would that necessarily or only probably happen? What are we assuming if that solution is used? From whose point-of-view would that solution be acceptable/unacceptable? Why? What would be necessary to convince them that solution is practical, necessary, etc.?" *S-24*

After the full discussion, the comparison/contrast paper from the original lesson plan will be assigned.

Speeches: Clarifying 'Equality'

Objectives of the remodelled plan

The students will:
- clarify the abstract concept: equality
- engage in a Socratic discussion of the concept
- discuss questions raised, and organize, compose, and give speeches
- practice listening critically by evaluating and discussing the speeches
- compare the perspectives expressed in the speeches

Standard Approach

In teaching speech, the emphasis is generally on mechanics and the attitudes necessary for successful delivery. As an introduction, students discuss the fears associated with giving a speech. The teacher asks questions like, "What don't you like about speaking in front of a group? What do you like ? Do you look forward to speaking in front of groups? Can you give some suggestions for overcoming your fears?" Various formats of speech are taught such as interviews, storytelling, oral reports, debate, parliamentary procedure, panel discussion and persuasive arguments.

To introduce the persuasive speech the students are asked to generate interesting topics. Prompts are given in the text for ideas. "_____ is a book everyone should read." "Each traveler should visit ____ ." "Nobody should miss the _____ concert." Students are asked to choose speech topics that would be of interest to particular groups: a meeting of a local sports club or a meeting of a citizen's group organized to fight pollution. They are told to begin with clear statements of what they want the listeners to do or think, including two or more reasons why they should think that way. They are then to prepare an outline for the topic they selected which they will share with the class. To prepare for actual delivery of the speech, the students brainstorm for the typical mistakes students make while giving a speech, such as, reading from a paper or forgetting to ask for questions. For practice, the students are asked to say their speeches aloud many times, pretending to speak to an audience or actually speaking to a friend.

Critique

Standard approaches to speech-making tend to overemphasize the mechanics of giving speeches at the expense of attention to content. This lesson unites speech-making and critical thinking by careful selection of topic. We present a speech lesson in which students clarify and analyze an abstract concept: equality. By first engaging in Socratic discussion of the concept, giving and hearing speeches on it, and discussing and comparing the speeches, students can begin to learn how to usefully analyze and clarify it.

People commonly experience great difficulty when attempting to use abstract concepts clearly, distinguishing different senses of the term — for example, numerical equality and economic equality — sorting out their relationships to related concepts, evaluating their use, applying them, exploring their implications, etc. They often incorrectly assume (or assert) that "everyone has his or her own definition" and request the speaker's definition. Definitions tend to be equally abstract and rarely useful in clarifying the concept or sense in which it is used in a particular context. We therefore suggest that the teacher help students begin to sort out the complexities of such concepts through guided discussions.

The following remodel can help students develop confidence in their ability to clarify an abstract concept.

Strategies used to remodel
S-14 clarifying and analyzing the meanings of words or phrases
S-27 comparing and contrasting ideals with actual practice
S-24 practicing Socratic discussion: clarifying and questioning beliefs, theories, or perspectives
S-22 listening critically: the art of silent dialogue
S-25 reasoning dialogically: comparing perspectives, interpretations, or theories
S-9 developing confidence in reason
S-8 developing intellectual perseverance

Remodelled Lesson Plan *S-14*

Before introducing the actual exercise to take place, the teacher could ask students to compare the characteristics of the prepared speech to other kinds of verbal communication. Write students' comments on the board. Among other things, students might notice that a speech is limited to a specific topic, is more formal, and has a beginning, middle, and end. Now ask what qualities an excellent speaker has. By this time, the students have begun to think about the mechanics of speech-making.

Lead students in an opening Socratic discussion which will elicit and separate aspects of and issues regarding the key concept. (The teacher should periodically relate to the concept specific points mentioned, indicating or eliciting the particular sense of 'equality' used or alluded to. The teacher can also periodically recap or have students recap the main points made in and directions taken by the discussion.) What does 'equality' mean? (Probe their responses with further questions.)

What different senses does this word have? In what ways are all people equal? Not equal? In what ways is equality an American ideal? Why? What issues and problems does our country face that relate to some sense of equality? (List these on the board.) What, exactly, does that issue have to do with equality? Why? What sense of equality? Is one side of the dispute against equality, or does the dispute rest on how to achieve it? What does 'equality under the law' mean? What would be an example of inequality under the law? What would we have to do to determine the extent to which American citizens are given equal treatment under the law? **S-27** What does 'equal opportunity' mean? Equal opportunity to do what? What interferes with equality of opportunity? In what ways does our society try to ensure that every citizen has equal opportunities? (During the course of an extended discussion, bring in other topics, issues, related concepts, beliefs, and values, such as the following: inequality, equal rights, "We are all equally human," one man one vote, autonomy, fairness, favoritism, elitism, racism, sexism, disadvantaged, affirmative action.) **S-24**

Explain to the students that they will be working in cooperative groups of four. You may want to have them divide responsibilities and chose a student to give the speech, a student to act as recorder or note-taker, a student to keep the group on task and keep track of time, and a student to report the group's progress to the instructor.

The group will have to decide how to narrow the topic by choosing an issue, a distinction, or a specific point. Once students have narrowed the topic, they will have to develop the speech: outlining the main points, offering and organizing their views, choosing clarifying examples, etc.

Students without this instruction would probably go on to produce a vague, rhetorical speech about equality that would be weak in construction. But because students narrow the topic, they can clarify it within their chosen context and give a more focused speech. The teacher should explain that the material in the speech should reflect the thought of everyone in the group, not just one person. It is important that students consider other people's opinions and that they work together cooperatively.

Before the speeches are given, tell students that they will discuss and evaluate them. Let the students decide the standards of evaluation, which should include things such as presence, clarity of voice, clarity of thought and its expression, strength of arguments, insightfulness, etc.

After each speech, the teacher may want to have students recap the main points (allowing the speaker or group to clarify any points inadequately understood). **S-22**

After the speeches are given and evaluated, the teacher should lead a discussion about the concept of equality as expressed in the speeches. In how many different ways was the concept presented? Was it used in the same sense in each speech? Did some opinions differ? How did the different points made in the speeches relate to each other? (Irrelevant to, supported or elaborated on, contradicted or conflicted with, compatible with, etc.) What were the strengths and weaknesses of the ideas? **S-25** Is it easy or difficult for us to talk about things like equality? Why? **S-9**

Students could later have dialogical or dialectical discussions (especially if a point of controversy among students arose in the speeches), synthesize points from different speeches, or write essays responding to points made in the speeches or discussions.

If you would like to repeat this lesson, then choose another abstract concept such as patriotism, love, friendship, security, success, progress, freedom, human being, etc. Whatever the topic, you can be sure that the results will never be the same and that students will have the opportunity to express their opinions in a critical way.

Socratic questioning should be available to the teacher at all times. Questions, not answers, stimulate the mind.

Analyzing Arguments: Beauty Pageants

Objectives of the remodelled plan

The students will:
- extract premises and conclusions from selected text
- formulate arguments
- argue both sides of an issue
- examine and evaluate those arguments

Standard Approach————————

> The student is introduced to a pro/con, debate, or issue-oriented format. Often the teacher would like the student to learn research techniques, and controversial topics are a likely vehicle. Among the most common topics are: abortion, gun control, capital punishment, euthanasia, nuclear energy, and animal rights. Presumably these are chosen because they are inflammatory, and because there is a wealth of information readily available. Even if a teacher suggests that students may do a paper on another topic, most will probably stay with the old standbys.
>
> The procedure for the research project may consist of the teacher spending a great deal of time discussing the requirements of the paper — thesis, length, required number of sources, footnotes, bibliography, warnings against direct quotations without proper accreditation, etc.

Critique

Clearly, such assignments as these, properly structured, are ideal for practice and synthesis of most aspects of critical thought, from examining assumptions to exercising fairmindedness.

Probably the most fatal flaw of standard lessons is that little or no time is spent on discussing the argument itself, how one formulates an issue, what constitutes relevant evidence, the value of the counter argument or the importance of justifying a conclusion. The student goes off to the library with an opinion — pro-gun control or anti-gun control, for example — collects the requisite information, thinly disguises the plagiarism, and types up a badly connected string of other people's work. The teacher takes home great piles of these papers and reads information seen countless times before. What has the student learned? Perhaps that research papers are dull or that footnotes and bibliographies are tedious. More than likely, students have learned nothing about formulating and examining an argument. They each began with a certain position on the issue and sought only to defend it, without testing its validity.

The debate format is worse, as it usually includes only the most sensational presentation of a case, replete with graphic horrors of animals being tortured in laboratories, for example. Usually no instruction is offered in argument analysis in this instance either. When argument analysis is addressed, discussion is often uselessly vague ("Be relevant!") or confused. (See the section "Text Treatment of Critical Thinking and Argumentation," in chapter 8.) Instead, students should be taught the skills of formulating and carefully evaluating a wide range of issues.

This is presented here as a speech lesson, though a written assignment could be given at the end. This lesson outlines a method of introducing students to argument and provides a model. A ten-step plan is suggested, but if you need to alter the procedure to thirteen steps or reduce it to eight, then do so without hesitation. The lesson is offered as a "formula" only because the task of introducing argument to students at this level seems difficult at first. Many things such as identifying assumptions, and testing the credibility of sources were omitted to keep the lesson simple. For another lesson on argument analysis, see "Writing an Argumentative Essay."

Strategies used to remodel

S-21 critical reading: clarifying and critiquing text
S-4   exploring thoughts underlying feelings and feelings underlying thoughts
S-31 distinguishing relevant from irrelevant facts
S-25 reasoning dialogically: comparing perspectives, interpretations, or theories
S-33 evaluating evidence and alleged facts
S-13 clarifying issues, conclusions, or beliefs
S-22 listening critically: the art of silent dialogue
S-3   exercising fairmindedness
S-9   developing confidence in reason

Remodelled Lesson Plan *S-18*

This plan consists of choosing an article from the newspaper and then extracting and examining an argument. It provides an extended example of reading critically.

1. Teacher finds a suitable newspaper article.

Ideally, the article should concern a current issue of interest to students. It should be long enough to contain the major points and have quotations from the parties concerned.

The selected article concerns a woman who disrupted a beauty pageant as a form of protest. She claimed that they are demeaning to women, encouraging them to starve and otherwise unnaturally change their appearances. Interviewees affiliated with the pageant countered her arguments and claimed that she hurt contestants and organizers. In this case, two issues were addressed: Do pageants hurt all women? Was Michelle Anderson justified in disrupting the pageant? Either issue can be chosen for discussion.

The article was chosen because it is timely, interesting to adolescents, clearly controversial, and easy to formulate. At the same time, the issue allows exploration of other issues such as the right to protest, gender equity, societal values, and commercialism. It is almost a page long, an ideal length. The story was followed for several days by the media, allowing the teacher to present new material if so desired.

2. Teacher prepares an introductory exercise.

Before introducing the lesson or the article, the teacher might devise an exercise as an anticipatory set. In this case, a class discussion on beauty pageants in general is suggested. How do you feel about beauty pageants? Why? **S-4** Does anyone know someone who was in a beauty pageant? If so, what did the experience involve? Does anyone want to be in one? Why? Do you ever watch them on T.V.? At the end of the discussion you could write "Beauty Pageants" on the board with plus and minus columns. Ask students to contribute positive and negative aspects.

3. Students and teacher read the text.

Students read the text, either aloud or silently. Ask, "What is the article about? What views were expressed?" ("Should Beauty Pageants be stopped? Was Anderson's action a justifiable form of protest?") **S-21**

4. Students, with the teacher facilitating, formulate a conclusion in such a way that pro/con positions are possible.

Begin by giving a definition of "conclusion" — the statement to be proven by means of the reasons the arguer is giving. Ask students (in groups or as individuals) to try to state Michelle Anderson's conclusion. "Pageants hurt all women," or "Disrupting the contest was justified." Avoid conclusions that state a position with a negative such as, "Beauty pageants are not worthwhile." If the conclusion is stated negatively, the pro and con sides become confusing. Keep students from inserting premises into the conclusion, e.g., "Beauty pageants are wrong because they demean women."

5. Students extract reasons or premises from the text.

Next define "premise" — a reason given for believing a conclusion. Students can work in groups to find the reasons, since it saves time and encourages a cooperative atmosphere. At first, reasons should be taken from the text with as little paraphrasing as possible.

6. Students formulate the counter argument.

A counter argument, the con side of the conclusion, may be formulated by examining the pro premises and by reading the text for supporting information.

Students should reread the article, listing details relevant to the conclusions. Have the class discuss these lists and distinguish what all agree is relevant from what is of disputed relevance. To use those points of disputed relevance, relevance itself must be argued. **S-31**

Encourage students to isolate key words and phrases (e.g., demeaning, indignities, cheating the contestants, right to protest, right to compete in the pageant). Examine the issue further, having students present reasons left out of the article, and discuss why the concepts do or don't apply.

7. Students prepare to argue both sides.

Students prepare to argue in groups or pairs. It is important that you impress upon students that they are expected to argue the case — *not just repeat the premises* — by *supporting* the premise. **S-25**

Perhaps they will argue that eating disorders are rampant in the United States and that, while the contestants themselves may or may not be starving, they serve as negative or unhealthy role models for the rest of American women. They may argue that it is rare for a non-white woman to win the contest. Or they may mention that women have to spend money to be in the contests and that only one woman wins the scholarship — the others lose. They should argue, for example, why bleaching hair is demeaning. Whatever points are made should be better developed than the premises.

On the con side, they may point out that everyone is judged in life in all sorts of different situations. The beauty pageant judges also score contestants on verbal ability and talent. They may even take issue with the wording of the conclusion itself, questioning a statement that pertains to all women; even if a few women object to beauty pageants, that doesn't mean *all* women are harmed.

Students will find the notion of supporting the premises difficult at first, because usually they are expected merely to repeat information, not think about it. After the first few times, students become quite good at argument skills and look forward to exploring the issue.

8. With a two-minute warning, students present either the pro or con side.

Give time for students to present their cases. The class should take notes on the strong and weak points in preparation for the evaluation. **S-22**

9. The class evaluates the presentation.

The evaluation may take any form the teacher wishes — written or oral. Remember that it is the presentation that is to be evaluated. The task is not to decide who won, pro or con. How well did the groups defend the premises? Did they argue irrelevant points? Did they bring in convincing information to supplement the premises? Did they address opposing arguments? **S-18**

You will notice that we have avoided having the students "choose" sides. Critical thinking requires students to enter into both points of view and understand what is strong and weak on both sides.

10. The class explores the underlying or tangent issues.

After this is done, the teacher may discuss the issue with the students and come to conclusions on which side is stronger. Have students discuss their own positions and evaluations of the points raised. Students could also discuss ways their thinking changed over the course of the assignment. **S-9**

This lesson can be structured in several different ways. For example, you may want the students to practice picking out the conclusions and premises of several articles before you try the ten-step approach. You may want to model much of the whole process yourself first. Using a video camera is always a good tool in lessons such as this, because it is possible to go back and replay sections of the presentations. Later, the element of library research may be added to more advanced lessons.

One cannot develop one's fairmindedness, for example, without actually thinking fairmindedly. One cannot develop one's intellectual independence without actually thinking independently. This is true of all the essential critical thinking traits, values, or dispositions. They are developmentally embedded in thinking itself.

News

Objectives of the remodelled plan

The students will:

- practice reading the news critically
- explore the consequences of working with and using different news media
- discussroot questions about the importance of following the news
- exercise independence of thought when evaluating the importance of, and emphasis on, news items
- analyze news stories by clarifying issues, claims, and criteria for evaluation, and by evaluating evidence

Standard Approach

Straight news is fact — who, what, when, where, and why. Often, however, news articles also interpret, analyze, or evaluate events, or describe an eyewitness' feelings. Texts emphasize the importance of the who, what, where, when, and why questions in news articles. Other purposes of the article are to show why an event was special, or how it was sad, funny, inspiring or unusual, and, in doing so, they make the story interesting. Texts point out that reporters sometimes tell more than the facts — they may tell how they themselves feel or how the eyewitness feels. Models of news writing are reprinted from actual articles written for different papers. The students are asked to analyze the models looking for vivid verbs, or imagining how the story would change if it were written by an eyewitness instead of the reporter.

Students are asked to bring in articles about new discoveries or to tell of a story they heard on the TV or the radio. Noting the pyramid structure of news stories, they are then to write their own stories based on one of the stories they found. They are to include the who, what, when, where and why questions as well as facts, quotes, and a catchy headline. Subsequent assignments are to write different kinds of news articles including lead paragraphs, complete news stories, and editorials. They are warned not to guess at the facts.

Some texts choose to focus on the mechanics of reading a newspaper. They emphasize the use of the index and the different sections of the paper as well as the format of the stories and the kinds of information presented. They assign such activities as finding particular services in the classified section or finding out about desirable vacation spots.

Critique

Critical thinking enables one to improve one's basic beliefs, and this requires having as complete information as possible. We chose this unit because of the important role that the news media have in shaping our view of the world. The earlier a person can learn to use news sources critically, the better. The critical thinker follows news, at least in part, for well-defined purposes. The critical spirit shapes one's use of news media.

When thinking about news, the critical thinker considers such questions as, "Why follow the news? What does 'news' mean? What situations and events are most important for me to know about? What can I believe? What should I doubt? What shapes the form and content of news I receive? What are the purposes of those who bring me news? How should I evaluate news sources?" Furthermore, the critical thinker realizes that the use of such terms as, 'news,' 'fact,' 'important,' and 'worth knowing,' all reflect one's perspective. The independent thinker makes these distinctions free of another's authority rather than blindly accepting reporters' and editors' evaluations. The critical thinker actively uses news media to develop an individual perspective, rather than passively accepting the perspective presented.

Independent thought

An enormous number of events occur everyday. No more than a small fraction can be printed or broadcast. Inclusion and placement of stories and order of details are editors' and reporters' decisions, and reflect *their* perspectives. Reporters and editors decide what to print and what to ignore, what to put on the front page and what inside. Yet texts repeatedly claim that the main or most important stories are on the front page; the most important details are in the first few paragraphs. By ignoring the effect of journalists' perspectives, texts inadvertently encourage students to unquestioningly accept others' judgments rather than making their own.

Another factor which determines the size and placement of an article is its popularity. A popular, though unimportant, issue may receive prominent and extended coverage. Gossip, celebrity news, fads, and other trivial events often receive more prominent coverage than serious issues and events. For example, a soft drink company that changed its recipe received time and space completely out of proportion to its importance. Emphasizing that the most important news receives the most extensive and prominent coverage discourages students from examining and evaluating the importance others place on news.

Texts tend to tell students such things as why people should be well-informed, and what functions or purposes news items serve. Students should be asked to develop their own views regarding the importance and purposes of news; and define their own categories of news stories.

Fact/opinion

Texts generally use or assume the "fact/opinion distinction" throughout their treatment of news. The sections on slanted news and news vs. editorials emphasize the distinction. The use of this distinction, as usual, is highly misleading. Activities on slanted news generally have students merely distinguish factual from evaluative claims. Texts encourage students to accept claims containing precise sounding language and doubt other kinds of claims. What sounds like a fact may be more doubtful than an inference or evaluation. Students should not be led to believe that they can judge the truth of claims merely by looking at their form. Instead, they should note the sources of claims and discuss the criteria for their evaluation. Here, texts provide little guidance.

Texts promote the commonly-held misconception that the news is fact (and therefore true) and opinion (usually understood as "mere opinion") is reserved for the editorial pages. This belief ignores the following points: *1)* Much of the news is quoted. Although it may well be true that this person did say that, what the person said may be false or misleading. Readers should remember whether "something they read in the paper" was quoted and from whom and in what context. *2)* Reporters make mistakes. They can get the facts wrong. *3)* Facts can be reported out of context.

Facts crucial to a fair understanding of an event can be left out, trivialized, or unfairly discredited. *4)* When a newspaper goes on a crusade, investigating and reporting a story to champion a cause, most of that work appears in the news sections. *5)* Editorial columns or letters to the editor may well contain facts (sometimes crucial facts not found elsewhere in the paper). *6)* A well-reasoned, clearly presented "opinion" column or letter to the editor may be as well worth reading, as new, insightful, and informative, as useful for understanding an issue, as is "straight news." *7)* Favored interpretations or explanations of events can be assumed or promoted, reasonable alternatives ignored. Students should learn to judge what they read on its own merit and in relation to evidence, not on the basis of the section in which it appears. (See the section on fact/ opinion, in "Thinking Critically About Teaching: From Didactic to Critical Teaching.")

Superficial explanations

Texts explain that news reports serve to inform and entertain. As they stand, such explanations offer little help toward understanding purposes and functions of various stories. The functions, rather than being clarified, are left vague. What is the purpose of the distinction between entertaining and informing? How should this distinction affect how each kind of story should be read, understood, or used? Such lessons leave students with a superficial, brief answer to root questions about the function of a wide variety of news stories.

The concept of slanted news is trivialized by the text treatment. According to most texts, news is slanted by use of misleading headlines or sentences (understood in light of the fact/opinion distinction). Even when texts do not limit the definition of 'slanting' to "emotive words used in headlines," student exercises and activities generally do. Texts ignore the subtler and much more common forms, such as placement, emphasis, introduction and use of details and quotes, lack of coverage, and the time at which stories are used or ignored. A neutrally phrased headline above seemingly factual statements may be slanted. The presence of evaluative language does not necessarily reflect bias. Though word choice often biases readers, the bias most frequently occurs in a larger context than in a single sentence. Writers may have double standards regarding the use of evaluative words or phrases, or such terms may simply be asserted without support. Texts generally ignore these factors in favor of applying the fact/opinion distinction to headlines and claims and having students "find emotive words."

Trivial activities

Too much time is spent having students write headlines, leads, and stories. Introducing reflective critical use of news media is more important than training reporters. Other forms of writing practice could be substituted (paraphrasing, summarizing, and writing argumentative essays).

The remodel which follows gives students the opportunity to assess and use news sources critically and reflectively. This unit promotes students' confidence in reason and in their abilities to think for themselves.

Strategies used to remodel
S-21 reading critically: clarifying or critiquing texts
S-9 developing confidence in reason
S-29 noting significant similarities and differences
S-8 developing intellectual perseverance
S-24 practicing Socratic discussion: clarifying and questioning beliefs, theories, or perspectives
S-1 thinking independently

S-17 questioning deeply: raising and pursuing root or significant questions
S-15 developing criteria for evaluation: clarifying values and standards
S-12 developing one's perspective: creating or exploring beliefs, arguments, or theories
S-30 examining or evaluating assumptions
S-13 clarifying issues, conclusions, or beliefs
S-16 evaluating the credibility of sources of information
S-18 analyzing or evaluating arguments, interpretations, beliefs, or theories
S-34 recognizing contradictions
S-35 exploring implications and consequences
S-23 making interdisciplinary connections
S-25 reasoning dialogically: comparing perspectives, interpretations, or theories

Remodelled Lesson Plan S-21

Teachers' introduction

We recommend that the teacher spend as much time as possible on this unit. News media themselves should be the main source of material, rather than textbooks. Students may also critique parts of the text after their study of news.

Although both the original and remodelled lessons focus on newspapers, we recommend that other sources of news also be used, discussed, and compared. "What are the differences between TV, radio, magazines, and newspapers? How do these differences affect presentation of the news? What are the consequences of the differences? In what ways is reading what people have said better or worse than hearing and/or watching them? How should these difference affect use of each medium?" **S-29**

Students could compare the perspectives reflected in different news magazines, newscasts, and newspapers. Videotapes of news reports could be used to introduce students to important stories.

Our remodelled unit is divided into the following sections: *1)* Preliminary work; *2)* Story placement; *3)* Individual items; *4)* Influence of media; *5)* Purposes of news; and *6)* Using news in other subjects.

1) Preliminary work

The class could spend the first week or so examining the news. The teacher may want to set up heterogeneous reading groups wherein stronger readers can help weaker readers. Groups may be formed to follow ongoing stories for the duration of the unit (and beyond). Such groups can make periodic reports to the rest of the class, and the subjects can be discussed. **S-8**

Work within such groups could be divided, with interested students doing background research, and others collecting, paraphrasing and analyzing articles, and looking up unfamiliar terms in dictionaries and encyclopedias. Students not interested in following an issue may cut and categorize stories (perhaps by subject, importance, or perspective of the source). Some students could keep running tallies on such things as use of wire services, journalists' sources, reports of opinion polls, what proportion of the news is quotes, or who is quoted most often.

The class could have an exploratory Socratic discussion of what 'news' means and why it is important. The teacher could ask questions like the following: "What is news? What are newscasts and newspapers for? What do they do? **S-1** (Follow up student responses with further questions or counter examples.) What kinds of stories or events make up the news? What kinds of stories do not make the news? **S-17** Why do people listen to, watch, and read news? What do people want to know about? What do people need to know about? (Encourage multiple responses, and encourage students to draw this distinction between want and need.) What kinds of things are important for people to know? Why?" **S-24**

When students have had sufficient time to familiarize themselves with newspapers and have shared their discoveries and impressions, the teacher can begin a series of more in-depth discussions about the significance of what students have found and about news media.

2) Story placement S-1

Students could apply insights gained through perusal of the news and preliminary discussions by discussing placement and emphasis of news. The teacher could use questions like the following: If you were an editor, and had a stack of stories, how would you decide which to print and which not to print? Why? Which to put on the front page and which inside the paper? Why? Which gets the biggest headline? If you were writing headlines, how would you figure out what to say? If you were a reporter, which details would you put first? Next? Last? Why? Would everyone make the same decisions? Have students discuss what kinds of stories everyone would agree are most important, least important, and which are of disputed importance. They can begin to generate criteria for judging the relative importance of news items. **S-17**

Students could compare front page stories with stories inside the paper, compare their ideas about what's most important to those of the editors, and generalize about their criteria. Ask questions like the following: "Why do you think these stories are on the front page? What, according to the editors of this paper, are the most important stories of the past week? Why, do you think, did they make these decisions? What other decisions could they have made instead? Are there stories or articles the editors thought were important, that you think are unimportant? Which stories inside of the paper do you think belong on the front page? Why? **S-12** What were the editors assuming? What could they have assumed instead? Which assumptions are better? **S-30** Why? (Similarly, students could compare different sources' coverage of specific stories.) Do any of the criteria conflict? If so, why might they conflict? Can they be reconciled? If so, how? What values underlie these criteria?" **S-15**

3) Individual items S-13

To develop students' sense of the requirements of fair coverage, the teacher could take a lead paragraph or headline, tell students the basic idea of the story, and ask questions like the following: "To research this story fairly, what would you have to do? Where could you get the information you need? Who would you have to talk to? What questions should you ask?" (The answers could be compared to the actual story, or stories from different sources — other papers, magazines, or TV.) If the story is one of conflict, the teacher might ask: "How are the sides portrayed in the story? Are they given equal space? Is each side portrayed neutrally? Why do you say so? Are the evaluations justified? Why or why not? How could we find out? How do the terms used influence the reader? Are the terms justified?" *S-9*

Students could discuss how the alleged facts in a story can be evaluated, rather than applying the fact/opinion distinction to statements. The teacher or students could select a story, and discuss questions like the following: What facts are mentioned in this story? (The teacher may want to record these.) What is the main point? Are all of the facts relevant, or are some irrelevant? Why do you say so? *S-31* Do the facts seem complete? Are there important questions left unanswered? What? Why? Are both sides represented? How does each side represent the issue? Do they agree about how to word the issue? Give an unbiased formulation of the issue. Is the report complete/does it tell you everything you need to know to be able to judge the situation? Why? What sources are used? Are these people in a position to know what they claim to know? Why or why not? Does anyone connected with the story have a vested interest in what people believe about it? *S-16* What evidence is presented to support or undermine the truth of the claims made? What conclusions, if any, can we reach about this story? *S-33*

For work on headlines, students could take actual newspaper articles, summarize or paraphrase them, and then assess the accuracy of the headlines. *S-21* Students could suggest better headlines, and compare different headlines for the same story. *S-1*

Examination of editorials, columns, and letters to the editor provide fruitful practice in argument analysis and critique. The class could discuss questions like the following: What is the writer's main point? How does he support it? What are the key terms or ideas? Are they used properly? Why or why not? Does anything said contradict something you know? *S-34* How can we find out which is true? Does the writer cite evidence/facts? What? Where does he get them? Are they clearly true, clearly false, or questionable? Why? Are the facts relevant? Why or why not? Are some relevant facts left out? *S-33* How would someone with an opposing view answer? (Students could practice dialogical or dialectical thinking here, if they are familiar enough with the subject of the passage.) What are the strengths of this argument? The weaknesses? Does the writer make a good case? Why or why not? *S-18*

4) Influence of media *S-35*

To explore some of the effects media have on reported news, the teacher could lead a discussion about "News as a business." Point out that most money comes from advertising and that news media with larger audiences get more money from advertisers. So news emphasizes stories that sell papers and attract viewers. And to maximize profits by spending less, news media tend to use cheaper sources such as press conferences and press releases, rather than investigation. The teacher may want to explain how AP and UPI are news-gathering services to which media subscribe. These services provide most of the news used by reporters.

Since two common sources of news are the press conference and press release, the teacher may want to explain what these are. Perhaps students could watch a videotape of a press conference. Students could look for and count mentions of press releases and press conferences, discuss why people give them, who gives them, who doesn't give them, and why they are relied on heavily.

"How does profit motive affect the news we recieve?" **S-35**

5) Purposes of news S-17

At or toward the end of the unit, the class could discuss, in greater depth than in the preliminary discussion, purposes of following the news. The class can discuss the news covered during the unit. Ask questions like the following: "What were the major stories? What other stories did you see? How important are the stories we've seen? Why?" For individual stories, ask, "Is this something people should be aware of? Why or why not? Why would people find this interesting or important? How important is this? What effect did it have? On whom? Which stories do you think are the most important for people to know about? Why? What does 'news' mean?" (Discuss at length.)

During the course of this discussion, the teacher may have students review the concept of 'democracy.' If necessary, explain the phrase 'informed decision.' The class can then discuss the kinds of news citizens of a democracy need to know — background for important decisions; actions of elected and appointed government officials. (Discuss at length.)

6) Using News in Other Subjects S-23

Social Studies

Students could write news reports of historical events under study. Different students or groups of students could write the reports from different points of view, for example, the Revolutionary War from the points of view of the English, Indians, and Revolutionaries. Students could compare and evaluate the results. **S-25**

Stories followed by students could be researched using back issues and other resources for background into the history of the country, conflict, or people involved. **S-8** Study of both the news and geography could be enhanced by having students read and discuss news about areas under study in geography, or by using their geography texts and other sources to research areas mentioned in important news stories.

Politics is an especially fruitful area for using news. Students can discuss different offices and to which branch of government each belongs, distinguish aspects of government mentioned in the Constitution from those not, and discuss any Constitutional issues which arise during the unit. Students can also learn about other governments, how they work and their similarities with and differences from ours, as well as our relationships to them.

Students could also relate discussion of political action groups and public opinion to government and history. Ask, "What is this group trying to accomplish? Why? Why hasn't it been done? How are they trying to accomplish their purpose? Do you think their goals are important? Why or why not? How would you evaluate their methods?"

The subjects anthropology, sociology, psychology are also covered in the news and could be introduced or discussed.

Science

Public opinion polls could be compared with scientific studies. Students could use news reports when studying weather and climate. Such subjects as energy, the environment, health and nutrition, astronomy, and physics are covered in the news. Students can use, discuss, and evaluate various charts, graphs, and diagrams presented in news reports.

When the powerful tools of critical thinking are used merely at the service of egocentrism, sociocentrism, or ethnocentrism, then genuine communication and discussion end, and people relate to one another in fundamentally manipulative, even if intellectual, ways.

8 Thinking Critically About Teaching: From Didactic to Critical Teaching

John Dewey once asked a class he visited, "What would you find if you dug a hole in the earth?" Getting no response, he repeated the question: again he obtained nothing but silence. The teacher chided Dr. Dewey, "You're asking the wrong question." Turning to the class, she asked, "What is the state of the center of the earth?" The class replied in unison, "Igneous fusion."

To begin to teach critical thinking one must critique present educational practices and the beliefs underlying them and develop a new conception of knowledge and learning. Educators must ask themselves crucial questions about the nature of knowledge, learning, and the human mind. Educators should reflect on their own thought processes, their own experiences of learning, misunderstanding, confusion, and insight. They should recall and analyze their successes and failures when attempting to teach. They should examine the conceptions and assumptions implicit in their educational practices and self-consciously develop their own theories of education through analysis, evaluation, and reconstruction of their understanding of education and what it means to learn.

Most instructional practice in most academic institutions around the world presupposes a didactic theory of knowledge, learning, and literacy, ill-suited to the development of critical minds and persons. After a superficial exposure to reading, writing, and arithmetic, schooling is typically fragmented thereafter into more or less technical domains, each with a large technical vocabulary and an extensive content or propositional base. Students memorize and reiterate domain-specific details. Teachers lecture and drill. Active integration of the students' daily non-academic experiences is rare. Little time is spent stimulating student questions. Students are expected to "receive" the knowledge "given" them. Students are not typically encouraged to doubt what they are told in the classroom or what is written in their texts. Students' personal points of view or philosophies of life are considered largely irrelevant to education. Classrooms with teachers talking and students listening are the rule. Ninety percent of teacher questions require no more thought than recall. Dense and typically speedy coverage of content is typically followed by content-specific testing. Interdisciplinary synthesis is ordinarily viewed as a personal responsibility of the student and is not routinely tested. Technical specialization is considered the natural goal of schooling and is correlated with getting a job. Few multi-logical issues or problems are discussed or assigned and even fewer teachers know how to conduct such discussions or assess student participation in them. Students are rarely expected to engage in dialogical or dialectical reasoning, and few teachers are proficient analysts of such reasoning. Knowledge is viewed as verified intra-disciplinary propositions and well-supported intra-disciplinary theories. There is little or no discussion of the nature of prejudice or bias, little or no discussion of metacognition, and little or no discussion of what a disciplined, self-directed mind or self-directed thought requires. The student is expected to develop into a literate, educated person through years of what is essentially content memorization and ritual performance.

The dominant pattern of academic instruction and learning is based on an uncritical theory of knowledge, learning, and literacy that is coming under increasing critique by theorists and researchers. Those who operate on the didactic theory in their instruction rarely formulate it explicitly. Some would deny that they hold it, even though their practice implies it. In any case, it is with the theory implicit in practice that we are concerned.

To illustrate, consider this letter from a teacher with a Master's degree in physics and mathematics, with 20 years of high school teaching experience in physics:

> After I started teaching, I realized that I had learned physics by rote and that I really did not understand all I knew about physics. My thinking students asked me questions for which I always had the standard textbook answers, but for the first time it made me start thinking for myself, and I realized that these canned answers were not justified by my own thinking and only confused my students who were showing some ability to think for themselves. To achieve my academic goals I had to memorize the thoughts of others, but I had never learned or been encouraged to learn to think for myself.

The extent and nature of "coverage" for most grade levels and subjects implies that bits and pieces of knowledge are easily attained, without any significant consideration of the basis for that knowledge. Speed coverage of content contradicts the notion that it is essential for the student to seriously consider content before accepting it. Most of us have experienced the difference between 'intellectual' or merely verbal 'knowledge' and true understanding — "Aha! So *that's* what that means!" Most teaching and most texts, designed to achieve the former kind of knowledge rather than the latter, are, in this sense, intellectually unrealistic, and hence foster intellectual arrogance in students, particularly in those who have a retentive memory and can repeat back what they have heard or read. Pretending to know is encouraged. Students rarely grapple with content. Much standardized testing, which frames problems isolated from their real-life contexts and provides directions and hints regarding their correct solution, validates this pretense.

This has led Alan Schoenfeld, for example, to conclude that "most instruction in mathematics is, in a very real sense, deceptive and possibly fraudulent." In "Some Thoughts on Problem-Solving Research and Mathematics Education," (Mathematical Problem Solving: Issues in Research, Frank K. Lester and Joe Garofalo, editors, © 1982 Franklin Institute Press), he cites a number of examples, including the following:

> Much instruction on how to solve worked problems is based on the "key word" algorithm, where the student makes his choice of the appropriate arithmetic operation by looking for syntactic cues in the problem statement. For example, the word 'left' in the problem "John had eight apples. He gave three to Mary. How many does John have left?"...serves to tell the students that subtraction is the appropriate operation to perform. (p.27)

In a widely used elementary text book series, 97 percent of the problems "solved" by the key-word method would yield (serendipitously?) the correct answer.

Students are drilled in the key-word algorithm so well that they will use subtraction, for example, in almost any problem containing the word "left." In the study from which this conclusion was drawn, problems were constructed in which the appropriate operations were addition, multiplication, and division. Each used the word 'left' conspicuously in its statement and a large percentage of the students subtracted. In fact, the situation was so extreme that many students chose to subtract in a problem that began "Mr. Left..." (p. 27)

I taught a problem-solving course for junior and senior mathematics majors at Berkeley in 1976. These students had already seen some remarkably sophisticated mathematics. Linear algebra and differential equations were old hat. Topology, Fourier transforms, and measure theory were familiar to some. I gave them a straightforward theorem from plane geometry (required when I was in the tenth grade). Only two of eight students made any progress on it, some of them by using arc length integrals to measure the circumference of a circle. (Schoenfeld, 1979). Out of the context of normal course work these students could not do elementary mathematics. (pp. 28-29)

In sum, all too often we focus on a narrow collection of well-defined tasks and train students to execute those tasks in a routine, if not algorithmic fashion. Then we test the students on tasks that are very close to the ones they have been taught. If they succeed on those problems we and they congratulate each other on the fact that they have learned some powerful mathematical techniques. In fact, they may be able to use such techniques mechanically while lacking some rudimentary thinking skills. To allow them and ourselves, to believe that they "understand" the mathematics is deceptive and fraudulent. (p. 29)

This approach to learning in math is too often paralleled in the other subject areas. Grammar texts, for example, present skills and distinctions, then drill students in their use. Thus, students, not genuinely understanding the material, do not spontaneously recognize situations calling for the skills and distinctions covered. Such "knowledge" is generally useless to them. They fail to grasp the uses of and reasoning behind the knowledge presented to them.

Most teachers made it through their college classes mainly by "learning the standard textbook answers" and were neither given an opportunity nor encouraged to determine whether what the text or the professor said was "justified by their own thinking."

Predictable results follow. Students, on the whole, do not learn how to work by, or think for, themselves. They do not learn how to gather, analyze, synthesize, and assess information. They do not learn how to recognize and define problems for themselves. They do not learn how to analyze the diverse logic of the questions and problems they face and hence how to adjust their thinking to those problems. They do not learn how to enter sympathetically into the thinking of others, nor how to deal rationally with conflicting points of view. They do not learn to become critical readers, writers, speakers, and listeners. They do not learn to use their native languages clearly, precisely, or persuasively. They do not, therefore, become "literate" in the proper sense of the word. Neither do they gain much in the way of genuine knowledge, since, for the most part, they could not explain the basis for what they believe. They would be hard pressed to explain, for example, which of their beliefs were based on rational assent and which on simple conformity to what they have been told. They have little sense as to how they might critically analyze their own experience or identify national or group bias in their own thinking. They are much more apt to learn on the basis of irrational than rational modes of thought. They lack the traits of mind of a genuinely educated person: intellectual humility, courage, integrity, perseverance, and confidence in reason.

If this is a reasonable characterization of a broad scholastic effect, then instruction based on a didactic theory of knowledge, learning, and literacy is the fundamental determining cause. Administrators and teachers need to explicitly grasp the differences that exist between instruction based on two very different sets of assumptions, the first deeply buried in the hearts and minds of most educators, parents, and administrators; the second emerging only now as the research base for a critical theory progressively expands. We express the basic difference as follows: "Knowledge can be 'given' to one who, upon receiving it, knows;" rather than, "Knowledge must be created, in a sense, and rediscovered by each knower."

Only if we see the contrast clearly, will we be empowered to move from the former conception to the latter. Now let us set out the two opposing theories systematically in terms of specific contrasting assumptions and practices.

Two Conflicting Theories of Knowledge, Learning, and Literacy: The Didactic and the Critical

The Scholastically Dominant Theory of Knowledge, Learning and Literacy assumes:

1 That the fundamental need of students is to be taught more or less directly *what* to think, not *how* to think. (That students will learn *how* to think if only they know *what* to think.) • Thus, students are *given* or told details, definitions, explanation, rules, guidelines, reasons to learn.

2 That knowledge is independent of the thinking that generates, organizes, and applies it. • Thus, students are said to know when they can repeat what has been covered. Students are given the finished products of others' thoughts.

3 That educated, literate people are fundamentally repositories of content analogous to an encyclopedia or a data bank, directly comparing situations in the world with "facts" that they carry about fully formed as a result of an absorptive process. That an educated, literate person is fundamentally a true believer, that is, a possessor of truth, and therefore claims much knowledge. • Thus, texts, assignments, lectures, discussions, and tests are detail-oriented, and content-dense.

The Emerging Critical Theory of Knowledge, Learning, and Literacy assumes:

1 That the fundamental need of students is to be taught *how*, not *what*, to think. • Thus, significant content should be taught by raising live issues that stimulate students to gather, analyze and assess that content.

2 That all knowledge or "content" is generated, organized, applied, analyzed, synthesized, and assessed by thinking; that gaining knowledge is unintelligible without engagement in such thinking. (It is *not* assumed that one can think without something, some content, to think about.) • Thus, students should be given opportunities to puzzle their way through to knowledge and explore its justification, as part of the process of learning.

3 That an educated, literate person is fundamentally a repository of strategies, principles, concepts, and insights embedded in processes of thought rather than in atomic facts. Experiences analyzed and organized by critical thought, rather than facts picked up one-by-one, characterize the educated person. Much of what is "known" is constructed by the thinker *as needed* from context to context, not *prefabricated* in sets of true statements about the world. That an educated literate person is fundamentally a seeker and questioner rather than a true believer, and is therefore cautious in claiming knowledge. • Thus, classroom activities should consist of questions and problems for students to discuss and discover how to solve. Teachers should model insightful consideration of questions and problems, and facilitate fruitful discussions.

4 That knowledge, truth, and understanding can be transmitted from one person to another by verbal statements in the form of lectures or didactic writing. • Thus, for example, social studies texts present principles of geography and historical explanations. Questions at the end of the chapter are framed in identical language and can be answered by repeating the texts. "The correct answer" is in bold type or otherwise emphasized.

4 That knowledge and truth can rarely, and insight never, be transmitted from one person to another by the transmitter's verbal statements alone. That one person cannot directly give another what he has learned; one can only facilitate the conditions under which people learn for themselves by figuring out or thinking things through. • Thus, students offer their own ideas, and explore ideas given in the texts, providing their own examples and reasons. Students come to conclusions by practicing reasoning historically, geographically, scientifically, etc.

5 That students do not need to be taught skills of listening in order to learn from others; they only need to learn to pay attention, which requires self-discipline or will power. Students should therefore be able to listen on command by the teacher. • Thus, students are told to listen carefully and are tested on their abilities to remember and to follow directions.

5 That students need to be taught how to listen critically, an active and skilled process that can be learned by degrees with various levels of proficiency. Learning what others mean by what they say requires questioning, trying on, and testing; hence, engaging in public or private debates with them. • Thus, teachers would continually model active critical listening, asking probing and insightful questions of the speaker.

6 That the basic skills of reading and writing can be taught without emphasis on higher-order critical thinking skills. • Thus, reading texts provide comprehension questions requiring recall of random details. Occasionally, "main point," "plot," and "theme" lessons cover these concepts. Literal comprehension is distinguished from "extras" such as inferring, evaluating, thinking beyond. Only after basic literal comprehension has been established is the deeper meaning probed.

6 That the basic skills of reading and writing are inferential skills that require critical thinking, that students who cannot read and write critically are defective readers and writers, and that critical reading and writing involve dialogical processes in which probing critical questions are raised and answered. (What is the fundamental issue? What reasons, what evidence, is relevant? Is this authority credible? Are these reasons adequate? Is this evidence accurate and sufficient? Does this contradict that? Does this conclusion follow? Should another point of view be considered?) • Thus, teachers should routinely require students to *explain* what they have read, to reconstruct the ideas, and to evaluate written material. Students should construct and compare interpretations, reasoning their way to the most plausible interpretations. Discussion moves back and forth between what was said and what it means.

7 That students who have no questions typically are learning well, while students with many questions are experiencing difficulty in learning; that doubt and questioning weaken belief.

7 That students who have no questions typically are not learning, while those who have pointed and specific questions are. Doubt and questioning, by deepening understanding, strengthen belief by putting it on more solid ground. • Thus, teachers can evaluate their teaching by asking themselves: Are my students asking better questions — insightful questions, questions which extend and apply what they have learned? ("Is that why...?" Does this mean that ...?" "Then what if ...?)

8 That quiet classes with little student talk are typically reflective of students learning, while classes with much student talk are typically disadvantaged in learning.

9 That knowledge and truth can typically be learned best by being broken down into elements and the elements into sub-elements, each taught sequentially and atomistically. Knowledge is additive. • Thus, texts provide basic definitions and masses of details, but have little back-and-forth movement between them. They break knowledge into pieces, each of which is to be mastered one by one: subjects are taught separately. Each aspect is further broken down: each part of speech is covered separately; social studies texts are organized chronologically, geographically, etc.

10 That people can gain significant knowledge without seeking or valuing it, and hence that education can take place without a significant transformation of values for the learner. • Thus, for example, texts tend to inform students of the importance of studying the subject or topic covered, rather than proving it by showing its immediate usefulness.

11 That understanding the mind and how it functions, its epistemological health and pathology, are not important or necessary parts of learning. To learn the basic subject matter of the schools, one need not focus on such matters, except perhaps with certain disadvantaged learners.

12 That ignorance is a vacuum or simple lack, and that student prejudices, biases, misconceptions, and ignorance are automatically replaced by the knowledge given them. • Thus, little if any attention is given to students' beliefs. Material is presented from the point of view of the authority, the one who knows.

8 That quiet classes with little student talk are typically classes with little learning, while student talk, focused on live issues, is a sign of learning (provided students learn dialogical and dialectical skills).

9 That knowledge and truth are heavily systemic and holistic and can be learned only by continual synthesis, movement back and forth between wholes and parts, tentative graspings of a whole guiding us in understanding its parts, periodic focus on the parts (in relation to each other) shedding light upon the whole, and that the *wholes* that we learn have important relations to other wholes as well as to their own parts and hence need to be frequently canvassed in learning any whole. (This assumption implies that we cannot achieve in-depth learning in any given domain of knowledge unless we grasp its relation to *other* domains of knowledge.) • Thus, education should be organized around issues, problems, and basic concepts which are pursued and explored through all relevant subjects. Teachers should routinely require students to relate knowledge from various fields. Students should compare analogous events or situations, propose examples, apply new concepts to other situations.

10 That people gain only the knowledge that they seek and value. All other learning is superficial and transitory. All genuine education transforms the basic values of the person educated, resulting in persons becoming life long learners and rational persons. • Thus, instruction poses problems meaningful to students, requiring them to use the tools of each academic domain.

11 That understanding the mind and how it functions, its health and pathology, are important, are necessary parts of learning. To learn the basic subject matter of the schools in depth requires that we see how we as thinkers and learners process that subject matter.

12 That prejudices, biases, and misconceptions are built up through actively constructed inferences embedded in experience and must be broken down through a similar process; hence, that students must reason their way out of them. • Thus, students need many opportunities to express their views, however biased and prejudiced, in a non-threatening environment, to argue their way out of their internalized misconceptions. Teachers should cultivate in themselves a genuine curiosity about how students look at things, why they think as they do, and the structure of students' thought. The educational process starts where the students are, and walks them through to insight.

13 That students need not understand the rational ground or deeper logic of what they learn in order to absorb knowledge. Extensive but superficial learning can later be deepened. • Thus, for example, historical and scientific explanations are presented to students as givens, not as having been reasoned to. In language arts, skills and distinctions are rarely explicitly linked to such basic ideas as 'good writing' or 'clear expression.'

13 That rational assent is essential for all genuine learning; that an in-depth understanding of basic concepts and principles is essential for rational assent to non-foundational concepts and facts. That in-depth understanding of root concepts and principles should organize learning within and across subject matter domains. • Thus, students are encouraged to discover how the details relate to basic concepts. Details are traced back to the foundational purposes, concepts, and insights.

14 That it is more important to cover a great deal of knowledge or information superficially than a small amount in depth. That only after the facts are understood, can students discuss their meaning; that higher order thinking can and should only be practiced by students who have mastered the material. That thought-provoking discussions are for the gifted and advanced, only.

14 That it is more important to cover a small amount of knowledge or information in-depth (deeply probing its foundation, meaning, and worth) than a great deal of knowledge superficially. That the "slowest," as well as the brighter, students can and must probe the significance and justification of what they learn.

15 That the roles of teacher and learner are distinct and should not be blurred.

15 That we learn best by teaching or explaining to others what we know; likewise students need many opportunities to teach what they know and formulate their understandings in different ways, and to respond to diverse questions from other learners.

16 That the teacher should correct the learners' ignorance by telling them what they don't know and correcting their mistakes.

16 That students need to learn to distinguish for themselves what they know from what they don't know. Students should recognize that they do not genuinely know or comprehend what they have merely memorized. Self-directed learning requires recognition of ignorance. • Thus, teachers respond to mistakes and confusion by probing with questions, allowing students to correct themselves and each other. Teachers routinely allow students the opportunity to supply their own ideas on a subject before reading their texts.

17 That the teacher has the fundamental responsibility for student learning. • Thus, teachers and texts provide knowledge, questions, and drill.

17 That students should have increasing responsibility for their own learning. Students should see that only they can learn for themselves and actively and willingly engage themselves in the process. • Thus, the teacher provides opportunities for students to decide what they need to know and helps them develop strategies for finding and figuring out.

18 That students will automatically transfer what they learn in didactically taught courses to relevant real-life situations. • Thus, for example, students are told to perform a given skill on a given group of items. The text will *tell* students when, how, and why to use that skill.

18 That most of what students memorize in didactically taught courses is either forgotten or inert, and that the most significant transfer requires in-depth learning which focuses on experiences meaningful to the student.

19 That the personal experience of the student has no essential role to play in education.

19 That the personal experience of the student is essential to all schooling at all levels and in all subjects, that it is a crucial part of the content to be processed (applied, analyzed, synthesized, and assessed) by the students.

20 That students who can correctly answer questions, provide definitions, and apply formulae while taking tests have proven their knowledge or understanding of those details. Since the didactic approach tends to assume, for example, that knowing a word is knowing its definition (and an example), didactic instruction tends to overemphasize definitions. By merely supplementing definitions with assignments that say "Which of these twelve items are X?", students do not come to see the usefulness of the concept and fail to use it spontaneously when appropriate.

20 That students can often provide correct answers, repeat definitions, and apply formulae while yet not understanding those questions, definitions, or formulae. That proof of knowledge and understanding are found in the students' ability to explain in their own words, with examples, the meaning and significance of the knowledge, why it is so, to *spontaneously* use it when appropriate.

21 That learning is essentially a private monological process in which learners can proceed more or less directly to established truth, under the guidance of an expert in such truth. The authoritative answers that teachers have are the fundamental standards for assessing students' learning.

21 That learning is essentially a public, communal dialogical and dialectical process in which learners can only proceed indirectly to truth, with much zigging and zagging, backtracking, misconception, self-contradiction, and frustration along the way. Not authoritative answers, but authoritative standards are the criteria for engagement in the communal, dialogical process of enquiry.

Common Problems with Texts

One crucial aspect of remodelling remains to be discussed: that of choosing which lessons to remodel. It is our view, after examining hundreds of High School lesson plans, that many of them ought to be abandoned rather than remodelled. Many of them are exercises in what might be called "trivial pursuit," wherein the student is presented with or led to discover random facts and esoteric vocabulary. The object behind many lesson plans seems to be to expose students to a wide variety of unassessed "facts," on the assumption that, since this constitutes new information for them, it is good in itself.

We, however, feel that school time is too precious to spend any sizeable portion of it on random facts. The world, after all, is filled with an infinite number of facts. No one can learn more than an infinitesimal portion of them. Random fact-collecting is therefore pointless. True, we need facts and information, but there is no reason why we cannot gain facts as part of the process of learning how to think, as part of broader cognitive-affective objectives. Problem-solving or exploring basic ideas or issues are effective ways to find and use facts and to discover why facts interest us in the first place. We ought not to overburden students' minds with facts that they cannot put to use in their thinking. If we don't apprehend the relevance and significance of facts, we tend to forget them rather quickly. We encourage the reader therefore to develop a skeptical eye for lesson plans that fall into the category of trivial pursuit or "fact-for fact's sake." Keep a wastebasket handy.

Often, though the lesson as a whole covers significant material, parts of it are trivial. The student's text provides insignificant details, the teacher's edition suggests trivial activities, which interrupts discussion of significant ideas. As a rule, texts fail to properly distinguish the trivial from the significant. Useless details receive equal time to basic concepts. End-of-chapter review questions especially confuse major with minor points. Structuring instruction around basic ideas and issues highlights crucial details.

Beyond the lessons and activities that need to be abandoned for their triviality, there are also lesson plans and activities that drill students — reading or filling out graphs, timelines, and charts, generalizing, categorizing, researching, experimenting, problem-solving. Such lessons turn skills of thought and crucial insights into mechanical procedures. Students practice the skills for practice itself, seldom in a context in which the skill aids understanding; thus, students fail to learn when to apply this or that procedure and so need to be told when to use it. The application of the skill is often merely memorized (and so easily forgotten), rather than understood. Students look for "indicator words," or verbal cues, rather than recognizing the logic of situations requiring use of the skill. Thus they can use the skill *on request,* that is, when given directions to do so, rather than learning to recognize contexts in which the skill is needed. Students read maps, charts, graphs, etc., at the most basic level, rattling off facts, but they do not discuss the meaning, significance, or implications of what they find. They copy charts and graphs, or formats for them, fill in graphs and timelines, but do not then use them as helpful displays. The purposes of skills, contexts within which they are needed, and reasons for applying them certain ways, should be discussed or discovered by students. Students should interpret the details they find, and explore their implications or significance.

This integration should be viewed, not as slowing down, but as deepening the understanding of the material. We should view the critical thinking that students practice as providing them with powerful concepts which they can use in a host of circumstances thereafter, and laying the foundation for the "I-can-figure-things-out-for-myself" attitude essential for education. Standard practice and testing methods, whenever possible, should be replaced with tasks and problems which require skills, insights, and information, presented to students with minimal direction given beforehand and minimal guidance given only when students are hopelessly bogged down.

Standard Treatment of Critical Thinking, Reasoning, and Argumentation

Finally, we recommend that the teacher keep an eye out for texts, questions, and activities that claim to emphasize or teach critical thinking, logic, reasoning, or argumentation. Often what is taught, or the way it is taught discourages clear and fairminded thought.

Texts generally lack an integrated theory of critical thinking or the critical person. Lessons fail to clarify the relationship of specific critical skills and insights to the idea of the critical thinker. Critical thinking should not be conceived merely as a set of discrete skills and ideas, but should be unified and grounded in a consistent, complete, and accurate theory of thought and reason, to the practical problem of deciding what to believe, question, or reject, the distinction between the reasonable and the unreasonable person. Particular distinctions and insights should be connected to that theory, specific skills placed within it. A unified conception of reasoning includes a unified conception of poor reasoning. Thus, each flaw in reasoning should be understood in terms of the underlying principles of good reasoning such as consistency, completeness, clarity, relevance, as well as being tied into a well developed conception of why we reason poorly and are influenced by poor reasoning.

The following problems are among the most common:

• Instruction in critical thinking should be integrated into the rest of the subjects whenever useful, rather than appear occasionally in separate lessons. Instead of consistently using such terms as conclusion, inference, interpretation, reasons whenever they apply, texts often restrict their use to too narrow contexts. Aspects of critical thinking are generally tacked on — taught in separate lessons and taught as drill, rather than brought in whenever relevant or taught in context. Lacking a complete and explicit theory of reasoning and the rational person, text writers limit the use of critical skills and insights, failing to bring them in when interpretation, exploration, organization, analysis, synthesis, or evaluation are discussed or most needed.

• Some texts give checklists for evaluating reasoning. They rarely mention looking at the argument as a whole and evaluating it as a whole. Students are asked to spot strengths and weaknesses in arguments but are given little guidance in figuring out how the points add up. Critical thinking lessons in texts have an overall lack of context when discussing arguments or conclusions. They use snippets rather than complete arguments, and ignore the larger context of the issue itself. Texts often seem to assume that students' final conclusions can be based solely on the analysis and evaluation of one piece of writing. Critical insight should lead to clearer and richer understanding, more rationally informed beliefs about the issue — not merely a critique of a particular argument.

• A common misconception found in texts is the problem of vagueness. Texts typically misunderstand the nature of the problem. Usually texts mistakenly claim that some words are "vague" because "people have their own definitions." The cure is to provide your definition. We, on the other hand, claim that words themselves are not vague. Claims are vague (in some contexts). A particular word or phrase within a vague claim may be the culprit requiring clarification *in the context of that issue* — the word itself is not vague in and of itself (nor are the words making up the phrase) but only in some contexts. Definitions, since worded abstractly, rarely usefully clarify a word used vaguely. We recommend discussions like those mentioned in the strategy "clarifying and analyzing the meanings of words or phrases."

• Many texts emphasize micro-skills. Yet they seldom attempt to teach critical vocabulary to students. Perhaps this is fortunate, since they often misuse the vocabulary of critical thinking or logic. Many texts use the words 'infer' or 'conclude' when requiring students to recall, describe, or guess. Micro-skills (like many other skills) are treated as things in themselves, rather than as tools which assist understanding. Many texts drill micro-skills but fail to mention or have students apply them when they are most useful. Instead, "analysis of arguments" too often consists of "separating fact from opinion," rather than clarifying or evaluating arguments.

• Teachers' notes often suggest debates. Yet traditional debate, with its emphasis on winning and lack of emphasis on rationality or fairminded understanding of the opposition, with its formal structure and artificial limits, rarely provides for the serious, honest, fairminded analysis and evaluation of ideas and arguments we want to foster. If afterward students merely vote on the issue, they need not rationally evaluate the views or justify their evaluations. Ultimately, such activities may encourage treatment of questions calling for reasoned judgment as questions of preference. Of course, the form of debate can be useful if students are required to sympathetically consider both sides of an issue, not just defend their side, and assess arguments for their rational persuasiveness rather than for mere cleverness.

• Many texts tend to simply ask students to agree or disagree with conclusions. They fail to require that students show they understand or have rationally evaluated what they agree or disagree with. Discussion is limited. Micro-skills are rarely practiced or orchestrated in these contexts which most require them. Argument evaluation is further oversimplified, since only two choices are presented: agreement or disagreement. Students are not asked "To what extent do you agree with this claim, or with what aspect of it?"

"Fact/Opinion," "Emotive Language," Value, and Bias

By far, the most all-pervasive, confused, and distorted ideas about critical thinking are found in the manner in which students are encouraged to "distinguish fact from opinion," and in the treatment of "emotive language," values, and bias. Texts generally set up or presuppose a false dichotomy with facts, rationality, and critical thinking on one side and values, emotions, opinions, bias, and irrationality on the other.

Texts give one or more of the following explanations of the "fact/opinion distinction": Facts are true; can be proven; are the most reliable source of information. Opinions are what someone thinks is true; are not necessarily true for everyone; are disputed; are judgments. Opinions are not necessarily either right or wrong. Often opinion is treated as equivalent to bias; *any* writing which expresses opinion, feeling, or judgment is biased.

Among our criticisms of the uses of the fact/opinion distinction are the following: 1) Students are often asked to judge the truth of claims they are not in a position to know; 2) the way the distinction is drawn in examples and exercises promotes uncritical thought, for example, the distinction often unhelpfully lumps together significantly different types of claims; 3) often neither category is presented so as to allow for rational assessment. (Facts are presented as true, and therefore need no debate; opinions are just opinions, so there is no "truth of the matter." Texts generally speak of exchanging opinions, but rarely of assessing them.)

When asked to make this distinction, students are typically given two or more statements. They are asked to read them and determine into which of the two categories each fits. Since the statements lack context, their truth or *reasonableness* typically cannot be rationally judged. Hence, as a rule, students are forced to make their judgments on superficial bases. In place of some reasoned assessment, students are given "indicators of fact." For example, statements judged to be facts are those which contain numbers or statements about observations or statements in "neutral" language. Statements judged to be opinions are those which contain such expressions as: 'I think,' 'good,' 'worst,' 'should,' 'I like,' or any evaluative term.

Since facts are defined as true, in effect, texts typically teach students to accept any statement with numbers, descriptions, etc., in it. Fact/opinion exercises typically teach students that every statement that "sounds like a fact" is *true* and *should be accepted*. Claims which seem factual are not open to question. Students are often not in a position to know whether or not the claim is true, but, since they need only look at the form of the statement and not its content, they can "get the right answers" to the exercises.

Students are often told that history is fact. (The evaluations and interpretations that appear in students' history books are forgotten.) Thus, if they read that a certain condition caused an historical event, they are in effect encouraged to believe it is fact and therefore true. But causes of historical events must be reasoned to. They are not written on the events for all to see. The interpretation, inextricably part of any historical account, is ignored.

This "distinction" has no single, clear purpose. Sometimes text writers seem to intend to teach students to distinguish acceptable from questionable claims, and at other times, statements which are empirically verifiable from those which are not (that is, whether evidence or observation alone verify the claim). In effect, many texts confuse these two distinctions by shifting from one to the other. Given the way texts usually teach the distinction, the claim, "I think there are four chairs in that room," would be categorized as opinion, since it begins with 'I think,' (an opinion indicator) and, since the speaker is unsure, the claim cannot be counted as true. Yet, by the second sense of the distinction, the claim is factual in a sense — that is, we need only look in the room to verify it. It requires no interpretation, analysis, evaluation, judgment; it expresses no preference.

Texts virtually never address claims that are certainly true, but are not empirical, for example: "Murder is wrong." or "A diet of potato chips and ice cream is bad for you." Students following the "indicator word" method of drawing the distinction, are forced to call these claims opinion. They are then forced to say that, although they agree with them, they may not be true for everybody; the opposite opinion is just as valid; no objective support can be marshalled for them or objective criteria or standards used to evaluate them. Students who look at the contents of the claims would call them "facts," because they are unquestionably true. These students would miss the distinction between these claims and claims that can be tested by experiment or observation.

The distinction is often drawn in such other guises as the distinction between accurate and biased or slanted accounts, news and editorials, history and historical fiction, knowledge or information and belief or value. Thus, on the criterion above, a passage, selection, article or book which contains nothing but "facts" could not possibly be biased or untrustworthy. Yet a "purely factual" account could well be biased. What the writer claims as facts could simply be false, or without basis — that is, I could simply say it, without verifying it. (When I claim that there are four chairs in that room, I may have pulled that number out of the sky.) Crucial facts which could influence one's interpretation of the facts could have been left out. Interpretations or inferences can be implied.

308

The distinction as typically covered lumps together too many completely different kinds of statements. Among the opinions we found were the following: "I detest that TV show." "Youth is not just a time, it is an age." "Jon is my best student." "Most children in Gail's class do not like her." Thus, expressions of preference, evocative statements, evaluations, and descriptions of people's attitudes are put in the same category, given the same status.

Many of the distinctions covered in a confused way might be covered so as to foster critical thinking. Unfortunately, as texts are presently written, this end is seldom achieved. We recommend that students distinguish acceptable from questionable claims and evidence from interpretation, and that the teacher use the applications such as those given in the strategy "clarifying issues, conclusions, or beliefs."

Texts often seem to assume that evaluation and emotion are antithetical to reason, always irrational or arational; that all beliefs, except belief in facts, are irrational, arational or mere whim. Values (like emotions) are "just there." They cannot be analyzed, clarified, assessed, or restructured. Judging another's opinions amounts to checking them against your own, rather than open-mindedly considering their support. Evaluative terms are often described as "emotive language" and are linked to the concepts of opinion and bias. Students are cautioned to look out for such terms and not allow their beliefs to be influenced by them. We recommend these points be replaced with the more pertinent distinction of rationally justified use of evaluative terms from unjustified, or supported from unsupported use of evaluative language, and that students analyze and assess values and discuss standards or criteria. Students can then share their views regarding the status of such claims and the significance of their disagreements. Students should be encouraged, not to abandon evaluative language, but to use it appropriately, when its use is justified; not to discount it, but to evaluate it. They should learn to analyze terms and determine what kinds of facts are required to back them up; set reasonable standards and apply them fairmindedly.

Texts are right about distinguishing when someone tries to influence belief from other kinds of writing and speech (as a basic distinction of critical thinking), but then they fall. They lump together what we would next separate: attempts to persuade, convince, or influence *by reason,* from other attempts to influence (such as by force, repetition, or obviously irrelevant association). Not all appeals to emotion are equivalent; they can be relevant or irrelevant, well-supported or unsupported.

According to texts, bias consists in a writer or speaker expressing a feeling on a topic. However developed the explanations of bias, however, students practice invariably consists of examining single sentences and underlining words that show bias, that is, "emotive" or evaluative words. Students do not evaluate passages for bias. Students do not distinguish contexts in which writers' conclusions and evaluations are appropriately expressed from when they are not, or when the feelings or opinions have rational grounds from when they reflect mere whim, impression, or prejudice, or when evaluations are supported from when they are merely asserted. Nor do students discuss *how* they should take bias into consideration — for example, by considering other views. The practical effect of the standard approach is to teach students to notice when someone uses evaluative terms, and then measure that use against their own beliefs. We suggest that instead, students consider questions like the following: What is wrong with bias? Why? How can I detect it? How does that fit in with the ideal of the fairminded critical thinker? What should I do when I realize the author is biased? What does the text mean by warning me against being "unduly influenced" by bias?

> *Everyone learning to deepen her critical thinking skills and dispositions comes to insights over time. We certainly can enrich and enhance this process, even help it to move at a faster pace, but only in a qualified way. Time to assimilate and grow is essential.*

Remodelling the Curriculum

Curricula can play a significant role in school life. Directed by a district's curriculum, instruction must meet the educational goals and objectives stated in the curriculum. It is crucial, therefore, that its articulation and interpretation conduce to critical thinking. A curriculum heavily loaded with detail, for example, may restrict the teacher's freedom to emphasize critical thinking by requiring large amounts of information to be covered quickly and superficially. Curriculum may also draw attention away from critical thinking by emphasizing goals, activities, and instruction contrary to critical thought or by being linked to tests that focus on recall. Some curricula mention critical thinking in vague, superficial, or narrow ways, creating confusion and mis-instruction. One of the most significant problems is the neglect of the essential role of critical thinking in the student's acquisition of knowledge. Rarely is the concept of knowledge analyzed. Instead, articulation assumes that all educators know what knowledge is and how it differs from opinion, belief, or prejudice. Any attempt to make critical thinking a significant part of the educational life of students must involve a restructuring of the curriculum, making explicit the philosophy of knowledge and learning that underlie its writing and direct its implementation. This chapter offers suggestions for analyzing, evaluating, and remodelling curricula to emphasize education based on principles of critical thought, coherently integrated into a rich philosophy of education.

Curriculum: What is it?

Written curricula can and do appear in a variety of forms. The *Oxford English Dictionary* defines curriculum as: "A course; specifically a regular course of study or training, as at a school or university." Some curricula written in this narrow sense list the particular courses students are to study, detailing the content of these courses, and perhaps even including course outlines. Curricula of this type are often restrictive and often rely heavily on a memorization/recall method of instruction, severely limiting teacher freedom, creativity, and individuality.

Most curricula are more complete than this, broader in scope, addressing much more than content and outline. Generally, curricula are best thought of as a conception, written or presupposed in practice, of what to teach and how to teach it. More complete curricula contain, therefore, all or most of the following elements, each of which is a possible source of problems: philosophy, goals, standards, curriculum and instructional objectives, assessment, and instructional examples. Let us first consider each element in order, from general to specific.

Philosophy: A theory or logical analysis of the principles underlying education, knowledge, teaching, and learning, including assumptions about educational purposes and practices intended to influence or direct all subsequent curriculum formulations and applications.

Commentary: There are two major problems to watch out for here: *1)* either the philosophy articulated is too vaguely expressed to be more than a set of empty platitudes, or *2)* it is so narrowly expressed that it forces many teachers to accede to an approach that they do not and should not accept. The philosophy should provide a defensible analysis of the principles underlying education, knowledge, teaching, and learning which is open to alternative teaching styles, respects the individual differences between teachers, and is sufficiently clear and specific to have clear-cut implications for teaching and learning.

Goals: Usually an abstract statement of expected student attainment as a result of education.

Commentary: Goals should be written as unambiguously as possible. If critical thinking is to be a significant element in the whole, some articulation of it must be visible throughout the goal statements.

Standards: A broad statement of expected student achievement on completion of a year's study within a specific subject area.

Commentary: If critical thinking is to play a significant role in instruction, then critical thinking standards must be explicit throughout. This is virtually never done.

Curriculum Objectives: A more specific statement of learning achievement shown by the student in any subject after completing the unit of study.

Instructional Objectives: Descriptions of minimal student achievement that should be demonstrated at the completion of one or more lessons.

Commentary: In both curriculum and instructional objectives, care must be taken not to imply lower order behavioral responses as the goal. These objectives should focus on the depth of student understanding, not, for example, on their ability merely to reproduce "correct" responses on recall oriented tests and assignments.

Assessment: Description of how student progress toward these goals, standards, and objectives is to be assessed; often used to assess teacher efficacy; rarely expressed, but implied by the Instructional Objectives.

Commentary: Again, care must be taken not to put the emphasis on lower order multiple choice testing.

Instructional Examples: Curriculum may end with examples of instruction appropriate to the attainment of these goals, standards, and objectives.

Commentary: If the curriculum contains model instructional examples, they should explicitly display methods that encourage independent and critical thought.

The Importance of Philosophy of Education to Curriculum Construction

All curricula reflect some philosophy of education; however, often this philosophy is not expressed, but uncritically assumed. Whether expressed or assumed, some philosophy is, *without exception*, the basis of any formulation of educational purposes, goals, and objectives. It determines, one way or another, the nature of educational practice. It is clear that most curriculum writers do not consider the statement of philosophy to be a significant element, since they are often satisfied with a vague, platitudinous treatment. Some curricula include under philosophy, statements that are not, properly speaking, definitive of a philosophical perspective. In these cases, what is called "philosophy" is nothing more than a broad and general educational objective. Failure to make assumed philosophy explicit often leads to the development of curricula based on unacceptable or questionable educational assumptions which would be rejected if openly stated.

Sometimes the expressed philosophy is inconsistent with the methods of instruction or assessment. In these cases, the goals are often vaguely defined, obscuring the contradiction between curriculum objectives, instructional examples, and philosophy. For example, an educational philosophy might emphasize the importance of autonomous and critical thought, while assessment focuses on testing which requires only recall and robotic practice of skills. Curriculua need, then, an articulate theory of education, knowledge, teaching, and learning that guides all subsequent articulations of goals, objectives, and instructional examples. At the same time, the philosophy should not rule out alternative teaching styles, except those incompatible with independence of thought and other fundamental educational values (truth, fairmindedness, empathy, rationality, self-criticism).

Knowing and Thinking: A Model Philosophical Statement

Of fundamental and critical importance in any discussion of educational philosophy is the conception of knowledge and learning guiding the formulation of the curriculum. Since we can roughly understand curriculum as a course of study which has knowledge as its objective, those involved in both curriculum development and teaching should be clear about their answers to such questions as these: "What is knowledge. How do humans acquire knowledge. How are students best taught so as to acquire genuine knowledge?" These questions may seem to have obvious answers or to be irrelevant to practical problems of instruction, but they are not. Indeed, one fundamental obstacle to educational reform is a set of misconceptions about knowledge embedded in teaching practice.

One persistent unexpressed misconception is that knowledge consists in bits and pieces of information to be implanted in the student's mind by the teacher and materials. Knowledge is unwittingly considered to be a thing that can be put into students' heads as some object might be put into their hands. Didactic instruction becomes dominant, and instruction reduces to giving students information (principles, values, facts, etc.) to accept as true and commit to memory. Memorization and recall then become the fundamental modes of thought, and students study to reproduce the "correct answers" given to them by the teacher or text. Curriculum based on this misconception of knowledge confuses the mere appearance of knowledge with genuine knowledge. A parrot or tape recorder, let us not forget, is not a knower. Many who verbally reject rote learning unwittingly continue to encourage it simply because they fail to examine the philosophy

313

underlying their instruction. Some practitioners also unknowingly undermine whatever effort they exert to break out of this mold by continually assessing student progress in ways that encourage memorization and recall rather than depth of understanding. A particularly significant misconception in this model is that if one has the "stuff" of knowledge, one will automatically reason well. The power of reasoning, in this view, naturally follows the acquisition of information, and need not, indeed cannot, precede or accompany it. Students are expected to get the information first, and then through it to start to think. Unfortunately, because of the amount of information taken to be essential, the time for thought is put off later and later. Furthermore, students who passively and uncritically accept information, do not go on to think critically once they learn to parrot it. The habits of learning they established in getting information transfer to subsequent learning. Information parrots become parrots of thinking.

Content dense curricula often create fragmented and unengaging instruction. Subjects become isolated units having little or no relation to each other, and are often defined in terms of a long list of fragmented specifics. Students rarely see how parts relate to the whole, or to their lives outside school. As a result, both teacher and student come to think of knowledge as bits of information grouped under the general heading of one or another subject. Under the heading "Science," for example, are many subheadings: Biology, Astronomy, Physiology, Chemistry, Physics, Geology, and so on, with each subheading containing the bits of information that constitute that field.

The conception of knowledge and learning presupposed in the didactic paradigm of memorization and recall is deceptive. It produces the illusion and confidence of knowledge without the substance, without the comprehension and understanding essential to any valid claim to knowledge. Remember, though people claim to know many things, a claim to know does not, in and of itself, certify actual knowledge. To claim knowledge is to imply not only that the thing claimed is true, but also that the knower understands the claim and the reasons for making it. The strength of one's conviction does not attest to its truth. There is often conviction in prejudice, certitude in gossip, rumor, and hearsay, confidence in unjustified authority, and blind faith in tradition. Students must grasp the difference between belief and knowledge. Blind memorization blurs that distinction.

Consider how a person moves from believing a rumor to ascertaining its truth, from believing the claim of some authority to verifying, and thus knowing, its truth. This shift from believing to knowing requires the active engagement of thought; it requires looking for and assessing reasons for and against the claim. The person who has moved from belief to knowledge understands the claim and the reason for the claim. This person can justify it. Knowledge exists, then, only in minds that have comprehended and justified it through thought. Knowledge is something we must think our way to, not something we can simply be given. Knowledge is produced by thought, analyzed by thought, comprehended by thought, organized by thought, evaluated, refined, maintained, and transformed by thought. The educational philosophy underlying educational goals, standards, and objectives should be based on an accurate and full conception of the dependence of knowledge on thought.

This conception of knowledge, that it exists only in and through critical thought, should pervade the whole of the curriculum. All of the disciplines — Mathematics, Chemistry, Biology, Geography, Sociology, History, Philosophy, Literature, Composition, and so on — are modes of thought. Remember, we *know* mathematics, not to the extent that we can recite mathematical formulas and apply them upon request, but only to the extent that we can *think mathematically*. We know science, not to the extent that we can recall information from our science textbooks and have gone through a series of actions described in a lab manual, but only to the extent that we can *think scientifically*. We understand sociology, history, and philosophy only to the extent that we can think sociologically, historically, and philosophically. We understand and can truly hold such values as freedom of speech and thought, tolerance for honest differences and plurality, and civic responsibility only to the extent that we have honestly examined the reasons for them and the practical consequences of holding them. When we teach courses in such a way that students pass without thinking their way into the knowledge that these subjects make possible, students leave without any more knowledge than they had initially. When we sacrifice thought to gain coverage, make no mistake, we sacrifice knowledge at the same time. The issue is not "Shall we sacrifice knowledge to spend time on thought?", but "Shall we continue to sacrifice both knowledge and thought for the mere appearance of learning, for inert, confused learning?"

As an illustrative example, consider history. In history classes, students expect to be given names, events, dates, places, causes, and explanations to repeat on papers and tests. Teachers typically tell students what events occurred, their causes, their results, and their significance. When asked, students can say that understanding the past is important to understanding the present, but they do not take this seriously. They see no useful application of what they study in history classes, and so are frequently bored. History seems to them a dull drudgery, with no real purpose or significance, except to those who need to know it: teachers.

Consider history taught as a mode of thought. Viewed from the paradigm of a critical education, blindly memorized content ceases to be the focal point. The logic of historical thought — that is, learning to think historically *by* thinking historically — becomes the focal point. Students learn the content of history, in other words, while learning to think historically. They learn by experience that history is not a simple recounting of past events, but also an interpretation of these events written from a point of view. In recognizing that each historian writes from a point of view, students can begin to identify and thus assess the points of view leading to various interpretations and propose their own interpretations based on alternative points of view. They can learn that historical accounts are not necessarily a matter of simple 'true or false.' The student of history has to assess the gain and loss of alternative conflicting accounts. To begin to recognize this fundamental logic of historical thought, students could explore the significance of their own personal history and the relationship of their past to their present. They could begin to see that their past and the way they interpret it significantly influences their perception of their present and anticipation of their future. Understanding their own interpretations and constructions of personal history becomes an important tool for understanding the present. From here it is a short step to recognizing the importance of cultural, national, and world history in understanding the present, as well as understanding the news as a mode of historical thinking. They learn, in short, to think historically. They gain not only historical information and insights, they also acquire skills, abilities, and values.

Knowledge, Skills, and Values: The Philosophical Statement Continued

Knowledge is a tool we use for many purposes: to explain, illuminate, answer, clarify, settle, solve, inform, perform, and accomplish. Divorced from its use, from the skills entailed by getting and using it, knowledge is empty. Indeed, one does not really know something if one does not understand its verification or purpose. To come to know anything, then, requires one to acquire the skills embodied in it. Schooling based on a didactic, lecture-drill-test, paradigm assumes that in giving students bits of information, they have, or will get, the skills embodied in the knowledge.

This is much too optimistic, for students frequently see no sense to, nor use for, the information they accumulate. Furthermore, not learning information in the context of its use, they have no sense of how to use it. This lack cannot be made up for by mere reiteration of those uses.

Also entailed by knowledge is the notion of value. No one learns what they do not in some sense value. Knowledge has value because of its use. We value what it allows us to accomplish. Consider, for example, the things that students *do* value, how quickly they learn these things, how much they know about them, and how well they retain and use what they really come to know. A list would include sports, both professional and personal (skateboarding, bicycling, etc.), music, television and movies, cars, fashions and styles, arcade games, and so on. Taking any one of these, say skateboarding, it is easy to see the connection between knowledge, skills, and values. Students who value skateboarding spend much time and energy learning the differences between available wheels, trucks, and boards, the advantages and disadvantages of each, the kind of riding best suited to each, and how well these components work together. They then use this knowledge to assemble a board adequate to the kind of riding they prefer. Difficulties do not dampen their enthusiasm to learn. Contrast this with someone who does not value skateboarding, but who must, for some reason, learn the same information about wheels, trucks, and boards. Although we can, with some difficulty, get the uninterested student to memorize some of the same information as the interested student, the difference in the level of understanding and retention between the two is large. We could say that those who simply memorize the information do not really know about skateboarding, but have only transitory — and typically confused — information. They do not value the information they have about skateboarding because they do not value skateboarding. They ineptly apply it. They confuse it. They distort it. They forget it.

Many skills and values gained by learning a body of knowledge have application beyond that body of knowledge. Many skills and values can be transferred to a wide variety of domains of thought. An education emphasizing critical thinking fosters transfer by stimulating students to use their own thinking to come to conclusions and solutions, to defend positions on issues, to consider a wide variety of points of view, to analyze concepts, theories, and explanations, to clarify issues and conclusions, to evaluate the credibility of authorities, to raise and pursue root questions, to solve nonroutine problems, to try out ideas in new contexts, to explore interdisciplinary connections, to evaluate arguments, interpretations, and beliefs, to generate novel ideas, to question and discuss each other's views, to compare perspectives and theories, to compare ideals with actual practice, to examine assumptions, to distinguish relevant from irrelevant facts, to assess evidence, to explore implications and consequences, and to come to terms with contradictions, paradoxes, and inconsistencies. These intellectual skills and abilities cut across traditional disciplinary boundaries apply equally well to science as to language, to mathematics as to social studies, and have relevance to and significance in nonacademic spheres of student life as well. To gain knowledge through critical thinking is to empower the student as a thinker, learner, and doer.

A Moment For Reflection

At this point, we recommend that the readers spend a few minutes reviewing the last two sections with the following question in mind: *"How does this expression of philosophy of education compare to those I have read in the curriculum statements I have seen?"* Most importantly, compare the above philosophy of education, the interrelation of knowledge, critical thinking, and values, to the sketchy objectives that often pass for a philosophy of education in standard curriculum.

Curriculum: Formulations and Reformulations

The problem with most of the goals and objectives of many curricula is that they are deeply vague and ambiguous. Lacking specificity, they are subject to many, even conflicting, interpretations and implementations. Ambiguous goals and objectives are often interpreted in ways that result in lecture and testing for retention of information, rather than in ways that emphasize principles of critical thought.

Another problem is that, though many of these goals and objectives complement each other, curricula present them as if they were separate and disconnected. A serious attempt to achieve any of the major goals involves linking goals with the other goals complementary to them. Otherwise, the result is superficial coverage of multiple topics. If nothing else, combining multiple but complementary goals and objectives saves time. Fortunately, whenever we approach our objectives deeply, we accomplish multiple goals simultaneously. By moving from the surface to depth, students learn more content skills, and see their value. They learn more, not because they "cover" more, but because they forget less and are able to *generate* more, that is, they see the implications of what they learn. This emphasis on depth of learning is now being called 'high content.'

A Model Case

What follows are examples of suggestions for curriculum development taken from the *Cooperative County Course of Study: Guide to a Balanced, Comprehensive, Curriculum*, (1984-1987 (California) Published by Office of the Alameda Superintendent of Schools, 1984. Kay Pacheco, project director) assembled and published by the California County Superintendents Association and the California State Steering Committee for Curriculum Development and Publications. This document provides some excellent suggestions for curriculum development and some well thought-out examples of instructional techniques. However, it lacks an over-arching philosophy of education and creates an unwitting vacillation between didactic and critical modes of instruction. At times it emphasizes rote learning, at others, deeper, more critical discussion of the material. There are also ambiguities and vaguenesses in it, contributing to potential confusion regarding the goals and objectives. Examples below illustrate how these problems can lead to confusion in instruction. A remodelled curriculum that eliminates much of the vagueness and ambiguity of the original follows each cited example. Questions and comments follow, to elucidate the kinds of problems inherent in the original curriculum. This serves as a model for the kind of questioning that could be done when evaluating curricula. We do not comment on all of the objectives listed under the goals.

English Language Arts/Reading

This section is divided into six areas, each with a goal for the area, several objectives for reaching that goal, and sample learner behaviors corresponding to the various grade levels. The six areas and their stated goals are:

(Original Curriculum)
Listening and Speaking: To develop listening and speaking skill.
Reading: Develop reading skill.
Writing: Develop writing skill.

317

Listening and Speaking: To develop listening and speaking skill.

Reading: Develop reading skill.

Writing: Develop writing skill.

Vocabulary/Grammar: Develop appropriate use of word.

Literature, Media, and Subjects: Respond critically and creatively to appropriate literature, media, and subject.

Study and Locational Skills: Use study and locational skills for independent living.

Under the first goal are five objectives students are to reach to have accomplished the goal. Contained in parentheses for each objective are the learner behaviors for students at the secondary school level.

(Original Curriculum)

Goal 1 "To develop listening and speaking skills"

Objectives:	*Learner Behaviors:*
1.1 To express facts and information received from listening.	Rates the value of information gained from each member of a panel.
1.2 To express personal and imaginative responses from listening.	Critiques the effectiveness of a media presentation.
1.3 To present ideas and information orally for varous settings and purposes.	Uses facts and challenges opinions in a debate.
1.4 To gather information by listening and questioning.	Interviews and researches a person and writes an article.
1.5 To develop interpersonal communication skills.	Understands the rules and procedures of formal groups, such as parliamentary procedure

These goals are very vague, ambiguous, and, if not further explained, superficial. Each can, and will, be construed in any number of ways, based on the teacher's background, operant educational philosophy, and past practice. Consider how this goal and its objectives might be reworded to explicitly emphasize critical thinking. We can do so by remembering that knowledge must be actively constructed, not passively acquired, and by understanding in what sense active listening is a mode of critical thinking.

Reading, writing, and listening presuppose a range of similar skills, abilities, and values. Passive, uncritical reading, writing, speaking, and listening have common failings. They fail to recognize the problems for thought that each involves. In each case, for example, we need to organize ideas, consider logical relationships, reflect upon experiences, and use imagination. If I am speaking to you I have to decide what to say and how to say it. To do this, I need to clarify my own thoughts, provide elaborations and illustrations, give reasons and explanations, and consider implications and consequences. I need to evaluate and rank my ideas, emphasizing the main points and ordering the rest. I need to anticipate questions or problems you might have. I need to consider your point of view and background. I even need to assess your interest in what I am saying to determine how long or how far to pursue a line of thought.

If I am listening to you, I need to be prepared to raise questions to you or to myself as I actively attempt to make sense of what you are saying. These questions reflect critical thinking skills, and might include the following:

What is she getting at?

What is her purpose?

Do I need any further elaboration of any point made?

Do I agree or disagree?
Should I pursue or drop the conversation?
Should I take this seriously or let it go in one ear and out the other?

(Remodelled Curriculum)

Goal 1.0: To develop critical listening and speaking skills

Objectives	*Learner Behaviors:*
1.1 In listening, to distinguish between a fact and a purported fact, between facts and conclusions; to critically assess conclusions; in speaking, to use facts and conclusions drawn from facts, using critical thinking principles whenever appropriate	Questions the facts and conclusions drawn from the facts given by members of a panel, or in debate; indicates the basis for questioning
1.2 To express well thought-out responses from listening, using critical thinking principles whenever appropriate	Students insightfully discuss the degree to which a situation comedy realistically approaches the problems of everyday life, asking themselves: What is the problem, how is it approached and handled, how would this problem be handled in real life?
1.3 To distinguish between opinions and judgments of varying strengths, as in a rationally defensible opinion and an irrational or indefensible opinion, using critical thinking principles whenever approapriate	Uses facts and defensible opinions to challenge less defensible opinions in class discussion or debate Demonstrates reasoned judgment by supporting things said with good reasons.

Several questions come to mind regarding both the goal and objectives stated in the original curriculum. For example, Objective 1.1 of the original refers to the gathering of facts, and the accompanying Learner Behaviors speaks of rating those facts. What *exactly* do both of these mean? Should any statement claimed to be factual be taken as factual? Not at all. How, then, is fact to be distinguished from purported fact? Do all facts stated in a conversation have relevance to the issue under discussion? Not necessarily, but how is relevance to be decided? Is there a difference between facts and conclusions drawn from the facts? Quite, but how are the two distinguishable? Is a conclusion drawn from facts always a reasonable or justifiable conclusion? No, not always, but how are conclusions to be assessed? By the agreement or disagreement with students' own beliefs, prejudices, and preferences? We hope not. By the strength of the conviction of the speaker? Never. By the charismatic persuasiveness or forceful personality of the speaker? By no means. Curriculum that does not address these questions, or that ambiguously mentions them, is very likely to lead to instruction that confuses facts with purported facts, that fails to distinguish facts from conclusions, and that promotes an unreasonable acceptance or rejection of conclusions drawn from facts.

The remodelled curriculum makes it clearer that a listener is not a passive receptor of information, but participates in the conversation, striving to understand and to clarify, to question, probe, and test, to grapple with ideas and claims. Not only do students better understand the topic discussed and retain the information, they also acquire valuable intellectual skills. As students use these skills, they better appreciate their value, making it more likely that they continue to use them in other contexts. Speaking, also, ceases to be concerned with confidence only, but is seen as a primary method of expressing ones' thoughts, ideas, and beliefs to another. Students not only recognize the importance of knowing how to express oneself *intelligibly* (grammar, syntax, vocabulary, etc.), but also *intelligently,* appreciating the connection between thought and language, that the thought itself is as important as its expression. Indeed, if one's thoughts are unclear, vague, contradictory, or confused, the expression of them will likewise be unclear, etc. Students should know how to formulate, assess, and express their thoughts and ideas clearly and accurately. This is more clearly the focus of the remodelled curriculum than the original.

History/Social Science

The History/Social Science curriculum in the *Cooperative County Course of Study* is superficial and vague, creating potential misunderstanding and mislearning. Critical thinking standards are not explicit in either the instructional objectives or Learner Behaviors. Lower order behavioral responses and a superficial understanding of history and social science are inadvertently encouraged.

The problem with vaguely stated objectives and Learner Behaviors is their likely interpretation, given the dominant mode of instruction in today's schooling. The didactic paradigm of instruction is still the operant paradigm in most instructional settings. Teachers who were themselves didactically taught are likely to teach didactically. This tendency can be reduced only by bringing principles of critical thought to the fore in philosophical statements, subject-matter curriculum, and instructional examples.

Selected objectives and learner behaviors from the first goal are reproduced below. Comments follow, as well as remodelled goal, objectives and behaviors.

(Original Curriculum)

Goal 1.0: To acquire knowledge drawn from history, social science, and the humanities

Objectives	Learner Behaviors
1.1 To understand the past and present of American, Western, and nonWestern civilizations	Recommends solutions to contemporary economic problems based on the historic ideas, traditions, and institutions of the United States
1.3 To know the democratic functions of local, state, and national government.	Lists the positive and negative aspects of a specific lobby, and supports one group by citing appropriate facts and figures
1.4 To know the historical development of issues and concerns of major cultrues	Compares the United States position on disarmament to the U.S.S.R. postition as related to political, geographic and economic factors

Objective 1.1 is very vague. It is given some specificity in the Learner Behavior which focuses on ideas, traditions, and institutions of the American past. However, the Learner Behavior is intended only as one example of what could be done with the objective. In what other ways are we to "understand the past?" This is not clear. It is susceptible to many and divergent interpretations, increasing the potential for shallow coverage.

The words 'to understand' in objectives 1.1, and 'to know' in objectives 1.3 and 1.4, are also vague and ambiguous. Is there a difference between knowing and understanding? We do not think there is. However, how might these two phrases be interpreted given the dominant mode of instruction in schools? In Bloom's taxonomy, 'knowledge' is synonymous with recall. Objective 1.3 might be interpreted something like this: "To be able to list the different branches and departments of government, and to describe the structure and purpose of each." Little more than memorization is required to fulfill this objective. The learner behavior becomes, literally, *listing* "positive and negative aspects of a specific lobby." This same criticism applies to Objective 1.4 and its accompanying Learner Behavior. A comparison of the Soviet and American position on disarmament may likewise become a list: "We think this, they think that." Simple lists do not require any understanding of the historical development of the positions, the assumptions underlying them, or the implications following from them. The list itself might not be fair, since Americans tend to think of America's weapons as defensive, and Soviet weapons as offensive. Neither is any assessment of the two positions likely to be fair, without significant sympathetic role-playing of the Russian point of veiw.

An important objective not included anywhere in this curriculum is insight into the notion that history is written from a point of view. America has a history, but accounts of this history vary with the point of view of the writer. A history of America written from the perspective of white settlers will be very different from one reflecting the perspective of Native Americans, Blacks, women, immigrants, or the British. Not only should students read historical accounts, they should also be sensitive to differences in perspective, be able to identify the perspective from which any historical report is written, assess this perspective, and, if necessary, rewrite it more objectively.

(Remodelled Curriculum)

Goal 1.0 To understand the meaning and significance of history, social science, and the humanities, and to acquire information drawn from them

Objectives	**Learner Behaviors**
1.1 To learn to think historically; to understand that historical accounts are interpretations of events; and to see how the past has shaped the present and how the present is shaping the future.	Rewrites historical accounts from a perspective other than the one from which it was written; assesses differing perspectives, and looks for relevant infromation that might have been left out of an account.
1.2 To understand the democratic functions of and purposes for the various branches and departments of local, state, and national government.	To defend, in writing or orally, the necessity of a branch or department of local, state, or national government to preserving democracy and individual rights; to argue against the necessity of one.
1.3 To understand the historical development of major issues and concerns of major cultures.	Compares, contrasts, and evaluates the United States and Soviet positions on disarmament, historically, politically, geographically, and eco nomically, retaining a sensitivity to their ten dency to favor the position of their own country.

Science

The science curriculum in the *Cooperative County Course of Study* is generally well done. The section reproduced below is representative of the rest of the science curriculum. At times, it tends to waver between didactic and critical modes of instruction, but does, overall, emphasize and promote independent, critical thought. Students devise experiments to test for various results, and do not merely follow step-by-step instruction on how to set up and conduct tests. They use precise terminology and data in expressing experimental conclusions. They locate, examine, and assess contradictions and discrepancies, and defend a conclusion. They formulate principles about the interdependence of organisms and the implications for survival. The emphasis is on original work, discovery, application, and critical evaluation. Students apply what they learn. They learn to think scientifically, and so better learn science.

(Original Curriculum)

Goal 2.0 To develop and apply rational and creative thinking processes

Objectives	*Learner Behaviors:*
2.1 To develop the ability to organize and generate data.	Organizes data on the basis of a continuous variable and uses an accepted classification system to order or identify objects or phenomena.
2.2 To develop the ability to apply and evaluate data and generate theories.	Examines data from different sources for discrepancies and contradictions and defends a conclusion.
2.3 To use data-gathering and theory building processes in problem solving.	Tests a hypothesis by designing an experiment, collecting and recording data, and applies the results to an appropriate theory
2.4 To demonstrate scientific information through the use of models, diagrams, and displays	Conducts an original experiment to answer one unresolved scientific question

Although these objectives and learner behaviors are desirable, there are some potential problems with this section. The science curriculum seems to assume a philosophy of knowledge and learning different from the rest of the curriculum. In the science curriculum the philosophy is more critical than didactic, emphasizing the connection between knowledge, skills, and value. It tends to encourage student discovery, application of knowledge, precision in method and terminology, evaluation of information, and original experimentation. This philosophy, however, is not explicit. Although it may have been assumed by the writers of this section, the possibility for didactic implementation is increased by the failure to explicitly state it.

This, however, is not the only problem with this section. The *Cooperative County Course of Study* science curriculum also has a lengthy list of content to be covered. How are teachers likely to cover this content given the dominant, unexpressed philosophy of education? Given that this dominant philosophy is didactic, instruction may tend toward the easier and quicker lecture-memorization approach. Content may be seen as an end in itself, that students having these bits of information know science. Although a more defensible and better philosophy may be assumed in the science curriculum, failure to state it explicitly may result in instruction contrary to it.

Conclusion

Curriculum can provide continuity, consistency, and focus in teaching. There must be, for example, some consistency in instruction and content between different sections of the same subject and level. Curriculum provides this consistency. Students must also be similarly prepared to move from one grade level to the next, one grade picking up where the previous ended. This continuity is also provided by the curriculum. All too often, however, the focus is blurred. Curricula are often vaguely and ambiguously written, with heavy emphasis on the specification of content to be covered. One significant reason for this is the absence of a clear and defensible philosophy of education.

The philosophy of education must be explicitly stated to avoid several problems. First, it must be explicit to ensure that the conception of knowledge and learning guiding curriculum development is reasonable and realistic. If we believe that knowledge is best conceived as bits of information, and that learning is the ability to reiterate these bits of information, then we should state it openly. If, on the other hand, deficiencies of the didactic conception are verbally acknowledged, the implications of this admission should be followed up. The philosophy of knowledge, learning, and teaching must be in harmony.

Second, the relation between knowledge, skills, and values must be explicit to ensure that conflicting conceptions of knowledge and learning do not creep in. Interestingly, in the *Cooperative County Course of Study,* discovery, application, precision, and critical evaluation have heaviest emphasis in the science curriculum. But, independent, critical thought is equally valuable and necessary in all subject areas. There appear to be two conceptions of knowledge and learning in this curriculum. The first is more didactic, and tacitly implied in all curriculum areas but science. The second is richer, and appears principally in the science section. Lacking explicit articulation, this conflict or contradiction is ignored. Remember, educational practice arises from some conception of knowledge, teaching, and learning. The dominant mode of instruction today is, as it has been for generations, didactic. Research has refuted this superficial approach, but we have not yet broken down the habits that instantiate it. We must now begin to write curricula so that we come to terms with a conception of knowledge, teaching, and learning that takes full cognizance of the intrinsic "thought-filled" nature of each.

We all know that reasons and evidence must be relevant to the conclusion. Telling people this doesn't help them learn how to make this distinction. People learn this distinction by discussing something, disagreeing on the relevance of a point, and trying to convince each other; by deciding what is and isn't relevant, and then analyzing and assessing those decisions.

Remodelling: A Foundation For Staff Development

The basic idea behind lesson plan remodelling as a strategy for staff development in critical thinking is simple. Every practicing teacher works daily with lesson plans of one kind or another. To remodel lesson plans is to critique one or more lesson plans and to formulate one or more new lesson plans based on that critical process. It is well done when the remodeller understands the strategies and principles used in producing the critique and remodel, when the strategies are well-thought-out, when the remodel clearly follows from the critique, and when the remodel teaches critical thought better than the original. The idea behind our particular approach to staff development of lesson plan remodelling is also simple. A group of teachers or a staff development leader who has a reasonable number of exemplary remodels with accompanying explanatory principles can design practice sessions that enable teachers to begin to develop new teaching skills as a result of experience in lesson remodelling.

When teachers are provided with clearly contrasting "befores" and "afters," lucid and specific critiques, a set of principles clearly explained and illustrated, and a coherent unifying concept, they can increase their own skills in this process. One learns how to remodel lesson plans to incorporate critical thinking only through practice. The more one does it the better one gets, especially when one has examples of the process to serve as models.

Of course, a lesson remodelling strategy for critical thinking in-service is not tied to any particular handbook of examples, but it is easy to indicate the advantages of having such a handbook, assuming it is well-executed. Some teachers do not have a clear concept of critical thinking. Some think of it as negative, judgmental thinking, which is a stereotype. Some have only vague notions, such as "good thinking," or "logical thinking," with little sense of how such ideals are achieved. Others think of it simply in terms of a laundry list of atomistic skills and so lack a clear sense of how these skills need to be orchestrated or integrated, or of how they can be misused. Rarely do teachers have a clear sense of the relationship between the component micro-skills, the basic, general concept of critical thinking, and the obstacles to using it fully.

325

It is theoretically possible but, practically speaking, unlikely that most teachers will sort this out for themselves as a task in abstract theorizing. In the first place, few teachers have much patience with abstract theory and little experience in developing it. In the second place, few school districts could give them the time to take on this task, even if they were qualified and motivated enough themselves. But getting the basic concept sorted out is not the only problem. There is also the problem of translating that concept into "principles," linking the "principles" to applications, and implementing them in specific lessons.

On the other hand, if we simply present teachers with prepackaged finished lesson plans designed by the critical thinking of someone else, by a process unclear to them, then we have lost a major opportunity for the teachers to develop their own critical thinking skills, insights, and motivations. Furthermore, teachers who cannot use basic critical thinking principles to critique and remodel some of their own lesson plans probably won't be able to implement someone else's effectively. Providing teachers with the scaffolding for carrying out the process for themselves and examples of its use, opens the door for continuing development of critical thinking skills and insights. It begins a process which gives the teacher more and more expertise and success in critiquing and remodelling the day-to-day practice of teaching.

Lesson plan remodelling can become a powerful tool in critical thinking staff development for other reasons as well. It is action-oriented and puts an immediate emphasis on close examination and critical assessment of what is taught on a day-to-day basis. It makes the problem of critical thinking infusion more manageable by paring it down to the critique of particular lesson plans and the progressive infusion of particular principles. It is developmental in that, over time, more and more lesson plans are remodelled, and what has been remodelled can be remodelled again; more strategies can be systematically infused as they become clear to the teacher. It provides a means of cooperative learning for teachers. Its results can be collected and shared, both at the site and district levels, so that teachers can learn from and be encouraged by what other teachers do. The dissemination of plausible remodels provides recognition for motivated teachers. It forges a unity between staff development, curriculum development, and student development. It avoids recipe solutions to critical thinking instruction. And, finally, properly conceptualized and implemented, it unites cognitive and affective goals and integrates the curriculum.

Of course, the remodelling approach is no panacea. It will not work for those who are deeply complacent or cynical, or for those who do not put a high value on students' learning to think for themselves. It will not work for those who have a low command of critical thinking skills coupled with low self-esteem. It will not work for those who are "burned out" or have given up on change. Finally, it will not work for those who want a quick and easy solution based on recipes and formulas. It is a long-term solution that transforms teaching by degrees as the critical thinking insights and skills of the teachers develop and mature. If teachers can develop the art of critiquing the lesson plans they use and learn how to use that critique to remodel those lesson plans more and more effectively, they will progressively *1)* refine and develop their own critical thinking skills and insights; *2)* re-shape the actual or "living" curriculum (what is in fact taught); and *3)* develop their teaching skills. (See diagram #2, page 19.)

The approach to lesson remodelling developed by the Center for Critical Thinking and Moral Critique is based on the publication of handbooks, such as this one, which illustrate the remodelling process, unifying well-thought-out critical thinking theory with practical application. The goal is to explain critical thinking by translating general theory into specific teaching strategies. The strategies are multiple, allowing teachers to infuse more strategies as they clarify more dimensions of critical thought. This is especially important since the skill at, and insight into, critical thought varies.

This approach, it should be noted, respects the autonomy and professionality of teachers. They choose which strategies to use in a particular situation and control the rate and style of integration. It is a flexible approach, maximizing the creativity and insight of the teacher. The teacher can apply the strategies to any kind of material: text lesson, lessons or units the teacher has created, discussion outside of formal lessons, discussion of movies, etc.

In teaching for critical thinking in the strong sense, we are committed to teaching in such a way that children, as soon and as completely as possible, learn to become responsible for their own thinking. This requires that they learn how to take command of their thinking, which in turn requires that they learn how to notice and think about their own thinking, as well as the thinking of others. Consequently, we teach so as to help children to talk about their thinking in order to be mindful and directive in it. We want them to study their own minds and how they operate. We want them to gain tools by which they can probe deeply into, and take command of their own mental processes. Finally, we want them to gain this mentally skilled self-control with a view to becoming more honest with themselves and more fair to others, not only to "do better" in school. We want them to develop mental skills and processes in an ethically responsible context. This is not a "good-boy/bad-boy" approach to thinking, for people must think their own way to the ethical insights that underlie becoming fairminded. We are careful not to judge the content of the student's thinking. Rather, we facilitate a process whereby the student's own insights can be developed.

The global objectives of critical thinking-based instruction are intimately linked to specific objectives. It is precisely because we want students to learn how to think for themselves in an ethically responsible way that we use the strategies we do; why we help them to gain insight into their tendency to think in narrowly self-serving ways (egocentricity); why we stimulate them to empathize with the perspectives of others; to suspend or withhold judgment when they do not have the evidence to justify making a judgment; to clarify issues and concepts, to evaluate sources, solutions, and actions; to notice when they make assumptions, how they make inferences and where they use, or ought to use, evidence; to consider the implications of their ideas; to identify the possible contradictions or inconsistencies in their thinking; to consider the qualifications or lack of qualifications in their generalizations; and why we do all of these things in encouraging, supportive, non-judgmental ways. The same principles of education hold for staff development.

Beginning to Infuse Critical Thinking

Let us now consider how we can incorporate these general understandings into in-service design. There are five basic goals or tasks teachers need to aim for to learn the art of lesson remodelling. Each can be the focus of some stage of in-service activity:

1) Clarifying the global concept — How is the fairminded critical thinker unlike the self-serving critical thinker and the uncritical thinker? What is it to think critically?

2) Understanding component teacher strategies that parallel the component critical thinking values, processes, and skills — What are the basic values that (strong sense) critical thinking presupposes? What are the micro-skills of critical thinking? What are the macro-processes? What do critical thinkers do? Why? What do they avoid doing? Why?

3) Seeing a variety of ways in which the various component strategies can be used in classroom settings — When can each aspect of critical thought be fostered? When are they most needed? What contexts most require each dimension? What questions or activities foster it?

4) Getting experience in lesson plan critique — What are the strengths and weaknesses of this lesson? What critical principles, concepts, or strategies apply to it? What important concepts, insights, and issues underlie this lesson? Are they adequately emphasized and explained? What use will the well-educated person make of this material? Will that usefulness be apparent to the students?

5) Getting experience in lesson plan remodelling — How can I take full advantage of the strengths of this lesson? How can this material best be used to foster critical insights? Which questions or activities should I drop, use, alter, or expand upon? What should I add to it? How can I best promote genuine and deep understanding of this material?

Let us emphasize at the outset that these goals or understandings are interrelated and that the achievement of any or all of them is a matter of degree. We therefore warn against trying to achieve "complete" understanding of any one of these in some absolute sense before proceeding to the others. Furthermore, we emphasize that understanding in each case should be viewed practically or pragmatically. One does not learn about what critical thinking is by memorizing a definition or a set of distinctions. The teacher's mind must be actively engaged at each point in the process — concepts, principles, applications, critiques, and remodels. At all of these levels, "hands-on" activities should immediately follow any introduction of explanatory or illustrative material. If, for example, teachers are shown a handbook formulation of one of the principles, they should then have an opportunity to brainstorm applications of the principle, or an opportunity to try out their own formulations of another principle. When they are shown the critique of one lesson plan, they should be given an opportunity to remodel it or to critique another. If they are shown a complete remodel — original lesson plan, critique, and remodel — they should be given an opportunity to do a full critique of their own, individually or in groups. This back-and-forth movement between example and practice should characterize the staff development process overall. These practice sessions should not be rushed, and the products of that practice should be collected and shared in some form with the group as a whole. Teachers need to see that they are fruitfully engaged in this process; dissemination of the products of the process demonstrates this fruitfulness. Of course, it ought to be a common understanding of staff development participants that initial practice is not the same as final product, that what is remodelled today by critical thought can be re-remodelled tomorrow and improved progressively thereafter as experience, skills, and insights grow.

Teachers should be asked early on to formulate what critical thinking means to them. You can examine some teacher formulations in the chapter, "What Critical Thinking Means to Me." However, be careful not to spend too much time on the general formulations of what critical thinking is before moving to the level of particular principles and strategies. The reason for this is simple. People tend to have trouble assimilating general concepts unless they are clarified through concrete examples. Furthermore, we want teachers to develop an *operational* view of critical thinking, to understand it as particular intellectual behaviors derivative of basic insights, commitments, and principles. Critical thinking is not a set of high-sounding platitudes, but a very real and practical way to think things out and to act upon that thought. Therefore, we want teachers to make realistic translations from the general to the specific as soon as possible and to periodically revise their formulations of the global concept in light of their work on the details. We aim at a process whereby teachers move back and forth from general formulations of what critical thinking means to them to specific strategies in specific lessons. We want teachers to see how acceptance of the general concept of critical thinking translates into clear and practical critical thinking teaching and learning strategies, and to use those strategies to help students develop into rational and fair thinkers.

For this reason, all the various strategies explained in the handbook are couched in terms of behaviors. The principles express and describe a variety of behaviors of the "ideal" critical thinker; they become applications to lessons when teachers canvass their lesson plans to find appropriate places where those behaviors can be fostered. The practice we recommend helps guard against teachers using these strategies as recipes or formulas, since good judgment is always required to apply them.

Some Staff Development Design Possibilities

1) Clarifying the global concept

After a brief exposition or explanation of the global concept of critical thinking, teachers might be asked to reflect individually (for, say, 10 minutes) on people they have known who are basically uncritical thinkers, those who are basically selfish critical thinkers, and those who are basically fairminded critical thinkers. After they have had time to think up meaningful personal examples, divide them up into groups of two to share and discuss their reflections with another teacher.

An alternative focus might be to have them think of dimensions of their own lives in which they are most uncritical, selfishly critical, and fairminded.

2) Understanding component teaching strategies that parallel the component critical thinking values, processes, and skills

Each teacher could be asked to choose one of the strategies to read and think about for approximately 10 minutes. Their task following this period is to explain the strategy to another teacher, without reading from the handbook. The role of the other teacher is to ask questions about the strategy. Once one has finished explaining his or her strategy, roles are reversed. Following this, pairs could link up with other pairs and explain their strategies to each other. At the end, each teacher should have a basic understanding of four strategies.

3) Seeing a variety of ways in which the various component strategies can be used in classroom settings

Teachers could be asked to reflect for about 10 minutes on how the strategies that they choose might be used in a number of classroom activities or assignments. Following this, they could share their examples with other teachers.

4) Getting experience in lesson plan critique

Teachers can be asked to bring one lesson, activity, or assignment to the inservice session. This lesson, or one provided by the inservice leader, can be used to practice critique. Critiques can then be shared, evaluated, and improved.

5) Getting experience in lesson plan remodelling

Teachers can then remodel the lessons which they have critiqued so that they can share, evaluate, and revise the results.

• Copy a remodel, eliminating strategy references. Groups of teachers could mark strategies on it; share, discuss, and defend their versions, etc. Remember, ours is not "the right answer." In cases where participants disagree with, or do not understand why we cited the strategies we did, they could try to figure out why.

- Over the course of a year, the whole group can work on at least one remodel for each participant.

- Participants could each choose several strategies and explain their interrelationships, mention cases in which they are equivalent, or when one could be used as part of another, etc.

- To become more reflective about their teaching, teachers could keep a teaching log or journal, making entries as often as possible, using prompts such as these: What was the best question I asked today? Why? What was the most effective strategy I used today? Was it appropriate? Why or why not? What could I do to improve that strategy? What did I actively do today to help create the atmosphere that will help students to become critical thinkers? How and why was it effective? What is the best evidence of clear, precise, accurate reasoning I saw a student do today? What factors contributed to that reasoning? Did the other students realize the clarity of the idea? Why or why not? What was the most glaring evidence of irrationality or poor thinking I saw today in a student? What factors contributed to that reasoning? How could I (and did I) help the student to clarify his or her own thoughts?

The processes we have described thus far presuppose motivation on the part of the teacher to implement changes. Unfortunately, we cannot presuppose this motivation. We must address it directly. This can be done by focusing attention on the insights that underlie the strategies in each case. We need to foster discussion of them so that it becomes clear to teachers not only *that* critical thinking requires this or that kind of activity but *why*, that is, what desirable consequences it brings about. If, for example, teachers do not see why thinking for themselves is of high importance for the well-being and success of their students, they will not take the trouble to implement activities that foster it, even if they know what these activities are.

To meet this motivational need, we have formulated "principles" so as to suggest important insights. For example, consider the brief introduction which is provided in the Strategy chapter for the strategy "exercising fairmindedness":

Principle: To think critically about issues, we must be able to consider the strengths and weaknesses of opposing points of view; to imaginatively put ourselves in the place of others in order to genuinely understand them; to overcome our egocentric tendency to identify truth with our immediate perceptions or long-standing thought or belief. This trait correlates with the ability to reconstruct accurately the viewpoints and reasoning of others and to reason from premises, assumptions, and ideas other than our own. This trait also correlates with the willingness to remember occasions when we were wrong in the past, despite an intense conviction that we were right, as well as the ability to imagine our being similarly deceived in a case at hand. Critical thinkers realize the unfairness of judging unfamiliar ideas until they fully understand them.

The world consists of many societies and peoples with many different points of view and ways of thinking. In order to develop as reasonable persons, we need to enter into and think within the frameworks and ideas of different peoples and societies. We cannot truly understand the world if we think about it only from *one* viewpoint, as Americans, as Italians, or as Russians.

Furthermore, critical thinkers recognize that their behavior affects others, and so consider their behavior from the perspective of those others.

If teachers reflect on this principle in the light of their own experience, they should be able to come up with their own reasons why fairmindedness is important. They might reflect upon the personal problems and frustrations they faced when others — spouses or friends, for example — did not or would not empathically enter their point of view. Or they might reflect on their frustration as children when their parents, siblings, or schoolmates did not take their point of view seriously. Through examples of this sort, constructed by the teachers themselves, insight into the need for an intellectual sense of justice can be developed.

Once the insight is in place, we are ready to put the emphasis on discussing the variety of ways that students can practice thinking fairmindedly. As always, we want to be quite specific here, so that teachers understand the kinds of behaviors they are fostering. The handbook, in each case, provides a start in the *application* section following the *principle*. For more of our examples, one can look up one or more remodelled lesson plans in which the strategy was used, referenced under each. Remember, it is more important for teachers to think up their own examples and applications than to rely on the handbook examples, which are intended as illustrative only.

Lesson plan remodelling as a strategy for staff and curriculum development is not a simple, one-shot approach. It requires patience and commitment. But it genuinely develops the critical thinking of teachers and puts them in a position to understand and help structure the inner workings of the curriculum. While doing so, it builds confidence, self-respect, and professionality. With such an approach, enthusiasm for critical thinking strategies will grow over time. It is an approach worth serious consideration as the fundamental thrust of a staff development program. If a staff becomes proficient at critiquing and remodelling lesson plans, it can, by redirecting the focus of its energy, critique and "remodel" any other aspect of school life and activity. In this way, the staff can become increasingly less dependent on direction or supervision from above and increasingly more activated by self-direction from within. Responsible, constructive critical thinking, developed through lesson plan remodelling, is a vehicle for this transformation.

In addition to devising in-service days that facilitate teachers developing skills in remodelling their lessons, it is important to orchestrate a process that facilitates critical thinking infusion on a long-term, evolutionary basis. As you consider the "big picture," remember the following principles:

✔ **Involve the widest possible spectrum of people** in discussing, articulating, and implementing the effort to infuse critical thinking. This includes teachers, administrators, board members, and parents.

✔ **Provide incentives to those who move forward in the implementation process.** Focus attention on those who do make special efforts. Do not embarrass or draw attention to those who do not.

✔ **Recognize that many small changes are often necessary before larger changes can take place.**

✔ **Do not rush implementation.** A slow but steady progress with continual monitoring and adjusting of efforts is best. Provide for refocusing on the long-term goal and ways of making the progress visible and explicit.

✔ **Work continually to institutionalize the changes made** as the understanding of critical thinking grows, making sure that the goals and strategies being used are deeply embedded in school-wide and district-wide statements and articulations. Foster discussion on the question of how progress in critical thinking instruction can be made permanent and continuous.

✔ **Honor individual differences among teachers.** Maximize the opportunities for teachers to pursue critical thinking strategies in keeping with their own educational philosophy. Enforcing conformity is incompatible with the spirit of critical thinking.

It's particularly important to have a sound long-range plan for staff development in critical thinking. The plan of the Greensboro City Schools is especially noteworthy for a number of reasons: *1)* it does not compromise depth and quality for short-term attractiveness, *2)* it allows for individual variations between teachers at different stages of their development as critical thinkers, *3)* it provides a range of incentives to teachers, *4)* it combines a variety of staff development strategies, *5)* it is based on a broad philosophical grasp of the nature of education, integrated into realistic pedagogy, and *6)* it is long-term, providing for evolution over an extended period of time. Infusing critical thinking into the curriculum cannot be done over night. It takes a commitment that evolves over years. The Greensboro plan is in tune with this inescapable truth.

Consider these features of the plan:

A good staff development program should be realistic in its assessment of time. Teachers need time to reflect upon and discuss ideas, they need opportunities to try out and practice new strategies, to begin to change their own attitudes and behaviors in order change those of their students, to observe themselves and their colleagues — and then they need more time to reflect upon and internalize concepts.

Furthermore, we think that teachers need to see *modeled* the teacher attitudes and behaviors that we want them to take back to the classroom. We ask teachers to participate in Socratic discussion, we ask teacher to write, and we employ the discovery method in our workshops. We do *not* imply that we have "the answer" to the problem of how to get students to think and we seldom lecture.

In planning and giving workshops, we follow these basic guidelines. Workshop leaders:

1. model for teachers the behaviors they wish them to learn and internalize. These teaching behaviors include getting the participants actively involved, calling upon and using prior experiences and knowledge of the participants and letting the participants process and deal with ideas rather than just lecturing to them.

2. use the discovery method, allowing teachers to explore and to internalize ideas and giving time for discussion, dissension, and elaboration.

3. include writing in their plans — we internalize what we can process in our own words.

Here is what Greensboro said about the Remodelling approach:

After studying and analyzing a number of approaches and materials, this nucleus recommends Richard Paul's approach to infusing critical thinking into the school curriculum (which has a number of advantages)

1. It avoids the pitfalls of pre-packaged materials, which often give directions which the teacher follows without understanding why or even what the process is that she/he is following. Pre-packaged materials thus do not provide an opportunity for the teacher to gain knowledge in how to teach for and about thinking, nor do they provide opportunity for the teacher to gain insight and reflection into his/her own teaching.

2. It does not ask teachers to develop a new curriculum or a continuum of skills, both of which are time-consuming and of questionable productivity. The major factor in the productivity of a curriculum guide is how it is used, and too many guides traditionally remain on the shelf, unused by the teacher.

3. It is practical and manageable. Teachers do not need to feel overwhelmed in their attempts to change an entire curriculum, nor does it need impractical expenditures on materials or adoption of new textbooks. Rather, the teacher is able to exercise his/her professional judgment in deciding where, when, at what rate, and how his or her lesson plans can be infused with more critical thinking.

4. It infuses critical thinking into the curriculum rather than treating is as a separate subject, an "add on" to an already crowded curriculum.

5. It recognizes the complexity of the thinking process, and rather than merely listing discreet skills, it focuses on both affective strategies and cognitive strategies.

This focus on affective and cognitive strategies may seem confusing at first, but the distinction is quite valid. Paul's approach recognizes that a major part of good thinking is a person's affective (or emotional) approach, in other words, attitudes or dispositions. Although a student may become very skilled in specific skills, such as making an inference or examining assumptions, he or she will not be a good thinker without displaying affective strategies such as exercising independent judgment and fairmindedness or suspending judgment until sufficient evidence has been collected. Likewise, Paul also emphasizes such behavior and attitudes as intellectual humility, perseverance, and faith in reason, all of which are necessary for good thinking.

Paul's approach also gives specific ways to remodel lesson plans so that the teacher can stress these affective and cognitive skills. Thirty-one specific strategies are examined and numerous examples of how to remodel lesson plans using these strategies are presented. These concrete suggestions range from ways to engage students in Socratic dialogue to how to restructure questions asked to students.

A critical factor in this approach is the way that a teacher presents material, asks questions, and provides opportunities for students to take more and more responsibility on themselves for thinking and learning. The teacher's aim is to create an environment that fosters and nurtures student thinking.

This nucleus recommends that this approach be disseminated through the faculty in two ways. First, a series of workshops will familiarize teachers with the handbooks. Secondly, nucleus teachers will work with small numbers of teachers (two or three) using peer collaboration, coaching, and cooperation to remodel and infuse critical thinking into lesson plans.

No two districts are alike, just as not two teachers are alike, so that any plan has to be adjusted to the particular needs of a particular district. Nevertheless, all teachers assess their lessons in some fashion or other, and getting into the habit of using critical thinking to assess their instruction cannot but improve it. The key is to find an on-going process to encourage and reward such instructional critique.

> *If a staff becomes proficient at critiquing and remodelling lesson plans, it can critique and 'remodel' any other aspect of school life and activity, and so become increasingly less dependent on direction or supervision from above and increasingly more activated by self-direction from within.*

The Greensboro Plan: A Sample Staff Development Plan

by Kim V. DeVaney and Janet L. Williamson

Greensboro, North Carolina is a city of medium size nestled in the rolling hills of the Piedmont, near the Appalachian Mountains. The school system enrolls approximately 21,000 students and employs 1,389 classroom teachers. Students in the Greensboro city schools come from diverse economic and balanced racial backgrounds. Forty-six percent of the students are White. Fifty-four per cent of the student population is minority; 52% is Black and 2% is Asian, Hispanic, or Native American. Every socio-economic range from the upper middle class to those who live below the poverty line is well-represented in the city schools. However, almost 28% of the student population has a family income low enough for them to receive either free or discounted lunches. Although our school system is a relatively small one, Greensboro has recently implemented a program that is beginning successfully to infuse critical thinking and writing skills into the K-12 curriculum.

The Reasoning and Writing Project, which was proposed by Associate Superintendent, Dr. Sammie Parrish, began in the spring of 1986, when the school board approved the project and affirmed as a priority the infusion of thinking and writing into the K-12 curriculum. Dr. Parrish hired two facilitators, Kim V. DeVaney, who had experience as an elementary school teacher and director of computer education and myself, Janet L. Williamson, a high school English teacher, who had recently returned from a leave of absence during which I completed my doctorate with a special emphasis on critical thinking.

Kim and I are teachers on special assignment, relieved of our regular classroom duties in order to facilitate the project. We stress this fact: we are facilitators, not directors; we are teachers, not administrators. The project is primarily teacher directed and implemented. In fact, this tenet of teacher empowerment is one of the major principles of the project, as is the strong emphasis on and commitment to a philosophical and theoretical basis of the program.

We began the program with some basic beliefs and ideas. We combined reasoning and writing because we think that there is an interdependence between the two processes and that writing is

335

an excellent tool for making ideas clear and explicit. We also believe that no simple or quick solutions would bring about a meaningful change in the complex set of human attitudes and behaviors that comprise thinking. Accordingly, we began the project at two demonstration sites where we could slowly develop a strategic plan for the program. A small group of fourteen volunteers formed the nucleus with whom we primarily worked during the first semester of the project.

Even though I had studied under Dr. Robert H. Ennis, worked as a research assistant with the Illinois Critical Thinking Project, and written my dissertation on infusing critical thinking skills into an English curriculum, we did not develop our theoretical approach to the program quickly or easily. I was aware that if this project were going to be truly teacher-directed, my role would be to guide the nucleus teachers in reading widely and diversely about critical thinking, in considering how to infuse thinking instruction into the curriculum, and in becoming familiar with and comparing different approaches to critical thinking. My role would not be, however, to dictate the philosophy or strategies of the program.

This first stage in implementing a critical thinking program, where teachers read, study, and gather information, is absolutely vital. It is not necessary, of course, for a facilitator to have a graduate degree specializing in critical thinking in order to institute a sound program, but it is necessary for at least a small group of people to become educated, in the strongest sense of the word, about critical thinking and to develop a consistent and sound theory or philosophy based on that knowledge — by reading (and rereading), questioning, developing a common vocabulary of critical thinking terms and the knowledge of how to use them, taking university or college courses in thinking, seeking out local consultants such as professors, and attending seminars and conferences.

In the beginning stages of our program, we found out that the importance of a consistent and sound theoretical basis is not empty educational jargon. We found inconsistencies in our stated beliefs and our interactions with our students and in our administrators' stated beliefs and their interaction with teachers. For example, as teachers we sometimes proclaim that we want independent thinkers and then give students only activity sheets to practice their "thinking skills;" we declare that we want good problem solving and decision-making to transfer into all aspects of life and then tend to avoid controversial or "sensitive" topics; we bemoan the lack of student thinking and then structure our classrooms so the "guessing what is in the teacher's mind" is the prevailing rule. We also noted a tendency of some principals to espouse the idea that teachers are professionals and then declare that their faculty prefer structured activities rather than dealing with theory or complex ideas. Although most administrators state that learning to process information is more important than memorizing it, a few have acted as if the emphasis on critical thinking is "just a fad." One of the biggest contradictions we have encountered has been the opinion of both teachers and administrators that "we're already doing a good job of this (teaching for thinking)," yet they also say that students are not good thinkers.

While recognizing these contradictions is important, it does not in and of itself solve the problem. In the spirit of peer coaching and collegiality, we are trying to establish an atmosphere that will allow us to point out such contradictions to each other. As our theories and concepts become more internalized and completely understood, such contradictions in thought and action become less frequent. In all truthfulness, however, such contradictions still plague us and probably will for quite a while.

We encountered, however, other problems that proved easier to solve. I vastly underestimated the amount of time that we would need for an introductory workshop, and our first workshops failed to give teachers the background they needed; we now structure our workshops for days, not hours. There was an initial suggestion from the central office that we use *Tactics for Thinking*. as a basis, or at least a starting point, for our program. To the credit of central office administration, although they may have questioned whether we should use an already existing program, they certainly did not mandate that we use any particular approach. As we collected evaluations of our program from our teachers, neighboring school systems, and outside consultants, however, there seemed to be a general consensus that developing our own program, rather than adopting a pre-packaged one, has been the correct choice.

Finally, teachers became confused with the array of materials, activities, and approaches. They questioned the value of developing and internalizing a concept of critical thinking and asked for specifics — activities they could use immediately in the classroom. This problem, however, worked itself out as teachers reflected on the complexity of critical thinking and how it can be fostered. We began to note and collect instances such as the following: a high school instructor, after participating in a workshop that stressed how a teacher can use Socratic questioning in the classroom, commented that students who had previously been giving unsatisfactory answers were now beginning to give insightful and creative ones. Not only had she discovered that the quality of the student's response is in part determined by the quality of the teacher's questions, she was finding new and innovative ways to question her students. Another teacher, after having seen how the slowest reading group in her fourth grade class responded to questions that asked them to think and reflect, commented that she couldn't believe how responsive and expressive the children were. I can think of no nucleus teacher who would now advocate focusing on classroom activities rather than on a consistent and reflective approach to critical thinking.

As the nucleus teachers read and studied the field, they outlined and wrote the tenets that underscore the program. These tenets include the belief that real and lasting change takes place, not by writing a new curriculum guide, having teachers attend a one day inspirational workshop at the beginning of each new year, adopting new textbooks that emphasize more skills, or buying pre-packaged programs and activity books for thinking. Rather, change takes place when attitudes and priorities are carefully and reflectively reconsidered, when an atmosphere is established that encourages independent thinking for both teachers and students, and when we recognize the complex interdependence between thinking and writing.

The nucleus teachers at the two demonstration schools decided that change in the teaching of thinking skills can best take place by remodelling lesson plans, not by creating new ones, and they wrote a position paper adopting Richard Paul's *Critical Thinking Handbook*. This approach, they wrote, is practical and manageable. It allows the teacher to exercise professional judgment and provides opportunity for teachers to gain insight into their own teaching. In addition, it recognizes the complexity of the thinking process and does not merely list discrete skills.

The primary-level teachers decided to focus upon language development as the basis for critical thinking. Their rationale was that language is the basis for both thinking and writing, that students must master language sufficiently to be able to use it as a tool in thinking and writing, and that this emphasis is underdeveloped in many early classrooms. This group of teachers worked on increasing teacher knowledge and awareness of language development as well as developing and collecting materials, techniques and ideas for bulletin boards for classroom use.

By second semester, the project had expanded to two high schools. This year, the second year of the program, we have expanded to sixteen new schools, including all six middle schools. Kim and I have conducted workshops for all new nucleus teachers as well as for interested central office and school-based administrators. Also, this year, at three of the four original demonstration sites, workshops have been conducted or planned that are led by the original nucleus teachers for their colleagues.

It is certainly to the credit of the school board and the central administration that we have had an adequate budget on which to operate. As I have mentioned, Kim and I are full-time facilitators of the program. Substitutes have been hired to cover classes when teachers worked on the project during school hours. We were able to send teachers to conferences led by Richard Paul and we were able to bring in Professor Paul for a very successful two-day workshop.

Our teachers work individually and in pairs, and in small and large groups at various times during the day. A number of teachers have video-taped themselves and their classes in action, providing an opportunity to view and reflect on ways that they and their colleagues could infuse more thinking opportunities into the curriculum.

Essentially, we have worked on three facets in the program: 1) workshops that provide baseline information, 2) follow-up that includes demonstration teaching by facilitators, individual study, collegial sharing of ideas, peer coaching, individual and group remodelling of lesson plans, teachers writing about their experiences both for their personal learning and for publication, team planning of lessons, peer observation, and 3) dissemination of materials in our growing professional library.

We are expanding slowly and only on a volunteer basis. Currently, we have approximately seventy nucleus teachers working in twenty schools. By the end of next year, 1988-1989, we plan to have a nucleus group in each of the schools in the system. Plans for the future should include two factions: ways for the nucleus groups to continue to expand their professional growth and knowledge of critical thinking and an expansion of the program to include more teachers. We plan to continue to build on the essential strengths of the program — the empowerment of teachers to make decisions, the thorough theoretical underpinnings of the program, and the slow and deliberate design and implementation plan.

Our teachers generally seem enthusiastic and committed. In anonymous written evaluations of the program, they have given it overwhelming support. One teacher stated:

> It is the most worthwhile project the central office has ever offered ....Because
> - it wasn't forced on me.
> - it wasn't touted as the greatest thing since sliced bread.
> - it was not a one-shot deal that was supposed to make everything all better.
> - it was not already conceived and planned down to the last minute by someone who had never been in a classroom or who hadn't been in one for X years.
>
> It was, instead,
> - led by professionals who were still very close to the classroom.
> - designed by us.
> - a volunteer group of classroom teachers who had time to reflect and read and talk after each session, and who had continuing support and information from the leaders, not just orders and instructions.

Short Range and Long Range Goals

Developing and sustaining a good critical thinking program is a long-range enterprise that takes a number of years. Accordingly, we have developed both long-range and short-range goals. Truthfully, we began the program with some confusion and hesitancy about our goals; we developed many of these goals as the program progressed and we continue to redefine our priorities.

Short range goals include:
- Staff development and workshops for all teachers, for school based administrators, and for central office administrators.

- Development of a professional library with materials and resources which teachers have identified as useful.
- Adoption of an elementary writing process model which can be used by all teachers.
- Adoption of a secondary writing model which can be used by teachers in all disciplines.
- Establishment of demonstration schools and demonstration classrooms.
- Development and encouragement of peer observations and peer coaching.
- Establishment of a network for communicating and sharing with other school systems.
- Adoption of instruments that encourage self-reflection and analysis of teaching.
- Adoption of processes and instruments for evaluating the project.
- Growth in knowledge and mastery of a number of programs and approaches to critical thinking as well as an expanded, common vocabulary of critical thinking terms.
- Participation of teachers in a number of experiences of remodelling lessons and sharing these remodelled lessons with colleagues.

Long range goals include:

- Development of a concept of critical thinking that allows for individual perceptions as well as for the differences between technical thinking and thinking dialectically.
- Development of ways to help students transfer good thinking from discipline to discipline and from school work to out-of-school experiences.
- Development of insight into our own thinking, including our biases and a consideration of contradictions in our espoused objectives and our behavior.
- Development of a supportive atmosphere that fosters good thinking for teacher, administrators, and students.

> *If we simply present the teacher with pre-packaged, finished lesson plans, designed by the critical thinking of someone else, someone who used a process that is not clearly understood by the teacher, then a major opportunity for the teacher to develop her own critical thinking skills, insights, and motivations will have been lost.*

What Critical Thinking Means to Me: Teachers' Own Formulations

Critical thinking is a process through which one solves problems and makes decisions. It is a process that can be improved through practice, though never perfected. It involves self-discipline and structure. Sometimes it can make your head hurt, but sometimes it comes naturally. I believe for critical thinking to be its most successful, it must be intertwined with creative thinking.

Kathryn Haines
Grade 5

Thinking critically gives me an organized way of questioning what I hear and read in a manner that goes beyond the surface or literal thought. It assists me in structuring my own thoughts such that I gain greater insight into how I feel and appreciation for the thoughts of others, even those with which I disagree. It further enables me to be less judgmental in a negative way and to be more willing to take risks.

Patricia Wiseman
Grade 3

Critical thinking is being able *and* willing to examine all sides of an issue or topic, having first clarified it; supporting or refuting it with either facts or reasoned judgment; and in this light, exploring the consequences or effects of any decision or action it is possible to take.

Kim V. DeVaney
Facilitator, WATTS

All of us think, but critical thinking has to do with becoming more aware of *how* we think and finding ways to facilitate clear, reasoned, logical, and better-informed thinking. Only when our thoughts are backed with reason and logic, and are based on a process of careful examination of ideas and evidence, do they become critical and lead us in the direction of finding what is true. In order to do this, it seems of major importance to maintain an open-minded willingness to look at other points of view. In addition, we can utilize various skills which will enable us to become more proficient at thinking for ourselves.

Nancy Johnson
Kindergarten

Critical thinking is a necessary access to a happy and full life. It provides me the opportunity to analyze and evaluate my thoughts, beliefs, ideas, reasons, and feelings as well as those of other individuals. Utilizing this process, it helps me to understand and respect others as total persons. It helps me in instructing my students and in my personal life. Critical thinking extends beyond the classroom setting and has proven to be valid in life other than the school world.

Veronica Richmond
Grade 6

Critical thinking is the ability to analyze and evaluate feelings and ideas in an independent, fairminded, rational manner. If action is needed on these feelings or ideas, this evaluation motivates meaningfully positive and useful actions. Applying critical thinking to everyday situations and classroom situations is much like Christian growth. If we habitually evaluate our feelings and ideas based on a reasonable criteria, we will become less likely to be easily offended and more likely to promote a positive approach as a solution to a problem. Critical thinking, like Christian growth, promotes confidence, creativity, and personal growth.

Carolyn Tarpley
Middle School
Reading

Critical thinking is a blend of many things, of which I shall discuss three: independent thinking; clear thinking; and organized Socratic questioning.

As for the first characteristic mentioned above, a critical thinker is an independent thinker. He doesn't just accept something as true or believe it because he was taught it as a child. He analyzes it, breaking it down into its elements; he checks on the author of the information and delves into his or her background; he questions the material and evaluates it; and then he makes up his own mind about its validity. In other words, he thinks independently.

A second criterion of critical thinking is clarity. If a person is not a clear thinker, he can't be a critical thinker. I can't say that I agree or disagree with you if I can't understand you. A critical thinker has to get very particular, because people are inclined to throw words around. For example, they misuse the word 'selfish.' A person might say: "You're selfish, but *I'm* motivated!" A selfish person is one who systematically *ignores* the rights of others and pursues his own desires. An unselfish one is a person who systematically *considers* the rights of others while he pursues his own desires. Thus, clarity is important. We have to be clear about the meanings of words.

The most important aspect of critical thinking is its spirit of Socratic questioning. However, it is important to have the questioning organized in one's mind and to know in general the underlying goals of the discussion. If you want students to retain the content of your lesson, you must organize it and help them to see that ideas are connected. Some ideas are derived from basic ideas. We need to help students to organize their thinking around basic ideas and to question. To be a good questioner, you must be a wonderer — wonder aloud about meaning and truth. For example, "I wonder what Jack means." "I wonder what this word means?" "I wonder if anyone can think of an example?" "Does this make sense?" "I wonder how true that is?" "Can anyone think of an experience when that was true?" The critical thinker must have the ability to probe deeply, to get down to basic ideas, to get beneath the mere appearance of things. We need to get into the very spirit, the "wonderment" of the situation being discussed. The students need to feel, "My teacher really wonders; and really wants to know what we think." We should wonder aloud. A good way to stimulate thinking is to use a variety of types of questions. We can ask questions to get the students to elaborate, to explain, to give reasons, to cite evidence, to identify their points of view, to focus on central ideas, and to raise problems. Socratic questioning is certainly vital to critical thinking.

Thus, critical thinking is a blend of many characteristics, especially independent thinking, clear thinking, and Socratic questioning. We all need to strive to be better critical thinkers.

Holly Touchstone
Middle School
Language Arts

Critical thinking is wondering about that which is not obvious, questioning in a precise manner to find the essence of truth, and evaluating with an open mind.

As a middle school teacher, critical thinking is a way to find out from where my students are coming (a way of being withit). Because of this "withitness" produced by bringing critical thinking into the classroom, student motivation will be produced. This motivation fed by fostering critical thinking will produce a more productive thinker in society.

Thus, for me, critical thinking is a spirit I can infuse into society by teaching my students to wonder, question, and evaluate in search of truth while keeping an open mind.

Malinda McCuiston
Middle School
Language Arts, Reading

Critical thinking means thinking clearly about issues, problems, or ideas, and questioning or emphasizing those that are important to the "thinker." As a teacher, I hope to develop Socratic questioning so that my students will feel comfortable discussing why they believe their thoughts to be valid. I hope that they will develop language skills to communicate with others and that they will be open to ideas and beliefs of others.

Jessie Smith
Grade 1

The spirit of critical thinking is a concept that truly excites me. I feel the strategies of critical thinking, implemented appropriately in my classroom, can enable me to become a more effective teacher. By combining this thinking process with my sometimes overused emotions and intuitive power, I can critically examine issues in my classroom as well as in my personal life. I feel it is of grave importance for us as educators to provide a variety of opportunities for our students to think critically by drawing conclusions, clarifying ideas, evaluating assumptions, drawing inferences, and giving reasons and examples to support ideas. Also, Socratic dialogue is an effective means of enabling the students to discover ideas, contradictions, implications, etc., instead of being told answers and ideas given by the teacher. Critical thinking is an excellent tool for the teacher to help the students learn how to think rather than just what to think. Hopefully critical thinking will help me be a more effective teacher as well as excite my students.

Beth Sands
Middle School
Language Arts

Critical thinking is what education should be. It is the way I wish I had been taught. Although I left school with a wealth of facts, I had never learned how to connect them or to use them. I loved learning but thought that being learned meant amassing data. No one ever taught me how to contrast and compare, analyze and dissect. I believed that all teachers knew everything, all printed material was true and authority was always right. It took me years to undo the habits of "good behavior" in school. I want to save my students the wasted time, the frustration, the doubts that I encountered during and after my school years. And teaching and using critical thinking is the way to do that.

Nancy Poueymirou
High School
Language Arts

For me, critical thinking is a combination of learning and applying a data base of learning to evaluate and interrelate concepts from diverse academic disciplines. Critical thinking is understanding that knowledge, wisdom, and education are not divided into math, science, English, etc. It is the fairness of tolerance combined with a strong sense of ethics and morals. It is the fun of feeling your mind expand as you accomplish intellectual challenges that attain your own standards. It is the zest of life.

Joan Simons
High School
Biology

Both as teacher and individual, I find critical thinking skills essential elements of a full and enjoyable life. With the ability to think critically, one can both appreciate and cope with all aspects of life and learning. When dealing with problems, from the most mundane to the most complex, the ability to think critically eliminates confusion, dispels irrational emotion, and enables one to arrive at an appropriate conclusion. At the same time, as we ponder the beauty and creativity of our environment, we are free to "wonder" and enjoy the complexity around us, rather than be perplexed or intimidated by it, because we have the mental capability to understand it. To live is to be ever curious, ever learning, ever investigating. Critical thinking enables us to do this more fully and pleasurably.

Mary Lou Holoman
High School
Language Arts

A critical thinker never loses the joy of learning, never experiences the sadness of not caring or not wondering about the world. The essence of the truly educated person is that of being able to question, inquire, doubt, conclude, innovate. And beyond that, to spread that enthusiasm to those around him, obscuring the lines that divide teacher and student, enabling them to travel together, each learning from the other.

Jane Davis-Seaver
Grade 3

Critical thinking is a means of focusing energy to learn. The learning may be academic (proscribed by an institutional curriculum or self-directed) or non-academic (determined by emotional need). It provides a systematic organization for gathering information, analyzing that information, and evaluating it to reach reasonable, acceptable conclusions for yourself.

Blair Stetson
Elementary
Academically Gifted

Critical thinking is the ability to reason in a clear and unbiased way. It is necessary to consider concepts or problems from another's point of view and under varying circumstances in order to make reasoned judgments. Awareness of one's own reasoning processes enables one to become a more fairminded and objective thinker.

Karen Marks
Elementary
Academically Gifted

Critical thinking is questioning, analyzing, and making thoughtful judgments about questions, ideas, issues or concepts. It refines thoughts to more specific or definite meanings. The critical thinker must be an active listener who does not simply accept what he/she hears or reads on face value without questioning, but looks for deeper meaning. Critical thinking also involves evaluating the ideas explored or problems addressed and better prepares a student to be able to think about the world around him or her.

Becky Hampton
Grade 6

Critical thinking has given me a broader means of evaluating my daily lesson plans. It has helped me better understand the thinking principles of each student I teach. It has also enabled me to practice strategies in lesson planning and to become a more effective classroom teacher.

Pearl Norris Booker
Grade 2

Critical thinking provides me the opportunity to broaden the thinking process of my students. It can be used to have the students to reason and to think about different ideas of a problem or a given situation.

Portia Staton
Grade 3

Critical thinking is a process that takes all the ideas, questions and problems that we are faced with each day and enables us to come up with solutions. It is the process by which we are able to search for evidence that support already-existing answers, or better yet, to come up with new solutions to problems. Through critical thinking, one begins to realize that many times there is more than one solution whereupon decisions can be made. To me, critical thinking has helped and will continue to help me understand myself and the world around me.

Debbie Wall
Grade 4

Critical thinking is a skill that involves the expansion of thoughts and the art of questioning. This skill must be developed over a period of time. It is a way of organizing your thoughts in a logical sequence. Knowledge is gained through this process.

Carolyn Smith
Grade 5

Critical thinking is questioning, analyzing and evaluating oral or written ideas. A critical thinker is disciplined, self-directed, and rational in problem solving. Reaching conclusions of your own rather than accepting everything as it is presented, is internalizing critical thinking.

Denise Clark
Grade 2

To think critically, one must analyze and probe concepts or ideas through reasoning. It makes one an *active* reasoner, not a *passive* accepter of ideas (or facts). It turns one into a doer, an evaluater, or re-evaluater. Critical thinking occurs everywhere, is applicable everywhere and while it can be tedious, need not be, because as one thinks critically, new ideas are formed, conclusions are drawn, new knowledge is acquired.

Janell Prester
Grade 3

Critical thinking means to think through and analyze a concept or idea. You are able to back up your reasoning and think through an idea in a manner which allows an over-all focus. If a person is a critical thinker, a yes-no answer is too brief. An answer to a problem or idea must have an explanation and reasoning backing it.

Donna Phillips
Grade 4

Critical thinking is a tool that teachers can use to offer a new dimension of education to their students: that of thinking about, questioning and exploring the concepts in the curriculum. When critical thinking is an integral part of the teaching-learning process, children learn to apply thinking skills throughout the curriculum as well as in their daily lives. Socratic dialogue fosters critical thinking and motivates the teacher and learner to share and analyze experiences and knowledge. Critical thinking involves the child in the learning process and makes education more meaningful to the individual, thus facilitating learning.

Andrea Allen
Grade 1

The most important part of critical thinking, to me, is *discovery*. We discover a deeper level of thinking. We discover the reasons for ideas instead of just accepting ideas. We are motivated by action, interaction, and involvement. We discover we have the ability to expand our thoughts to include all aspects and perspectives of our beliefs.

Mandy Ryan
Grade 5

Critical thinking, to me, is the process of analyzing new and old information to arrive at solutions. It's the process of learning to question information that you may have taken for granted. It's being independent. Critical thinking is letting people think for themselves and make judgments for themselves.

Leigh Ledet
Grade 4

Critical thinking is the process of taking the knowledge you have gained through past experience or education and re-evaluating conclusions on a certain situation or problem. Because students must evaluate the reasons for their beliefs, they become actively involved in learning through the teacher's use of Socratic questioning. Allowing students to clarify their reasons through the writing process further stimulates the students to become critical thinkers. The ultimate goal for students to understand in using critical thinking is to become active thinkers for themselves.

Robin Thompson
Middle School
Language Arts

Critical thinking, to me, is to be open-ended in my thoughts. It is like opening a door which leads to many other doors through which ideas may evolve, move about, change, and come to rest. It is like a breath of freshness in which one can gain new insight over long-established opinions. It stimulates and generates endless new possibilities.

Eutha M. Godfrey
Grades 2-3

346

Critical thinking is thinking that demonstrates an extension of an idea or concern beyond the obvious. A critical thinker's values are significant to his learning.

Frances Jackson
Grade 2

To me, critical thinking means independence. It gives me a tool which lets me explore my own mind extending beyond basic recall to a higher level of reasoning. I then feel more in touch with myself and my own inner feelings. This results in my becoming a better decision-maker.

Jean Edwards
Grade 5

Critical thinking is the process of working your mind through different channels. It is the process of thinking logically. Critical thinking is analyzing your thoughts through questions. It is the process of seeing that your ideas and concepts may not be the same as another's. It is opening your mind to those who have different views and looking at their views.

Cathy L. Smith
Grade 3

Critical thinking is to question in-depth at every possible angle or point of view, to look at someone else's point of view without making hasty judgments. Critical thinking is to logically and fairly re-orient your own personal point of view, if necessary. To think critically, you are self-directed in your thinking process, as well as disciplined.

Mary Duke
Grade 1

Critical thinking is the vehicle by which I encourage students to become active participants in the learning process. I allow more time for and become more aware of the need for students to express ideas verbally and in written form to clarify ideas in their own minds. I recognize the importance of developing skills for analyzing and evaluating. Ultimately, once students become comfortable using critical thinking skills, they assume greater responsibility for their learning.

Dora McGill
Grade 6

Critical thinking is clear, precise thinking. I believe that all human actions and expressions involve in some way, thinking. For example, I believe that feelings, emotions and intuitions are much the results of earlier thought (reactions) to stimuli. I think that this, in one way, explains the variations of emotional responses in some people to similar stimuli. Thus, I believe that critical thinking not only has the potential to clarify new and former conscious thoughts but also to effect/change likely (future) emotive and intuitive reactions/responses.

More concrete and less theoretical outcomes of critical thinking may be more relevant to me as an educator. Better questioning skills on the part of the students and the teacher is an obvious outcome. There seem to be several positive outcomes of better questioning: more opportunity for in-depth understanding of content, a natural (built-in) process for accessing the effectiveness of lessons, and more opportunity for student participation, self-assessment, and direction are three apparent outcomes. There are, of course, many other outcomes of developing better questioning skills, and from the other skills of critical thinking.

I simply believe that critical thinking improves the overall integrity of the individual and the collective group, class, school, community, etc.

Richard Tuck
High School
Art

347

I perceive critical thinking in teaching as a tool for my learning. As I attempt to develop the critical thinker, I will become more aware of the students' thoughts, values, and needs. I must learn from what students offer, and develop acceptance and sensitivity to the individual. The knowledge I gain from the student will determine what I utilize as strategies or principles of critical thinking.

Loretta Jennings
Grade 1

Critical thinking is the ability to look at a problem or issue with a spirit of open-mindedness and to take that problem and analyze or evaluate it based on the facts or good "educated" hypotheses. Critical thinking is being flexible enough to suspend one's bias towards an issue in order to study all sides to formulate an opinion or evaluation.

Mark Moore
Grade 4

Critical thinking to me involves mental conversations and dialogues with myself. I try first to establish the facts. Then I try to search for criteria to examine my "facts." The next question is whether or not there are distortions and irrelevancies. I have to examine whether I have a personal bias which has led me to select only certain facts and leave others out.

I then try to mentally list facts and arguments on both sides of a question and, finally, draw logical questions and conclusions.

Barbara Neller
Middle School
Social Studies

Critical thinking is a systematic, logical approach to life in which an individual, using this method, truly learns and understands a concept rather than imitates or mimics. Knowledge and intellectual growth are achieved by a variety of strategies which include examining a variety of viewpoints, making assumptions based on viable evidence and forming well thought out conclusions.

Jane S. Thorne
High School
Math

Critical thinking allows students to become active participants in their learning. Socratic dialogue stimulates communication between teacher and students, thus creating an atmosphere where everyone is encouraged to become risk-takers. A teacher needs to become a model of critical thinking for the students. Through this interaction, content can be analyzed, synthesized, and evaluated with thinking.

Carol Thanos
Grade 6

Critical thinking is the complex process of exploring an issue, concept, term or experience which requires verbal as well as non-verbal involvement from the participant. It involves listing ideas related to the subject, so that the person involved could objectively examine the relationship of the ideas thought of. It demands the person involved in the process to investigate the certain issue, concept, or process from varied vantage points, in order that intuitions, assumptions, and conclusions are presented with reasoned opinions or experienced evidences. Critical thinking is a task that involves the participant's in-depth assessment of his or her body of knowledge, experience and emotions on the subject in question.

Ariel Collins
High School
Language Arts

Critical thinking is thinking that is clear, fairminded, and directed. It is not sloppy or self-serving thinking, but deep and probing thought aimed at finding the truth. It is skillful thinking aimed at genuine understanding, not superficial head-shaking. It is *the* tool used by and descriptive of an educated person whose mantra would be "veritas."

Helen Cook
Middle School
Science

Critical thinking is a process of questioning and seeking truth and clarity. It is a continual endeavor as one is constantly exposed to new knowledge which must be reconciled with prior conclusions. As one's body of knowledge grows, it is all the more important to be able to critically consider and determine *what is truth*.

Critical thinking demands certain prerequisites: open-mindedness, willingness to withhold snap judgments, commitment to explore new ideas. The development of such qualities empowers me to participate in the various facets of critical thinking, e.g., clarifying ideas, engaging in Socratic discussions. These skills are not nearly so difficult as achieving the mindset which must precede them. Only a *commitment* to question and persevere and honestly pursue truth will supply the impetus necessary to delve beneath the surface of issues and concepts. Yet this predisposition is difficult to achieve, because it necessitates taking risks, making mistakes, being wrong and being corrected — activities very threatening to our safe ego boundaries.

Only in transcending these ego boundaries does growth occur and genuine learning transpire. Critical thinking is comprised of a sense of wonderment, daring and determination. It is undergirded by a value of truth and personal growth. It is the continual learning process of the individual.

Deborah Norton
High School
Social Studies

The definition of critical thinking that I now hold is one that explains some things that I have felt for some time. I am convinced that everything that I know, that is a part of my education, I have figured out or found for myself. I have had close to twenty years of formal, didactic education, but I could tell you very little about anything that was presented to me in lecture through all those classes, except perhaps some trivia. In college, I did my real learning through the writing that I did, either from research or from contemplation. I have felt that this was true, but a lot of my own teaching has continued to be didactic and students have learned to be very accepting and non-questioning and to *expect* to be told what the right answer is, what someone else has decided the right answer is. I hope that I can change that now. I now feel that it is imperative that my students learn to be critical thinkers, and I hope that I can model that belief and, through all my activities in class, lead them in that direction. We all need to be open-minded, to realize that there are often many sides to a problem, many points of view and that there are strategies and techniques for analyzing, making decisions, and making learning our own. I want to be, and I want my students to be, questioning, open-minded, fairminded, synthesizing individuals — in other words, critical thinkers.

Liza Burton
High School
Language Arts

This is not a "good-boy/bad-boy" approach to thinking, for everyone must think his own way to the ethical insights that underlie becoming a fairminded thinker. We are careful not to judge the content of the student's thinking. Rather, we facilitate a process whereby the student's own insights can be developed.

Regarding a Definition of Critical Thinking

Many people who feel that they don't know what critical thinking is, or means, request a definition. When they realize there is no *one* definition of critical thinking given by all theorists, many people feel frustrated and confused. "Even the experts can't agree about what they're talking about. How can I teach it if *I* don't know what it is, and no one else can tell me?" What such a reaction misses, however, is that although theorists provide a variety of definitions, they do not necessarily reject each others' definitions. They feel that their particular definition most usefully conveys the basic concept, highlighting what they take to be its most crucial aspects, but they do not necessarily hold that other definitions are "wrong" or lacking in usefulness. Novices, on the other hand, typically get caught up in the wording of definitions and do not probe into them to see to what extent their meanings are compatible. The various proposed definitions, when examined, are in fact much more similar than they are different.

Furthermore, because of the complexity of critical thinking, its relationship to an unlimited number of behaviors in an unlimited number of situations, its conceptual interdependence with other concepts (such as the critical person, the reasonable person, the critical society, a critical theory of knowledge, learning, literacy, and rationality, not to speak of the opposites of these concepts) — it is important not to put too much weight on any one particular definition of critical thinking. A variety of useful definitions have been formulated by distinguished theoreticians, and we should value these diverse formulations as helping to make important features of critical thought more apparent.

Harvey Siegel, for example, has defined critical thinking as "thinking appropriately moved by reasons." This definition helps us remember that our minds are often inappropriately moved by forces other than reason: by desires, fears, social rewards and punishments, etc. It points out the connection between critical thinking and the classic philosophical ideal of rationality. Yet, clearly, the ideal of rationality is itself open to multiple explications. Similar points can be made about Robert Ennis' and Matthew Lipman's definitions.

Robert Ennis defines critical thinking as "rational reflective thinking concerned with what to do or believe." This definition usefully calls attention to the wide role that critical thinking plays in everyday life, for since all behavior is based on what we believe, all human action is based upon what we in some sense *decide* to do. However, like Siegel's definition, it assumes that the reader has a clear concept of rationality and of the conditions under which a decision can be said to be a "reflective" one. There is also a possible ambiguity in Ennis' use of 'reflective.' As a person internalizes critical standards — sensitivity to reasons, evidence, relevance, consistency, and so forth — the application of these standards to action becomes more automatic, less a matter of conscious effort and, hence, less a matter of overt "reflection" (assuming that Ennis means to imply by 'reflection' a special consciousness or deliberateness).

Matthew Lipman defines critical thinking as "skillful, responsible thinking that is conducive to judgment because it relies on criteria, is self-correcting, and is sensitive to context." This definition is useful insofar as one has a clear sense of the difference between responsible and irresponsible thinking, as well as what to encompass in the appropriate self-correction of thought, the appropriate use of criteria, and appropriate sensitivity to context. Of course, it would not be difficult to find instances of thinking that were self-correcting, used criteria, and responded to context *in one sense* but nevertheless were *uncritical* in some other sense. For example, one's particular criteria might be uncritically chosen or the manner of responding to context might be critically deficient in a variety of ways.

We make these points not to underestimate the usefulness of these definitions but to point out limitations in the process of definition itself when dealing with a complex concept such as critical thinking. Rather than working solely with one definition of critical thinking, it is more desirable to retain a host of definitions, and this for two reasons: 1) in order to maintain insight into the various dimensions of critical thinking that alternative definitions highlight, and 2) to help oneself escape the limitations of any given definition. In this spirit, we will present a number of definitions which we have formulated of the cluster of concepts whose relationship to each other is fundamental to critical thinking. Before reading these definitions, you might review the array of teachers' formulations in the chapter "What Critical Thinking Means to Me." You will find that virtually all the teachers' definitions are compatible with each other, even though they are all formulated individualistically.

Critical thinking is disciplined, self-directed thinking which exemplifies the perfections of thinking appropriate to a particular mode or domain of thinking. It comes in two forms. If the thinking is disciplined to serve the interests of a particular individual or group, to the exclusion of other relevant persons and groups, we call it *sophistic* or *weak sense* critical thinking. If the thinking is disciplined to take into account the interests of diverse persons or groups, we call it *fairminded* or *strong sense* critical thinking.

In thinking critically, people use their command of *the elements of thinking* to adjust their thinking successfully to the logical demands of a type or *mode of thinking*. As they come to habitually think critically in the strong sense, they develop special *traits of mind* : intellectual humility, intellectual courage, intellectual perseverance, intellectual integrity, and intellectual faith in reason. A sophistic or weak sense critical thinker develops these traits only in a restricted way, in accordance with egocentric and sociocentric commitments.

It is important not only to emphasize the dimension of skills in critical thinking but also to explicitly mark out the very real possibility of a one-sided use of the skills associated with critical thought. Indeed, the historical tendency for skills of thought to be systematically used in defense of the vested interests of dominant social groups and the parallel tendency of all social groups to develop one-sided thinking in support of their own interests, mandates marking this tendency with explicit concepts. It should be clearly recognized that one-sided critical thinking is much more common in the world of affairs than is fairminded critical thought.

Critical Thinking is:

a) skilled thinking which meets epistemological demands irrespective of the vested interests or ideological commitments of the thinker;

b) skilled thinking characterized by empathy into diverse opposing points of view and devotion to truth as against self-interest;

c) skilled thinking that is consistent in the application of intellectual standards, holding oneself to the same rigorous standards of evidence and proof to which one hold's one's antagonists;

d) skilled thinking that demonstrates the commitment to entertain all viewpoints sympathetically and to assess them with the same intellectual standards, without reference to one's own feelings or vested interests, or the feelings or vested interests of one's friends, community or nation;

e) the art of thinking about your thinking while your're thinking so as to make your thinking more clear, precise, accurate, relevant, consistent, and fair;

f) the art of constructive skepticism;

g) the art of identifying and removing bias, prejudice, and one-sidedness of thought;

h) the art of self-directed, in-depth, rational learning;

i) thinking that rationally certifies what we know and makes clear wherein we are ignorant;

j) the art of thinking for one's self with clarity, accuracy, insight, commitment, and fairness.

This is by no means all, for sometimes it is important to know whether a question is being raised against the background of a given social system, a given socio-logic. Sometimes, in other words, people think as Americans or as Iranians, or Russians. When people think like the other members of their social group, it is often to their advantage to believe what they believe even when it is *false*. We have alluded to this variable before in terms of the use within social systems of "functional falsehoods." What is justified as an answer to a question, given one social system as the defining context, may very well be different within the logic of another social system. We need to know, therefore, whether we seek to reason within the logic of a given social system or, on the other hand, are asking the question in a broader way. A question may be answerable within one system and not within another, or not in the same sense, or in the same sense but with a different answer. We sometimes forget this complexity when talking about critical thinking.

Going still further, it may be important for a critical thinker to recognize, in asking a question, whether the question is framed within the logic of a technical or natural language. The question, 'What is fear?' asked with the technical language of physiology and biology in mind, may well be a different question than that same interrogative sentence asked in ordinary English, a *natural* language. This is yet another dimension to critical thinking.

Finally, we often need to know, when reasoning about a question, whether that question is most appropriately treated by an established procedure (monological issues), or whether it is plausible for people to approach it from the perspective of diverse points of view (multilogical issues). If there is one dominant theory in a field or an established procedure or algorithm for settling a question, the rational thing to do would be to use that theory, procedure, or algorithm. Many of the routine problems of everyday life as well as many of the standard problems in highly technical or scientific disciplines are of this sort. However, it is crucial for students to learn how to identify those higher order problems for which there are multiple theories, frames of reference, or competing ideologies as the instrumentality for settling the issue, and hence cannot legitimately be approached monologically. Instruction rarely addresses these multilogical issues, even though most of the pressing problems of everyday social, political, and personal life are of this order. Moreover, there is good reason to foster a multilogical approach even to monological issues when students initially approach them. Students learn better when they struggle to understand things on their own terms, so even when we can immediately show them the "best" way to proceed, it is often better to let them argue about alternative ways first.

The Perfections and Imperfections of Thought

clarity _____ vs _____ unclarity

precision _____ vs _____ imprecision

specificity _____ vs _____ vagueness

accuracy _____ vs _____ inaccuracy

relevance _____ vs _____ irrelevance

consistency _____ vs _____ inconsistency

logical _____ vs _____ illogical

depth _____ vs _____ superficiality

completeness _____ vs _____ incompleteness

significance _____ vs _____ triviality

fairness _____ vs _____ bias or one-sidedness

adequacy (for purpose) _____ vs _____ inadequacy

Each of the above are general canons for thought. To develop one's mind and to discipline one's thinking to come up to these standards requires extensive practice and long-term cultivation. Of course, coming up to these standards is typically a relative matter and often has to be adjusted to a particular domain of thought. Being *precise* while doing mathematics is not the same thing as being precise while writing a poem or describing an experience. Furthermore, there is one perfection of thought that may come to be periodically incompatible with the others, and that is adequacy to the purpose. Because the social world is often irrational and unjust, because people are often manipulated to act against their interests, because skilled thought is often used in the service of vested interest, thought adequate to these purposes may require skilled violation of the common standards for good thinking. Skilled propaganda, skilled political debate, skilled defense of a group's interests, or skilled deception of one's enemy may require the violation or selective application of any of the above standards. The perfecting of one's thought as an instrument for success in a world based on power and advantage is a different matter from the perfecting of one's thought for the apprehension and defense of fairminded truth. To develop one's critical thinking skills merely to the level of adequacy for success is to develop those skills in a lower or *weaker* sense. It is important to underscore the commonality of this weaker sense of critical thinking, for it is dominant in the everyday world. Virtually all social groups disapprove of members who make the case for their competitors or enemies, however justified that case may be. Skillful thinking is commonly a tool in the struggle for power and advantage, not an angelic force that transcends this struggle. It is only as the struggle becomes mutually destructive and it comes to be the advantage of all to go beyond the one-sidedness of each that a social ground is laid for fairmindedness of thought. There is no society yet in existence that, in a general way, cultivates fairness of thought in its citizens.

It is certainly of the nature of the human mind to think — spontaneously, continuously, and pervasively — but it is not of the nature of the human mind to think critically about the standards and principles which guide its spontaneous thought. It has no built-in drive to question, for example, its innate tendency to believe what it wants to believe, what makes it comfortable, what is simple rather than complex, what is commonly believed, what is socially rewarded, etc. The human mind is ordinarily at peace with itself as it internalizes and creates biases, prejudices, falsehoods, half-truths, and distortions. Compartmentalized contradictions do not, by their very nature, disturb the mind of those who take them in and selectively use them. The human mind spontaneously experiences itself as being in tune with reality, as though it is directly observing and faithfully recording it. It takes a special intervening process to produce the kind of self-criticalness that enables the mind to effectively question its own constructions. The mind spontaneously but uncritically invests itself with epistemological authority with an even greater ease than the ease with which it accepts authority figures in the world into which it is socialized. The process of learning to think critically is therefore an extraordinary process that cultivates capacities merely potential in human thought and develops them at the expense of capacities spontaneously activated from within and reinforced by normal socialization. It is not normal and inevitable nor even common for a mind to discipline itself within a rational perspective and direct itself toward rational rather than egocentric beliefs, practices, and values. Yet it is increasingly possible to describe the precise conditions under which critical minds can be cultivated. The nature of critical thought, in contrast to uncritical thought, is becoming increasingly apparent.

We should recognize, therefore, that the process of encouraging critical thinking is a slow, evolutionary one — one that proceeds on many fronts simultaneously. We should recognize that built into our students' minds will be many egocentric and sociocentric tendencies. They will need time and encouragement to come to terms with these. A definition of critical thinking will never be our fundamental need, but rather a sensitivity to the many ways we can help students to make their thinking more clear, accurate, consistent, relevant and fair.

> *All the various strategies explained in the handbook are couched in terms of behaviors. The principles express and describe a variety of behaviors of the 'ideal' critical thinker; they become applications to lessons when teachers canvass their lesson plans to find appropriate places where those behaviors can be fostered. The practice we recommend helps guard against teachers using these strategies as recipes or formulas, since in each case good judgment is required in the application process.*

14 Glossary: An Educator's Guide to Critical Thinking Terms and Concepts

accuracy: Free from errors, mistakes, or distortion. Accuracy is an important goal in critical thinking, though it is almost always a matter of degree. It is important to recognize, in addition, that making mistakes is an essential part of learning and that it is far better that students make mistakes of their own, than that they parrot the thinking of the text or teacher. It should also be recognized that some distortion usually results whenever we think within a point of view or frame of reference. Students should think with this awareness in mind, with some sense of the limitations of their own, the text's, the teacher's, the subject's perspective.

ambiguity: A sentence having two or more possible meanings. Sensitivity to ambiguity and vagueness in writing and speech is essential to good thinking. **A continual effort to be clear and precise in language usage is fundamental to education.** Ambiguity is a problem more of sentences than of words. Furthermore, not every sentence that can be construed in more than one way is problematic and deserving of analysis. Many sentences are clearly intended one way; any other construal is obviously absurd and not meant. For example, "Make me a sandwich." is never seriously intended to request metamorphic change. For an example of a problematic ambiguity, consider the statement, "Welfare is corrupt." Among the possible meanings of this sentence are the following: Those who administer welfare programs take bribes to administer welfare policy unfairly; Welfare policies are written in such a way that much of the money goes to people who don't deserve it, rather than to those who do; A government that gives money to people who haven't earned it corrupts both the giver and the recipient. If two people are arguing about about whether or not welfare is corrupt, but interpret the claim differently, they can make little or no progress; they aren't arguing about the same point.

analyze: To break up a whole into its parts, to examine in detail so as to determine the nature of, to look more deeply into an issue or situation. **All learning presupposes some analysis of what we are learning**, if only by categorizing or labelling things in one way rather than another. Students should continually be asked to analyze their ideas, claims, experiences, interpretations, judgments, and theories.

argue: There are two meanings of this word that need to be distinguished: *1)* to argue in the sense of **to fight** or to emotionally disagree; and *2)* to give reasons for or against a proposal or proposition. In emphasizing critical thinking, we continually try to get our students to move from the first sense of the word to the second; that is, we try to get them to see the importance of **giving reasons** to support their views without getting their egos involved in what they are saying. This is a fundamental problem in human life. To argue in the critical thinking sense is to use logic and reason, and to bring forth facts to support or refute a point. It is done in a spirit of cooperation and good will.

argument: A reason or reasons offered for or against something, the offering of such reasons. This term refers to a discussion in which there is disagreement and suggests the use of logic and bringing forth of facts to support or refute a point. See **argue.**

to assume: To take for granted or to presuppose. Critical thinkers can and do make their assumptions explicit, assess them, and correct them. Assumptions can vary from the mundane to the problematic: I heard a scratch at the door. I got up to let the cat in. I assumed that only the cat makes that noise, and that he makes it only when he wants to be let in. Someone speaks gruffly to me. I feel guilty and hurt. I assume he is angry *at me*, that he is only angry at me when I do something bad, and that if he's angry at me, he dislikes me. **Notice that people often equate making assumptions with making false assumptions.** When people say, don't assume." this is what they mean. In fact, we cannot avoid making assumptions and some are justifiable. (We have assumed that people who buy this book can read English.) Rather than saying "Never assume," we say, "be aware of and careful about the assumptions you make, and be ready to examine and critique them." See **assumption.**

assumption: A statement accepted or supposed as true without proof or demonstration; an unstated premise or belief. **All human thought and experience is based on assumptions**. Our thought must begin with something we take to be true in a particular context. We are typically unaware of what we assume and therefore rarely question our assumptions. Much of what is wrong with human thought is to be found in the uncritical or unexamined assumptions that underlie it. For example, we often experience the world in such a way as to assume that we are observing things just as they are, as if we were seeing the world without the filter of a point of view. People we disagree with, of course, we recognize as **having a point of view.** One of the key dispositions of critical thinking is the on-going sense that as humans we always think within a perspective, that we virtually never experience things totally and absolutistically. There is a connection therefore between thinking so as to be **aware of our assumptions** and being **intellectually humble.** Assumptions generate inferences.

358

authority: *1)* The power or supposed right to give commands, enforce obedience, take action, or make final decisions. *2)* A person taken to have much knowledge and expertise in a field, hence taken to be reliable. Critical thinkers recognize that ultimate authority rests with reason and evidence, since it is only on the assumption that purported experts have the backing of reason and evidence that they rightfully gain authority. Much instruction discourages critical thinking by encouraging students to believe that whatever the text or teacher says is true. As a result students do not learn how to assess authority.

bias: A mental leaning or inclination. There are two different senses of the word 'bias' that need to be clearly distinguished: one is neutral, the other negative. In the neutral sense we are referring simply to the fact that, **because of one's point of view, one notices some things rather than others,** emphasizes some points rather than others, and thinks in one direction rather than others. This is not in itself a criticism because **thinking within a point of view is unavoidable.** In the negative sense, we are implying **blindness or irrational resistance to weaknesses within one's own point of view** or to the strength or insight within a point of view one opposes. Fairminded critical thinkers try to be aware of their bias (in sense one) and try hard to avoid bias (in sense two). Many people confuse these two senses and confuse bias with emotion or with evaluation, perceiving any expression of emotion or any use of evaluative words to be biased.

clarify: To make easier to understand, to free from confusion or ambiguity, to remove obscurities. **Clarity** is a fundamental perfection of thought and **clarification** a fundamental aim in critical thinking. Students often do not see why it is important to write and speak clearly, why it is so important to **Say what you mean and mean what you say.** See **accuracy, ambiguity, vague.**

concept: An idea or thought, especially a generalized idea of a thing or of a class of things. Humans think within concepts or ideas. **We can never achieve command over our thoughts if we do not learn how to achieve command over our concepts or ideas.** Thus we must learn how to identify the concepts or ideas we are using, contrast them with alternative concepts or ideas, and clarify what we include and exclude by means of them. For example, most people say they believe strongly in democracy, but few can clarify with examples what that word does and does not imply. **Typically, people confuse the meaning of words with cultural associations,** with the result that 'democracy' means to people whatever we do in running our government — any country that is different is undemocratic. We must distinguish the concepts implicit in the English language from the psychological associations surrounding that concept in a given social group or culture. The failure to achieve this ability is a major cause of uncritical and selfish critical thinking.

conclude: To decide by reasoning, to infer, to deduce: See **Conclusion.**

conclusion: The last step in a reasoning process. A judgment, decision, or belief formed after investigation or reasoning. All beliefs, decisions, or actions are formed on the basis of human thought, but rarely as the result of conscious reasoning or deliberation. **All that we believe is,** one way or another, **based on conclusions** that we have come to during our life time. Typically, however, we do not monitor our thought processes, we don't critically assess the conclusions we come to, to determine whether we have sufficient grounds or reasons for accepting them. People rarely recognize when they have come to a conclusion. They confuse their conclusions with evidence, and so cannot assess the reasoning that took them from evidence to conclusion. To recognize that **human life is inferential**, that we are continually coming to conclusions about ourselves and the things and persons around us, is essential to thinking critically and reflectively.

consistency: To think, act, or speak in agreement with what has already been thought, done, or expressed; to have intellectual or moral integrity. Human life and thought is filled with inconsistency, hypocrisy, and contradiction. We often say one thing and do another, judge ourselves and our friends by one standard and our antagonists by another, lean over backwards to justify what we want or to negate what does not serve our interests. Similarly, we often confuse desires with needs, treating our desires as equivalent to needs, putting what we want above the basic needs of others. **Logical and moral consistency are fundamental values of fairminded critical thinking.** Social conditioning and native egocentrism often obscure social contradictions, inconsistency, and hypocrisy. See **personal contradiction, social contradiction, intellectual integrity, human nature.**

correct: Connotes little more than absence of error; *accurate* implies a positive exercise of one to obtain conformity with fact or truth; *exact* stresses perfect conformity to fact, truth, or some standard; *precise* suggests minute accuracy of detail.

criterion (criteria, pl): A standard, rule, or test by which something can be judged or measured. Human life, thought, and action are based on human values. The standards by which we determine whether those values are achieved in any situation represent criteria. Critical thinking depends upon making explicit the standards or criteria for rational or justifiable thinking and behavior. See **evaluation.**

critical listening: A mode of monitoring how we are listening so as to maximize our accurate understanding of what another person is saying. By understanding the logic of human communication — that **everything spoken expresses point of view,** uses some ideas and not others, has implications, etc. — critical thinkers are able to listen so as to enter sympathetically and analytically into the perspective of others. See **critical speaking, critical reading, critical writing, elements of thought, intellectual empathy.**

critical person: Any person who has mastered a range of intellectual skills and abilities. If such a person uses those skills generally to advance his or her own selfish interests, that person is a critical thinker only in a weak or qualified sense. If such a person uses those skills generally in a fairminded fashion, entering empathically into the points of view of others, he or she is a critical thinker in the strong or fullest sense. See **critical thinking.**

critical reading: Most people read uncritically and so miss some part of what is expressed while distorting other parts. A critical reader realizes the way in which **reading, by its very nature, means entering into a point of view other than our own,** that of the writer. A critical reader actively looks for assumptions, key concepts and ideas, reasons and justifications, supporting examples, parallel experiences, implications and consequences, and any other structural features of the written text, to interpret and assess it accurately and fairly. **Critical reading is an active, intellectually engaged process** in which the reader participates in an inner dialogue with the writer. See **elements of thought.**

critical society: A society which rewards adherence to the values of critical thinking and hence **does not use indoctrination and inculcation as basic modes of learning** (rewards reflective questioning, intellectual independence, and reasoned dissent). Socrates is not the only thinker to imagine a society in which independent critical thought became embodied in the concrete day-to-day lives of individuals; William Graham Sumner, America's distinguished anthropologist, explicitly formulated the ideal:

> The critical habit of thought, if usual in a society, will pervade all its mores, because it is a way of taking up the problems of life. Men educated in it cannot be stampeded by stump orators and are never deceived by dithyrambic oratory. They are slow to believe. They can hold things as possible or probable in all degrees, without certainty and without pain. They can wait for evidence and weigh evidence, uninfluenced by the emphasis or confidence with which assertions are made on one side or the other. They can resist appeals to their dearest prejudices and all kinds of cajolery. Education in the critical faculty is the only education of which it can be truly said that it makes good citizens. (*Folkways*, 1906.)

Until critical habits of thought come to pervade our society, however, there will be a tendency for schools as social institutions to transmit the prevailing world view more or less uncritically, to transmit it as reality, not as a picture of reality. Education for critical thinking, then, requires that the school or classroom become a microcosm of a critical society. See **didactic instruction, dialogical instruction, intellectual virtues, knowledge.**

critical thinking: 1) Disciplined, self-directed thinking which exemplifies the perfections of thinking appropriate to a particular mode or domain of thinking. 2) Thinking that displays mastery of intellectual skills and abilities. 3) The art of thinking about your thinking while you are thinking in order to make your thinking better: more clear, more accurate, or more defensible. Critical thinking can be distinguished into two forms: "selfish" or sophistic, on the one hand, and "fairminded," on the other. In thinking critically we use our command of the elements of thinking to adjust our thinking successfully to the logical demands of a type or mode of thinking. See also **critical person, critical society, critical reading, critical listening, critical writing, perfections of thought, elements of thought, domains of thought, intellectual virtues.**

critical writing: To express oneself in language requires that one arrange ideas in some relationships to each other. When accuracy and truth are at issue, then it is essential that we understand what our thesis is, how we can support it, how we can elaborate it to make it intelligible to others, what objections can be raised to it from other points of view, what the limitations are to our point of view, and so forth. **Disciplined writing requires disciplined thinking; disciplined thinking is achieved through disciplined writing.** See **critical listening, critical reading, logic of language.**

critique: An objective judging, analysis, or evaluation of something. The purpose of critique is the same as the purpose of critical thinking: to appreciate strengths as well as weakness, virtues as well as failings. **Critical thinkers critique in order to remodel, redesign, and make better.**

cultural association: Undisciplined thinking often reflects associations, personal and cultural, which are absorbed or uncritically formed. If a person who was cruel to me as a child had a particular tone of voice, I may find myself disliking a person who has the same tone of voice. Media advertising juxtaposes and seeks to join any number of logically unrelated things in order to influence our buying habits. Raised in a particular country or within a particular group within it, we form any number of mental links which, if they remain unexamined, are apt to unduly influence our thinking. See **concept, critical society.**

cultural assumption: Unassessed (often implicit) belief adopted by virtue of upbringing in a society. Raised in a society, we unconsciously take on its point of view, values, beliefs, and practices. At the root of each of these are assumptions of a wide variety of sorts. Not knowing that we perceive, conceive, think, and experience within assumptions we have taken in, we take ourselves to be perceiving "things as they are," not "things as they appear from a cultural vantage point." Becoming aware of our cultural assumptions so that we might critically examine them is a crucial dimension of critical thinking. It is, however, a dimension almost totally absent from schooling. Lip service to this ideal is common enough; a realistic emphasis is virtually unheard of.

data: Facts, figures, or information from which conclusions can be inferred, or upon which interpretations or theories can be based. As critical thinkers we must make certain to distinguish what we have in the way of hard data from the inferences or conclusions we draw from those data.

dialectical thinking: Dialogical thinking conducted in order to test the strengths and weaknesses of opposing points of view. (Court trials and debates are, in a sense, dialectical in nature.) When thinking dialectically, reasoners pit two or more opposing points of view in competition with each other, developing each by providing support, raising objections, countering those objections, raising further objections, and so on. Dialectical thinking or discussion can be conducted so as to "win" by defeating the positions one disagrees with — using critical insight to support one's own view and point out flaws in other views (associated with critical thinking in the restricted or weak sense), or fairmindedly, by conceding points that don't stand up to critique, trying to integrate or incorporate strong points found in other views, and using critical insight to develop a fuller and more accurate view (associated with critical thinking in the fuller or strong sense).

dialogical instruction: Instruction that fosters dialogical or dialectic thinking. Thus, when considering a question, the class brings all relevant subjects to bear and considers the perspectives of groups whose views are not canvassed in their texts — for example, "What did King George think of the *Declaration of Independence,* the Revolutionary War, Continental Congress, Jefferson and Washington, etc.?" or, "How would an economist analyze this situation? A historian? A psychologist? A geographer?" See **critical society, didactic instruction, higher order learning, lower order learning.**

dialogical thinking: Thinking that involves a dialogue or extended exchange between different points of view or frames of reference. Students learn best in dialogical situations, in circumstances in which they have continuous opportunities to express their views to others and to try to fit other's views into their own. See **Socratic questioning, monological thinking, multilogical thinking, dialectical thinking.**

didactic instruction: A form of teaching by telling. In didactic instruction the teacher directly tells the student what to believe and think about a subject. The student's task is to remember what the teacher said and reproduce it on demand. In its most common form, this mode of teaching falsely assumes that one can directly give a person knowledge without that person having to think his or her way to it. It falsely assumes that knowledge can be separated from understanding and justification. It confuses the ability to state a principle with understanding it, the ability to supply a definition with knowing a new word, and the act of saying that something is important with recognizing its importance. See **Knowledge.**

domains of thought: Thinking can be oriented or structured with different issues or purposes in view. **Thinking varies in accordance with purpose and issue.** Critical thinkers learn to discipline their thinking to take into account the nature of the issue or domain. We see this most clearly when we consider the difference between issues and thinking within different academic disciplines or subject areas. Hence mathematical thinking is quite different from, say, historical thinking. Mathematics and history, we can say then, represent different domains of thought. See the **logic of questions.**

egocentric: A tendency to view everything else in relationship to oneself. One's desires, values, and beliefs (seeming to be self-evidently correct or superior to those of others) are often uncritically used as the norm of all judgment and experience. To think egocentrically is one of the fundamental impediments to critical thinking. As one learns to think critically in a strong sense, one learn to become more rational, in contrast to being egocentric. See **human nature, strong sense critical thinker, ethnocentrism, sociocentrism, personal contradiction.**

elements of thought: All thought has a universal set of elements, each one of which can be monitored for possible problems: Are we clear about our **purpose or goal?** about the **problem or question at issue?** about our **point of view or frame of reference?** about our **assumptions?** about the **claims** we are making? about the **reasons or evidence** upon which we are basing our claims? about our **inferences and line of reasoning?** about the **implications and consequences** that follow from our reasoning? Critical thinkers develop skills of identifying and assessing these elements in their thinking and in the thinking of others.

emotion: A feeling aroused to the point of awareness, often a strong feeling or state of excitement. When our egocentric emotions or feelings get involved, when we are excited by anger, fear, jealousy, etc., our objectivity typically decreases. Critical thinkers need to be able to monitor their egocentric feelings and use their rational passions to reason themselves into feelings appropriate to the situation as it really is, rather than to how it seems to their infantile ego. Emotions and feelings themselves are not irrational; however, it is common for people to feel strongly when their ego gets stimulated. One way to understand the goal of strong sense critical thinking is as the attempt to develop rational feelings and emotions at the expense of irrational, egocentric ones.

empirical: Relying or based on experiment, observation, or experience rather than on theory or meaning. **It is important to continually distinguish those considerations based on experiment, observation, or experience from those based on the meaning of a word or concept or the implications of a theory.** One common form of uncritical or selfish critical thinking involves distorting the facts or experience in order to preserve a preconceived meaning or theory. For example, a conservative may distort the facts that support a liberal perspective to prevent empirical evidence from counting against a theory of the world that he or she holds rigidly. Indeed, within all perspectives and belief systems there are a large number who will distort the facts before they will admit to a weakness in their favorite theory or belief. See **data, fact, evidence.**

empirical implication: That which follows from a situation or fact, not due to the logic of language, but from experience or scientific law. The redness of the coil on the stove empirically implies dangerous heat.

ethnocentric: A tendency to view one's own race or culture as central, based on the deep-seated belief that one's own group is superior to all others. Ethnocentrism is a form of egocentrism extended from the self to the group. Much uncritical or selfish critical thinking is either egocentric or ethnocentric in nature. Ethnocentrism and sociocentrism are used synonymously, for the most part. The "cure" for egocentrism or sociocentrism is empathic thought within the perspective of opposing groups and cultures. Such empathic thought is rarely cultivated in the societies and schools of today. Instead, many people develop an empty rhetoric of tolerance, saying that others have different beliefs and ways, but without seriously considering those beliefs and ways, what they mean to those others, and their reasons for maintaining them.

evaluation: To judge or determine the worth or quality of. **Evaluation has a logic and should be carefully distinguished from mere subjective preference.** The elements of its logic may be put in the form of questions which may be asked whenever an evaluation is to be carried out: *1)* Are we clear about **what precisely we are evaluating?**; *2)* Are we clear about what **our purpose** is? Is our purpose legitimate?; *3)* Given our purpose, what are the **relevant criteria or standards** for evaluation?; *4)* Do we have **sufficient information** about that which we are evaluating? Is that **information relevant to the purpose?**; and *5)* Have we **applied our criteria accurately and fairly to the facts** as we know them? Uncritical thinkers often treat evaluation as mere preference or treat their evaluative judgments as direct observations not admitting of error.

evidence: The data on which a judgment or conclusion might be based or by which proof or probability might be established. Critical thinkers distinguish the evidence or raw data upon which they base their interpretations or conclusions from the inferences and assumptions that connect data to conclusions. Uncritical thinkers treat their conclusions as something given to them in experience, as something they directly observe in the world. As a result, they find it difficult to see why anyone might disagree with their conclusions. After all, the truth of their views is, they believe, right there for everyone to see! Such people find it difficult or even impossible to describe the evidence or experience without coloring that description with their interpretation.

explicit: Clearly stated and leaving nothing implied; *explicit* is applied to that which is so clearly stated or distinctly set forth that there should be no doubt as to the meaning; *exact and precise* in this connection both suggest that which is strictly defined, accurately stated, or made unmistakably clear; *definite* implies precise limitations as to the nature, character, meaning, etc. of something; *specific* implies the pointing up of details or the particularizing of references. Critical thinking often requires the ability to be explicit, exact, definite, and specific. Most students are not able to make what is implicit in their thinking explicit. This deficiency affects their ability to monitor and assess their thinking.

fact: What actually happened, what is true; verifiable by empirical means; distinguished from interpretation, inference, judgment, or conclusion; the raw data. There are distinct senses of the word 'factual:' "True," (as opposed to "claimed to be true"); and "empirical" (as opposed to conceptual or evaluative). You may make many "factual claims" in one sense, that is, claims which can be verified or disproven by observation or empirical study, but I must evaluate those claims to determine if they are true. People often confuse these two senses, even to the point of accepting as true statements which merely "seem factual," for example, "29.23 % of Americans suffer from depression." Before I accept this as true, I should assess it. I should ask such questions as "How do you know? How *could* this be known? Did you merely ask people if they were depressed and extrapolate those results? How exactly did you arrive at this figure?" Purported facts should be assessed for their accuracy, completeness, and relevance to the issue. Sources of purported facts should be assessed for their qualifications, track records, and impartiality. Education which stresses retention and repetition of factual claims stunts students' desire and ability to assess alleged facts, leaving them open to manipulation. See **intellectual humility, knowledge.**

fair: The general word, implies the treating of both or all sides alike, without reference to one's own feelings or interests; *just* implies adherence to a standard of rightness or lawfulness without reference to one's own inclinations; *impartial* and *unbiased* both imply freedom from prejudice for or against any side; *dispassionate* implies the absence of passion or strong emotion, hence, connotes cool, disinterested judgment; *objective* implies a viewing of persons or things without reference to oneself, one's interests, etc.

faith: *1)* Unquestioning belief in anything. *2)* Confidence, trust, or reliance. A critical thinker does not accept faith in the first sense, for every belief is reached on the basis of some thinking, which may or may not be justified. Even in religion one believes in one religion rather than another, and in doing so implies that there are good reasons for accepting one rather than another. A Christian, for example, believes that there are good reasons for not being an atheist, and Christians often attempt to persuade non-Christians to change their beliefs. In some sense, then, everyone has confidence in the capacity of their own mind to judge rightly on the basis of good reasons, and does not believe simply on the basis of blind faith.

fallacy/fallacious: An error in reasoning; flaw or defect in argument; an argument which doesn't conform to rules of good reasoning (especially one that appears to be sound). Containing or based on a fallacy; deceptive in appearance or meaning; misleading; delusive.

higher order learning: Learning through exploring the foundations, justification, implications, and value of a fact, principle, skill, or concept. **Learning so as to deeply understand.** One can learn in keeping with the rational capacities of the human mind or in keeping with its irrational propensities, cultivating the capacity of the human mind to discipline and direct its thought through commitment to intellectual standards, or one can learn through mere association. Education for critical thought produces higher order learning by helping students actively think their way to conclusions; discuss their thinking with other students and the teacher; entertain a variety of points of view; analyze concepts, theories, and explanations in their own terms; actively question the meaning and implications of what they learn; compare what they learn to what they have experienced; take what they read and write seriously; solve non-routine problems; examine assumptions; and gather and assess evidence. Students could learn each subject by engaging in thought with in that subject. They could learn history by thinking historically, mathematics by thinking mathematically, etc. See **dialogical instruction, lower order learning, critical society, knowledge, principle, domains of thought.**

human nature: The common qualities of all human beings. People have both a primary and a secondary nature. Our primary nature is spontaneous, egocentric, and strongly prone to irrational belief formation. It is the basis for our instinctual thought. People need no training to believe what they want to believe: what serves their immediate interests, what preserves their sense of personal comfort and righteousness, what minimizes their sense of inconsistency, and what presupposes their own correctness. People need no special training to believe what those around them believe: what their parents and friends believe, what is taught to them by religious and school authorities, what is repeated often by the media, and what is commonly believed in the nation in which they are raised. People need no training to think that those who disagree with them are wrong and most probably prejudiced. People need no training to assume that their own most fundamental beliefs are self-evidently true or easily justified by evidence. People naturally and spontaneously identify with their own beliefs and experience most disagreement as personal attack. The resulting defensiveness interferes with their capacity to empathize with or enter into other points of view.

On the other hand, **people need extensive and systematic practice to develop their secondary nature, their implicit capacity to function as rational persons.** They need extensive and systematic practice to recognize the tendencies they have to form irrational beliefs. They need extensive practice to develop a dislike of inconsistency, a love of clarity, a passion to seek reasons and evidence and to be fair to points of view other than their own. People need extensive practice to recognize that they indeed have a point of view, that they live inferentially, that they do not have a direct pipeline to reality, that it is perfectly possible to have an overwhelming inner sense of the correctness of one's views and still be wrong. See **intellectual virtues.**

idea: Most general of these terms, may be applied to anything existing in the mind as an object of knowledge or thought; *concept* refers to generalized idea of a class of objects, based on knowledge of particular instances of the class; *conception,* often equivalent to concept, specifically refers to something conceived in the mind or imagined; *thought* refers to any idea, whether or not expressed, that occurs to the mind in reasoning or contemplation; *notion* implies vagueness or incomplete intention; *impression* also implies vagueness of an idea provoked by some external stimulus. Critical thinkers are aware of what ideas they are using in their thinking, where those ideas have come from, and how to go about assessing them.

imply/implication: A claim or truth which follows from other claims or truths. One of the most important skills of critical thinking is the ability to distinguish between what is actually implied by a statement or situation from what may be carelessly inferred by people. Critical thinkers try to **monitor their inferences to keep them in line with what is actually implied** by what they know. When speaking, critical thinkers **try to use words that imply only what they can legitimately justify.** They recognize that there are established word usages which generate established implications. To say of an act that it is murder, for example, is to imply that it is unjustified. See **clarify, precision, logic of language, critical listening, critical reading, elements of thought.**

infer/inference: An inference is a step of the mind, an intellectual act by which one concludes that something is so in the light of something else's being so, or seeming to be so. If you come at me with a knife in your hand, I would probably infer that you mean to do me harm. Inferences can be strong or weak, justified or unjustified. Inferences are based upon assumptions. See **imply/implication.**

insight: The ability to see and clearly and deeply understand the inner nature of things. Instruction for critical thinking fosters insight rather than mere performance; it cultivates the achievement of deeper knowledge and understanding through insight. **Thinking one's way into and through a subject leads to insights** as one synthesizes what one is learning, relating one subject to other subjects and all subjects to personal experience. Rarely is insight formulated as a goal in present curricula and texts. See **dialogical instruction, higher order learning, lower order learning, didactic instruction, intellectual humility.**

intellectual autonomy: Having rational control of ones beliefs, values, and inferences. The ideal of critical thinking is to learn to think for oneself, to gain command over one's thought processes. Intellectual autonomy does not entail willfulness, stubbornness, or rebellion.

It entails a commitment to analyzing and evaluating beliefs on the basis of reason and evidence, to question where it is rational to question, to believe when it is rational to believe, and to conform when it is rational to conform.

(intellectual) confidence in reason: Confidence that in the long run **one's own higher interests and those of humankind at large will be served best by giving the freest play to reason** — by encouraging people to come to their own conclusions through a process of developing their own rational faculties; faith that (with proper encouragement and cultivation) people can learn to think for themselves, form rational viewpoints, draw reasonable conclusions, think coherently and logically, persuade each other by reason, and become reasonable, despite the deep-seated obstacles in the native character of the human mind and in society. Confidence in reason is developed through experiences in which one succeeds at reasoning one's way to insight, at solving problems through reason, at using reason to persuade, at being persuaded by reason. Confidence in reason is undermined when one is expected to perform tasks without understanding why, to repeat statements without having verified or justified them, to accept beliefs on the sole basis of authority or social pressure.

intellectual courage: The willingness to face and assess fairly ideas, beliefs, or viewpoints to which we have not given a serious hearing, regardless of our strong negative reactions to them. This courage arises from the recognition that **ideas considered dangerous or absurd are sometimes rationally justified** (in whole or in part), and that **conclusions or beliefs espoused by those around us or inculcated in us are sometimes false or misleading.** To determine for ourselves which is which, we must not passively and uncritically "accept" what we have "learned." Intellectual courage comes into play here, because inevitably we will come to see some truth in some ideas considered dangerous and absurd and some distortion or falsity in some ideas strongly held in our social group. It will take courage to be true to our own thinking in such circumstances. Examining cherished beliefs is difficult, and the penalties for non-conformity are often severe.

intellectual empathy: Having a consciousness of the need to imaginatively put oneself in the place of others in order to genuinely understand them. We must recognize our egocentric tendency to identify truth with our immediate perceptions or longstanding beliefs. Intellectual empathy correlates with the ability to reconstruct accurately the viewpoints and reasoning of others and to **reason from premises, assumptions, and ideas other than our own.** This trait also requires that we remember occasions when we were wrong, despite an intense conviction that we were right, and consider that we might be similarly deceived in a case at hand.

intellectual humility: Awareness of the limits of one's knowledge, including sensitivity to circumstances in which one's native egocentrism is likely to function self-deceptively; sensitivity to bias and prejudice in, and limitations of one's viewpoint. Intellectual humility is based on the recognition that **no one should claim more than he or she actually knows.** It does not imply spinelessness or submissiveness. It implies the lack of intellectual pretentiousness, boastfulness, or conceit, combined with insight into the strengths or weaknesses of the logical foundations of one's beliefs.

368

intellectual integrity: Recognition of the need to be true to one's own thinking, to be consistent in the intellectual standards one applies, to hold one's self to the same rigorous standards of evidence and proof to which one holds one's antagonists, to practice what one advocates for others, and to honestly admit discrepancies and inconsistencies in one's own thought and action. This trait develops best in a supportive atmosphere in which people feel secure and free enough to honestly acknowledge their inconsistencies, and can develop and share realistic ways of ameliorating them. It requires honest acknowledgment of the difficulties of achieving greater consistency.

intellectual perseverance: Willingness and consciousness of the need to pursue intellectual insights and truths despite difficulties, obstacles, and frustrations; firm adherence to rational principles despite irrational opposition of others; a sense of the need to struggle with confusion and unsettled questions over an extended period of time, to achieve deeper understanding or insight. This trait is undermined when teachers and others continually provide the answers, do the thinking for students, or substitute easy tricks, algorithms, and short cuts for careful independent thought.

intellectual sense of justice: Willingness and consciousness of the need to entertain all viewpoints sympathetically and to assess them with the same intellectual standards, without reference to one's own feelings or vested interests, or the feelings or vested interests of one's friends, community, or nation; implies adherence to intellectual standards without reference to one's own advantage or the advantage of one's group.

intellectual virtues: The traits of mind and character necessary for right action and thinking; the traits of mind and character essential for fairminded rationality; the traits that distinguish the narrowminded, self-serving critical thinker from the openminded, truth-seeking critical thinker. These **intellectual traits are interdependent.** Each is best developed while developing the others as well. They cannot be imposed from without; they must be cultivated by encouragement and example. People can come to deeply understand and accept these principles by analyzing their experiences of them: learning from an unfamiliar perspective; discovering you don't know as much as you thought, and so on. They include: intellectual sense of justice, intellectual perseverance, intellectual integrity, intellectual humility, intellectual empathy, intellectual courage, (intellectual) confidence in reason, and intellectual autonomy.

interpret/interpretation: To give one's own conception of, to place in the context of one's own experience, perspective, point of view, or philosophy. Interpretations should be distinguished from the facts, the evidence, the situation. (I may interpret someone's silence as an expression of hostility toward me. Such an interpretation may or may not be correct. I may have projected my patterns of motivation and behavior onto that person, or I may have accurately noticed this pattern in the other.) The best interpretations take the most evidence into account. Critical thinkers recognize their interpretations, distinguish them from evidence, consider alternative interpretations, reconsider their interpretations in the light of new evidence. **All learning involves personal interpretation, since whatever we learn we must integrate into our own thinking and action.** What we learn must be given a meaning by us, must be meaningful to us, and hence involves interpretive acts on our part. Didactic instruction, in attempting to directly implant knowledge in students' minds, typically ignores the role of personal interpretation in learning.

intuition: The direct knowing or learning of something without the conscious use of reasoning. We sometimes seem to know or learn things without recognizing how we came to that knowledge. When this occurs, we experience an inner sense that what we believe is true. The problem is that sometimes we are correct (and have genuinely experienced an intuition) and sometimes we are incorrect (having fallen victim to one of our prejudices). A critical thinker does not blindly accept the inner sense that what one thinks or believes, but cannot account for, is necessarily true. A critical thinker is aware of the ease with which we can confuse intuitions and prejudices. Critical thinkers may follow their inner sense that something is so, but only with a healthy sense of intellectual humility.

irrational/irrationality: *1)* Lacking the power to reason. *2)* Contrary to reason or logic. *3)* Senseless, absurd. An uncritical thinker has failed to develop the ability or power to reason well. His or her beliefs and practices, then, are often contrary to reason and logic, and are sometimes senseless or absurd. It is important to recognize, however, that in societies with irrational beliefs and practices, it is not clear whether challenging those beliefs and practices — and therefore possibly endangering oneself — is rational or irrational. Furthermore, suppose one's vested interests are best advanced by adopting beliefs and practices that are contrary to reason. Is it then rational to follow reason and negate one's vested interests or follow one's interests and ignore reason? These very real dilemmas of everyday life represent on-going problems for critical thinkers. Selfish critical thinkers, of course, face no dilemma here because of their consistent commitment to advance their narrow vested interests. Fairminded critical thinkers make these decisions self consciously and honestly assess the results.

irrational learning: All rational learning presupposes rational assent. And, though we sometimes forget it, all learning is not automatically or even commonly rational. **Much that we learn in everyday life is quite distinctively irrational.** It is quite possible — and indeed the bulk of human learning is unfortunately of this character — **to come to believe any number of things without knowing how or why.** It is quite possible, in other words, to believe for irrational reasons: because those around us believe, because we are rewarded for believing, because we are afraid to disbelieve, because our vested interest is served by belief, because we are more comfortable with belief, or because we have ego identified ourselves, our image, or our personal being with belief. In all of these cases, our beliefs are without rational grounding, without good reason and evidence, without the foundation a rational person demands. We become rational, on the other hand, to the extent that our beliefs and actions are grounded in good reasons and evidence; to the extent that we recognize and critique our own irrationality; to the extent that we are not moved by bad reasons and a multiplicity of irrational motives, fears, and desires; to the extent that we have cultivated a passion for clarity, accuracy, and fairmindedness. These global skills, passions, and dispositions, integrated into a way of acting and thinking, are what characterize the rational, the educated, and the critical person.

judgment: *1)* The act of judging or deciding. *2)* Understanding and good sense. A person has good judgment when they typically judge and decide on the basis of understanding and good sense. Whenever we form a belief or opinion, make a decision, or act, we do so on the basis of implicit or explicit judgments. All thought presupposes the making of judgments concerning what is so and what is not so, what is true and what is not. To cultivate a person's ability to think critically is to foster their judgment, to help them to develop the habit of judging on the basis of reason, evidence, logic, and good sense. Good judgment is developed, not by merely learning about principles of good judgment, but by frequent practice judging and assessing judgments.

justification/justify: The act of showing a belief, opinion, action, or policy to be in accord with reason and evidence and/or to be ethically acceptable. Education should foster reasonability in students. This requires that both teachers and students develop the disposition to ask for and give justifications for beliefs, opinions, actions, and policies. Asking for a justification should not then be viewed as an insult or attack, but rather as a normal act of a rational person. Didactic modes of teaching that do not encourage students to question the justification for what is asserted fail to develop a thoughtful environment conducive to education.

know: To have a clear perception or understanding of, be sure of, to have a firm mental grasp of; *information* applies to data that are gathered in any way, as by reading, observation, hearsay, etc. and does not necessarily connote validity; *knowledge* applies to any body of facts gathered by study, observation, etc. and to the ideas inferred from these facts, and connotes an *understanding* of what is known. Critical thinkers need to distinguish knowledge from opinion and belief. See **knowledge.**

knowledge: The act of having a clear and justifiable grasp of what is so or of how to do something. Knowledge is based on understanding or skill, which in turn are based on thought, study, and experience. 'Thoughtless knowledge' is a contradiction. 'Blind knowledge' is a contradiction. 'Unjustifiable knowledge' is a contradiction. Knowledge implies justifiable belief or skilled action. Hence, when students blindly memorize and are tested for recall, they are not being tested for knowledge. **Knowledge is continually confused with recall in present-day schooling.** This confusion is a deep-seated impediment to the integration of critical thinking into schooling. **Genuine knowledge is inseparable from thinking minds.** We often wrongly talk of knowledge as if it could be divorced from thinking, as if it could be gathered up by one person and given to another in the form of a collection of sentences to remember. When we talk in this way, we forget that knowledge, by its very nature, depends on thought. Knowledge is produced by thought, analyzed by thought, comprehended by thought, organized, evaluated, maintained, and transformed by thought. Knowledge exists, properly speaking, only in minds that have comprehended and justified it through thought. Knowledge is not to be confused with belief nor with symbolic representation of belief. Humans are quite capable of believing things that are false or believing things to be true without knowing them to be so. A book contains knowledge only in a derivative sense, only because minds can thoughtfully read it and through that process gain knowledge.

logic: *1)* Correct reasoning or the study of correct reasoning and its foundations. *2)* the relationships that exist between propositions (supports, assumes, implies, contradicts, counts against, is relevant to ...). *3)* the system of principles, concepts, and assumptions that underlie any discipline, activity, or practice. *4)* the set of rational considerations that bear upon the truth or justification of any belief or set of beliefs. *5)* the set of rational considerations that bear upon the settlement of any question or set of questions. The word 'logic' covers a range of related concerns all bearing upon the question of rational justification and explanation. **All human thought and behavior is to some extent based on logic** rather than instinct. Humans try to figure things out using ideas, meanings, and thought. Such intellectual behavior inevitably involves "logic" or considerations of a logical sort: some sense of what is relevant and irrelevant, of what supports and what counts against a belief, of what we should and should not assume, of what we should and should not claim, of what we do and do not know, of what is and is not implied, of what does and does not contradict, of what we should or should not do or believe. **Concepts have a logic** in that we can investigate the conditions under which they do and do not apply, of what is relevant or irrelevant to them, of what they do or don't imply, etc. **Questions have a logic** in that we can investigate the conditions under which they can be settled. **Disciplines have a logic** in that they have purposes and a set of logical structures that bear upon those purposes: assumptions, concepts, issues, data, theories, claims, implications, consequences, etc. The concept of logic is a seminal notion in critical thinking. Unfortunately, it takes a considerable length of time before most people become comfortable with its multiple uses. In part, this is the result of people's failure to monitor their own thinking in keeping with the standards of reason and logic. This is not to deny, of course, that logic is involved in all human thinking. It is rather to say that the logic we use is often implicit, unexpressed, and sometimes contradictory.

the logic of a discipline: The notion that every technical term has logical relationships with other technical terms, that some terms are logically more basic than others, and that every discipline relies on concepts, assumptions, and theories, makes claims, gives reasons and evidence, avoids contradictions and inconsistencies, has implications and consequences, etc. Though all students study disciplines, most are ignorant of the logic of the disciplines they study. This severely limits their ability to grasp the discipline as a whole, to think independently within it, to compare and contrast it with other disciplines, and to apply it outside the context of academic assignments. Typically now, students do not look for seminal terms as they study an area. They do not strive to translate technical terms into analogies and ordinary words they understand. They do not look for the basic assumptions of the disciplines they study. Indeed, on the whole, they do not know what assumptions are nor why it is important to examine them. What they have in their heads exists like so many BB's in a bag. Whether one thought supports or follows from another, whether one thought elaborates another, exemplifies, presupposes, or contradicts another, are matters students have not learned to think about. They have not learned to use thought to understand thought, which is another way of saying that they have not learned how to use thought to gain knowledge. **Instruction for critical thinking cultivates the students' ability to make explicit the logic of what they study.** This emphasis gives depth and breath to study and learning. It lies at the heart of the differences between lower order and higher order learning.

the logic of language: For a language to exist and be learnable by persons from a variety of cultures, it is necessary that **words have definite uses and defined concepts that transcend particular cultures.** The English language, for example, is learned by many peoples of the world unfamiliar with English or American cultures. Critical thinkers must learn to use their native language with precision, in keeping with educated usage. Unfortunately, many students do not understand the significant relationship between precision in language usage and precision in thought. Consider, for example, the manner in which students relate to their native language. If one questions them about the meanings of words, their account is typically incoherent. They often say that people have their own meanings for all the words they use, not noticing that, were this true, we would not be able to understand each other. Students speak and write in vague sentences because they have no criteria for choosing words other than that one word popped into their head rather than another word. They do not realize that every language has a highly refined logic which must be learned to express oneself precisely. They do not realize that even words similar in meaning typically have different implications. Consider, for example, the words explain, expound, explicate, elucidate, interpret, and construe. *Explain* implies the process of making clear and intelligible something not understood or known. *Expound* implies a systematic and thorough explanation, often by an expert. *Explicate* implies a scholarly analysis developed in detail. *Elucidate* implies a shedding of light upon by clear and specific illustration or explanation. *Interpret* implies the bringing out of meanings not immediately apparent. *Construe* implies a particular interpretation of something whose meaning is ambiguous.

the logic of questions: The range of rational considerations that bear upon the settlement of a given question or group of questions. A critical thinker is adept in analyzing questions to determine what, precisely, a question asks and how to go about rationally settling it. A critical thinker recognizes that different kinds of questions often call for different modes of thinking, different kinds of considerations, and different procedures and techniques. Uncritical thinkers often confuse distinct questions and use considerations irrelevant to an issue while ignoring relevant ones.

lower order learning: Learning by rote memorization, association, and lock-step practice. There are a variety of forms of lower order learning in the schools, which we can understand by understanding the relative **lack of logic informing them.** Paradigmatically, lower order learning is learning by sheer association or rote. Hence students come to think of history class, for example, as a place where you hear names, dates, places, and explanations of events; where you try to remember them and state them on tests. Math comes to be thought of as numbers, symbols, and formulas — mysterious things you mechanically manipulate as the teacher told you, to get the right answer. Literature is often thought of as uninteresting stories to remember along with what the teacher said is important about them. The result is that students leave with a host of undigested fragments, scraps left over after they have forgotten most of what they stored in their short-term memories for particular tests. Virtually never do they grasp the logic of what they learn. Rarely do they relate what they learn to their own experience or critique each by means of the other. Rarely do they try to test what they learn in everyday life. Rarely do they ask "Why is this so? How does this relate to what I already learned? How does this relate to what I am learning in other classes?" To put the point in a nutshell, very few students think of what they are learning as worthy of being arranged logically in their minds.

monological (one-dimensional) problems: Problems that can be solved by reasoning exclusively within one point of view or frame of reference. For example, consider the following problems: *1)* Ten full crates of walnuts weigh 410 pounds, whereas an empty crate weighs 10 pounds. How much do the walnuts alone weigh?; and *2)* In how many days of the week does the third letter of the day's name immediately follow the first letter of the day's name in the alphabet? I call these problems and the means by which they are solved 'monological:' They are settled within one frame of reference with a definite set of logical moves. When the right set of moves is performed, the problem is settled. The answer or solution proposed can be shown by standards implicit in the frame of reference to be the "right" answer or solution. **Most important human problems are multilogical rather than monological,** nonatomic problems inextricably joined to other problems, with some conceptual messiness to them and very often with important values lurking in the background. When the problems have an empirical dimension, that dimension tends to have a controversial scope. In multilogical problems it is often arguable how many facts ought to be considered and interpreted, and how their significance ought to be determined. When they have a conceptual dimension, there tend to be arguably different ways to pin the concepts down. Though life presents us with predominanatly multilogical problems, shcooling today over-emphasizes monological problems. Worse, and more frequently, present instructional practices treat multilogical problems as though they were monological. The posing of multilogical problems, and their consideration from multiple points of view, play an important role in the cultivation of critical thinking and higher order learning.

monological (one-dimensional) thinking: Thinking that is conducted exclusively within one point of view or frame of reference. How much will this $67.49 pair of shoes with a 25% discount cost me? What does signing this contract oblige me to do? When was Kennedy elected President? A person can think monologically whether or not the question is genuinely monological. The strong sense critical thinker would avoid monological thinking when the question is multi-logical. The process of higher order learning requires multi-logical thought, even when the problem is monological (for example, learning a chemical concept), allowing students to explore and assess their original beliefs while developing insight into new ideas.

multilogical (multi-dimensional) problems: Problems that can be analyzed and approached from more than one, often from conflicting, points of view or frames of reference. For example, many ecological problems have a variety of dimensions to them: historical, social, economic, biological, moral, political, etc. A person comfortable thinking about multilogical problems is comfortable thinking within multiple perspectives, in engaging in dialogical and dialectical thinking, in practicing intellectual empathy, in thinking across disciplines and domains. See **monological problems, the logic of questions, the logic of disciplines, intellectual empathy.**

multilogical thinking: Thinking that sympathetically enters, considers, and reasons within multiple points of view. See **multilogical problems.**

national bias: Prejudice in favor of one's country, it's beliefs, traditions, practices, image, and world view; a form of sociocentrism or ethnocentrism. It is natural, if not inevitable, for people to be favorably disposed toward the beliefs, traditions, practices, and world view within which they were raised. Unfortunately, this favorable inclination commonly becomes a form of prejudice: a more or less rigid, irrational, ego-identification which significantly distorts one's view of one's own nation and the world at large. It is manifested in a tendency to take the side of one's own government, to uncritically accept governmental accounts of the nature of disputes with other nations, to uncritically exaggerate the virtues of one's own nation while playing down the virtues of "enemy" nations. National bias is reflected in the press and media coverage of every nation of the world. Events are included or excluded in accordance with what appears significant within the dominant world view of the nation, and are shaped into stories in such a way as to validate that view. Though constructed to fit into a particular view of the world, the stories in the news are presented as neutral, objective accounts, and uncritically accepted as such, because people tend to uncritically assume that their own view of things is the way things really are. To become responsible critically thinking citizens and fairminded people, students must practice identifying national bias in the news and in their texts, and to broaden their perspective beyond that of uncritical nationalism. See **ethnocentrism, sociocentrism, bias, prejudice, world view, intellectual empathy.**

opinion: A belief, typically one open to dispute. Sheer unreasoned opinion should be distinguished from reasoned judgment — beliefs fromed on the basis of careful reasoning. See **evaluation, judgment, justification, know, knowledge, reasoned judgment.**

the perfections of thought: Thinking, as an attempt to understand the world as it is, has a natural excellence or fitness to it. This excellence is manifest in its **clarity, precision, specificity, accuracy, relevance, consistency, logicalness, depth, completeness, significance, fairness, and adequacy.** These perfections are general canons for thought; they represent legitimate concerns irrespective of the discipline or domain of thought. To develop one's mind and discipline one's thinking with respect to these standards **requires extensive practice and long-term cultivation.** Of course, achieving these standards is a relative matter and varies somewhat among domains of thought. Being *precise* while doing mathematics is not the same as being precise while writing a poem or describing an experience. Furthermore, one perfection of thought may be periodically incompatible with the others: adequacy to purpose. Time and resources sufficient to thoroughly analyze a question or problem is all too often an unafordable luxury. Also, since the social world is often irrational and unjust because people are often manipulated to act against their interests, and because skilled thought is often used in the service of vested interest, thought adequate to these manipulative purposes may require **skilled violation of the common standards for good thinking.** Skilled propaganda, skilled political debate, skilled defense of a group's interests, skilled deception of one's enemy may require the violation or selective application of any of the above standards. The perfecting of one's thought as an instrument for success in a world based on power and advantage is a different matter from the perfecting of one's thought for the apprehension and defense of fair-minded truth. **To develop one's critical thinking skills merely to the level of adequacy for social success is to develop those skills in a lower or *weaker* sense.**

personal contradiction: An inconsistency in one's personal life, wherein one says one thing and does another, or uses a double standard, judging oneself and one's friends by an easier standard than that used for people one doesn't like. Typically a form of hypocrisy accompanied by self-deception. Most personal contradictions remain unconscious. People too often ignore the difficulty of becoming intellectually and morally consistent, preferring instead to merely admonish others. Personal contradictions are more likely to be discovered, analyzed, and reduced in an atmosphere in which they can be openly admitted and realistically considered without excessive penalty.

perspective (point of view): Human thought is relational and selective. It is impossible to understand any person, event, or phenomenon from every vantage point simultaneously. Our purposes often control how we see things. Critical thinking requires that this fact be taken into account when analyzing and assessing thinking. This is not to say that human thought is incapable of truth and objectivity, but only that human truth, objectivity, and insight is virtually always limited and partial, virtually never total and absolutistic. The hard sciences are themselves a good example of this point, since qualitative realities are systematically ignored in order to explicate quantitative realities.

precision: The quality of being accurate, definite, and exact. The standards and modes of precision vary according to subject and context. See **the logic of language.**

prejudice: A judgment, belief, opinion, point of view — favorable or unfavorable — formed before the facts are known, which is resistant to evidence and reason, or in disregard of facts which contradict it. Self-announced prejudice is rare. Prejudice almost always exists in obscured, rationalized, socially validated, functional forms. It enables people to sleep peacefully at night even while flagrantly abusing the rights of others. It enables people to get more of what they want, or to get it more easily. It is often sanctioned with a superabundance of pomp and self-righteousness. Unless we recognize these powerful tendencies toward selfish thought in our social institutions, even in what appear to be lofty actions and moralistic rhetoric, we will not face squarely the problem of prejudice in human thought and action. Uncritical and selfishly critical thought are often prejudiced. Most instruction in schools today, because students do not think their way to what they accept as true, tends to give students prejudices rather than knowledge. For example, partly as a result of schooling, people often accept as authorities those who liberally sprinkle their statements with numbers and intellectual-sounding language, however irrational or unjust their positions.

premise: A proposition upon which an argument is based or from which a conclusion is drawn. A starting point of reasoning. For example one might say, in commenting on someone's reasoning, "You seem to be reasoning from the premise that everyone is selfish in everything they do. *Do* you hold this belief?"

principle: A fundamental truth, law, doctrine, value, or commitment, upon which others are based. Rules, which are more specific, and often are superficial and arbitrary, are based on principles. Rules are more algorithmic; they needn't be understood to be followed. Principles must be understood to be appropriately applied or followed. Principles go to the heart of the matter. Critical thinking is dependent on principles, not rules and procedures. Critical thinking is principled, not procedural, thinking. Principles cannot be truly grasped through didactic instruction; they must be practiced and applied to be internalized.

problem: A question, matter, situation, or person that is perplexing or difficult to figure out, handle, or resolve. Problems, like questions, can be divided into many types. Each has a (particular) logic. See **the logic of questions, monological, multilogical problems.**

problem-solving: Whenever a problem cannot be solved formulaically or robotically, critical thinking is required: first, to determine the nature and dimensions of the problem, and then, in the light of the first, to determine the considerations, points of view, concepts, theories, data, and reasoning relevant to its solution. Extensive practice in independent problem-solving is essential to developing critical thought. Problem-solving is rarely best approached as a series of steps. For example, problem-solving schemas typically begin, "State the problem." Rarely can problems be precisely and fairly stated prior to analysis, gathering of evidence, and dialogical or dialectical thought wherein several provisional descriptions of the problem are proposed, assessed, and revised.

proof (prove): Evidence and/or reasoning so strong or certain as to demonstrate the validity of a conclusion beyond a reasonable doubt. How strong evidence or reasoning have to be to demonstrate what they purport to prove varies from context to context, depending on the significance of the conclusion or the seriousness of the implications following from it. See **domain of thought.**

rational/rationality: That which conforms to principles of good reasoning, is sensible, shows good judgment, is consistent, logical, complete, and relevant. Rationality is a summary term like 'virtue' or 'goodness.' It is manifested in an unlimited number of ways and is based on a host of principles. There is some ambiguity in it, depending on whether one considers only the logicalness and effectiveness by which one pursues one's ends, or whether it includes the assessment of ends themselves. There is also ambiguity in whether one considers selfish ends to be rational, even when they conflict with what is just. Does a rational person have to be just or only skilled in pursuing his or her interests? Is it rational to be rational in an irrational world? See **perfections of thought, irrational/irrationality, logic, intellectual virtues, weak sense critical thinking, strong sense critical thinking.**

rational emotions/passions: R. S. Peters has explained the significance of the affective side of reason and critical thought in his defense of the necessity of "rational passions:"

There is, for instance, the hatred of contradictions and inconsistencies, together with the love of clarity and hatred of confusion without which words could not be held to relatively constant meanings and testable rules and generalizations stated. A reasonable man cannot, without some special explanation, slap his sides with delight or express indifference if he is told that what he says is confused, incoherent and perhaps riddled with contradictions.

Reason is the antithesis of arbitrariness. In its operation it is supported by the appropriate passions which are mainly negative in character — the hatred of irrelevance, special pleading and arbitrary fiat. The more developed emotion of indignation is aroused when some excess of arbitrariness is perpetuated in a situation where people's interests and claims are at stake. The positive side of this is the passion for fairness and impartial consideration of claims. ...

A man who is prepared to reason must feel strongly that he must follow the arguments and decide things in terms of where they lead. He must have a sense of the giveness of the impersonality of such considerations. In so far as thoughts about persons enter his head they should be tinged with the respect which is due to another who, like himself, may have a point of view which is worth considering, who may have a glimmering of the truth which has so far eluded himself. A person who proceeds in this way, who is influenced by such passions, is what we call a reasonable man.

rational self: Our character and nature to the extent that we seek to base our beliefs and actions on good reasoning and evidence. Who we are, what our true character or predominant qualities are, is always to some extent, and sometimes to a very large extent, different from who we think we are. Human egocentrism and accompanying self-deception often stand in the way of our gaining more insight into our selves. We can develop a rational self, become a person who gains significant insight into what our true character is, only by reducing our egocentrism and self-deception. Critical thinking is essential to this process.

rational society: See **critical society.**

reasoned judgment: Any belief or conclusion, reached on the basis of careful thought and reflection, distinguished from mere or unreasoned opinion on the one hand, and from sheer fact on the other. Few people have a clear sense of which of their beliefs are based on reasoned judgment and which on mere opinion.

reasoning: The mental processes of those who reason; especially the drawing of conclusions or inferences from observations, facts or *hypotheses*. The evidence or arguments used in this procedure. A critical thinker tries to develop the capacity to transform thought into reasoning at will, or rather, the ability to make his or her inferences explicit, along with the assumptions or premises upon which those inferences are based. Reasoning is a form of explicit inferring, usually involving multiple steps. When students write a persuasive paper, for example, we want them to be clear about their reasoning.

reciprocity: The act of entering empathically into the point of view or line of reasoning of others; learning to think as others do and by that means sympathetically assessing that thinking. (Requires creative imagination as well as intellectual skill and a commitment to fair-mindedness.)

relevant: Bearing upon or relating to the matter at hand; *relevant* implies close logical relation-ship with, and importance to, the matter under consideration; *germane* implies such close natural connection as to be highly appropriate or fit; *pertinent* implies an immedi-ate and direct bearing on the matter at hand (a pertinent suggestion); *apposite* applies to that which is both relevant and happily suitable or appropriate; *applicable* refers to that which can be brought to bear upon a particular matter or problem. Students often have problems sticking to an issue and distinguishing information that bears upon a problem from information that does not.

self deception: The deceiving of oneself as to one's true motivations, character, identity, etc. One possible definition of the human species is "The Self-Deceiving Animal." Self-decep-tion is a fundamental problem in human life and the cause of much human suffering. Overcoming self-deception through self-critical thinking is a fundamental goal of strong sense critical thinking. See **egocentric, rational self.**

social contradiction: An inconsistency between what a society preaches and what it practices. In every society there is some degree of inconsistency between its image of itself and its actual character. Social contradiction typically correlates with human self-deception on the social or cultural level. Critical thinking is essential for the recognition of inconsis-tencies, and recognition is essential for reform and eventual "integrity."

sociocentric: When a group or society sees itself as superior and thus considers its way of seeing the world as correct, or as the only reasonable or justifiable way, and all its actions justi-fied, there is a tendency to presuppose this superiority in all of its thinking and thus to think closed-mindedly. All dissent and doubt are considered disloyal, and rejected with-out consideration. Few people recognize the sociocentric nature of their thinking.

Socratic questioning: A mode of questioning that deeply probes the meaning, justification, or logical strength of a claim, position, or line of reasoning. Socratic questioning can be car-ried out in a variety of ways and adapted to many levels of ability and understanding.

specific: Limiting or limited; specifying or specified; precise; definite. Student thinking, speech, and writing tend to be vague, abstract, and ambiguous rather than specific and clear. Learning how to state one's views specifically is essential to learning how to think clearly, precisely, and accurately.

specify: To mention, describe, or define in detail.

strong sense critical thinker: One who is predominantly characterized by the following traits: *1)* an ability to question deeply one's own framework of thought; *2)* an ability to recon-struct sympathetically and imaginatively the strongest versions of points of view and frameworks of thought opposed to one's own; and *3)* an ability to reason dialectically (multilogically) in such a way as to determine when one's own point of view is at its weakest and when an opposing point of view is at its strongest. Strong sense critical thinkers are not routinely blinded by their own points of view. They know that they have points of view and therefore recognize on the basis of what framework of assumptions and ideas their own thinking is based. They realize the necessity of putting their own assumptions and ideas to the test of the strongest objections that can be leveled against them. Teaching for critical thinking in the strong sense is teaching so that students explicate, understand, and critique their own deepest prejudices, biases, and misconceptions, thereby discovering and contesting their own egocentric and sociocentric tendencies. Only if we contest our inevitable egocentric and sociocentric habits of thought can we hope to think in a genuinely rational fashion. Only dialogical thinking about basic issues that genuinely matter to the individual will provide the kind of practice and skill essential to strong sense critical thinking.

Students need to develop all critical thinking skills in dialogical settings if they are to achieve ethically rational development, that is, genuine fairmindedness. If critical thinking is taught simply as atomic skills separate from the empathic practice of entering into points of view that students are fearful of or hostile toward, they will simply find additional means of rationalizing prejudices and preconceptions, or convincing people that their point of view is the correct one. They will be transformed from vulgar to sophisticated (but not to strong sense) critical thinkers.

teach: The basic inclusive word for the imparting of knowledge or skills. It usually connotes some individual attention to the learner; *instruct* implies systematized teaching, usually in some particular subject; *educate* stresses the development of latent faculties and powers by formal, systematic teaching, especially in institutions of higher learning; *train* implies the development of a particular faculty or skill or instruction toward a particular occupation, as by methodical discipline, exercise, etc.

theory: A systematic statement of principles involved; a formulation of apparent relationships or underlying principles of certain observed phenomena which has been verified to some degree. Often without knowing it, we form theories that help us make sense of the people, events, and problems of our lives. Critical thinkers put their thoeires to the test of experience and give due consideration to the theories of others. Critical thinkers do not construe their theories as facts.

think: The general word meaning to exercise the mental faculties so as to form ideas, arrive at conclusions, etc.; *reason* implies a logical sequence of thought, starting with what is known or assumed and advancing to a definite conclusion through the inferences drawn; *reflect* implies a turning of one's thoughts on or back on a subject and connotes deep or quiet continued thought; *speculate* implies a reasoning on the basis of incomplete or uncertain evidence and therefore stresses the conjectural character of the opinions formed; *deliberate* implies careful and thorough consideration of a matter in order to arrive at a conclusion. Though everyone thinks, few people learn to think critically. We don't need instruction to think; we think spontaneously. We need instruction to learn how to discipline and direct our thinking on the basis of sound intellectual standards.

truth: Conformity to knowledge, fact, actuality, or logic: a statement proven to be or accepted as true, not false or erroneous. Most people uncritically assume their views to be correct and true. Most people, in other words, assume themselves to possess the truth. Critical thinking is essential to avoid this, if for no other reason.

uncritical person: One who has not developed intellectual skills (naive, conformist, easily manipulated, dogmatic, easily confused, unclear, closed-minded, narrow-minded, careless in word choice, inconsistent, unable to distinguish evidence from interpretation). Uncriticalness is a fundamental problem in human life, for when we are uncritical we nevertheless think of ourselves as critical. The first step in becoming a critical thinker consists in recognizing that we are uncritical. Teaching for insight into uncriticalness is an important part of teaching for criticalness.

vague: Not clearly, precisely, or definitely expressed or stated; not sharp, certain, or precise in thought, feeling, or expression. Vagueness of thought and of language usage is a major obstacle to the development of critical thinking. We cannnot begin to test our beliefs until we recognize clearly what they are. We cannot disagree with what someone says until we are clear about what they are saying. Students need many techniques for transforming vague thoughts into clear ones.

verbal implication: That which follows, according to the logic of the language. If I say, for example, that someone used flattery on me, I *imply* that the compliments were insincere and given only to make me feel positively toward that person, to manipulate me against my reason or interest, for some end, such as a job promotion.

weak sense critical thinkers: 1) Those who do not hold themselves or those with whom they ego-identify to the same intellectual standards to which they hold "opponents." 2) Those who have not learned how to reason empathically within points of view or frames of reference with which they disagree. 3) Those who tend to think monologically. 4) Those who do not genuinely accept, though they may verbally espouse, the values of critical thinking. 5) Those who use the intellectual skills of critical thinking selectively and self-deceptively to foster and serve their vested interests (at the expense of truth); able to identify flaws in the reasoning of others and refute them; able to shore up their own beliefs with reasons.

world view: All human action takes place within a way of looking at and interpreting the world. As schooling now stands very little is done to help students to grasp how they are viewing the world and how those views determine the character of their experience, their interpretations, their conclusions about events and persons, etc. In teaching for critical thinking in a strong sense, we make the discovery of our own world view, and the experience of other people's world views, a fundamental priority.

> *The analytical vocabulary in the English language, with such terms as 'assume,' 'infer,' 'conclude,' 'criteria,' 'point of view,' 'relevance,' 'interpretation,' 'issue,' 'contradiction,' 'credibility,' 'evidence,' 'distinguish,' enables us to think more precisely about our thinking.*

Resources for Teaching Critical Thinking

Videotape Library

Videotapes are one of the most important developing resources for critical thinking in-service education. They can be used in a variety of ways: *1)* as discussion starters, *2)* as sources of information on the nature of critical thinking, *3)* as models of critical thinking, and *4)* as models for classroom instruction. All of the following videotapes have been developed as low-cost resources. No attempt has been made to achieve broadcast quality. An order form follows the tape descriptions.

1. Critical Thinking in Science

Professor Richard Paul, Chemistry Professor Douglas Martin, and Sonoma State University student Eamon Hickey discuss ways in which critical thinking may be applied in science education. The following issues are raised: "To what extent is there a problem with science education being an exercise in rote memorization and recall? Is there a conflict between preparing science students to become critical thinkers and preparing them for specialized scientific work? To what extent is science being taught monologically? Does monological instruction alienate students from the overall goal of becoming educated thinkers?" This tape is an excellent discussion-starter for in-service use. (50 minutes)

2. Critical Thinking in History

In this videotape, Professor Richard Paul is joined by History Professor Robert Brown and Sonoma State University student Eamon Hickey to discuss the relation of critical thinking to the interpretation, understanding, and construction of history. The following issues are discussed: "What is the place of value judgments in history? To what extent is history written from a point of view or frame of reference? Can students come to understand history from a critical vantage point? How would history be taught if this were the goal? To what extent should history be used to inculcate patriotism? What is it to learn how to think historically? Have teachers been adequately prepared to teach history from a critical vantage point? What can be done to facilitate historical thinking rather than memorization of 'facts'?" (50 minutes)

3. Dialogical Practice I

One of the most important skills of critical thinking is the ability to enter into and reason within opposing viewpoints. In this videotape, Sonoma State University students Stacy Goldring and Jean Hume practice dialogical reasoning, using the Israeli-Arab conflict as the subject. (50 minutes)

4. Dialogical Practice II

In this videotape, Sonoma State University students Hub Lampert and Dave Allender practice dialogical reasoning, using the issue of abortion as the subject. (29 minutes)

(Both of these dialogical practice tapes are excellent illustrations of what it is for students to integrate a host of critical thinking skills and dispositions into their spontaneous thinking.)

5. Critical Thinking: The State of the Field

In this welcoming address to the Third International Conference on Critical Thinking and Educational Reform, Professor Richard Paul addresses the following issues: "What fundamental changes are necessary to give students the incentive to develop critical thinking skills? How does the very nature of belief pose difficulty for critical thinking? How does traditional intra-disciplinary education provide an obstacle to independence of thought? How is critical thinking fundamental to all forms of reference, and how can we use it to think across and beyond disciplinary boundaries? How is the field of critical thinking developing so as to cut across subject matter divisions? What are the social and institutional barriers to the development of critical thinking as a field and as an educational reality?" (65 minutes)

6. Socratic Questioning In Large Group Discussion (4ᵗʰ Grade)

Professor Richard Paul leads a 4ᵗʰ Grade class discussion, using Socratic questions. Issues such as the following are discussed: "What is your mind? Does it *do* anything? Where does your personality come from? Is thinking like an American kid different from thinking like an Eskimo kid? Do you choose to be the kind of person you are going to be? Can you be a good person and people think you're bad? How do you find out what's inside a person?" (60 minutes)

7. Socratic Questioning in Large Group Discussion (6ᵗʰ Grade)

Professor Richard Paul leads a 6ᵗʰ Grade class discussion, using Socratic questions. Issues such as the following are discussed: "Who does the 'our' in the textbook title *Our World* refer to? Are people easy or hard to understand? Are all members of a group alike? Do some groups think they are better than other groups? Are there any groups of people that you think are bad? If you had to list the qualities of most Americans, what would they be? If you had to list the qualities of Germans, what would they be? Italians? Russians? Now imagine all of you are Russian boys and girls: how would you describe Americans?" The students' stereotypes and biases are probed. When contradictions begin to emerge, the students struggle to reconcile them or go beyond them. (70 minutes)

8. Socratic Questioning in Large Group Discussions (7ᵗʰ and 8ᵗʰ Grades)

Professor Richard Paul writes a definition of critical thinking on the board — "Critical thinking is seeing through the surface of things, events, and people to the deeper realities" — and then leads the class to probe the definition by Socratic questioning: "Can anyone give an example of a person you met that you thought was one way whom you later came to think was very different? Have you ever seen a toy advertised on TV that you later saw was very different from the way it appeared on TV? Do people ever try to make things look different from the way they are? Is it common or not common for people to try to trick other people? How can we check to see if people or things are really the way they appear to be? Do we always know what we really want? What we are really like? Are all people around the world basically alike or basically different? How could we check? How could we find out if we are right or wrong?" (65 minutes)

17. Coaching Teachers Who Teach Critical Thinking — John Barell, David Perkins

If we wish students to engage in critical thinking in the 'strong sense,' how do we nurture this intended outcome through teacher-supervisor-coach interactions? Assuming experienced teachers are aware of the nature of critical thinking and find it difficult to engage students in this process, how do we help them become more flexible, empathic analysts and problem solvers? A model coaching process will be demonstrated and related to research on staff development, teacher growth, metacognition and achievement motivation. (90 minutes)

20. Effective Design for Critical Thinking Inservice — Chuck Blondino, Ken Bumgarner

A team approach has been used effectively in the State of Washington to institute and improve the teaching of critical thinking in elementary, secondary, and higher education. Central to this team is effective networking that exists between and among the educational service districts (ESDS) and the curriculum and instruction leadership of the state office. Employee and curriculum organizations as well as parent, citizen and business associations have joined in this team effort focused on the teaching of thinking skills at all levels. Organizing and networking techniques employed are discussed along with approaches taken to garner support of the educational groups, citizen organizations, and outside enterprises. (90 minutes)

22. Bridging the Gap Between Teachers' Verbal Allegiance to Critical Thinking and Their Actual Behavior — M. Neil Browne, Stuart Keeley

Faculty and administrators regularly rank critical thinking as a preeminent educational objective. They claim it is the core of what teachers should be doing. Unfortunately, their talk is rarely supported by their teaching behavior. An initial obstacle to transforming verbal devotion to critical thinking into classroom performance is the mistaken belief that the discontinuity between prescription and practice is illusory. Professors Browne and Keeley summarize research done by themselves and others concerning the extent of critical thinking activity in secondary and post-secondary classrooms, and discuss strategies that offer promise for actually integrating critical thinking into the classroom. Especially important is the need to addresss the dominance of the 'coverage model' in shaping teaching practice. The presenters include suggestions for dialogic conversation with those who are motivated by the 'coverage model.' (90 minutes)

23. Teaching Critical Thinking Across the Curriculum — John Chaffee

Professor Chaffee explores an established interdisciplinary program which teaches and reinforces fundamental thinking skills and critical attitudes across the curriculum. The program is centered around *Critical Thought Skills,* a course specifically designed to improve the thinking, language, and symbolic abilities of entering college students. The course has been integrated into the curriculum through an NEH funded project of faculty training and curriculum re-design. In addition to reviewing the structure, theoretical perspective and evaluative results of the program, special attention is given to exploring practical approaches for developing thinking abilities. (90 minutes)

24. Critical Thinking and the History-Social Sciences Curriculum, Grades 9-12 — Ira Clark, Jerry Cummings

Using the Model Curriculum Standards for Grades 9-12, History-Social Science, the presenters and audience discuss and develop clasroom activities and strategies for getting students to enlarge their views through critical thinking skills. (90 minutes)

25. Language Arts and Critical Thinking for Remedial and Bilingual Students — Connie DeCapite

This workshop focuses on two specific components. Initially, Ms. DeCapite discusses the benefits of using critical thinking skills to help low-achieving or ESL students develop language, reading, and writing proficiency. The second part of the workshop focuses on how to develop and implement a language arts program consisting of activities utilizing critical thinking strategies and interdisciplinary materials. (90 minutes)

26. A Conception of Critical Thinking — Robert H. Ennis

On the assumption that a liberally educated person should be able to think critically in handling the civic and personal problems of daily life, as well as those of the standard subjects as taught in school, Robert Ennis offers a conception of critical thinking that bridges all of these concerns. Starting with the idea that thinking critically is reflectively and reasonably going about deciding what to believe or do, he suggests a number of dispositions and abilitites that might well constitute a critical thinking set of goals for the school, K-U. (90 minutes)

27. How To Write Critical Thinking Test Questions — Robert H. Ennis

Dr. Ennis offers suggestions on how to frame questions that test critical thinking skills. (90 minutes)

30. Philosophy For Children — Thomas Jackson

Professor Jackson presents a brief introduction to the Philosophy for Children program followed by a 'hands-on' demonstration of how the program actually works. Participants then read from a section of the novel, *Pixie*, raise questions from the reading, group these questions, and work a follow-up exercise together. (90 minutes)

31. Critical Thinking in Math and Science — Douglas Martin, Richard Paul

A discussion of the sense in which routine and non-routine mathematical and scientific thinking presuppose critical thinking. Consideration is given not only to the 'ultimate' nature of such thinking, but to the forms that thinking takes (or ought to take) as students approach it at various levels of 'ignorance' and incomplete understanding. (90 minutes)

32. Projects for Integrating Critical Thinking — Ogden Morse, Geoffrey Scheurman

The projects discussed help enable teachers to foster the deliberate teaching and integration of thinking skills with the presentation of normal content material. The projects offer several avenues to aid teachers in developing units of study and integrating them into specific subject areas. Mr. Scheurman discusses the Wyoming Critical Thinking Project. Mr. Morse discusses a model he developed for transferring critical thinking theory into practical application in the classroom. (90 minutes)

33. Varieties of Critical Thinking Tests: Their Design and Use — Stephen Norris

Critical thinking tests can serve different purposes. They might be used to examine, for example, critical thinking skills or critical thinking dispositions, or to examine either several aspects of critical thinking or only a few aspects. In addition, the information provided by a critical thinking test might be used to make decisions about individual students, to assess the critical thinking curricula, to evaluate teachers, or to compare the quality of schools.

Dr. Norris argues that not all types of critical thinking tests can serve equally well all of the purposes for which such tests might be used. A systematic matching of type of test to the intended use can help make currently available critical thinking tests more effective. The bottom line in all cases, no matter what type of test is used and no matter what the purposes for using it, is that the reasons be known for students' responses to the tasks on the tests. (90 minutes)

34. Teaching Critical Thinking in the Strong Sense in Elementary, Secondary, and Higher Education — Richard Paul

In his opening address to the Fourth International Conference on Critical Thinking and Educational Reform, Richard Paul argues for the importance of teaching critical thinking at all levels in such a way as to foster the critical spirit and the application of that spirit to the foundations of our own beliefs and actions. He argues that it is inadequate to conceive of critical thinking simply as a body of discrete academic skills. The synthesis of these skills and their orchestration into a variety of forms of deep criticism is accentuated. He comments on the application of strong sense critical thinking to personal and social life as well as to academic subject domains. In this perspective, the strong sense critical thinker is conceived of as having special abilities and a special commitment to becoming an integrated and moral person. (60 minutes)

35. Workshop on the Art of Teaching Critical Thinking in the Strong Sense — Richard Paul

In this workshop, emphasis is placed on strategies which enhance strong sense critical thinking abilities and skills. First, the distinction between weak and strong sense critical thinking is explained. Then, exercises are used to explain and demonstrate how one can use the macro-abilities of critical thinking (Socratic quesitoning, reciprocity, and dialogical reasoning) to orchestrate micro-skills in achieving 'strong sense' objectives. (90 minutes)

36. Critical Thinking's Original Sin: Round Two — David Perkins, Richard Paul

At the Third International Conference on Critical Thinking and Educational Reform, Richard Paul and David Perkins debated the psychological sources of closed-mindedness and superficial thinking. Paul contended that deep motivational factors such as egocentricity are the culprit. Perkins contended that powerful cognitive factors such as the avoidance of cognitive load lead to one-sidedness and oversimplification. Here, the two review, broaden, and deepen the debate. To demonstrate the spirit of fair thinking, however, each argues the other's side. (90 minutes)

37. Knowledge as Design in the Classroom — David Perkins

This workshop introduces participants to the basic strategies of "knowledge as design," a systematic approach to integrating the teaching of critical and creative thinking into subject-matter instruction. The key notion is that any piece of knowledge or product of mind — Newton's laws, the Bill of Rights, a sonnet by Shakespeare — can be viewed as a design, a structure adapted to a purpose. By examining the purpose of Newton's laws, the Bill of Rights, or a sonnet, analyzing structure, and assessing how and how well the structure serves the purpose, students can achieve genuine insight into such products and into the way knowledge works in general. By redesigning existing designs (for example, make up your own Bill of Rights) and devising new ones, students can learn the art of inventive thinking. (90 minutes)

38. The Possibility of Invention — David Perkins

"How can something come out of nothing?" is a fundamental question not only for physicists pondering the origins of the universe but for psychologists, philosophers, and educators pondering the nature of creative thinking. How can a person invent something genuinely new, or is it so that nothing we invent is really new? This presentation explores the basic 'logic' of invention, arguing that there are fundamental patterns of information processing that can be found in human thought, and some of them even in computers and biological evolution. (90 minutes)

39. The Role of Thinking in Reading Comprehension — Linda M. Phillips

Dr. Phillips discusses the intimate relation between critical thinking and reading comprehension, using case studies to illustrate how the same passage of text is interpreted differently by a critical reader and an uncritical reader. Thinking should not be separated from reading, she concludes, and reading well is thinking well. (90 minutes)

41. Teaching Thinking Strategies Across the Curriculum: The Higher Order Thinking (H O T) Project: Elementary Level — Edys Quellmalz

Dr. Quellmalz describes the Higher Order Thinking (H. O. T.) Projects currently underway in San Mateo County, Sacramento County and the San Juan Unified School District. The projects involve teachers in a collaborative effort to develop and monitor students' higher order thinking skills in school subjects. In the instructional component, teachers examine textbooks and other classroom resources in order to design activities that will involve students in sustained reasoning about significant concepts and problems typically encountered in academic and practical situations. Following an overview of the projects, teachers describe lessons developed and discuss samples of student work. (90 minutes)

43. Why Not Debate? Strong Sense Critical Thinking Assignments — Dianne Romain

After defining strong sense critical thinking values such as fairmindedness, truth, and autonomy, Dr. Romain argues that student debates tend to emphasize some of these values. She presents a dialogue paper assignment, small group projects, and guidelines for class discussion that encourage strong sense critical thinking values. (90 minutes)

44. **Introducing Affective Awareness** — Vivian Rosenberg

This presentation is based on the assumption that Critical Thinking in the 'strong' sense is more than simply constructing, criticizing and assessing arguments. It involves: *1)* understanding how our minds work *2)* developing insight into different ways of thinking about problems and ideas and *3)* developing strategies to analyze different kinds of problems and ideas. To illustrate how affective awareness can be taught in the classroom, Professor Rosenberg describes a program in which students are directed *consciously and systematically* to focus on feelings — to identify how they feel as they deal with ideas and problems, and to understand how others feel. She concludes that affective awareness is a teachable skill, and that it can — and should — be taught and practiced in critical thinking courses. (90 minutes)

46. **A Holistic Approach to Thinking Instruction** — Vincent Ryan Ruggiero

Because the development of thinking instruction has taken place in two separate disciplines (philosophy and psychology), it has produced two models of the thinking process — a critical model and a creative model. Unfortunately, neither model is by itself adequate for problem-solving and issue-analysis, which demand both the production and evaluation of ideas. This workshop presents a holistic approach to thinking instruction that combines creative and critical thinking and demonstrates how that approach applies to problems and issues across the curriculum. (90 minutes)

51. **Solving Problems in Writing** — Joseph Williams

Real life problem solving differs from laboratory problem solving in several ways: real life problems are not easily identified or defined; they have no one right solution nor is there a standard way to solve the problem. There is no way to determine easily the goodness of the solution because the problem is so deeply embedded in a wider context of problems. Teachers who ask students to solve problems in writing often fail to understand that some students think that they are being asked to solve a laboratory-like problem when the instructor is looking for evidence that they appreciate that a problem is ambiguous, complex and open-ended. Or vice-versa.

This workshop addresses the ways to think through the context of a writing problem, ways to anticipate a student's simply following a "set of rules" for solving a writing problem, and ways to demonstrate those rhetorical conventions that most of us take to be the signs of thoughtful problem solving — of good critical thinking. (90 minutes)

Mini Critical Thinking Course

At the Fourth International Conference on Critical Thinking and Educational Reform, several authors of critical thinking texts and other experienced critical thinking instructors were asked to speak on particular aspects of critical thinking. The series of lectures, presented as a mini-course in critical thinking, is now available in video format.

52. **Using Arguments to Decide What to Believe** — J. Anthony Blair

Faced with contentious claims, there is a tendency to respond with immediate reaction, and also to consider only a few of the pros and cons. Moreover, the reflection that goes into such an examination when it does occur is seldom thorough or tenacious. What seems needed are some easily-understood and readily-applied methods that will extend and deepen the critical examination of contentious claims. The method suggested by Dr. Blair is a systematic collection and examination of *1)* the pros and cons of a contentious opinion or claim, *2)* the merits of those pros and cons, *3)* the overall strengths and weaknesses of the best case for the claim. Dr. Blair describes the theory of the method, then participants are given a chance to apply it and see how it works in practice. (90 minutes)

53. Critical and Creative Problem-Solving — John Chaffee

Solving problems effectively involves an integrated set of critical and creative thinking abilities. This workshop introduces a versatile problem-solving approach which is useful for analyzing complex problems in a creative and organized fashion. Participants work through a sequence of problems, individually and in small groups, and are given the opportunity to discuss and critically reflect on the learning process. In addition, participants explore ways of incorporating problem-solving approaches into the courses that they teach. (90 minutes)

54. Learning About Good Arguments Through the Fallacies — Edward Damer

This session is devoted to the treatment of a selected number of informal fallacies. Since a fallacy is defined as a violation of one of the three criteria of a good argument, the emphasis is upon the ways in which an understanding of the fallacies can help one to develop abilities to construct good arguments and to detect bad ones. (90 minutes)

57. Information and the Mass Media — Ralph Johnson

Professor Johnson makes the following assumption: That in order to be a critical thinker, one must have the following things: first, certain intellectual and logical skills and the propensity to use them appropriately; second, a basis of knowledge and information; third, vigilance against ego- and ethno-centric bias. Professor Johnson concentrates on the second of the above-mentioned items, specifically on how the critical thinker deals with information and the mass media. The idea would be to give the students a crash course in how the critical thinker uses the mass media in such a way as to benefit from their strengths, while avoiding being seduced into thinking we know more than we do. He outlines the elements that go into being a RACON: a reflective and aggressive consumer of the news. (90 minutes)

58. Practical Reasoning — Carol LaBar, Ian Wright

Critical thinking includes reasoning about what ought to be done, as well as what to believe. This sort of reasoning, sometimes called practical reasoning, involves two logically different kinds of reasons: *1)* motivating reasons in the form of value standards which the agent accepts, and *2)* beliefs about the degree to which the actions under consideration will fulfill the value standard. These two different kinds of reasons lead to a conclusion about what ought to be done; that is a practical judgment. This session focuses on the practical syllogism and the use of principle 'tests' as a way of assessing the value standard. (90 minutes)

59. The Nature of Critical Thinking Through Socratic Interrogation — Richard Paul

Professor Paul interrogates the audience Socratically in order to elicit collective insights into the nature of critical thinking. This parallels the first couple of sessions of his introductory course in critical thinking in which Professor Paul uses a similar strategy for getting his students to begin to come to terms with some of the basic issues. (90 minues)

60. Dispositions: The Neglected Aspect of Critical Thinking — Vincent Ruggiero

All the understanding of creative and critical thinking and all the skill in applying that understanding to problems and issues will profit students little if they lack the *motivation* to think well. This fact has led a growing number of authorities on thinking instruction to urge that classroom instructors give special attention to the *dispositions* that underlie effective thinking. This workshop identifies these dispositions and suggests ways for instructors to assist students in developing them. It also examines the obstacles to such development and ways in which they can be overcome. (90 minutes)

61. Epistemological Underpinnings of Critical Thinking — Harvey Siegel

To be a critical thinker is to base one's beliefs, opinions and actions on relevant reasons. The notions of 'reason' and 'rationality' are, however, philosophically problematic. Just what is a reason? How do we know that some consideration constitutes a reason for doing or believing something? How do we evaluate the strength or merit of reasons? What is it for a belief or action to be *justified*? What is the relationship between justification and *truth*? Dr. Siegel examines these epistemological questions, and explores their relevance for critical thinking. (90 minutes)

63. Designing Faculty Development Programs for Integrating Critical Thinking Across the Curriculum — M. Neil Browne

Many teachers who desire to encourage critical thinking have no formal training in either critical thinking or pedagogical techniques that might stimulate such thinking. Administrators often respond with some form of weakness. What works? What kinds of pitfalls do faculty development programs typically encounter? What can be done to encourage long-term effects of faculty development?

Professor Browne's presentation is a dialogue between someone planning a faculty development program and a potential participant in the program. The content of the dialogue reflects both the author's research on effective faculty development, as well as his own experience as a facilitator at numerous faculty development workshops. (90 minutes)

64. What Human Beings Do When They Behave Intelligently and How They Can Become More So — Art Costa

Studies of efficient thinkers by Feuerstein, Sternberg, Glatthorn and Baron, and others have yielded some rather consistent characteristics of effective human performance. Studies of home, school, and classroom conditions, and the significance of mediative behaviors of parents and teachers are increasing our understanding of how to enhance the acquisition and performance of intelligent behavior. In this session, twelve qualities of human intelligent behavior are cited; indicators of their presence and increased performance in the classroom are identified; and school, home, and classroom conditions that promote their development are presented. (90 minutes)

66. Critical Thinking Staff Development: Developing Faculty Critical Thinking and Critical Teaching Skills — Richard Paul

The problem of long term staff development is a central problem in any attempt to bring critical thinking into the curriculum. Whatever else, we want critical thinking to be infused into all subject matter instruction. But we cannot do this unless, and to the extent that, faculty become comfortable articulating and utilizing critical thinking skills and dispositions. The standard mindset to instruction is an impediment. In this session, Professor Paul presents a general model for staff development and discusses ways of adapting it to different educational levels: elementary, secondary, and university. (90 minutes)

67. Lesson Plan Remodelling: A Strategy for Critical Thinking Staff Development — Richard Paul

The basic idea behind lesson plan remodelling as a strategy for staff development in critical thinking is simple. To remodel lesson plans is to develop a critique of one or more lessons and formulate one or more new lessons based on that critical process. A staff development leader with a reasonable number of exemplary remodels with accompanying explanatory principles can develop a series of staff development sessions that enable teachers to begin to develop new teaching skills as a result of their experience in lesson remodelling. In this session, Dr. Paul illustrates this mode of staff development using the Center's *Critical Thinking Handbook: K-3, A Guide For Remodelling Lesson Plans in Language Arts, Social Studies, and Science.* (40 minutes)

68. Teaching Critical Thinking: Skill, Commitment and the Critical Spirit, Kindergarten through Graduate School — Richard Paul

In his opening address to the 5th International Conference on Critical Thinking and Educational Reform, Professor Paul explains the significant opportunities that critical thinking

390

instruction provides as well as the obstacles it faces. He begins by tracing his own intellectual development in terms of critical thinking. He then illustrates the application of critical thinking to productive, synthetic, and meaningful learning in general. He explains how and why critical thinking represents not only a set of skills but also a set of commitments and mental traits. He discusses the significance, for example, of intellectual courage, intellectual humility, and fairmindedness, which he argues we as educators often don't foster.

Professor Paul uses a variety of everyday examples to make clear how critical thinking cuts across the curriculum and is significant at every grade level. He underscores the growing consensus in the field as to the meaning and nature of critical thinking as well as the wide variety of dimensions of it that need further exploration. (50 minutes)

69. Supervision for Critical Self-Reflection upon Teaching — Richard Paul, David Perkins

How do we help teachers engage in critical thinking in the strong sense and develop those dispositions, such as intellectual humility and openess to diversity, that are fundamental to critical inquiry? In this session, Professors Paul and Perkins model a teaching episode followed by a post observation conference. The purpose of the conference is to exemplify processes designed to help adults become more analytic and reflective about their own performance. This process is related to the research on staff development, adult growth, metacognition and achievement motivation. (90 minutes)

70. Culture and Critical Thinking: The Danger of Group- or Culture-bound Thought — Richard Paul, Carol Tavris

One danger for thought is social or cultural blindness. In this case our critical thinking results in misjudgments of others. Another, but opposite, danger is the refusal to make any judgments about any culture but our own. In this session, Richard Paul and Carol Tavris discuss the nature and significance for education of these deepseated problems. The issue is, in other words, how can we so structure instruction so that students learn how to recognize and overcome their group-bound and culture-bound thinking? (90 minutes)

71. What Makes Science Concepts Hard to Understand? — David Perkins

The learning of science with genuine understanding has emerged as a pressing educational problem not only in pre-university education but even at the university level. Science "misconceptions" prove prevalent in students even after a year or two of physics or chemistry. In this session, Professor Perkins explores through examples some of the factors that lead to deeply rooted misunderstandings of scientific concepts and examines some of the educational strategies that might serve to help students toward real comprehension. (90 minutes)

72. What the Mind is Made Of — David Perkins

The mind can be conceived and modeled in innumerable ways. Two contemporary views of the nature of mind strike a particularly provocative contrast. Alan Newell, in his SOAR model, proposes that the mind is a "production system," a computer-like mechanism that operates by checking for what the situation of the moment is and then "firing" an action that responds more or less appropriately to the situation. In seemingly stark contrast, Marvin Minsky, in his "society of mind" model, proposes that the mind is composed of a loose society of semi-autonomous sub-minds — "agencies" that have very specialized jobs. In this session, Professor Perkins ponders whether the question, "What is the mind made of?" even makes sense, and what kind of sense it might make. (90 minutes)

75. The Administrator's Role in Thinking Instruction — Vincent R. Ruggiero

In this session, Professor Ruggiero advances the idea that administrators have an important role to play in the thinking movement, a role upon which the ultimate success of the movement could well depend. He examines the nature of this role, identifies numerous ways in which administrators can promote and facilitate thinking instruction in their schools or colleges, and discusses the benefits such initiatives will bring to administrators themselves and to their institutions. (90 minutes)

76. What is the Appropriate Role of Critical Thinking in Pre-Service Education? — Richard Paul, Robert Swartz

In this session, Dr. Swartz and Dr. Paul examine the following: if public school teachers are to foster critical thinking in all of their teaching, how should pre-service education be designed to accomplish this end? What are some of the obstacles and dilemmas to be faced in moving in this direction? (90 minutes)

77. Thinking Critically about Emotion — and the Role of Emotion in Critical Thinking — Carol Tavris

Historically, philosophers and psychologists have divided emotion and cognition into two camps: the "bestial" and the "human," the irrational and the rational, the bad and the good. One implication of this perspective has been that emotion is death to critical thinking; that human beings would be able to think logically and solve their problems if only they didn't have those nasty old mammalian emotions in the way. In her presentation, Dr. Tavris discusses how new research is breaking down old dichotomies: for example, the role of cognition in generating emotion; the role of emotional arousal in influencing thought; and ways in which cognition can be "irrational" and emotion "rational." (90 minutes)

81. What Are State Departments of Education Doing About Critical Thinking? — Ken Bumgarner, Fran Claggett, William Geffrey, Mark Weinstein

This panel explores the general approaches being used to facilitate the infusion of critical thinking into the curriculum in three vanguard states: Washington, California and New York. (90 minutes)

84. State Wide Critical Thinking Testing in California: What Has It and What Has It Not Accomplished? — Robert Ennis, Jan Talbot, Perry Weddle

The nature and impact of mandated statewide critical thinking testing in California is considered by the panel. (90 minutes)

90. Integrating Teaching for Thinking into Mainstream Classroom Instruction — Robert Swartz and Jane Rowe

Robert Swartz and Jane Rowe of the Critical and Creative Thinking Program at the University of Massachusetts, Boston demonstrate and discuss lessons and techniques that infuse a focus on critical thinking into classroom instruction by restructuring traditional content. The concept of critical thinking that is utilized is discussed as well as issues about the structure of instructional programs in schools and school systems that can foster this kind of integration. (90 minutes)

91. Infusing Critical Thinking into Subject Matter Instruction: The Problem of Restructuring Instruction — Richard Paul

Putting the critical thinking movement into a historical perspective, Richard Paul gives his assessment of what is most essential: the need to transform instruction in all academic subjects. He argues for the following changes: *a)* from a content-dense to a content-deep curriculum, *b)* from a data-oriented to issue-oriented content, *c)* from teacher-centered to student-centered instruction, *d)* from recitation-centered or lecture-centered to activity-centered learning, *e)* from thought-discouraging to thought-provoking assignments, *f)* from lock-step to flexibility-paced instruction, and *g)* from a didactic to a critical concept of education. This requires school-wide or college-wide articulations of a philosophy of education that makes clear how the basic critical thinking objectives are harmonized with each other and infused in a coherent and concrete way into all subject matter instruction. (90 minutes)

92. Designing an Elementary or Middle School Inservice Program for Infusing Critical Thinking into Subject Matter Instruction — Richard Paul

Richard Paul provides a general model for designing an inservice program for elementary or middle schools. After sketching out a brief overview of the problem, discussion follows. Practical, long-range strategies for a progressively deeper integration of critical thinking into subject matter instruction is emphasized. (90 minutes)

94. Facilitating Critical and Creative Thinking Dispositions in Children — Alma M. Swartz

While many in the field of critical and creative thinking acknowledge the importance of the need to teach for critical and creative thinking *dispositions*, the stress has been on the discrete critical and creative thinking *skills*. Based on the assumption that teaching for critical and creative thinking attitudes and dispositions, such as openmindedness, or the tendency to seek reasons, is a necessary precondition to the acquisition and transfer of the discrete skills, Alma Swartz explores the idea of *primary* critical and creative thinking dispositions which underly and impel critical and creative thought.

The primary dispositions are categorized and explored as these interact with critical and creative thinking skills. A discussion of the ways in which cultural bias, as expressed in our schools, often runs counter to the child's natural inclination toward critical and creative thought is provided, with suggestions for the encouragement and facilitation of the dispositions as a means of ensuring the attainment of critical and creative thinking skills in the classroom. (90 minutes)

95. The Pre-Service Preparation of Teachers for Critical Thinking: The Montclair State College Model — Nicholas Michelli, Wendy Oxman, Mark Weinstein, John Barell

This session is a presentation and discussion of the model adopted at Montclair State College for infusing the teaching of critical thinking into the undergraduate pre-service teacher education program. Building upon a tradition of work in the field of critical thinking at Montclair State College, including the Institute for the Advancement of Philosophy for Children and Project THISTLE: Thinking Skills in Teaching and Learning, faculty have worked to revise the undergraduate program in light of proposed national standards for the preparation of teachers and recommendations of such groups as the Carnegie Forum on Education and the Economy. Key features of the program, including: the training of public school personnel to work with prospective teachers, the development and implementation of a new course within the undergraduate teacher education sequence on teaching for critical thinking, and revisions of all elements of the undergraduate teacher education curriculum are designed to foster and support teaching for critical thinking. A definition of critical thinking, goals for the program, and a philosophy for the program is shared with participants and discussed. (90 minutes)

97. Critical Thinking Staff Development — Charlie Blatz, Ken Bumgarner, Matthew Lipman, John Barell, Mark Weinstein, Nicholas Michelli

This panel surveys both short-term development projects, such as awareness workshops, and long-term projects, such as district-wide planning, assessment, and budgetary support, K-12. (90 minutes)

103. Think and Think Again! — Jan Talbot

Jan Talbot presents exciting materials and innovative strategies for strong sense critical thinking that teachers have found to be most effective in K-12 classrooms in Sacramento

County's seventeen school districts and in districts throughout the state. The materials are aligned with California's new Frameworks for math, science, language arts, and history-social science. Student work and new ways of assessing the effectiveness of student efforts to think critically are also presented. (90 minutes)

105. Preparing Teachers for Critical Thinking: A National Perspective — David Martin, Nicholas Michelli, David Imig

If we are to be successful in infusing the teaching of critical thinking into our schools, we must prepare new teachers to be sensitive to critical thinking and skilled in its implementation across the disciplines at the elementary level and within their disciplines at the secondary level. This need is especially critical if the projections that 50% of the work force of teachers will change within the next five to ten years are accurate. In addition to attending to the needs of new teachers, we must continue to assist in the professional development of practicing teachers as well. Efforts to develop national standards for the preparation of teachers who are capable of teaching for critical thinking are described and discussed. Model programs for the pre-service and in-service preparation of teachers are also discussed. (90 minutes)

106. A Critical Connection — George Hanford

There is a critical connection between what the Scholastic Aptitude Test measures and what critical thinking is all about. Those who call either for the abolition of our major modifications in the SAT or for a substantial decrease in its use overlook that important connection between the assessment of verbal and mathematical reasoning and the infusion of critical thinking into sub-ject matter instruction. Is the connection, as suggested, critical? Is it understood? Does it need clarification? What will happen to SAT scores if the infusion succeeds? (90 minutes)

107. Teaching Critical Thinking Across the Curriculum: an Approach Through Specific Courses — Gerald Nosich

Initiating a program in critical thinking across the curriculum requires doing two tasks that often seem opposed. First, you need to induce a unified idea of critical thinking (skills, attitudes, values) in both teachers and students, so that what is learned in one course can be seen to be transferable to other, different courses and situations. Second, if you're teaching a course in the social sciences, you want the critical thinking skills to be integrated with the needs of teaching social sciences, and so you need methods and examples geared specifically to that discipline. Gerald Nosich covers both tasks but, instead of concentrating on what all critical thinking has in common, he concentrates on individual courses in Social Sciences (History, Psychology, Sociology), Humanities (English Literature, Fine Arts, Music), Natural Sciences, and Physical Education. In each case, Professor Nosich offers some specific and practical methods for teaching critical thinking in that particular discipline. (90 minutes)

108. The American High School: What Needs to Be Done to Prepare Students for College — George Hanford, Richard Paul

George Hanford and Richard Paul informally discuss what high schools need to do to prepare students for college. (90 minutes)

110. Social Constraints on Critical Thinking and Educational Reforms: An International Perspective — Marek Zelazkiewicz

There is no society without constraints on critical thinking. Ethnocentrism, areas of "taboo," unnoticable blank spots, unrevealed routine thinking, etc., can differ in various societies but do exist in each one. There is no social system without limitations on educational reforms. Conservative social groups, dependence of schools on other institutions, limited resources, complexity of the changes, the time factor, etc., can bury even the best reform. Marek Zelazkiewicz demonstrates how experiences from the Soviet Union, Poland and other countries can help to identify social obstacles for successful educational change and what can be done to avoid these obstacles. (90 minutes)

111. Critical Thinking Across the Disciplines: An Ecological Approach — Mark Weinstein, Wendy Oxman

The relevance of critical thinking requires its broad application. A natural adjunct to a specialized course in critical thinking is its infusion in courses in various academic disciplines. An ecological approach affords a model for infusion. the goal is to empower students to understand the principles and values implicit in the subjects they take and to expose the presuppositions that structure the educational milieu in which they function. (90 minutes)

114. Why Is It Imperative to Distinguish Weak Sense from Strong Sense Critical Thinking? A Challenge to All Comers — Richard Paul

Various reasons have been advanced for abandoning the distinction between weak sense and strong sense critical thinking. Richard Paul responds to these concerns and explains why the distinction is essential to the field. (90 minutes)

115. Mini-Critical Thinking Course: Assignments that Stimulate Critical Thinking — M. Neil Browne, Stuart Keeley

Most of the time spent practicing critical thinking is focused on out-of-class assignments. To be effective, those assignments must be consistent with a coherent method of critical thinking. This workshop uses the model of critical thinking, presented in *Asking the Right Questions*, as a basis for organizing assignments to develop specific critical thinking skills and attitudes. Numerous assignments that can be used in any classroom are illustrated. Participants share critical thinking assignments that they have found to be effective. (90 minutes)

116. Critical Thinking and Literature — Stephen Marx, Jonah Raskin, Donald Lazere

This panel surveys means of emphasizing critical thinking in high school and college literature courses. (90 minutes)

117. On the Nature of Critical Thinking — Richard Paul, Connie Missimer, Robert Ennis, Gerald Nosich

This panel discusses definitions of critical thinking and their applications to classroom practice at all levels, K-U. (90 minutes)

118. Designing Staff Development that Models Thinking Skills — Ken Bumgarner

This presentation features a practical and workable design for staff development in thinking skills that can be adapted to any level—school, district, regional or state. Based on information processing theory, the components of effective staff development design suggested by Joyce and Showers, Knowles and others are coupled with techniques for managing change effectively. The design involves participants in immediate active processing and moves them to an application level with commitment to implement, using an adaptation of Fogarty's "Thinking Log." The techniques designed for workshop presentation are equally adaptable for classroom teaching. Actual conferences employing the design are described. (90 minutes)

119. Mini-Critical Thinking Course: Critical Thinking and Advertising — Ralph Johnson

Why should a mini-course on critical thinking bother with advertising? First, advertising is an important part of the cultural and information environment and, hence, cannot be ignored. Second, advertising is one of the most powerful communications, persuaders, and shapers of values and attitudes that has ever existed. Third, advertising often presents itself as argumentation and reasoning but, in fact, rarely works at that level. The logic of advertising is not the logic of argumentation. Students need to learn how to analyze advertisements and what to watch for, and this does not mean combing ads for fallacies, as some have suggested. Finally, there is a fair amount of mythology and self-deception in consumer attitudes about and responses to advertising. The premise of the mini-course, then, is that advertising is a territory rich in materials for the student of critical thinking. The instructor demonstrates why and brings with him numerous examples. (90 minutes)

120. Remodeling Lesson Plans in Middle School and High School to Infuse Critical Thinking — Richard Paul

To remodel lesson plans is to develop a critique of one or more lessons and formulate one or more new lessons based on that critical process. This process allows teachers to take existing material and restructure it to incorporate critical thinking strategies. In this presentation, Richard Paul maximizes participant involvement in analyzing, assessing, and constructing remodelled lesson plans. (90 minutes)

122. The Montclair State College Institute for Critical Thinking's Approach to Critical Thinking Across the Curriculum — Nicholas Michelli, Wendy Oxman, John Barell, Mark Weinstein

The Institute for Critical Thinking has been established at Montclair State College, to support and enrich faculty development efforts toward critical thinking as an educational goal. The primary purpose of the Institute is to serve as a catalyst in the development of educational excellence across the curriculum at the college level. A collaborative, multi-disciplinary approach has been initiated, with attention to the study of both the theoretical aspects of critical thinking across the disciplines and their implications for teaching and learning at the college level. In addition, the Institute has assumed a leadership role in helping other colleges and schools to incorporate thinking skills into their curricula.

As a state-funded project designed to promote educational reform at a multipurpose state college, as a faculty development project involving interdepartmental collegial collaboration, and as a project with inter-institutional responsibilities, the Institute for Critical Thinking serves as a model for understanding the effects of selected change efforts within similar institutional settings. (90 minutes)

125. Empowering Teachers and Students Toward Critical Thinking: K-12 — John Barell

This session introduces participants to a program that focuses upon empowering students, teachers and administrators with strategies for improving performance, achievement, and the quality of life in schools. Based upon research on staff development, the nature of thinking, and strategic planning for success, this program fosters more self-direction and independent thinking through goal-setting, infusion of problem solving/critical inquiry throughout the curriculum, and written reflection upon our own thinking processes. Participants will practice these programmatic elements. (90 minutes)

127. Teaching Critical Thinking in the Strong Sense: The Practitioner's Perspective — Noreen Miller, Ross Hunt, Karen Jensen, Chris Vetrano

In this panel, teachers share classroom ideas they have successfully implemented for teaching strong-sense critical thinking in grades K-12. (90 minutes)

128. Cultural Literacy and Critical Thinking: Where E.D. Hirsch Is Right, Where He Is Wrong, and What Is Likely to Come of His Influence — Richard Paul

E.D. Hirsch's recent best seller, *Cultural Literacy*, has sent educators scurrying around, making enormous lists of names, events, and facts to which students are to be exposed on the theory that even a superficial recognition of these is essential to reading what is in print. On this view, the fundamental reason why students are poor readers is that they lack the background information presupposed in what they read. Richard Paul spells out where Hirsch's analysis is misleading and apt to reinforce more "trivial pursuit" in the classroom. (90 minutes)

133. Critical Thinking Testing: Recent Developments — Robert Ennis, Stephen Norris, George Hanford

A panel of experts in critical thinking testing discuss positive developments toward testing for strong-sense critical thinking. (90 minutes)

Order Form

(Photocopy This Form to Order)

Rates: **Purchase —** $38.00/each, 4-9 tapes $30.00/each
10 or more $25.00/each

            Rental — $25.00/each

            Postage and Handling — $2.00 for first tape, add $.50 for each additional tape

            California Residents add 6% sales tax

Make check or Purchase Order Payable To: SSU Academic Foundation (U.S. dollars only please; no stamps or foreign monies)

Please Mail Order Form and Payment To: Center for Critical Thinking & Moral Critique, Sonoma State University, Rohnert Park, CA 94928 USA

Tape #	Title

NAME: _____

ADDRESS: _____

_____

_____

PHONE: _____

RENTAL _____ PURCHASE _____ TOTAL ENCLOSED _____

Note: Please do not give Post Office Boxes. UPS will not deliver to them.

Audiotape Library

1. Richard Paul **Teaching Critical Thinking in the Strong Sense in Elementary, Secondary, and Higher Education**

2. Stephen Norris **Varieties of Critical Thinking Tests: Their Design and Use**

8. Gus Bagakis **The Myth of the Passive Student**

10. Dianne Romain **Faculty Development in Critical Thinking**

12. Vincent Ryan Ruggiero **A Holistic Approach to Thinking Instruction**

13. Joseph Williams **Solving Problems in Writing**

14. Ralph Johnson **Mini Critical Thinking Course: Information and the Mass Media**

16. Gerald Nosich **On Teaching Critical Thinking**

17. Edward Damer **Can a Creationist Be a Critical Thinker?**

18. Debbie Walsh **The AFT Critical Thinking Project: The Hammond, IN Pilot**

20. Edys Quellmalz **Teaching Thinking Strategies Across the Curriculum — The Higher Order Thinking (H O T Project: Secondary Level**

22. David Hyerle **Design for Thinking: Making Sense in the Classroom**

23. Richard Paul **Workshop on the Art of Teaching Critical Thinking in the Strong Sense**

24. Edys Quellmalz **Teaching Thinking Strategies Across the Curriculum — The Higher Order Thinking (H O T) Project: Elementary Level**

28. M. Neil Browne, Stuart Keeley **Classroom Assignments that Encourage Critical Thinking**

29. Jack Lochhead **Teaching Kids to Argue: Inciting Riot in the Classroom**

30. Elinor McKinney **Models for Teaching Higher Order Thinking: Introduction**

33. Vivian Rosenberg **Introducing Affective Awareness as a Critical Thinking Skill**

34. Robert H. Ennis **A Conception of Critical Thinking**

35. Richard Paul **Mini Critical Thinking Course: The Nature of Critical Thinking Through Socratic Interrogation**

36. Connie DeCapite **Language Arts and Critical Thinking for Remedial and Bilingual Students**

37. Ralph Johnson **Getting Clear About Vagueness**

41. Dianne Romain **Strong Sense Critical Thinking in Junior High School Social Studies**

43. David Perkins **Knowledge as Design in the Classroom**

45. Vincent Ryan Ruggiero **Mini Critical Thinking Course: Dispositions: The Neglected Aspect of Thinking Instruction**

46. Chuck Blondino, Ken Bumgarner **Effective Design for Critical Thinking Inservice**

50. Perry Weddle **How to Appeal to Authority**

51. Debbie Walsh **Integrating Critical Thinking Skills into the K-12 Curriculum**

63. Thomas Jackson **Philosophy for Children**

64. J. Anthony Blair **Mini Critical Thinking Course: Using Arguments to Decide What to Believe**

65. Michael Rich **Moral Arguments as a Means of Introducing Critical Thinking Skills to Elementary School Students**

66. Judy Hirsch **Teaching Critical Thinking Skills to Students in Remedial Classes: Feuerstein's Theories on Cognitive Modifiability**

67. John Feare **Counseling as a Critical Thinking Activity**

68. Ira Shor **A Paolo Freire Workshop in Critical Thinking: "Dialogue" and "Desocialization" in the Classroom**

73. David Perkins, Richard Paul **Critical Thinking's Original Sin: Round Two**

74. Robert Swartz, Jane Rowe **Integrating Teaching for Thinking into Mainstream Classroom Instruction**

79. Peter E. Kneedler **California State Department of Education Program: Overview of K-12 Critical Thinking Assessment in California**

85. Linda M Phillips **The Role of Critical Thinking in Reading Comprehension**

86. John Barell, David Perkins **Coaching Teachers Who Teach Critical Thinking**

89. Diane F Halpern **Critical Thinking Across the Curriculum: Practical Suggestions for Promoting Critical Thinking in Every Classroom**

90. Peter Kneedler **California State Department of Education Program: Evaluation of Critical Thinking in California's New Statewide Assessment of History and Social Science**

94. Ogden Morse, Geoffrey Scheurman **Projects for Integrating Critical Thinking**

96. Jane Rowe **Reshaping the Elementary School Curriculum to Infuse Teaching for Thinking**

102. Robert Ennis **How to Write Critical Thinking Test Questions**

104. John Chaffee **Mini Critical Thinking Course: Critical and Creative Problem-Solving**

109. M. Neil Browne, Stuart Keeley **Bridging the Gap Between Teachers' Verbal Allegiance to Critical Thinking and Their Actual Behavior**

111. J. Anthony Blair **Problems with Teaching How to Use Arguments to Decide What to Believe**

112. Jerry Cummings, Ira Clark **Critical Thinking and the History-Social Science Curriculum, K-8**

114. Alita Letwin **A Conceptual Citizenship Education Curriculum: Examining and Evaluating the Fundamental Ideas of Privacy and Responsibility**

121. Jerry Cummings, Ira Clark **Critical Thinking and the History Social Science Curriculum, 9-12**

122. Linda Zimmerer, Zack Taylor **California State Department of Education Program: Process Skill Assessment in Science**

123. Peter Blewett **Learning is a Crystal: A Project Method for Teaching Critical and Creative Thinking in the Social Sciences**

130. Elinor McKinney **Models for Teaching Higher Order Thinking, Demonstration**

134. David Perkins **The Possibility of Invention**

135. John Chaffee **Teaching Critical Thinking Across the Curriculum**

136. Richard Paul **Critical Thinking: The State of the Field**

137. David Perkins **Real World Reasoning and How it Grows**

139. Albert Shanker **Critical Thinking and Educational Reform**

140. Edward Glaser **The Watson-Glaser Critical Thinking Appraisal**

141. Edys Quellmalz **Teaching Critical Thinking K-3**

142. Ronald Brandt **Approaches to Teaching Thinking**

143. Vincent Ruggiero **Teaching Critical Thinking Across the College Curriculum**

144. David Perkins, Richard Paul **Critical Thinking's Original Sin: An Exploration of the Causes of Monological Thinking**

146. Kevin O'Reilly **Teaching for Critical Thinking about Historical Interpretation**

147. Michael Rich **Critical Thinking in Grades 4-6**

148. Richard Paul, Perry Weddle, Robert Ennis **A Continuum of History-Social Science Critical Thinking Skills for Grades 3-12**

149. Tony Johnson **Philosophy for Children: An Approach to Critical Thinking**

150. Ronald Brandt **Issues in Teaching Thinking**

151. Ronald Giere **Understanding Scientific Reasoning**

153. Mary Ann Wolff **According to Whom? — Analyzing Our Own and Other's Frames of Reference**

154. Art Costa **Teaching for Intelligent Behavior**

159. Joseph Williams **Writing and Thinking: 3 Myths/3 Tru(?)ths**

161. David Perkins **Knowledge as Design**

166. Dan Dolan **Teaching Problem Solving Strategies**

167. Jonathan Adler **Philosophical Problems in Everyday Reasoning**

169. Stephen Norris **Validating Critical Thinking Tests**

170. Richard Paul **Overview of K-12 Critical Thinking Assessment in California**

173. Connie DeCapite **Using Critical Thinking with Remedial and/or Bilingual Students**

175. Mary Ann Wolff **Beyond the Scientific Method: Can Our Schools Encourage Reflective Thinking?**

176. Stephen Norris **Evaluating Ability to Appraise Observations**

177. Antoinette Worsham, Anita Stockton **The Thinking Skills Inclusion Process — An Instructional Model**

179. Ralph Johnson **On Reasoning**

182. Dennis Rohatyn **Critical Thinking in Radio & Television**

184. Tej Pandey **Problem Solving in Statewide Math Assessment**

185. Tom Sachse **Process Skill Assessment in Science**

363. Stephen Norris, Douglas Martin, Robert Ennis, Robert Swartz **Infusing Critical Thinking into Math and Science**

364. Alma M. Swartz **Facilitating Critical and Creative Thinking Dispositions in Children**

366. John Barell, Nicholas Michelli, Wendy Oxman, Mark Weinstein **The Pre-Service Preparation of Teachers for Critical Thinking: The Montclair State College Model**

367. John Chaffee **Practical Strategies for Teaching Critical Thinking in the Disciplines**

368. Linda M. Phillips **Improving Inference Ability in Reading Comprehension**

369. Matthew Lipman **Critical Thinking and Reliance upon Criteria**

370. Joe Edwards **The Challenges of Keeping a Strong Staff Development/Critical Thinking Program On-Going with Enthusiasm and Energy**

371. Howard Kahane **Critical Thinking Courses as Preparation for Adult Life in a Democratic Society**

372. Kate Sandberg **Collaborative Learning: Making a Difference in Student Thinking**

379. Charlie Blatz, Ken Bumgarner, Matthew Lipman, John Barell, Mark Weinstein, Nicholas Michelli **Critical Thinking Staff Development**

381. Gus Bagakis, Bernice Goldmark, Paul Baker, Dean Dorn, Eugene Labovitz **Infusing Critical Thinking into Social Studies**

382. Wendy Oxman **Project THISTLE: Thinking Skills in Teaching and Learning**

383. Sandra Black **Teaching Analytical and Critical Thinking: An Inservice Training Program**

384. Stephen P. Norris **The Disposition to Think Critically in Science**

385. Richard Paul **Designing a High School or College Inservice Program for Infusing Critical Thinking into Subject Matter Instruction**

387. Thomas Jackson **Philosophy for Children: A Hands-On Demonstration, K-2 Level**

388. Kenneth Chuska, John Meehan **Activating Knowledge and Thinking In and Through Reading and Writing Activities**

392. John Meehan, Ken Bumgarner, John Barell, Wendy Oxman, Peter Kneedler **Critical Thinking: What States are Doing**

395. Mark Weinstein **Integrating Thinking Skills into the Schools**

396. Jan Talbot **Think and Think Again!**

398. Charlie Blatz **Enhancing the Use of Critical Thinking, K-12: Understanding and Designing a Schoolwide Staff Development Program**

400. Vincent Ryan Ruggiero **"Ha! Ha! I'm Thinking"**

404. John K Wilson **Developing Critical Thinking Skills with Developmental Students**

407. Nigel Dower, Richard Paul, James Gray **Critical Thinking and Global Problems**

408. David Martin, Nicholas Michelli, David Imig **Preparing Teachers for Critical Thinking: A National Perspective**

409. Clinton Vickers **Using the Mind Well: An Essential School**

412. Charlie Blatz **Enhancing the Use of Critical Thinking, K-12: Matters of Perspective**

414. Vincent Ryan Ruggiero **Will Thinking Instruction Succeed?**

Order Form

(Photocopy This Form to Order)

Rates: **Purchase —** $7.50 per tape

Postage and Handling — $1.50 for first tape, add $.25 for each additional tape

California Residents add 6% sales tax

Make check or Purchase Order Payable To: SSU Academic Foundation (U.S. dollars only please; no stamps or foreign monies)

Please Mail Order Form and Payment To: Center for Critical Thinking & Moral Critique, Sonoma State University, Rohnert Park, CA 94928 USA

Tape #	Title

NAME: _____

ADDRESS: _____

_____

_____

PHONE: _____

TOTAL # TAPES ORDERED _____ TOTAL ENCLOSED _____

Note: Please do not give Post Office Boxes. UPS will not deliver to them.

Annual Conference on Critical Thinking

Every year in the first week of August, the Center hosts the oldest and largest critical thinking conference. In 1988, the conference had over 100 presenters, nearly 300 sessions, and over 1,000 registrants. The conference is designed to meet the needs and concerns of the widest variety of educational levels. Practitioners, administrators, professors, and theoreticians regularly attend the conference. Many registrants have responsibilities for curriculum design and inservice training or particular subject matter concerns: math, science, language arts, social studies, humanities, fine arts, ... Others are principally concerned with assessment issues, remediation, or preservice education. Still others want information about the relation of critical thinking to citizenship, to vocational or professional education, or to personal development. Some are eager to explore the relation of critical thinking to the classic ideals of the liberally educated person and the free society or to world-wide social, economic, and moral issues. The conference discussions and dialogues that result from bringing together such a large number of committed critical thinkers with such a broad background of concerns are not only truly exciting but also rich in practical pay-offs.

Please send me more information on the Center's annual conferences on Critical Thinking:

NAME: _____

ADDRESS: _____

_____

_____

SPECIAL INTERESTS (GRADE LEVELS, SUBJECT, ETC.)

_____

_____

*Newly Released
for Staff Development*

Lesson Plan Remodelling Videotape

VHS 40 minutes

*to accompany the
Critical Thinking Handbooks*

*Write or call
The Center
for Critical Thinking
(707) 664-2940
Sonoma State University
Rohnert Park, CA 94928*

Help Us "Remodel" this Handbook

In the spirit of good critical thinking, we want your assessment of this handbook and ideas for its improvement. Your ideas might be rewarded with a scholarship to the next International Conference on Critical Thinking!

Evaluation:

Here's what I found most useful about the handbook:

_____

_____

_____

This is what I think is in need of change:

_____

_____

_____

Here are my ideas for improving the handbook:

_____

_____

_____

Send evaluation to: Center For Critical Thinking; Sonoma State University; Rohnert Park, CA 94928.

Information About the Center for Critical Thinking and Moral Critique

Sonoma State University

The Center conducts advanced research, inservice education programs, professional conferences, and disseminates information on critical thinking and moral critique. It is premised on the democratic ideal as a principle of social organization. That is, that it is possible

> so to structure the arrangements of society as to rest them ultimately upon the freely-given consent of its members. Such an aim requires the institutionalization of reasoned procedures for the critical and public review of policy; it demands that judgments of policy be viewed not as the fixed privilege of any class or elite but as the common task of all, and it requires the supplanting of arbitrary and violent alteration of policy with institutionally channeled change ordered by reasoned persuasion and informed consent.*

It conducts its research through an international network of fellows and associates, as follows:

Honorary Fellows

Max Black, Professor of Philosophy, Cornell University, Ithaca, NY

Robert Ennis, Director, Illinois Thinking Project, University of Illinois, Champaign, IL

Edward M. Glaser, Psychologist, Founder, Watson-Glaser Critical Thinking Appraisal, Los Angeles, CA

Mathew Lipman, Professor of Philosophy, Founder and Director, Institute for the Advancement of Philosophy for Children, Montclair, NJ

Israel Scheffler, Thomas Professor of Education and Philosophy, Harvard University, Cambridge, MA

Michael Scriven, Professor of Philosophy, University of Western Australia, Nedlands, Australia

Research Associates

J. Anthony Blair, Professor of Philosophy, University of Windsor, Ontario, Canada

Carl Jensen, Associate Professor of Communications Studies, Sonoma State University, Rohnert Park, CA

Ralph Johnson, Professor of Philosophy, University of Windsor, Ontario, Canada

Don Lazere, Professor of English, California Polytechnic State University, San Luis Obispo, CA

Perry Weddle, Professor of Philosophy, California State University, Sacramento, CA

Ian Wright, Professor of Education, University of British Columbia, British Columbia, Canada

Joel Rudinow, Assistant Professor of Philosophy, Sonoma State University, Rohnert Park, CA

Teaching Associates

Carl Jensen, Center Research Associate

Don Lazere, Center Research Associate

Richard Paul, Director

Dianne Romain, Assistant Professor of Philosophy, Sonoma State University

Douglas Martin, Associate Professor of Chemistry, Sonoma State University

Joel Rudinow, Center Research Associate

*Israel Scheffler, *Reason and Teaching* 1973, (Bobbs-Merril Co, Inc.) page 137.

Research Assistants

A. J. A. Binker, Sonoma State University

Ken Adamson, Sonoma State University

Director

Richard W. Paul, Center for Critical Thinking and Moral Critique and Professor of Philosophy, Sonoma State University

The work of the Center includes an annual international Conference on Critical Thinking and Education; Master's Degree in Education with emphasis in Critical Thinking; Supplementary Authorization Program in the teaching of critical thinking (under the Single Subject Waiver Credential Program of the State of California); inservice programs in the teaching of critical thinking; Research Intern program (for graduate students in the field of critical thinking and moral critique); a resource center for the distribution of tests, documents, position papers; and research in the field of critical thinking and moral critique and in the reform of education based upon the teaching of reasoning and critical thinking skills across the curriculum. Other recent contributors include the historian Henry Steele Commager and George H. Hanford, President of the College Board.

Center for Critical Thinking and Moral Critique
Sonoma State University
Rohnert Park, CA 94928

Our Science Consultant

Douglas R. Martin is a Professor of both Chemistry and Education at Sonoma State University, Rohert Park, California. After receiving his Ph.D. in Physical Chemistry from the University of California at Berkeley, he taught biology, chemistry, and physics at the high school level for five years. During this time, his theoretical and practical interests in reasoning development, particularly in the work of Jean Piaget, led to publications in journals like *The Physics Teacher* and the *Journal of Chemical Education*. He subsequently taught in the sciences and in philosophy of science at the university level.

Professor Martin is actively involved with science education in several ways. He has directed two National Science Foundation-funded projects and has been involved with several others. These projects have been concerned with issues ranging from curriculum development to inservice teacher education and from the elementary grades to high school. Professor Martin's research interests focus on students' naive understanding of basic science concepts and how this naive understanding influences their ability to understand concepts and relationships more accurately. He is also concerned with understanding how the goals of the critical thinking movement are best expressed in science education.

His publications include:

1. "A Primer on Elementary Science," monograph published in curricular materials developed for Project MAST, an elementary science curriculum project supported by the National Science Foundation. 1988.
2. "Encouraging Critical Thought: Alternative Problem Forms," *The Physics Teacher, 26,* 5, 1988.
3. "Teacher Helping Teachers in Science," *Teacher Education Quarterly,* Summer, 1987.
4. "Critical Thinking in Science Through the Construction of Meaning," accepted for publication in the *Proceedings* of the Fourth International Conference on Critical Thinking and Moral Critique, Sonoma State University, 1986.
5. "Status of the Copernican Theory Before Galileo, Kepler, and Newton," *American Journal of Physics,* 52, 982, 1984.
6. "'How Far Can You See?' An Activity Involving Approximate Reasoning," *The Physics Teacher,* 20, 318, 1982.
7. "A Piagetian Approach to Physics Teaching," *The Physics Teacher,* 18, 34, 1980.
8. "A Group-Administered Reasoning Test for Classroom Use," *Journal of Chemical Education,* 56, 179, 1979.